French Folktales

Pantheon Fairy Tale and Folklore Library

French

From the

collection of

Henri Pourrat

◆

Selected by

C. G. Bjurström

◆

Translated and

with an introduction

by Royall Tyler

P a n t h e o n   B o o k s

Folktales

New York

The folktales translated in this work were selected from the seven-volume French collection, *Le trésor des contes*, originally published by Editions Gallimard, Paris. Copyright © 1977, 1978, 1979, 1981, 1983, 1986 by Editions Gallimard

Each part division of *French Folktales* corresponds to a volume title of the seven-volume Gallimard edition. For a listing of each tale by volume followed by its original French title and the page on which it can be found in the French edition, see "Tales Classified by Volume" on pages 477–80.

Library of Congress Cataloging-in-Publication Data

Pourrat, Henri, 1887–1959.
[Trésor des contes. English. Selections]
French folktales from the collection of Henri Pourrat / selected by C. G. Bjurström; translated and with an introduction by Royall Tyler.
(Pantheon fairy tale and folklore library)
p.   cm.
Selected from: Le trésor des contes.
Bibliography: p.
ISBN 0-394-54451-X
1. Tales—France. I. Bjurström, Carl Gustaf, 1919–   . II. Tyler, Royall. III. Title. IV. Title: French folk tales from the collection of Henri Pourrat. V. Title: French folktales.
GR161.P6213   1989b
398.2'0944—dc20   89-42560

BOOK DESIGN BY CHRIS WELCH

Manufactured in the United States of America

First American Edition

Contents

Part Two
THE DEVIL

Part Three
BANDITS

Part Four
AROUND THE VILLAGE

Part Five
. . . .
THE MAD AND THE WISE

P a r t   S i x
· · · · · · · · · · · · ·
BESTIARY

P a r t   S e v e n
· · · · · · · · · · · · ·
LOVE AND MARRIAGE

Introduction

A N OLD MAN I know, past eighty now, lives in a hamlet in
Burgundy. Admirers call him "le sage du village," which rhymes
much better than "the village sage." He remembers the time when
in all that countryside only the schoolmaster had a bicycle. No one had
been to Paris then. People seldom got to the county seat, either, since the
walk there and back took all day. The language they spoke was not exactly
French, and the dialect two and a half kilometers away in the neighboring
hamlet was recognizably different. In those days, each village had a mole
catcher and a blacksmith, just as the villages in these stories do; and, just
as in these stories, you ate your dinner with your knife. One summer day
in 1988, the village sage graced with his presence a festive meal in the
great house nearby, amid polished furniture and fine china. At first he tried
out the silver knife and fork. Then, being among friends, he gave up and
finished the meal comfortably with his Swiss army knife. These are stories
to eat with your pocket knife, among friends. They are delicious, and the
days they taste of will never come again.

Auvergne and Henri Pourrat

Henri Pourrat (1887–1959) started collecting folktales in his native Auvergne when "le sage du village" was a boy, in 1910, and continued for
nearly fifty years. His work, from which *French Folktales* is a selection, came
out complete in thirteen volumes between 1948 and 1964 under the title

Le trésor des contes ("The Treasury of Tales"). Recently, *Le trésor des contes* has been republished, differently organized and slightly larger, in seven weighty volumes containing 1,009 tales. These range from short jokes like "The Ill-Lodged Goat" to long stories of magic and romance like "The Black Mountain." Each chapter of *French Folktales* corresponds to a volume title of the seven-volume edition.

This treasury was to be, in Pourrat's words, "the original mythology of the French people," or again, "a compendium of the peasant imagination." The Auvergne region lies at the geographical heart of France. By gathering its folklore he hoped to capture the very mind of rural France, which even then was changing fast. (Once there had been no schoolmaster and no bicycle at all.) His labor produced one of the finest folktale collections ever published by anyone anywhere.

There may be no more beautiful region in all the world than the Auvergne which so inspired Henri Pourrat. He was born in the quiet town of Ambert on the river Dore, where his family's shop sign advertised "Notions, Hosiery, Quality Groceries, Hardware, Art Objects." East and north of Ambert rise the Monts du Forez, where "The False Child" is probably set. The distraught mother in that story goes for help to "a certain old woman who lives in the mountains":

Up there it's all wilderness. Through the blossoming plum trees you see water whiten as it tumbles down the rocks. There are steep ravines, deep shadows, pines clinging for dear life to cliffs, and perhaps a few gliding coils of cloud.

West of Ambert, beyond the Monts du Livradois, you come to Issoire on a rich plain watered by the Allier. Further on, past Issoire, a spectacular chain of volcanic pinnacles known as *puys* stretches roughly north and south. The vast, grassy bulk of the Puy du Cantal—ablaze in June, like all these mountains, with sweeping expanses of golden broom—rises to the south; while to the north, above the city of Clermont-Ferrand, towers the mighty Puy de Dôme (1,465 m.), which once supported a Roman temple to Mercury. On a mountainside nearby lived the old carpenter in "Three Very Clever Lads":

Evenings, he'd sit in his doorway smoking a pipe and gaze down the winding road that led far off toward all of France: toward terraced villages climbing the slopes of lava cones, with stout, square belfries rising gallantly above them; toward distant spurs and towns, crystal clear like scenes glimpsed through a glass of water; toward great sweeps of space, blue and inviting, out at the edge of the world.

Out that way too you may find the kingdom of "Pimpon d'Or and the Three Ogres":

Once in the land of sheep and rocks—yonder beyond the Aubrac range, you know, among the wild box and the blue thistles, on the sunny side— there lived a king and a queen and their little daughter.

Travel south from Ambert, and you pass the old abbey of La Chaise-Dieu ("Seat-of-God") to reach Le Puy, where, long ago, a woman asleep on a dolmen (a prehistoric table-stone) dreamed of the Virgin.

It was sickness that freed Henri Pourrat to roam this glorious world. Tuberculosis, which at that time was killing so many people, including Pourrat's younger brother, struck Pourrat in 1905. For a year he hung between life and death, and though he eventually pulled through, a normal career was out of the question. His delicate health kept him to what he once called "a very quiet and regular, almost monastic life." On pain of relapse he had not only to lie long morning hours in bed, but also, each afternoon, "to wander hill and dale."

Soon, he turned to writing. Poems and stories began to flow from his pen. In his rambles he gathered folktales and folksongs. With the years he became a well-established regional literary figure. His massive and absorbing novel *Gaspard des montagnes* ("Gaspard from the Mountains," 1922–31), woven from dozens of local folktales, won a national literary prize in 1922; and in 1941 he won another national prize for his novel *Vent de mars* ("March Wind"). Pourrat's copious output over the years included several other novels as well as essays, reminiscences, ethnological accounts, and historical studies.

In fact, Henri Pourrat became one of the major regional writers of twentieth-century France. What is a "regional writer"? In France, it is a writer who does *not* migrate to Paris and who does *not* join the literary or intellectual trends of the capital, but who instead celebrates his or her own region and its concerns. Actually, Pourrat's concerns far transcended his own region. In his case, it is more that he saw Ambert rather than Paris as the center of the world.

A characteristic feature of a region is often its language. I noted before that when "le sage du village" was young, people in his region spoke a distinctive dialect, now all but gone. In Auvergne, not far away, many people speak a variety of Occitan, one form of which is the well-known and richly literary language called Provençal. Occitan still has its champions and its writers today. Here is a sample of the Ambert dialect taken from a tale Pourrat published early in his career: "Ha! Chose, qu'aucu t'aye liceno!" This means, "Say! Chose, someone's been teaching you a lesson!" The French version (which Pourrat himself supplied) would be, "Ha! Chose, quelqu'un t'a fait la leçon!"

Le Félibrige, a vigorous literary movement formed around the great Provençal writers Théodore Aubanel (1829–1886) and Frédéric Mistral (1830–1914), had adherents in the Auvergne region. Pourrat was in touch with them, especially with "le bon félibre livradois," his friend Régis Michalias. Some informants told Pourrat their tales in Occitan. Although Pourrat himself did not speak Occitan, since he was from an urban merchant family who conversed in French, he understood it well and practiced writing it. The great Occitan (or Provençal) literary heritage, with all its celebration of rustic virtue and romance, undoubtedly fed his own sympathy for the soil and those who live directly from its fruits.

This sympathy fueled the central project of Pourrat's life, begun first and finished last of all, which was *Le trésor des contes*. His purpose in compiling *Le trésor* was not that of the academic folklorist. As the decades passed after 1910, he saw his growing collection more and more as representing all of France in a deep (perhaps one should say literary or even religious) sense foreign to the academic researcher. *Le trésor des contes* actually includes some tales from beyond Auvergne, although they are not particularly numerous or prominent. More than that, however, Pourrat's aim was to grasp and convey, through the eternal verities of peasant life, the uncorrupted, universal mind of true mankind. Not that he had sentimental illusions about the peasantry of the past. He wrote, for example, in 1928:

I doubt that one should lament the past, mired as it was too often in poverty, isolation, and at times, horrible brutality. I have no wish to mock the good old days when people blew their noses on their sleeves, but I can hardly believe that that age was one of exemplary virtue.

What he had in mind, instead, was spiritual renewal through a return to the earth and to peasant *ideals*.

A Little History of the French Folktale

How, then, does *Le trésor des contes* fit into the history of French folklore— a history still poorly known in the English-speaking world, apart from the tales published so long ago by Charles Perrault? And even more important, where does *Le trésor* stand among the work of modern French folklorists? To answer the first question, I will rely on an authoritative survey of the subject by Paul Delarue.

In the mid-sixteenth century the Breton writer Noël du Fail evoked a scene of winter evening storytelling which would have delighted Pourrat. Du Fail first described the farmer Robin Chevet and his family at work after supper: Robin scutching hemp with his back to the fire or singing as he fixes his shoes; his wife Jouanne, nearby, spinning and singing too; and the other family members and servants tidying up their threshing flails, cutting teeth for rakes, or making whips. Then comes story time:

> And as they worked at their several tasks, the good Robin first called for silence. Then he began a fine tale from the time when animals talked: how Fox stole fish from the fishmongers, for instance; how he had Wolf beaten by the washerwomen when he was teaching Wolf to fish; how the Dog and the Cat traveled far. Or Robin told about Crow losing his cheese when he began to sing; about Mélusine; about the Werewolf; or about Little Donkey-Hide (Cuir d'Anette, i.e. Peau d'Ane or Cinderella).

In those days country folk told stories in daily life, as some still did even in Pourrat's youth. Tales like these had been widely known among the upper classes until the Renaissance, somewhat before du Fail's time. From then on, however, the cult of classical antiquity completely overshadowed tales among cultivated people (with the exception of Rabelais). Writers had only contempt for what they called "contes de la cigogne" ("stork tales") or "contes de ma mère l'Oye" ("Mother Goose tales"), which they associated with the chatter of nurses and old women. The widespread assumption that folktales are for children, though often inaccurate, is far from new.

In the late seventeenth century a vogue for tales caught on—not folktales at first, but fantasies made up by literary people. Then in 1697 Charles Perrault published (under his son's name) his famous *Histoires ou Contes du temps passé* ("Stories or Tales of Times Past"). Though gussied up to please salon society, almost all Perrault's stories are real folktales, and for most people they have represented French folklore ever since. At the time, they started a bit of a fad for tales based on popular motifs. After all, nurses and old servant-woman informants were never lacking. Shortly, however, interest flagged again. In 1699 one Madame de Murat published *Histoires sublimes et allégoriques dédiées aux fées modernes* ("Tales Sublime and Allegorical, Dedicated to Modern Fairies"), in which she heaped scorn on "Mother Goose tales" and the cooks, nursemaids, and butter-churning, stable-sweeping peasants who told them.

A craze for "Oriental" tales swept the reading public early in the eighteenth century, thanks to the French translation of the *Thousand and One Nights* which appeared between 1704 and 1712. Expansive tale collections followed, with titles like *Les mille et une heures, contes péruviens* ("The Thousand and One Hours: Peruvian Tales") or *Les aventures d'Abdalla, fils d'Hanif, envoyé par le Sultan des Indes à la découverte de l'Ile Borico . . .* ("The Adventures of Abdalla, Son of Hanif, Sent by the Sultan of the Indies to Seek Out the Isle of Borico . . ."). One volume, entitled *Les soirées bretonnes, nouveaux contes de fées* ("Breton Nights: New Fairy Tales"), actually made free use of a Near Eastern collection published in Venice a hundred and fifty years before. On the other hand, some of the "Oriental" fantasies, if not purely imaginary, were really traditional French or at least Western tales in extravagantly oriental guise. This was the only form in which high society would accept them. At last, the whole corpus of literary tales, from Perrault to a very dubious "continuation" of the *Thousand and One Nights*, was gathered together in the vast *Cabinet des fées* ("The Fairies' Chamber," 41 volumes, 1785–89).

In the countryside, meanwhile, tales were beginning to circulate not only orally but in books and pamphlets published for distribution by traveling salesmen. Tales which Perrault or other writers had turned into literature were returned to the common people in this form. Their influence naturally grew as education spread. Late nineteenth-century or early twentieth-century folklore collectors, including Pourrat, gathered tales clearly taken from such written sources alongside older, purely oral versions.

Between 1812 and 1815 the Brothers Grimm published their famous collection of German folktales. Partial French translations soon delighted a broad range of readers. Yet in the 1860s France still had nothing comparable. Few people realized that tales of equal distinction could be found all over France. On the contrary, most assumed that Perrault and his followers had exhausted the possibilities of the folktale long ago, and that French tales consisted of what had appeared in the powdered-and-painted *Cabinet des fées*.

But in France, too, the nineteenth-century rediscovery of the medieval and popular past eventually turned some minds toward folklore. Serious study of the French folktale (in the modern sense) began in 1870 with the publication of Luzel's *Contes bretons* ("Breton Tales," real ones this time) and the founding of two folklore journals. During this golden age of French folklore, which lasted until the First World War, folklorists like E. Cosquin (d. 1918) or Paul Sébillot (d. 1919) established folklore studies as a respectable academic discipline. No French province was neglected, each ending up covered by at least one carefully compiled folktale collection. It is no accident that Henri Pourrat began his work during this same golden age. The rediscovery of France's folk heritage, fueled no doubt by all the corrosive menace of industrializing modernization, was in the air.

Yet between the two world wars, French folklore studies lapsed once more. Researchers abandoned the folktale, the one outstanding exception being the French ethnologist Arnold van Gennep. Soon, scholars from other countries, where folklore studies still flourished, were complaining about recent French neglect of the field and reminding their French colleagues of the need for international cooperation. France responded to their call after the end of the Second World War. In the meantime Henri Pourrat, who hardly ever left Ambert and his Auvergne, and who remained relatively distant from the war, quietly continued his collecting.

The publication of *Le trésor des contes*, starting in 1948, therefore came at the beginning of a new era for France and for French folklore studies. How was Pourrat's work received?

Pourrat and the Folklorists

Paul Delarue, commenting in 1953 on the first three volumes of the collection, accorded the work some value but concluded that Pourrat had "taken great liberties with his popular material," so that "a researcher can use his tales only with a certain caution." In 1964 Delarue's successor,

Marie-Louise Ténèze, urged "extreme caution" and soon abandoned the tales altogether. As a result, a standard, readily accessible history of the French folktale published in 1981 (Michèle Simonsen, *Le conte populaire français*) does not mention *Le trésor des contes* at all.

The root of the problem is clear. Paul Delarue defined it in 1957 (without overt reference to Pourrat) when he discussed what sort of collections are, for the folklore scholar, beyond the pale:

> In general, one must reject those collections which do not give their sources in accordance with the practice followed by folklorists and researchers ever since Luzel and Sébillot: the name, dwelling place and age of the teller; the date when the tale was recorded; and an appropriate citation when the tale was taken from a printed source.

This is precisely the information which Pourrat did not provide in *Le trésor des contes*.

He did, however, record it. Until well into the 1920s, Pourrat scrupulously noted all these details in each case and continued to do so, although less consistently, until 1951. In all, he collected tales from fifty-three women and fifty-three men, and songs from fifty-seven women and twenty-nine men. His voluminous papers, now stored at the Centre Henri Pourrat in Clermont-Ferrand, include not only notes on sources and informants, but countless raw transcriptions of the tales he collected—often several for one title in *Le trésor*. These materials help to establish the true value of a major folklore collection. But why did he not share all this information with his readers?

Henri Pourrat simply did not understand why anyone should want to know such things. At least, that is what he wrote more than once. The truth is actually a little more complicated. In a sense he obviously understood very well. From 1911 to 1913 Pourrat corresponded with Arnold van Gennep, offering information and materials, and receiving sound advice on how the conscientious folktale collector should proceed. Pourrat learned the lesson, as his records prove. However, the real interests of the two men were too different and the correspondence lapsed.

As Pourrat saw it, van Gennep treated folktales as dead specimens good only for the laboratory or the museum case. Pourrat wanted folktales alive— alive in a world from which they were obviously fading. He seems to have approached folktales rather as those in the idealistic craft movement of the time approached folk pottery, which was also fading as a functional craft.

In an age of strident individualism, the folk potter was to be anonymous, his works expressing simply the collective genius of the folk. For the same sort of reason, Henri Pourrat surely did not so much fail to understand why people wanted source information, as object in principle to giving it. Source identification would only reduce a tale to an accident of time, place, and person, instead of restoring it to its rightful place as a timeless expression of the genius of a whole people, or even of humanity itself.

This intellectual position resembles that taken by others, in other fields, during Pourrat's lifetime. Jung's "collective unconscious," for example, is of the same period. Moreover, Pourrat's position is not unattractive. One need not blame him for having parted company with the folklorists, however valuable their own enterprise may be. On the other hand, Pourrat's procedure affected the reputation of his work, and that is not a result he would have welcomed. He certainly wanted the tales in *Le trésor des contes* to be widely read and enjoyed.

The Tales of Le trésor des contes

Perhaps it is irreducibly true that if a body of tales is to be well loved as a book, it must be well written. And perhaps it is also true that tales transcribed from oral telling seldom read really well. Pourrat reached both these conclusions in the course of his career, and that is why he rewrote all the tales in *Le trésor des contes*. With immense talent and patience he turned what had been diffuse, halting, or flat into absorbing literature.

It is important to understand that Pourrat was scrupulously faithful to the tales as he received them, according to his own understanding of fidelity. He even noted that in his mountains, a *pourra* (which sounds like Pourrat) was a sort of wandering storyteller. He wrote in 1949:

> I can speak of these popular tales without modesty because, after all, with respect to them I am only a scribe. I believe that this has never been done in France and may leave its mark. The task is to give body to these inspirations of the people, to give them voice, and to establish thereby a sort of classic of the imagination and rhetoric proper to the ancient people of the countryside.

In those days there were no tape recorders. Pourrat learned from experience that taking notes on the spot made a teller nervous. Instead, he recommended writing out the tale only that evening, or better, the following morning. Under such circumstances he could hardly have reproduced every detail of the teller's language, even had he wished to. Still, in his correspondence with van Gennep, Pourrat considered the problems of exact transcription very seriously. In the end, they seemed to him at once overwhelming and beside the point. Pourrat took it for granted that there is a critical difference between speech and the written word. "Literal fidelity," he wrote, "kills literary fidelity." For him, literal transcription more often than not *betrayed* the teller.

> To transcribe a tale exactly as the teller told it but without her miming gestures, without the fragrance of ferns or that woodpecker yonder, hammering away with its beak as it clings to an oak—that is to betray the tale. . . . You must restore the tale's character, make it something flowing, something shapely.

And that is what he did. As a result, the tales in *Le trésor des contes* are beautifully *written*.

About 1912, Pourrat published locally several tales transcribed exactly from his informants' telling, just as van Gennep himself would have wished. Seventy years later, the French folklorist Dany Hadjadj compared these versions with the rewritten ones included by Pourrat in *Le trésor*. Hadjadj's study shows how Pourrat went about rewriting the tales, why he did so, and how right he was. Its concluding paragraph sums up the matter perfectly:

> Thus, a careful comparison between a few tales written by Pourrat and their oral originals helps us to appreciate the steadfast patience of this writer-teller of tales. In reworking and enriching the raw material provided by his informants, Pourrat succeeded, thanks to his writing, in bringing these tales back to life. Of course, bearing as they do their author's stamp, the tales in *Le trésor* lack the folklorist's scholarly fidelity. Instead, they attain the faithfulness of the poet. . . . The reader has the illusion of reading a true folktale—a splendid illusion indeed! . . . Thanks to [Pourrat's] work, the old, all-but-smothered wellsprings of the *told* tale run clear and full once more before the amazed eyes of the modern reader.

It is easy to understand Hadjadj's enthusiasm. To evoke a rough parallel, the tales in *Le trésor* are like ruins lovingly taken apart, then reassembled and restored to perfection by an immensely learned archaeologist-architect. What did Pourrat actually do? First, he used his deep knowledge of the region and its ways to fill out in the tales many things which to the tellers themselves were too obvious to need saying, but which readers like ourselves (whether in French or English) are certainly glad to have put in words. For example, since outsiders do not know what a rich Auvergnat farmer really looked like, Pourrat might paint his portrait. In the same way, the beautiful evocations of nature found in the tales are not the spontaneous eloquence of Pourrat's informants. They are the voice of Henri Pourrat, painting for us the world his tellers lived in. Sometimes Pourrat localized a tale much more thoroughly than his teller did. A radical example is "The Miller's Three Sons," in which a widely known story is woven tightly into the local geography. In this way Pourrat drew distant readers like ourselves into the landscape, hence the mentality, of his beloved Auvergne.

Second, Pourrat polished the language of the tales. Some tales, of course, had to be translated anyway from Occitan. But even the majority told in French were often filled with unfamiliar vagaries of grammar or vocabulary. Pourrat described in a letter to van Gennep, written in 1911,

> a French compounded of provincialisms, bristling with barbarisms, fractured with solecisms—a rough, limping and confused language, as Montaigne puts it, but seasoned with striking images and touches of wit.

For *Le trésor* he brought the language of the tales much closer to standard French. At same time, he preserved the general flavor of his tellers' speech not only by keeping some mild archaisms they favored but by drawing freely on a vast card file of peasant words, expressions, and idioms which he had gathered in the field. He also took images and expressions from older literary sources, including La Fontaine or Rabelais. The result, a remarkably lively, "homespun" style, is actually a sophisticated literary creation.

Pourrat also collected, wherever he could find them, not only orally transmitted tales but popular songs, jokes, riddles, or proverbs. Material from these, too, often found its way into *Le trésor*. Of course, he included jokes like "The Sick Vine Grower" intact. As for songs, he sometimes rewrote them into complete prose tales like "The Beauty and the Thirty Mariners" or "Jeanne d'Aymet." (He noted down mainly the words of songs, although he sometimes had others transcribe melodies.) But he also enlivened the orally transmitted tales with proverbs or with passages of songs he had collected elsewhere. Examples are surely the two snatches of song which the hero of "The Wooden-Clog Maker and the King's Daughter" sings to himself early in the tale. Sometimes Pourrat also took from such sources the little rhymes (in French *formulettes*, often couplets) which punctuate tales like "The Man with the Bean" or "The Black Mountain." At other times, of course, the teller herself included such *formulettes*, but Pourrat might still improve them or make them rhyme nicely if they had not done so before.

Further items in Pourrat's huge collection of local folklore were popular books, pamphlets, and broadsides. Not all the tales in *Le trésor* are from oral sources. Pourrat included many written stories, often from books originally distributed in the region by traveling salesmen. Examples in *French Folktales* include "The Village of the Damned" and "The Flight into Egypt."

"Mary-in-the-Ashes"

To return to the oral folktales, which are the heart of the matter, it is interesting to see Pourrat at work in a specific instance. Let us look at "Mary-in-the-Ashes" ("Marie-Cendron"), Pourrat's version of "Cinderella."

Reviewing in 1949 the very first volume of *Le trésor des contes*, Paul Delarue noted Pourrat's inclusion of "a good version of Cendrillon, with traditional features found in other French versions but absent from the version of Perrault." Pourrat had actually gathered three versions of the tale. The first was told to him by Marie Claustre, age seventy-eight, a lacemaker at Marsac, on November 22, 1912; the second was told by Antoinette Rocher, age seventy-five, at Pacros, on December 14, 1936; and the third was told by Alphonsine Dapzol, age fifty-two, a seamstress at Champétières, on October 24, 1943.

On the whole it was Alphonsine Dapzol's version which Pourrat adopted, but he inserted into it the passage in which Marie throws salt on the fire to drive away her evil sisters. This came from the telling by Marie Claustre, who gave the little girl the picturesque name of Gratassin de Moutassou "or else Pé d'Ane." He rejected the sketchy version given him by Antoinette Rocher.

The opening paragraph of Alphonsine Dapzol's and of Pourrat's "Marie-Cendron" reveals Pourrat's manner. In this case, the field version is quite good. You can hear the quiet voice of an old lady talking. But Pourrat's version, which says nothing startlingly different, has the density and beauty that are characteristic of his style. "Once upon a time," Dapzol began, "a very long time ago, there were a husband and wife who had a very pretty

little girl. We'll just call her Mary." Pourrat specifies that the husband was
a lord—presumably, a local squire. As to Mary herself, Pourrat elaborates
a bit, calling her "a sweet Mary, ever so pretty and clever." The following
sentence is about the same in both versions, but Pourrat adds the lyrical
flourish, "on this dreary earth of ours." Then Dapzol notes plainly, "The
mother died, the girl was young." Pourrat, for his part, inserts an appeal
to an imaginary audience: "La dame est morte, bonnes gens" ("Yes, good
people, the lady died"). One catches him here recreating imaginatively the
sort of scene described by Noël du Fail in the sixteenth century, in which
the storyteller addresses a "real," plural audience instead of one aging
folktale collector. This fiction, for Pourrat, undoubtedly served a truth
higher than that of the ethnologists, for it evokes a time when the telling
of tales had a natural place in everyone's life. Finally, Pourrat concluded
this opening paragraph with the concrete detail that Marie was "going on
seven."

The whole tale goes this way. Pourrat consistently transformed Dapzol's
pleasant but somewhat plain ingredients into thoroughly tasty fare. Two
more examples will do to illustrate the point.

First, where Dapzol described the evil sisters merely as "ugly, nasty,
jealous, and bossy," Pourrat wrote, "As puffed-up as turkeys they were,
as envious as owls, and as nosy as one-eyed rats." Dapzol here will do, but
Pourrat's version makes genuinely good reading. He succeeded beautifully
in making up for the missing "fragrance of ferns or that woodpecker yonder,
hammering away with its beak as it clings to an oak." Second, at the end
of Dapzol's version, "Everyone was invited [to the wedding] and the animals
ran around with knives in their backs." Pourrat developed this into, "Little
roast pigs roamed all crispy through the streets with an orange in their
mouth, a sprig of parsley in each ear, and a knife and fork stuck upright
in their back." No doubt that is exactly how roast pigs were prepared for
a feast in Pourrat's Auvergne, but it takes a writer to make them so mouth-
watering right there on the page. It is worth noting too that whereas Dapzol
had Mary and her prince going to the town hall to be married, Pourrat
sent them (quite properly) to the church.

Pourrat's treatment of the *formulettes* which are dotted through "Marie-
Cendron" is also revealing. Dapzol's do not scan or rhyme very well, while
the other two field versions lack them entirely. Pourrat did much more
than simply tidy up Dapzol's versification. Here again, two examples will
prove the point.

First, when the stepmother and the evil sisters come home from church,

Dapzol's stepmother speaks to Mary a cruel and tricky triplet in Occitan. Pourrat turned this *formulette* into prose ("Ah, Mary-in-the-Ashes, there you are in your corner as always . . . !"). On the other hand, it appears to be Pourrat who gave Mary the couplet which comes next ("However pretty she may be,/ She's no prettier than me.") and who added the two follow-up paragraphs which develop it. Dapzol's version barely hints at all this. Pourrat's exquisite touch brings the little girl so intensely to life that she fairly melts your heart even as you burst out laughing. Second, near the end of the tale Pourrat expanded a plain, nonrhyming phrase into the more elaborate and much more effective quatrain which starts, "You've taken the ugly one,/ Left the beauty all alone . . ." By punctuating the prose with musically rhymed verse, Pourrat greatly increased the appeal of the whole tale.

Pourrat's Sense of Decency and Fun

In short, Pourrat had edited thoroughly a tale which passed the initial scrutiny even of Paul Delarue. What, then, did he do with the occasionally gross passages which, as everyone knows, have their own place in folklore, or with risqué lampoons of priests and the Church? Did he pass such material on to his readers uncensored, or did he (as one might well suspect) tone it down or eliminate it?

To take up the matter of religion first, *Le trésor des contes* (and *French Folktales*) includes a good many religious tales. Pourrat had deep respect for the Catholic Church and all it meant in peasant society. His collection, as he knew better than anyone, would have been incomplete without such appeals to Catholic piety. These devotional tales are from written sources and some, like "The Flight into Egypt," "The Finch in May" or "Péquelé" are particularly fine. It was only when a tale reflected unfavorably on the Church that Pourrat exercised any serious censorship. Some popular tales, including ones Pourrat himself collected, joke about the unsavory sexual predicaments of priests. Pourrat kept tales like that out of *Le trésor des contes* or else modified them. One story, for example, tells how a village priest gave birth to a calf. Pourrat kept the tale but turned the priest into a mere sacristan. He also toned down, on similar grounds, a scatological moment in "The Stupid Wife." The wife, up in a tree with her husband hiding from bandits, cannot refrain from defecating. Down plops the re-sulting substance, straight into the pot where the bandits' dinner is simmering away. "Bubble, bubble, rich and brown," sing the astonished bandits, "God's own fat is tumbling down!" Pourrat's "God's own fat" ("la graisse de Dieu") is in the field version "God's own grace" ("la grâce de Dieu"). That *grâce* was too much.

Still, though respectful toward the Church and keen on "good taste," Pourrat was no prude. Although he occasionally softened crude vocabulary, he did not necessarily suppress a suggestive scene. On the contrary, he could make a suggestive description much more evocative even as he made it less flatly direct. In any case, he sometimes quarreled with editors who demanded prudish revisions. In one tale he published before the war, a king had to kiss a donkey *under* its tail. When the editors demanded that the king kiss the donkey *above* its tail instead, Pourrat was outraged. Unfortunately, he had to compromise in the end.

Henri Pourrat, who insisted that when truth demands it even a king should kiss a donkey in the you-know-what, was not above a little hoax, either. Detesting tourists and folkloric displays for summer visitors, he once suggested that newspapers should report frightful viper infestations in the Auvergne region, together with the resulting tragic deaths. He even published a tongue-in-cheek celebration of tourism, ending it with a resigned sigh, "What a pity that our countryside should be so infested with vipers!"

Remarks and Acknowledgments

Perhaps only one thing about these English translations needs explaining. The original stories are filled with such monetary units as sous, francs, écus, pistoles, and louis. Since no familiar counterparts exist in English, I translated most of these only vaguely. However, I preserved écu as "crown," kept "pistole," and left a few louis around too. For what it is worth, a franc was twenty sous; an écu was three francs; a pistole was ten francs; and a louis was twenty-four francs. Actually, the pistole never existed as an official unit of currency.

I wish to thank two scholars who answered my questions about Henri Pourrat and his work, and who kindly provided me with vital written materials. Bernadette Bricout of the University of Paris, who has exhaustive knowledge of *Le trésor des contes* and its background, discussed Pourrat and his work with me at length, provided me with xerox copies of the three field versions of "Mary-in-the-Ashes," and airmailed to me (in Japan) a second copy of volume 1 of her doctoral thesis when the first copy was swallowed up by a postal strike. Anne-Marie Thiesse, of the Centre d'Ethnologie Française in Paris, prepared for me an excellent briefing on Pourrat, xeroxed a set of articles and reviews, and swiftly sent me another important article when, by a circuitous route, I at last found out about it.

Finally, I would like to dedicate these translations to my daughter Clare.

Royall Tyler

Part One

FAIRY

ENCHANTMENTS

1. The Green Peacock

There once was a man so lost in worry that he set off wherever the path would lead him, and wandered through the forest up there in the mountains without even knowing where he was going. On and on he went, rolling his hat along before him with the end of his stick. Suddenly he looked up, and there was a lady under a huge tree—the loveliest lady one could ever hope to see.

"What's the matter and what are you looking for, my good man?" said she. "You seem very worried and downcast."

"Ah, lady," he replied, "I've a whole houseful of children at home, and now another's on the way. I have to find this new one a godmother, and I don't know where to look."

"I'll be the godmother. When the child is born, good man, simply call me."

"Oh, lady, I'll call you with all my heart."

"All you need do is come and show yourself under this tree."

He went straight home, greatly relieved to have found a way out of his trouble.

The child came into the world three days later. It was a boy. The father hurried under the tree to tell the lady. She appeared as she'd promised, and became the godmother. She had him named Little-John. And what a godmother she made! She was so beautiful! She'd suddenly arrive on her horse all caparisoned with gold, come to fetch Little-John for a day or more.

"My godmother! My godmother's here!" He'd have vaulted over walls to get to her, he was so happy to see her.

Perhaps they rode off together to the Land of Dancing Water, or the Land of the Singing Apple, or the Land of the Little Blue Bird Who Knows

All. Who can say? Anyway, one day Little-John and his godmother were strolling about when they saw a peacock with his tail spread wide: a peacock all green, all blue, all rainbow-colored. (My late mother, you know, saw two peacocks at a castle. I've never seen one myself, but anyway, I say this peacock was green because that's how my mother described them.)

"Oh, godmother, what a beautiful peacock! I wish he were mine!"

> Little-John, Little-John, leave that peacock alone!
> He'll make you weep and groan!

But it was no use. Little-John had to have that peacock or he'd have practically jumped out of his skin; and never mind *who* might try to stop him, even the horned devil himself. So he caught the bird and carried it off to his father's garden, just as proud as if he'd been given all of Paris for his own.

But there came a day when the king said to his servant, "Go and fetch me Little-John. I've had enough of his airs, with that peacock of his. Why, now he even boasts he could go all by himself, with his peacock, and bring me back my daughter from Castle-on-the-Water, though I've besieged the place in vain with all my army. Well, I'll take him at his word. If he *doesn't* bring me back my daughter, I'll see his head fly from his shoulders!"

The servant leaped into the saddle and galloped at full speed to bring Little-John the king's message.

"Oh no, oh no!" cried Little-John. "I swear I never said anything of the kind! *I'm* supposed to have talked about the king's daughter and Castle-on-the-Water?"

"Well, it's the king's will," replied the servant, "whatever the truth may be. If you don't bring him back his daughter, you and your life will be parting company."

Now Little-John's back was to the wall. He ran to his godmother, who, of course, was a fairy. She could do lots of things, but not everything.

"I *told* you," she said.

> Leave that peacock alone!
> He'll make you weep and groan!

"But tell me, godmother, what shall I do now?"

"I don't quite know."

"Godmother, my godmother, oh, what *am* I going to do?"

"You're going to take three boats and load one with flour, the second with white bread, and the third with all sorts of goods. When you get to the edge of the sea, you'll find there hundreds and hundreds of little fishes, all of them starving. You'll give them your flour and your white bread. Then you'll cry, 'Goods for sale! Fine goods of all kinds for sale!'"

So Little-John went down to the sea in his three boats, and he found there just what his godmother had foretold: hundreds and hundreds of fishes, gulping desperately. He gave them all the bread and flour he'd brought. The fish revived, greeted him, and thanked him.

"Good sir," they cried, "only tell us what we can do for you! Your kindness has saved us!"

"Never fear, little fishes," he replied. "Since you wish me so well, I'll surely have favors to ask of you."

Then Little-John stood on the shore and shouted as loud as he could, like a peddler, "Fine goods of all kinds for sale!"

The fishes carried the news to Castle-on-the-Water, where the king's daughter was. She got straight into her boat and came to look at all the treasures. Perhaps Little-John had put his peacock up on top of the mast, to give his ship a more gallant air. And when she saw Little-John, the peacock, and all the wonderful goods his godmother had given him, well, she had the keys to Castle-on-the-Water with her, and she dropped them into the deep, deep sea. She crossed over onto Little-John's boat, to go with him wherever he might take her. So he took her back to the king, just as happy as he could be, and then went to thank his godmother.

Before he even got there, the king called his servant again.

"Go tell Little-John," he said, "who boasted so loudly he'd bring back my daughter all by himself, with that peacock of his, from Castle-on-the-Water, when I with my whole army had failed—go tell him he must bring me the castle itself. And if he doesn't, I'll see his head fly from his shoulders."

The servant jumped on his horse, galloped at top speed after Little-John, caught up with him on the road, and told him what the king had said.

Little-John was as crushed with grief as he'd been dizzy with joy but a moment before, and he went to complain to his godmother.

"I *told* you," she said.

> Leave that peacock alone!
> He'll make you weep and groan!

"But tell me, godmother, what shall I do now?"

"I don't quite know."

"Godmother, my godmother, oh, what *am* I going to do?"

"You'll have to take three more boats filled with flour, bread, and wine, because wine gives strength, you know. You'll find lots and lots of fishes, and you'll give them all they want. Perhaps they'll help you."

Little-John went back down to the sea with his three boats, and, yes, he did find fishes! Starving fishes had come from everywhere, once they heard he was giving food away. And when he'd given them his flour, bread, and wine, they hardly knew what to do with themselves, they were so eager to find words to thank him, and nice things to do for him.

"You've done everything for us, kind sir!" they cried. "If only we could do something for *you*!"

"Dear little fishes, you *can*, you *can*. Do me the kindness of picking up Castle-on-the-Water and bringing it to me! But there'll have to be millions and millions of you!"

Well, they didn't mind that a bit—no, nothing seemed too much to them as long as it was for their Little-John. Such a horde of them got to work that they loaded the castle on their backs, and on it came, sailing

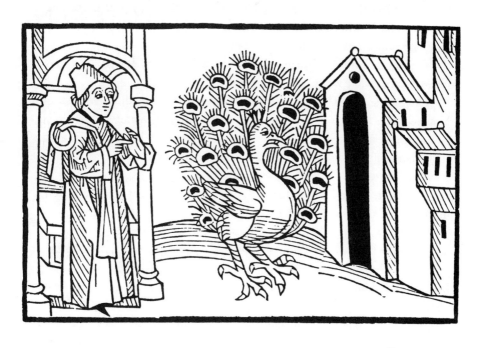

over the water! Little-John was very happy, and so was the king's daughter, and so was His Majesty the king.

But Little-John had hardly set off to thank his godmother when the king started looking angry and called his servant back again.

"Go tell Little-John," he said, "that he's made his point. Yes, he certainly did bring back my daughter from Castle-on-the-Water, all by himself with his peacock, though I with all my army failed; and he certainly did then bring me the castle itself. So now he's won himself this task: if he doesn't bring along the *keys* to this castle, I'll see his head fly from his shoulders!"

Little-John knew he hadn't done any preening or boasting; he swore great oaths to that. But the servant could do nothing about it. Little-John was going to have to do as the king wished. Ah, those keys so deep down at the bottom of the sea! Sad and crestfallen, Little-John went straight to his godmother.

"I *told* you, didn't I!" she replied.

> *Leave that peacock alone!*
> *He'll make you weep and groan!*

"You're the one who wanted it this way, so manage as you think best."

He got his three boats again, filled them with flour, bread, and wine, and went back down to the sea. The poor fishes, who'd had such a bad year, ate and drank their fill.

"Oh good, kind sir," they cried, "you do so much for us! How we'd love to know what we can do for you!"

"Dear little fishes," he answered, "yes, there *is* something you can do. You see, I'm here to find the keys to Castle-on-the-Water."

Just then some more fishes arrived, very late. "Why, we came across such a pile of old discarded metal in the sea," they complained, "that we could hardly get by!"

"That's it!" cried Little-John. "We're in luck! That discarded metal must be just the keys I need so badly!"

And it was. The whole tribe of fishes threw themselves into the task and brought the keys up from the deep, deep waters, very happy to be of service! As happy, in fact, as fish in the sea are bound to be when they've had a good dinner and find themselves able to do their generous host a good turn.

Little-John, happier even than the fishes, took the keys to His Majesty the king. The king's daughter gave him a sweet smile, but the king himself turned away. All the thanks Little-John got was to hear the king tell him, "Little-John, you're too much the magician, and magicians like you don't live long."

You could tell he meant he was going to rid the earth of Little-John. More crestfallen than ever, Little-John could think of nothing better to do than to go to his godmother for help.

"And what do you want me to tell you *this* time?" she cried. "All right, here's my wand. If ever the king mounts his throne and orders that you be put to death, you have only to touch him with this wand and say, 'Let the king be dry as a stick of wood!' "

So Little-John returned to the king's court. He got the king's daughter, who loved him so much, and he got Castle-on-the-Water with the key in every door. And when the king passed away, he got the kingdom. In fact, he got every last thing.

2. Mary-in-the-Ashes (Marie-Cendron)

There was once a man, a lord, and he and his wife had a little girl named Mary: a sweet Mary, ever so pretty and clever. They were so happy that of course, on this dreary earth of ours, their happiness couldn't last. Yes, good people, the lady died. The girl might have been going on seven at the time. The father, wanting to do the right thing, married again.

At first, the new wife treated Mary as she treated her own daughters—she herself had lost her husband, and she had two. *Her* daughters, though, were as repulsive as Mary herself was charming. As puffed-up as turkeys they were, as envious as owls, and as nosy as one-eyed rats. By the time three weeks had passed they'd turned their sister, who wasn't their sister, into their own servant. It was up to Mary to sweep their room, to polish their shoes, to wash their skirts . . . In fact, they even wanted Mary to comb their hair.

Mary's godmother told her:

"When they call you, sit in the corner by the hearth and make sure you've tossed a handful of salt on the fire. Then pretend to pick lice. You'll see, they'll leave you alone."

It worked. The salt crackled like thunder. The two others thought they were hearing lice popping between Mary's fingernails, and shrieked with horror. "Don't you come near us!" they cried. "Don't you come anywhere near us! You'll get your bugs all over us too!"

That's how Mary fended them off. She wanted nothing better than to stay by herself in her corner. Sometimes, too, she hid in the closet among the pots, pans, and rags; or in the laundry room behind the great washtub. But as the months went by, she more and more often had to wash the dishes, then the table linen, then all the dirty clothes in the house. She ended up the regular laundry and kitchen girl. Winters passed, and summers, and years. No one noticed her any more. Now her place was in the corner among the ashes, the only name they gave her was Mary-in-the-Ashes or, sometimes, Ash Girl.

The two others, as they grew up, despised her so! That pair of hussies had to show themselves off at every gathering. If they weren't as pretty as they might have been, they certainly acted as though they were. You'd have thought it was their sacred duty to display their beauty wherever they could. God knows, though, how ugly their faces really were, especially when they came to say to poor Mary:

"Well, Mary-in-the-Ashes, are you coming to the dance?"

"No, no, I'm not going."

"That's just as well. You were made to stay in your corner with your nose to the wall and your fingers in the ashes!"

Mary-in-the-Ashes bore this life patiently. As for her father, he dressed in grey, let his beard grow, and noticed nothing. At least, he didn't dare say anything. Often enough, a man's a coward toward his wife. There are rude women and there are crude women, but that second wife of his was just plain bad.

One Sunday she and her hussies had decided to go early to church. There was supposed to be a solemn high mass and a very fine sermon. First thing that morning, she could tell that Mary-in-the-Ashes wanted very much to go too. So out of pure meanness that stepmother spilled a whole sack of peas in the kitchen.

"Pick them up, Mary-in-the-Ashes, and do it fast before any get squashed. Leave out just one and you'll pay for it!"

Poor Ash Girl could only obey. She set about picking up the peas. But they rolled into corners, under the firewood and behind the basket of turnips; or else they slipped into every crack between the flagstones. The more she picked up, the more there were. (Actually, the stepmother was a bit of a sorceress.) After a while, Mary-in-the-Ashes couldn't stand it any more and her heart broke. It wasn't that she was resentful, it's just that she felt such terrible malice bearing down on her. The others had gone to church, and there she was, stuck in a corner full of ashes and dishwater! It seemed to Mary that no one would *ever*, in all the days of her life, come to chat with her or keep her company.

Just then her godmother appeared. The truth is that her godmother was a fairy—and what a *good* fairy! Perhaps she believed a little suffering was good for her goddaughter's upbringing. But when, out in her fairyland, she began to feel her goddaughter was just too sad for words, she came right away.

"You're crying, dear? Why aren't you at mass?"

"Oh, dear godmother, I wanted to go so badly! But you see, I have to pick up all these peas, and the more I pick up, the more there are. There won't be any mass for me this Sunday."

Her godmother stepped toward her:

> *By the power of my wand,*
> *Let those peas go back where they belong!*

All the peas popped straight back into their sack. A mouse scouring the house from the broom behind the door to the three pots on the hearth wouldn't have found a single one.

The godmother took another step. She touched Mary with her wand, and suddenly Mary-in-the-Ashes was changed into a fine lady so beautiful, in looks and dress, that no princess could have surpassed her! Her gown shone like a field of stars! And her slippers, why, they were glass!

The fairy sent her to church looking like *that*, though she told her she should leave before the last lesson. Perhaps the gown was enchanted, or perhaps the enchantment would only last exactly the length of the mass. Anyway, if Ash Girl didn't leave at the right moment, something awful would happen to her.

Mary, of course, was delighted, and promised to leave the church in time.

She got there just as the people were about to go in. Everyone ran to stare at her and wonder who she was. They even climbed on each other's shoulders for a better look. No one knew her, not even her two sisters. She could see that well enough when she went to sit down beside them.

But she hadn't forgotten. Her godmother's words were too well lodged in her head. Once the Ite Missa Est was said, she disappeared.

By the time her stepmother and her two sisters got home, she was busy around the house as usual, in her coarse apron.

"Ah, Mary-in-the-Ashes, there you are in your corner as always, scratching at the ashes! If only you'd come to church with us, you'd have seen such a fine lady, so splendidly dressed! Oh, wasn't she ever! And she was so pretty!"

> However pretty she may be,
> She's no prettier than me!

"What's that you're singing, Mary-in-the-Ashes? Not prettier than you? Oh, you should have seen her! You should have seen her gown and her slippers! They shone like stars!"

Each sister cut the other short, breathlessly elaborating on the lady's skirt, her ribbons, her grace, and her pretty ways. "They can't be very smart if they didn't recognize me," said Mary-in-the-Ashes to herself. But she kept her eyes lowered for fear they might catch a glint of laughter in them, and went on peeling the turnips.

The next Sunday she wanted very much to go back to church. Her stepmother could see that, of course. So the horrid woman took ashes from the ash bin near the oven and spilled a whole bushel of them all over the house.

"Ah, you Ash Mary, you scratcher in the ashes, look, here's a job for you! Pick them up, pick them up! And if I see any trace of ashes when I get back, I'll let you know about it with the broom handle!"

The poor girl got to work. Poor, poor Mary cried her eyes out. Still, she must have had *some* hope at least in her godmother. Heavens, when your godmother's a fairy . . . Her godmother would manage to get her to church!

She was just beginning to sweep and mop when she saw her godmother in the doorway.

"You're not at mass this Sunday either?"

"Look, dear godmother, just *look* at all these ashes. And I'm supposed to clean them up so you could never tell they'd been there at all."

Her godmother stepped toward her:

> By the power of my wand,
> Let those ashes go back where they belong!

Then she took another step and touched Mary-in-the-Ashes. Mary was beautiful again—even more splendidly beautiful than the Sunday before. She had her glass slippers and a gown more lustrous than the stars in the sky.

"Look out now, my girl, it's only for as long as the mass goes on. Make sure you leave in time! Goodness, be careful!"

Ash Girl promised. But she was sixteen, or seventeen, maybe. Is anyone careful at that age? Anyway, there with her secret among the congregation, with all the lights and the singing, she certainly couldn't be blamed if she forgot the promise she'd made her godmother. And that's not all, either, because that Sunday the king's son was there. Talk of the lovely lady you could see at church on Sundays had run like wildfire through the land. The king's son had heard it, too. He came and waited on the square, and was charmed by her at first sight.

How eyes do meet and speak sometimes! She too, at her first sight of him . . . Dear Lord, what dazzling sunlight burst forth then! It really made her head spin. And now, oh heavens, she had so many prayers to say if she was to find her way through it all! She had so much to ask God for! And that's why she very nearly let the moment slip by. She only just got up and out in time. Ash Girl didn't run, she flew!

The king's son had wanted to see her again on the way out from mass. He ran after her, and almost caught her, too, by the heel, as she raced down the church steps. All he got, though, was a glass slipper left behind in his hand.

Outside the town, under a great oak by the roadside, he rejoined his valet and his saddled horse.

"Valet, valet, didn't you see a lady who is beauty itself?"

"All I saw was a girl—not one for you to keep company with, but a country girl."

Because when the time came the fairy dress fell away. Mary turned back into Ash Girl with her coarse apron and her clogs.

There was the king's son, now, alone with his glass slipper. But that slipper was certainly something, it was so dainty and wonderful. He told himself that the one who wore this slipper was surely dainty in every way— dainty and lovely enough to become a princess, a queen, or even more.

"I shall marry the girl who lost this slipper! I shall have no other wife! She's the one for me!"

The sisters, meanwhile, got back to the house, all primping, pompous, and puffed up. They strutted about as though *they* were the ones who'd brought the princess to church—in fact, as though they'd made her themselves!

"Ah, poor Ash Girl. All you're good for is sitting in your corner, scratching away at the ashes. Now, that princess in church, *she* shone like a star! Oh, she was pretty, so pretty—yes, prettier still than she was Sunday last!"

Mary kept her eyes downcast, afraid she'd give herself away by the way they twinkled and laughed.

> *However pretty she may be,*
> *She's no prettier than me!*

"What's that she's saying? No prettier than she? Ha, ha, Mary-in-the-Ashes, Slop Mary, ha, ha, Ash Girl!"

Oh, those hussies laughed and mocked her so!

Then they turned once more to the beautiful lady and the prince.

"They say the king's son wants to marry her. If he sees *you*, he'll probably come asking for *you* instead!"

That week, the king's son had the drum beaten through all the streets of the town. He had it cried abroad that the slipper would be tried on all the girls roundabout. Not one was to be missed.

He had someone go from house to house, the way they invite people to a funeral mass. This had nothing to do with a funeral, though, but with a wedding. How all the girls longed that their foot might fit that slipper! But when they tried it on, they all found their foot was too big.

At last, the turn came round to Mary's sisters. Those sneaky creatures knew Mary's feet were quite a bit smaller than theirs. So they shut her up in the back of the closet, they stuffed her behind the big washtub. "Goodness, the king's messenger has better things to do than to kneel before that scratcher in the ashes. Anyway, she wasn't even in church."

The messenger came. He tried the glass slipper on the elder sister, but not even her toes would go in.

The younger sister was next. Confound it! Her foot didn't go in too well, either. But never mind. All the other girls had already failed the test. There had to be *one*. The sisters' mother, Ash Girl's stepmother, decided to do something about it. She was a bit of a sorceress, you remember. She whittled away at the younger sister's heel, and somehow, one way or another, she got the foot into the slipper.

At least, they say it went in.

Well, someone went straight to fetch the king's son, and he came. Then he saw the girl. The wretched lad had given his word! You can imagine how the mother pressed him to keep it. There was no way out. They had to head right off to the church.

Ash Girl, meanwhile, was at the back of the closet. "This is where I'll be stuck all my life," she was saying to herself, "without company or friends." She wept floods of tears.

But her godmother wasn't a fairy for nothing. As the wedding party stepped out the door, they heard a little bird twittering its song. From the top of the lilac tree the little bird was singing:

> You've taken the ugly one,
> Left the beauty all alone
> In the closet, rub-a-dub,
> Behind the big washtub.

"Stop!" cried the king's son. "What's that bird saying?"

"Idle chatter, nothing more," answered the stepmother. "Never mind its jabbering. What we *do* have to worry about is hurrying. We might be late. Father might not wait for us."

But as the wedding party passed through the courtyard gate, they heard the bird again. From the top of the big linden tree the bird was singing:

> You've taken the ugly one,
> Left the beauty all alone
> In the closet, rub-a-dub,
> Behind the big washtub.
> You've taken the ugly one,
> Left the beauty all alone . . .

The stepmother rushed along, already in a horrible temper. She knew what would happen if they went into that closet. This time, though, there was nothing she could do about it. The king's son had listened. He ran back to the closet with the washtub in it and found Mary-in-the-Ashes. The messenger told him he hadn't tried the slipper on her. He did it then, and the glass slipper slipped right on! Mary-in-the-Ashes took the other slipper from her pocket—she'd kept it right with her for fear her sisters would find it—and put it on the other foot. Both slippers fit as though she'd been born wearing them.

"The one who wears these slippers is the one I must marry," said the king's son.

The two sisters and the ladies, young and old, all exchanged glances and began to murmur and groan. "Is it possible? The king's son wants to marry Mary-in-the-Ashes! Ash Mary and the king's son! Dear God, can it really be?"

But the godmother now appeared and touched the Ash Girl with her wand. The Ash Girl in her glorious gown shone brighter than the sun.

Everyone stared wide-eyed. They knew her now for that dazzling beauty, the beauty in the church! There were cries of wonder and admiration. Those people couldn't have been more confounded if all the ashes in the ash bin had turned before their eyes to flakes of gold.

There was no holding back the king's son now.

The wedding was celebrated that very morning (he insisted), and very grandly, too. Perhaps the fairy had something to do with it as well. Little roast pigs roamed all crispy through the streets, with an orange in their mouth, a sprig of parsley in each ear, and a knife and fork stuck upright in their back. If you wanted a piece you just carved yourself one. For eight days everything was joy, dancing, and feasting, with bagpipes playing, pigs roasting, and glasses clinking!

Then there were the two sisters and the stepmother. Their spite ate at them till they got jaundice, and by the end of the week they were dead. Mary-in-the-Ashes mourned them a little, but before another week was out the king's son, so dear and tender, had comforted her very nicely indeed.

3. The False Child

Once a woman was nursing a little baby, so pretty a baby that you could have gazed at him for hours. His sweet little face was as bright as a flower, and then there were those big, surprised eyes of his, and their way of looking at you, and the smile that followed. It seemed to light up the whole house. For his mother, such a smile was like a sunbeam straight from God. Her heart burned with a sweet warmth whenever her dear child greeted her that way.

It was March, when sap runs in the willows, and along the hedges you can smell the first violets among the sprouting nettles. That day the restless wind was gusting over meadows green with new grass—grass as green as grass ever can be. The mother showed her child three red leaves dancing in the gusts on a big oak tree, then lost herself playing with his tiny fingers. "This little hen laid the egg," she chanted, "this one put it on to boil . . ."

Then it was time to peel the leeks and next to hang the pot. And the water jug under the stone sink was empty. Night was falling. The mother ran to the well. She didn't lock the door, because after all, this was in the mountains, and what did people there know about locks? In those days there was one thief per village. He picked up things left carelessly outside— a strap, the blade of a plow—but he never would have gone into a house to steal.

Off she went, never thinking harm might strike while she was gone. But when she got back to the dark house she heard a sort of snuffling from the cradle and knew something terrible had happened. That sound couldn't be her own child's breathing.

Paler than her white headdress, she piled wood on the fire, then peered down into the cradle. What did she see? A tiny thing with a ruddy face— like a toad's, you know—all wrinkled and shriveled the way bad apples are, the ones you just leave on the tree. It was looking at her with grey, wild eyes, its expression drawn and sly. Poor woman, she could only bury her face in her hands to stifle her screams.

No one could doubt it for a minute, she said. In any case she, the mother, knew that creature wasn't her baby. Night or day, it neither spoke nor cried, but clung to her breast with its little clawed hands, butted her cruelly with its head, and never, never had enough. Again and again and again it wanted more. Instead of her good little baby, she had this clawing glutton that could only snuffle like a wildcat!

The poor mother was choked with tears. Come evening she couldn't stand the house any longer, but fled over the meadows to a certain old woman who lived in the mountains. Up there it's all wilderness. Through the blossoming plum trees you see water whiten as it tumbles down the rocks. There are steep ravines, deep shadows, pines clinging for dear life to cliffs, and perhaps a few gliding coils of cloud.

"Such an awful thing's happened to my little Johnny! In his place I found this other one who stares at me like an old man. Why, he's not even weaned, and he must be five or maybe even seven years old!"

"Oh yes, he's five, or seven, or perhaps far older still! He doesn't say a word? Who knows? An old man with white hair in his ears might speak in a less quavering voice. You'll have to find out. You'll have to make him talk."

"But what do you think?"

"What do I think? You see the mouths of those caves, under the pines? At twilight the fairies left the ravine and at dark they slipped into your house. They took your baby and left the glutton in his place. You've got to find out what he is!"

"And how am I to do that?"

"Listen to me!"

She drew the mother up close to her and whispered some instructions.

"Go, my girl, and do it right! May the Good Lady help you and give you back your child!"

Three days and three nights the poor mother pretended the glutton was her own dear child. The third day she made a show of having ten strong laborers over to eat who were to work her fields. She busied herself between cupboard and stove, rushed all over the house, darted about, fussed, and complained she was going out of her head. Six pails she filled with milk and four basins with cream. She carved away at the side of lard and took down the rope of onions. "Oh, where'd I put the salt?" she cried. "And the herbs? And the butter? Where's the flour? Oh dear, oh dear, what a job, with ten strong laborers coming, to cook dinner in an eggshell!"

All her scurrying turned around this eggshell. Sometimes she put it in the middle of the table and sometimes she picked it up in her fingers.

Dinner for ten laborers in an eggshell! The glutton looked on, so amazed that his mouth hung half open. Finally he couldn't stand it. He had to speak. And in a hoarse, worn-out voice he murmured:

> Three hundred days, six thousand years
> I've lived, and seen sprout swell to ear;
> Before the great tree seen the seed,
> Before the highroad seen the mead,
> Before the cottage seen the plot,
> But never seen a white cooking pot!

That's what the old woman had said: "Have him watch you pretend to cook for ten laborers in an eggshell, and you'll force him to speak. If he watches you without surprise, he's a Christian child. But if he's some fairy creature, then he'll have seen a bit of the world, and so he'll be surprised and will speak. If he speaks, whip him. Whip him hard. If he's whipped he'll cry out, and if he cries out he'll be heard. If he's heard they'll come to take him back, and if they take him back they'll return your baby. But if he doesn't speak, be sure not to touch him, not even with the tip of your finger!"

He spoke and repeated twice:

> *Three hundred days, six thousand years*
> *I've lived, and seen sprout swell to ear;*
> *Before the great tree seen the seed,*
> *Before the highroad seen the mead,*
> *Before the cottage seen the plot,*
> *But never seen a white cooking pot!*

"Aha, you talker, you've seen too much! I've got you now! You've betrayed yourself. You're only a fairy waif, boy, a dwarf, an old man, older than the roads and the wells. Yes, I've got you now! Take that, and that, and that!"

Blow after blow smacked into his hide, as he kicked and squalled. She spanked him furiously, without mercy; she beat him like washing spread on a rock. Oh yes, she showed him the heat of her hand!

"Stop, stop, woman, don't beat him so! Do we ever beat yours? He's like a king in our own kingdom! Return this one to us now. You have yours back!"

In a whirl of wild wind the fairy passed; the flame hissed as it went by. The gust and the fairy carried off the false child. They vanished through the banging front door, and after them flew the ashes from the hearth.

Turning back to the cradle, the mother saw her little one looking at her with eyes so full of goodness: dear eyes, filled with dreams of red apples and hazelnuts, looking at her, yes, laughing—her little smiler of dazzling smiles!

4. The Children from the Sea

There once was a woman with an only daughter, still at the breast. Her cabin stood at the sea's edge, on the island shore, and there she lived off her goats and what the sea brought her.

One night there was a storm. Surely a ship had broken up on the rocks. She went to see whether the ocean had brought her some wreckage, some smashed timbers, or some bits of wood for her fire. But what she saw, floating in over the waters, was a cradle with two infants lying in it, asleep.

The pair, a boy and a girl, looked just alike. They were brother and sister, no doubt—in fact, clearly twins. Their diapers were of fine linen, fastened with gold pins. Otherwise the cradle held only the miniature portrait of a beautiful lady, crowned with diamonds. Why, she looked like a young queen! The woman rummaged around but found nothing else.

All the others on board must have perished. She took the two babies home to her cabin, nursed them at her breast, and fed them the milk from her goats. She brought them up with her own daughter, Marotte.

"They'll work for me when they're big and strong," thought she. And later they did just that. They planted a garden for her among the rocks: three fig trees leaning in the wind, two tufts of rosemary, a border of flowers like drops of blood, and three beds of vegetables.

The almost-deserted island supported no one but them, their goats, and one old man. The children grew up wholly ignorant of the world. They would only trade a word or two with the old man when they met him, and he taught them to garden a bit. The boy enjoyed the work so much that he became very good at it. He learned to grow lettuce, cucumbers, and beans, and to graft and trellis pears. The old man came to see him and give him advice.

"He's such a good boy," mused the old man, "that he hasn't turned brutish in this wild spot. But he oughtn't to stay here much longer." And he whispered in the boy's ear, "You'd be better off at the king's. Go, leave. Cross the sea. I've lived over there, in the king's garden. I'd like to return one day."

"But I couldn't leave Marinette, my sister," said Marin—for those were the names the woman had given them. "I'll never leave her."

Everything Marin did, and everything he found, was for Marinette. And if Marinette picked up some pretty shell, she wove it into a rush hat for Marin. If she clotted a cheese with the milk from her goats, that too was for her Marin. Both had but one single heart.

The old man tried to bring the boy around to his point of view, and the boy, being so bright, more or less understood.

"Yes," he said, "I ought to leave. But really, how could I possibly leave my sister behind?"

He thought it over a day, a month, and a year.

"I know what I'll do," he told the old man. "I'll go, but I'll take along this portrait that was in our cradle. Anyone would now swear it's a picture of my sister. In a year I'll come back for her."

He told the woman in the cabin that he was going to cross the sea, to be the king's gardener.

"That's a good idea," she replied. "And when you're at the king's—they say he's young and kind—remember us here, Marotte and me. I've fed you, you and your sister. Don't abandon me!"

"Oh no, I promise I'll take you with me too!"

"Do you swear it?"

"Yes, I swear!"

He sailed away, torn by this parting from his sister and happy (though he never said so) to breathe different air than Marotte and the woman. Above all, he was glad to go before the king: this king who was no older than he, but whose praise floated like a song over the islands and the sea. Standing forward on the bridge with his hair streaming in the wind, he sailed away. Everything began to open before him: the sea, the world, and perhaps the king's own favor. And under his shirt he wore the portrait which so resembled his sister. He gazed at it when no one was looking.

On landing he went straight to the castle, and the king received him. Marin liked him at once and swore himself to his service. As for the king, he liked Marin as well. He took him on right away as a gardener and told Marin all his duties. There was so much work to be done! Gardening is never finished. You spend the whole day at it, then the next day, then the next, and still you can hardly tell anyone's been there. You manure, spade, hoe, weed, rake, according to the season; or set out seedlings or prepare vegetable beds. There in the king's garden, Marin worked from dawn to dusk.

Sometimes, behind a nicely trained pear tree or a clump of big sunflowers, he'd straighten up, take off his hat, and wipe his forehead. That's when he'd take out the portrait and think of his sister and their garden on the island. He'd wonder what she was doing just then. Perhaps the woman and Marotte weren't treating her well. Perhaps she was dying of loneliness with him so far away.

One evening, far down a path, he was lost in thought this way, gazing at the portrait, when suddenly he sensed someone behind him, looking over his shoulder. He turned and saw the king.

"Show me," said the king. "Whose picture is it?"

"My twin sister's, sire."

"Let me have it. You no longer need it. Go at once, take my ship, and fetch her from your island. Bring her straight back here. She was born to be queen over all who see her. I swear I'll have no other wife!"

The king was still gazing at the portrait.

"Why is she crowned with diamonds, like a queen? Was this wedding then decreed long ago?"

"I don't know, sire. I only know that a woman found us in a cradle washed in from the sea. The cradle held this portrait, which has become my sister's own."

The king stared at Marin, studied his face.

"I believe you, you who look so like her. I'll always believe what you say!"

He had the sail hoisted and Marin went aboard, full of joy. In no time he was off on the royal ship. Three days later, toward midday, he reached his island and rushed to the cabin, where he found Marinette, Marotte, and Marotte's mother eating their fish soup.

"Sister, sister, you're to follow me to the king's castle! He saw your portrait and wants you for his wife!"

He shouldn't have said all that, especially in front of the other two. But he was so loyal a young man that he couldn't even imagine pretense or treachery.

The mother stood and put down her spoon like someone who's finished eating.

"You'll take us all," she said, putting on her clogs. "I fed you in your need. Now you're going to help us in your good fortune. Besides, you swore."

"How evil I am!" thought Marin. "It's true, she *did* feed us when we were little. It gives me a shiver just to see the two of them, her and Marotte. I don't know why, but I feel something—I feel in their hearts they don't much care for my sister. But how could I think such a thing? This woman saved us and fed us, and I swore to her I'd take her to the king."

Still, he couldn't help himself. He wanted to tell them he couldn't take them to the castle, that he wasn't allowed to. But all red as he was with confusion and embarrassment, he just couldn't say it. He was so stuck that his tongue got all tangled up in his mouth. Then from red he turned pale and altogether lost the power of speech. Standing right there in the cabin, he found he was as mute as a fish.

All four boarded the royal vessel.

Marinette's stroke of good fortune had filled Marotte and her mother with envy. They stood high on the bridge, with nothing to do but watch the waves.

Idle girl,
Spiteful girl.

All day they brooded and brooded about Marinette, and their hearts were full of venom. Their thoughts were only of malice, rage, and death.

As twilight fell, but before the lantern was lit, the old woman lay in wait. The captain was at the wheel and the sailors in the rigging, for the wind was rising. Marin's back was turned. The old woman slipped to Marinette's side, then suddenly leaned over the rail as though she'd just dropped her handkerchief. When Marinette leaned over too, the old women grabbed her by the feet and pitched her overboard.

Just then, Marin turned around and saw what was happening, or thought he saw. He hurled himself at the woman, but couldn't cry out or speak. That instant there came a terrific clap of thunder and a storm broke with such fury that it was all he could do to hold on for dear life. It lasted till the morning.

Marin now knew only one thing: his sister was gone. He felt in his heart that the old woman must have thrown her into the sea, but he couldn't swear that he'd seen it happen. And how was he to make himself understood when he was mute and had never been taught to write? Being only sixteen and unused to life in the wide world, he was wild with grief and frustration.

After a storm like that the sailors had enough to do without counting the women. Anyway, they'd hardly noticed the group that had got on board. The king's orders had just been to bring him one woman. So three days later the ship reached port. Marin, Marotte, and the old woman went up to the castle.

The king hardly knew what to do before this girl who didn't look at all like the portrait. As for the gardener, he had nothing to say and seemed completely lost.

"The storm got his tongue," explained the old woman. "The lightning nearly killed us all. You see, sire, how it sort of cooked her face a bit— not that she doesn't look still lovelier for it! But all she needs to recover are patience and rest."

The king had given his word. The lightning, which had turned his

gardener mute, wasn't going to make him take back his oath just because
it had twisted and hardened the features of his betrothed. Still, his heart
hardly sang. How could he love this stubborn-looking girl with her beady
little eyes and her skin pimplier than a turkey's neck? Fond as he was of
Marin, he wanted so much to hear his story. But Marin seemed half dazed,
like someone who's been clubbed over the head.

> *Do you care?*
> *Are you there?*

As far as the young king was concerned, these were the only questions
worth asking Marin, and he asked them each time he came upon the young
man wandering sadly through the castle courtyard or along the avenue lined
with black trees.

Now, the king had a talking bird, a very rare creature he dearly prized.
This bird got into the habit of asking Marin in the same way.

> *Do you care?*
> *Are you there?*

Still, the wedding was celebrated. A splendid wedding it was, too, but
the king was not happy. As for Marin, he seemed duller than ever. When
the king asked him to make the queen a bouquet, his hand shook as he
worked. More than ever, the bird beat his ears with

> *Do you care?*
> *Are you there?*

The old woman heard this so often that she came to fear the bird. She
got the idea that by pestering Marin it would finally make him speak. Or
perhaps the bird kept at it because it already knew everything.

One evening she could stand it no longer, and she drove a sharp knife
into the bird's heart. Then she hid the bloody knife under Marin's pillow
and told the king that Marin had killed his bird.

The king had two servants bring Marin before him. His only defense
was the look in his eye and the expression on his face, but this look and
expression spoke loud.

The king gazed past Marin at the garden and sky behind, as though searching yonder for some truth he couldn't quite grasp. "Anyway," he said to himself, "even if Marin did kill the bird, I forgive him. He probably couldn't bear being tormented all the time with

Do you care?
Are you there?

It troubled the old woman that Marin hadn't been put to death. "Imagine what'll happen if he ever regains his speech!" said she to her daughter. "Just think! We'll be finished. No, I just can't stand to have him walking about on this earth."

When you've started down the path of crime, as she had by throwing Marinette into the sea, you end up traveling a long way. She brooded and brooded, in a black fever of fear and hate. She and her daughter constantly put their heads together to find some way of destroying Marin.

Now, Queen Marotte had just had a son. "Don't be too pleased!" whispered her mother. "Now that the kingdom has an heir, the king won't even look at you any more. He's never loved you, you know. Oh, I've got eyes. And I can see this baby could help us get rid of that mute. As long as the mute's alive, our own lives hang by a thread—the thread of his tongue. Give me the baby before you get too fond of him. Yes, I know what I'm going to do."

And what *did* the old hag do? She slipped that same knife, the one she'd used to pierce the bird's heart just the month before, into the heart of the baby. Then she hid the knife under Marin's pillow, worked herself into a fury of screams and tears, and ran to throw herself at the feet of the king.

"I knew it!" she shrieked. "I knew that cursed mute was bound to do something terrible! He's the one, yes, he's the one who killed your son! He hates his poor sister ever since she became his queen. He can't forgive her her crown—why, just see the looks he gives her! Oh, but how could he have taken it out on the poor innocent child!"

The king glanced at the bloody knife found under Marin's pillow. This time he didn't even want Marin brought before him. He ordered a stone tied around Marin's neck, and Marin thrown from a cliff into the sea.

"All right then, I'll take the sea," thought Marin. "At least I'll join my sister. I don't know what moon we were born under, but this earth did us no good. Perhaps the water will be kinder." It was as though he realized that he and his sister, in truth the son and daughter of a king, had had for

their godmother a sea fairy. Their mother and father had been forced to flee before another king's attack, and when the vessel they all sailed in sank in a storm, the children alone were saved thanks to the fairy.

Servants carried Marin, tied hand and foot and with a stone around his neck, to the top of the cliff. From there they hurled him into the sea.

He ended up, he never knew how, in a wave-washed cave. There he hid, living off shellfish and grasses.

One day as he sat sadly dreaming deep within the cave, the sea suddenly churned before him. Up rose a girl, who ventured as far as the sand of his cave. She could come no closer because a chain of rippling gold held her back by the ankle. Marin recognized his sister, Marinette.

They kissed, both trembling, half laughing and half crying. To be twins means a lot, and they felt the bond so strongly.

"You see," said she, "our godmother, the sea fairy, caught me and saved me from the waters. But I have to live with her in her sea castle. Today I've only a quarter of an hour to be with you. Tomorrow I'll have a half-hour, and perhaps I'll tell you how you can free me. The day after tomorrow I'll have an hour. But if you don't free me that day, I'll have to go back forever to the castle in the sea."

Marin was so amazed and so transported with joy that his tongue was loosened. He began to speak. Together they talked, sitting side by side, hand in hand. He told her all his troubles, all that had happened since she'd disappeared from the ship. But he'd hardly finished when she had to return to the sea, drawn back by the rippling chain.

Alone again in his cave, Marin felt a new boldness fill him. Still, he said to himself, "What am I to do? If I go to the castle, Marotte and her mother will have me killed before I can get to the king. Oh, if I can just free Marinette and the two of us can make it back to the garden . . ."

He couldn't keep himself from going out to roam the dunes along the beach. And as he wandered, he caught sight of a cabin tucked away behind a dune. It was made of rushes like the one on his island. He stole toward it, trying to stay out of sight, till finally he spotted the owner and saw it was the old man who'd taught him to garden.

They met under a peach tree, and under a fig tree they ate together a fish grilled over the coals. To poor Marin it seemed a feast.

"I'll help you as best I can," the old man promised him. "Tomorrow I'll join you in your cave at the time when you expect your sister. Perhaps Marinette will tell you how to free her."

Well, she did tell him, that second day. The golden chain was still rippling at her ankle.

"I'll come again a third time," she said, "and that'll be the day when you can free me. You'll need a three-hundred-pound anvil, a fifteen-pound hammer, and a pair of golden scissors. But take care, take care! If you don't break the chain with one stroke, it'll drag me back to the bottom of the sea, this time forever!"

Anvil, hammer, and scissors. Where was he to get them?

The old man planned everything, sitting cross-legged on the sand. Then he got up and set off for the castle. Turning his hat round and round in his hands, he came before the king.

"Sire," said he, "I was once your gardener, long ago. Would you, in your generous goodness, lend me for just one day a three-hundred-pound anvil, a fifteen-pound hammer, and a pair of golden scissors? I'll return them tomorrow before midday."

The king was not unkind. He commanded that the old man should be lent these things.

The cock crowed in the new day. Out came Marinette from the sea, and Marin was waiting for her in his cave in front of the three-hundred-pound anvil, with the fifteen-pound hammer in his hand. The old man held the golden scissors.

It had to be done with one stroke of the hammer. Marin struck without flinching. The golden chain leaped like a snake and vanished into the waters. Marinette was free.

"Oh my sister," said Marin, "let's go back to the island, let's just go back to our garden there!"

"I'll follow you anywhere, my brother. But I'd like the king to see the truth with his own eyes. I'd like him to know that you didn't lie."

"Yes," the old man agreed, "you must go before the king."

This wasn't necessary, because the king himself appeared in the cave. He'd grown very curious as to what on earth his old gardener could want with an anvil, a hammer, and golden scissors.

At the sight of Marinette he recognized the queen in the portrait, and he knew Marin too. They had to tell him everything. Never was a man more amazed, and set more free as well, as though the golden scissors had cut his own chains too.

"Follow me to the castle," he cried, "all three! With these hands of mine I will work justice!"

They wanted to stop him, but again they didn't have to trouble themselves. Anxious to know where the king had gone, the old woman and her Marotte had climbed the highest tower. From there they saw him striding toward them, not like a man on his way home but like a lion coming in for the kill. They could hardly believe their eyes when they first saw Marin and Marinette. Then the ground tilted under their feet, as though the tower were crumbling. They threw themselves into the sea below, but no sea fairy came to catch them!

The old man became the king's gardener once more, but he didn't do the spading himself. Strong servants spaded for him while he directed the grafting and the sowing as the moon and the seasons turned.

The king took Marinette for his queen, and Marin rejoiced to see them so happy. All three lived together in peace and were never again parted.

5. The Talking Bone

There once lived a queen and she had two children: two handsome sons, pink-cheeked and straight as arrows. One cool May morning she took them both walking in the Forest of Ardenne, in Charlemagne's Grove.

Now, on her finger the queen wore a ring with a stone as green as the inner bark of a willow. She treasured this ring as she treasured her own heart. But by the first brook they came to, under the tall trees of the wood, the ring slid around on her finger; just past the second brook, under the trees, the ring slipped off; and she'd already crossed the third brook when she saw the ring was gone. "My sons, my sons," she cried, "you must find me my ring! Whoever finds it and brings it back to me shall win his father's kingdom!"

Both began searching, searching through the Forest of Ardenne—league after league of bending grasses, swaying branches, rolling drops of dew. Under a beech tree the elder thought he saw the ring sparkle, but it was under a poplar the younger found it gleaming. He cried out.

His brother ran up, saw the ring, and held out his hand. "Have you found our mother's ring?"

"Yes, brother, I have."

"Then give it to me."

"No, I'll keep it."

"Give it up, or I'll have your life."

"We'll see about that. You'll take my life before I let you take the ring!"

At the first reply the elder had drawn his dagger. At the second he plunged it into the younger's heart. He washed the ring in the dew of the grass, and his blade in the running stream. Then, trembling, he dug a grave with his dagger under the poplar tree. As he buried his brother, he shook.

At sundown, as night came on, he made his way back to the castle. "The ring, mother," he cried, "I've found the ring! Here in the Forest of Ardenne, it's I who've won my father's kingdom!"

"Yes, my son, that's the ring, yes it is. But your brother, now—where's your brother?"

They shouted from the great gateway, they blew horns from the highest tower. The elder clapped his hands over his ears.

"Your brother's not coming, not coming! Why didn't you bring your brother home?"

But he shrugged his shoulders. "Was I supposed to look after my brother? I lost him in the thickets of Charlemagne's Grove. He vanished under the trees in the Forest of Ardenne. Perhaps a wolf caught him. Perhaps a bear ate him up."

The queen had them seek her younger son three days, with great noise and sounding of horns, over the fields alive with birds, through the woods filled with fluttering leaves. But the third evening, she had to tell the elder that in seven weeks and a day a feast would be held, and he would be crowned king.

The seven weeks passed. A shepherd on his daily walk with his flock to the Forest of Ardenne noticed his pair of dogs digging furiously under a green poplar tree. The moss flew, and he, ten paces off, thought he saw a white finger beckoning to him. From three paces off he saw a dug-up bone and picked it out of the earth.

He bored a hole in the bone with his awl and carved it with his knife. When he put it to his lips and blew, the whistle began to sing:

> *Whistle, shepherd, whistle on!*
> *'Twas my brother killed me.*
> *Yes, my noble father's kingdom*
> *Rightfully belongs to me.*
> *And all for my mother's ring*
> *I found beneath the poplar tree!*
> *In the Forest of Ardenne,*
>   *tirralee,*
> *I'm still lively as can be!*

That evening when the shepherd brought his cows home to the village, he went on blowing on the bone. The count heard the song from the door of his castle—the count who the next day was to attend the elder brother's coronation feast. The first time he heard it, he pricked up his ears. The second time, he called to the shepherd. "Shepherd," he said, "sell me your whistle. I must have it. I'll give you a gold piece for it; no, *three* pieces of shining gold."

So the count went to the feast with the whistle hidden under his shirt. When the first course was served, he laid the whistle on the table. When the glasses were first filled, he put the whistle to his lips and the bleached bone sang its song:

> *Whistle, dear count, whistle on!*
> *'Twas my brother killed me.*
> *Yes, my noble father's kingdom*
> *Rightfully belongs to me.*
> *And all for my mother's ring*
> *I found beneath the poplar tree!*
> *In the Forest of Ardenne,*
> > *tirralee,*
> *I'm still lively as can be!*

The first time he blew, the guests exchanged glances. The second time, they all stared at the elder son.

The queen took the bleached bone and she too put it to her lips:

> *Whistle, mother, whistle, queen!*
> *'Twas my brother killed me.*
> *Yes, my noble father's kingdom*
> *Rightfully belongs to me.*
> *And all for my mother's ring*
> *I found beneath the poplar tree!*
> *In the Forest of Ardenne,*
> > *tirralee,*
> *I'm still lively as can be!*

The guests and all the people beyond the castle walls set off straight for the Forest of Ardenne, to Charlemagne's Grove. The whistle's song, sweeter than the warbler's trill, led them through the trees. They'd crossed the first brook when it told them the path to take; they'd crossed the second brook when it sang of the poplar tree. Before them walked the king's elder son, as though lost in a dream. The grasses withered behind him, and blood ran from the stones. Then a murmur rose from the poplar, and again the white bone began to speak.

They set to work with their swords and staves, and with the first blow they struck, they found the grave. With the second, they found the child, his heart pierced through, amid his bloody clothes.

The whole company rose up to exact justice for the murder. They gathered deadwood and living wood, and they made a great roaring fire. Then they threw the elder son, bound hand and foot, into the pitiless blaze.

And the bleached bone sang again:

> *From his corpse they took me:*
> *So set me upon his lips,*
> *And once more he'll living be.*
> *For now you can make him your king,*
> *Crowned, beneath the poplar tree!*
> *In the Forest of Ardenne,*
>   *tirralee,*
> *I'm still lively as can be!*

And it was done. Once the white bone touched his mouth the little king rose to his feet, pink-cheeked and straight as an arrow. They shouted their praise, clapped their hands, and crowned him there in Charlemagne's Grove, in the Forest of Ardenne.

6. The Wooden-Clog Maker and the King's Daughter

Once a maker of wooden clogs lived at the entrance to a village. All day long, behind his shop window, he carved clogs with his gouges, or smoothed them with his knife. And as he worked he gaily sang that song which says that clog makers do nothing all week long:

> *The clog maker's worse than a bishop . . .*

and all the rest. The girl next door laughed to hear him. Her eyes got all soft as she watched the good shoemaker working away so merrily.

He'd noticed this himself, and he thought he'd rather like to be married to this Guillemette, fresh and lively as she was. But they wouldn't have much to set up housekeeping with!

I've but four pennies,
My love has but five.
What will we do
When we're man and wife?

Well, they'd just follow the dance: buy a pan, then a bowl, next a cooking pot, and then, God willing, eat together in peace and joy.

In those days clogs made of walnut sold for seven pennies a pair, while the ones made of beech cost four.

One fine morning as he was singing his song,

Then on Sunday they're sick with a headache . . .

a shadow fell on his window. The clog maker looked up. An old beggar woman was standing there in rags, the poor thing, and all wrinkled, with enough dirt in the wrinkles to start a garden. She was looking at him.

He lifted two fingers politely to his fur cap. Painfully she shuffled in, for beneath the dust from the road her feet were all wounded by stones and scratched by thorns.

"Handsome clog maker," said she, "for how much will you sell me a pair of clogs?"

"Good day, kind mother," he replied. "Oh, I won't sell you a pair, I'll give you one."

"Thank you, handsome clog maker. Here, take this for your reward. No, don't laugh, it's a peach stone. You shall plant the stone in your garden."

"Of course I will, kind mother, for love of you."

"And the peach tree you'll have will bear you fruit in every season."

The old woman put the peach stone in his hand, then went about choosing herself the right pair. She must have chosen fast, the clogs must have fit her beautifully, and she must then have been able to step livelier than a girl; because when the clog maker looked up from turning the stone over a time or two (imagine, a peach tree that would bear even in winter!), he saw she was gone. No, she wasn't in the shop, or on the road, or anywhere.

That same evening he planted the stone in the sunniest corner of his garden. He'd put an oat seed with it, the way a clever gardener does, to make the sprout come up better.

The peach tree did sprout, and grew amazingly fast. Next came the miracle: the following year, in the dead of winter, it was loaded with peaches—red, juicy, fragrant peaches! Good heavens! There had never been peaches like that.

It happened that the king of that country got a craving for peaches. He was a great eater, this king, and history tells us that he ate his dinner four times a day: the first time when he ordered it from the cook, the second when he dropped by the kitchen to see how things were going, the third when he gobbled it up with his eyes as it sat on the table, and the fourth when he actually dug in. And now that he had this craving for peaches, he could talk and even think of nothing else.

But it was between Christmas and Twelfth Night, during the twelve days which, so they say, foretell the weather for the year's twelve months. It certainly wasn't July, when the first peaches ripen. Nonetheless, mad though it was, the king's craving simply wouldn't leave him.

One Saturday like any other, he was watching the market in front of his castle—all those fat geese, those sausages, those baskets of walnuts and chestnuts . . . He shrugged his shoulders, raised his hand, and said (everyone heard him), "Why, king's faith: to the man who brings me a basket of peaches, I'll give my daughter for his wife!"

The next day, Sunday, no one in the whole country could talk about anything else. The shoemaker had just taken a basket of peaches to Guillemette (for after all, neighbors owe each other a little gift or two), he'd kissed her on the cheek as good manners require, and she'd turned redder than the fruit in the basket.

Now, this peach tree bearing fruit in December had caused a sensation in the village. When mass was over, those who'd been there at the market the day before, in front of the castle, started in on the clog maker.

"You've got to go! You've got to go! You've got to take him your peaches!"

"He said so! A king's word! He can't take it back! He'll give you his daughter!"

"But his daughter, well, I don't know if I . . ."

"You're mad to hang around here, shuffling your feet! You should already be on your way!"

They took him back to his place and made him pick peaches. The best ones had been for Guillemette, but the rest were fit enough for a king. His aunt put them in a basket and his cousin covered them with a white napkin.

"Just imagine! Son-in-law to the king! The best position in the whole kingdom!"

They put the basket on his arm, took him by the shoulders, and pushed him off toward the castle. He walked on as though in a dream. He had to go, of course, they were all so eager . . . When he went up to the guard at the gate, and then to the captain of the guards, he could only lift up a corner of the napkin and show them the peaches. Then he found himself before the king.

The king's eyes got bigger than saucers. He just couldn't believe what he saw.

He had to believe his sense of taste, though. He put his hand in the basket, took a peach, and ate it. He ate three, then four, then a dozen, then a second dozen, then another. In short, he ate them all. When he was done (he'd unbuckled his belt), he stroked his stomach. Then, without really looking at the clog maker, he pulled from his pocket a rather fat purse and held it out. The clog maker took it (it was worth taking), saluted the king with his fur cap in hand, and moved to leave.

His aunt, who'd been behind him the whole time, stepped smartly forward. "Your Majesty," she said, "would you be good enough to recall what you said?"

"What *did* I say?" asked the king with a solemn air, settling back onto his throne.

He remembered perfectly well, but he didn't much care for the common people. To give a village boy his daughter—well, that seemed a bit much.

His daughter was there, too, and the pretty damsel was as quiet as a mouse. Did I say pretty? She could hardly help it, with her white velvet dress, her headdress of lace, and her satin slippers with their blue ribbons!

"Your Majesty," the aunt began boldly, with a toss of her head, "you said it! You said you would give your daughter to the man who, in the dead of winter, could bring you a basket of peaches. My nephew brought you the basket you wished for."

"And he wants my daughter? Did I really say that?" asked the king, glancing over his court. No one said a word. You could have heard a pin drop.

"My daughter, my daughter . . . Mind you, my boy, I'm not going back on my word. It's just that we can all see about what you're worth. You've just two shirts, haven't you? One on your back and the other in the wash. You'll have to prove yourself a little before you marry my daughter. You, good woman, go home. You, my boy, tell me what you can do."

"Well, Your Majesty, my trade is making wooden clogs."

"Neither I nor my daughter," said the king, "wear clogs at home. What else can you do?"

"I can catch trout, Your Majesty, by damming the stream. I can plant trees and make a fine orchard, and yes, I can herd sheep. I've watched flocks in the fields of stubble."

"We've no sheep for you to watch, my boy. But my daughter has twelve little white rabbits. Take them to graze in the pasture beyond the castle grounds. Watch them, by all means, and bring them back this evening, every one of them."

The king's minister took out the rabbits and let them go at the edge of the pasture. That instant, of course, they made themselves scarce, darting off to the east, to the west, toward the rocks or toward the pond. The clog maker ran high and low, right and left, backwards and forwards, till he finally stopped, panting for breath, at the crossing of four green paths. He was so fed up he could have hurled his fur cap across the pasture. "I'm going back to the castle," thought he. "I'll pick up my basket and go home myself. But no, I won't give him the pleasure. Now I'm mixed up with the king, I'll do what I can till I can do no more."

Now he was decided, he saw before him . . . guess who? The old beggar woman who'd come for the pair of clogs. Suddenly she turned into a fairy, more radiantly beautiful than the dawn.

"Handsome clog maker," she cried, "stop worrying about those twelve little white rabbits! Do you see this hazel wand? This evening, strike the ground with it three times. The twelve rabbits will all come back. The king will have you do many more things. Don't be surprised. Just keep hold of the wand and get on with it."

As for the rabbits, that evening, by the power of the wand, he got them back together and brought them to the king.

When the king and his daughter saw him coming, herding the twelve little white rabbits before him with his wand, they opened their eyes even wider than when they'd seen the peaches.

"Yes, yes," said the king after a pause, "but before we ring the wedding bells, there's just one more small thing I'd like to have you do. I'll see you tomorrow, my boy." Then he turned his back and walked out, with his daughter behind him.

The next morning he once again called the clog maker before him.

"My boy, I remember you're good at planting trees. Well, today, clear my wood, get all the stumps out, and since I'm so fond of fruit, plant me an orchard that'll yield me plenty of peaches, apricots, apples, pears, and plums."

All right then, a big, beautiful orchard, by the power of the wand! The clog maker, his head high, set off for the wood beyond the grounds. And there, in a trice, he cleared, prepared, planted, and smoothed the whole orchard. Toward evening (that's they way they tell it, anyhow), everything was done.

The king came with his daughter, and how he stared! He didn't look too happy, either, this high-and-mighty king. The clog maker knew perfectly well what was going on. The king was searching desperately for a way not to keep his word.

"I remember," said the king the next morning, "that you know how to catch trout and build dams. Take out the rocks up there in back of the wood, level the earth, and dig me a nice fishpond. I'm very fond of fish. This evening, my daughter and I will come and see how you're doing."

So they came that evening, and this time their eyes really popped! They didn't know the wand had been at work, but they could see everything was done.

"Hmph," said the king, "very good, very good. But, king's faith, the fishpond won't be much of a fishpond till it has a whole crowd of fish swimming around in it, just the way the orchard won't be much of an orchard till it has fruit. Get me some carp, some tench, some eels, and some perch. Come to think of it, I'd like a pike or two as well, to keep the carp moving."

The clog maker bowed, lifted his head high again, and put his fur cap back on. He had a glint in his eye now, and was feeling up to a little mischief. What a wand, that wand of his!

The next day he went to the orchard and touched the branches, went to the fishpond and touched the water. By the power of the wand the branches were suddenly loaded with butter pears, duchesses, greengages, pippins, and bergamots; and the pond was suddenly full of carp, barbel, and chub.

The king's minister raced to him with the news, and the king came running, all red-faced and with his crown askew. His eyes opened so wide it looked as though they might roll right out on the ground! "Ah, well then," he muttered to himself, "this boy must be a magician! Better not play games with magicians!" He was getting flustered.

The king inspected everything. First the orchard with its branches bend- ing under the weight of the apples and pears, the way a girl's arm bends as she comes home from the well with a big jug of water. Next the pond, with its waters dancing in the sun as the tench leaped and the carp turned pirouettes. The clog maker, fur cap in hand, stared into space without even looking at the king.

"Enough, enough," the king stammered, quite frightened. "Perhaps I asked for a little too much."

"That's easily remedied, Your Majesty."

The shoemaker put on his cap, and with his wand struck the ground three times. Instantly, the work was undone. What an uproar! The orchard turned back into a wild wood, the fishpond dried and crinkled up into bush-covered rocks. Everything was shaking and rumbling.

The clog maker had overdone it a bit himself. But you see, the only thing he wanted now was to go home. He didn't care if he had just one bowl. That would do for him and his real love, Guillemette, to drink their soup from! The castle with its big pointed towers (tottering now) meant nothing to him. Neither did the damsel (sobbing with fright) on her way through the wood to join her father. The king staggered about, trying to catch hold of his scepter and crown.

"Enough! Enough! Stop! Stop! Even if all you've got is yourself and your shirt, my daughter's yours!"

But the clog maker was dying to get back to Guillemette and his shop.

"Your Majesty," said he, turning on his heel, "no thank you. Where I'm from we've prettier girls!"

7. Péquelé

There was once a poor juggler people called Péquelé. He lived off the little shows he put on in village squares, when he rolled out his mat with the rope drawn on it. Heaven knows what acrobatics he launched into then, leaping and somersaulting, walking on his hands, twisting himself up, tying himself into knots like a snake and then untying himself again, or springing about like a squirrel.

He lived off these tricks but he didn't live well. People always look down a bit on those who wander the countryside, though they may admit the wanderers keep the rest of us amused. For themselves, their work is to grow bread. With the strength of *their* arms they struggle mightily with wheatgrass, brambles, and thistles. They can hardly think much of strolling entertainers. Poor Péquelé didn't see many coins fall on his carpet. He now only knew by rumor what a roast of beef might be, or even a nice steaming bowl of thick soup. As pale as a church candle he was, and as thin as a draft through a keyhole. But he roamed on, hawking and coughing, hair in his eyes, like a skinny cat. He really was almost like a ghost, or like one of those scarecrows made of crossed sticks and a few rags that people put up in cherry orchards to keep jays and orioles off the fruit.

Lightly though he wandered, one December evening at nightfall Péquelé fell. He stumbled in some brambles and collapsed a few paces farther on, on the steps of a roadside cross. There he fainted.

Happily two begging friars on the way home to their cloister found him, just as it was beginning to snow, and loaded him on their donkey. At the monastery he got some wine to drink and some hot soup. The next day he tried walking again, but his legs were all rubbery and wouldn't hold him up. The abbot said he could stay a week to get his strength back.

The week went by and the snow melted. The south wind cleared the roads. One fine morning the abbot had Péquelé brought to the locutory, the cloister's visiting room.

"My good Péquelé," said he, "all friends must part. We're going to fill your pack and you're going to set out on the road again."

"But you see, Father Abbot, I'd rather stay here," replied Péquelé.

"You'll come and see us again next year, and we'll give you three days on retreat. Our rule won't let us keep a passing traveler for more than three days."

Poor Péquelé was dreaming of good round bread on the table, of bowls full of lentils, and of chunks of cheese washed down with a little wine. There was especially the peace of the monastery, like the peace of a room where you sit by the fire while it's snowing outside. How miserable it is then, on the road! The wind whistles, the rain beats in your face, and the dogs people loose at the sight of you bark savagely and snap at your heels. And above all, there's the whole countryside's sullen ill-will. Here, in the white-vaulted passageways, there was peace always present and always found; sweet, assured peace.

But there was still more in the monastery to capture the heart of poor Péquelé. Ever since he was a tiny boy, doing somersaults in the grass, he'd loved Our Lady and had given her his heart. There before her image, in the cloister's beautiful chapel with its red and blue stained-glass windows, he felt closer to her than anywhere else in the world.

"Oh please, Father Abbot, won't you keep me, so I can be a friar with the others?"

"My poor Péquelé, weren't you born instead to roam the highways and byways? You're good at somersaults, but that's all. Do you think Our Lady needs an acrobat in this monastery of ours?"

Péquelé hung his head. One tear, then another and another, ran down his cheeks.

"All right," said the abbot after a moment. "Listen. Will you promise me you'll be a good monk, worthy of the name?"

"Oh yes, yes, Father! I so love the Holy Virgin!"

"All right, we'll keep you here as a novice, and in three months' time we'll see."

Péquelé shone with happiness. Carried away by joy he flipped upside down, walked on his hands, then turned cartwheels round and round the locutory. Nothing like that had ever been seen in the room before.

"Enough, enough, Péquelé! We'll overlook your gamboling this once. But now you're a novice, we'll have no more of your mountebank tricks. Do you understand me, Péquelé?"

"I understand you, Father."

"No more leaps or somersaults!"

"Absolutely not. No, no."

"You're going to put on the habit, and you must stop acting like a carnival buffoon. Agreed?"

"Yes, Father Abbot, agreed!"

Péquelé had promised with all his heart, like a child. And with all his heart he kept the rule three days, three weeks, and three months. But winter was past now and spring was coming. Soon there'd be no more snowflakes sailing by on the wind, but instead petals of hawthorn and plum. Already you could hear the blackbird, the first bird to sing in the year's first thaw, like a little flute in the trees still bare and stirred by the wind. Far off, in the heart of the woods, cuckoos were calling forth yellow flowers to bloom in the grass. Wet garden paths, drying now, were running off toward the sun.

Something got into Péquelé's legs—something like the fife's mad magic, when the music comes to life before your eyes, dancing to each measure and phrase. The abbot, whose eye watched everything, saw well enough that Péquelé had quicksilver in his veins.

"Listen, my son," said he, "your work for today is to prune the orchard.

Get up there in the tops of the apple trees and take out all the dead or weak branches."

So Péquelé got up in the trees, pruning hook in hand. Here and there he hopped, like a tightrope dancer. And all at once, in the spring wind, he discovered he was lighter than down. He ended up leaping from apple tree to apple tree like a squirrel.

When he got to the end of the orchard, of course, he had to come down and put back on the habit he'd taken off for climbing. But first, on the grass in his shirt and breeches, all alone, free and full of fun, he just couldn't resist. Off he went, standing on his head, walking on his hands, doing leaps and twists and flip-flops of all sorts, filling the orchard with acrobatics as a goldfinch fills its cage with song.

The abbot came to check on Péquelé's progress. He saw everything.

Péquelé promised very contritely that he'd never do it again. No more somersaults, oh no! In fact he apologized so humbly and so sincerely that the abbot couldn't help relenting. He sighed a big sigh and drew his hands back into his sleeves.

"Very well," he said, "I'll keep you on probation awhile longer. But if you don't keep your promise, out you go! Remember that, my son, if you hope to stay."

The abbot thought the problem was quicksilver in the veins, did he? No, it wasn't so much that as heartfelt joy. Some evenings, Péquelé's heart was just bursting with joy.

The weather was fine, cool, and bright with a nice breeze. The setting sun, as red as a red-hot iron quoit, was turning the air in the distance all pink. You could see, beneath a few homing birds, the blue countryside settling into evening calm, and all space opening to the peace of God. Poor Péquelé (so he told himself) didn't know how to offer up dignified prayers like the other monks. But somehow he had to thank the Lord who made

all things so beautiful. And it seemed to him that he could do this only by doing the one thing he was good at in this world: his tricks of a showman and a carefree child.

The abbot called the chapter together. The matter seemed clear to him and to all the monks: it was wiser not to keep at the monastery a monk who leaped about like a goat—in a word, a mountebank.

"Surely he's no great sinner," one monk objected.

"Ah," replied another, "but there are all these somersaults of his. That's what he was born to and he can't help it!"

"We haven't been able to get him to mend his ways," concluded the abbot. "He's still a madcap, and no madcap will ever make a monk."

Péquelé confessed his fault and wept. He didn't dare try to defend himself. All he had were his tears. He wept at the very idea of leaving the monastery; his white, vaulted cell; the little garden full of box and pansies; and all the peaceful, kindly friars. Poor Péquelé wept like the spring at the back of the orchard.

The abbot, his eyes on Péquelé, felt a quiver in the pit of his stomach. More than one friar was close to tears, and so was he. But this mad spate of flip-flops seemed just too outrageous to let pass. Péquelé hadn't managed to keep on the path of wisdom and live like a monk, so he'd have to go back to his old path as a strolling acrobat.

They stripped off his habit and gave him back his mat and pack.

The abbot left right away and went to pray in the chapel. "I had to do it," he kept repeating, sunk in his stall. "Poor Péquelé's still a child. And we, Our Lady's servants, can't be romping children any more."

He'd gotten that far in his thoughts when from his dark corner he heard a slight noise. Not far away, Péquelé was unrolling his mat on the chapel's flagstones. He was right in front of the column which supported the Virgin's wooden image.

"Our Lady Mary," said Péquelé, "I wanted to live in your house all the days of my life, but as you can see, I'm not worthy. Still, I mean to thank you for the time I've spent here almost as your little boy."

Believing himself alone in the chapel, he addressed Our Lady as volubly as a child. And what did he do next but start in on his tricks. Bending and stretching, rolling and leaping, he did every trick he knew, but with so much spirit, so much *soul*, that the abbot, who was about to get up and stop the whole thing, stayed right where he was.

Suddenly, dazzled and bathed in light, the abbot slid from his seat down onto his knees. For at a certain moment Péquelé had come down on his feet, his face streaming with sweat and almost breathless. And at that very moment (the abbot saw it happen), the Virgin left her stone column and came to Péquelé on a ray of light. She leaned over him and, with the edge of her veil, gently wiped his streaming forehead.

Like a mother caressing her child, she caressed the strolling acrobat. The chapel was ablaze with light.

"Forgive me, Our Lady, forgive me," murmured the abbot, bowing his head to touch with his forehead the rail of his stall. "I thought I was truly wise, and yet could not see wisdom. What do we really know, after all, except to gather at your feet like children, innocently and with joy? That's all the saints have ever known—to love God with all their heart, and God's Mother, and everything that is of God. This mountebank is a greater saint than us all."

Péquelé stayed at the monastery to pray and to do his leaps and tricks, which in spirit were easily worth any prayers. Then, one fine day, he died. They say Our Lady appeared at his bedside and the abbot saw her there again, as he had that evening in the chapel when to wipe away with her shining veil the sweat of exhaustion, Our Lady had come and leaned down over her poor acrobat.

8. The Golden Twig

There once lived a king (poor fellow!) whose only son was a deformed freak, so ill-made that his parents had wondered for a good while whether he really ought to be christened.

CNo—Crickneck was the only name people called him by. His godfather, the magician, hadn't been able to help him much, beyond giving him a golden twig. This was a twig with the power to cut through all evil enchantments. But the golden twig didn't smooth away the little prince's hump.

Humpbacked, twisted, and deformed as he was, this son of a king, there came a time when he had to take a wife. The king had seemed very downcast since Crickneck's birth, but he'd gotten so tyrannical that it wasn't a good idea to contradict him. So no one said a word when he decided to marry his son off to a princess known as Princess Bootface. She was so shriveled and ugly that her parents too had had to wonder whether she was worth christening. Bootface and Crickneck—what a couple! One lord dared to remark that he wouldn't want to keep any of *their* babies. Everyone agreed.

Although the kind wanted this match, Crickneck couldn't bring himself to agree. He declared (in the princess' presence, since he had no other choice) that he'd rather die. The poor princess was so hurt by this insult that she fainted on the spot.

"Take them both out of my sight!" shouted the furious king. "My son's not exactly entitled to be finicky about looks. Remove him immediately to the tower. It'll help him think."

"As for the princess," he went on to himself, "she obviously doesn't think much of herself either. But this wedding will take place, or I'm not the king!"

Prince Crickneck was taken straight to the tower, which for a long, long time had been empty and abandoned. Having nothing else to do, he went exploring. The tower was all stone staircases alive with rats; stone vaults with fluttering bats; stone passageways with owl eyes gleaming far, far down them in the gloom; and stone chambers where a single spider hung from a thread of web. Crickneck climbed from room to room right to the top. He saw nothing but owls, mice, and grey dust; he heard nothing but woodworms boring through the beams, or drafts whistling under the doors.

He was about to come down again when he took it into his head to lift up a corner of blue and green tapestry that hung there all in tatters. Behind it, in a bay let into the wall, he saw a bed.

On the bed lay a lady. Covered with spiderwebs, she seemed dead or at least sunk in a very, very long sleep.

Crickneck touched her with the golden twig.

Instantly she awoke. She was a fairy, betrayed and put under a spell by the evil fairy with whom she was at war. She thanked Crickneck, bid him tell her his story, and touched him in turn with her wand. Suddenly Crickneck was made new. In one stroke his whole body straightened. Now he was as slender as a reed, with a well-turned leg and a smiling face—in short, the handsomest king's son in the world.

"From now on you'll be known as Peerless," said the fairy. "I can't keep you with me in my fairyland, but I appoint you a shepherd. That's the happiest fate you could have. But never lose your golden twig. Don't forget it protects you."

The next morning, the king remembered his son.

"I must go to him," thought he. "Surely he's seen reason. Anyway, I swear he'll have to obey me!"

So off went the king to the tower. Crickneck wasn't there.

They searched everywhere but found nothing, neither blood nor body. There were just a few footprints in the dust of the flagstones: the prince's and the smaller ones of a woman.

"It must be the princess," the king decided. "Bootface must have come and strangled my son to avenge his insult. Who else could it be?"

On the spot he ordered the princess fetched, refused to hear her, and had her shut up in the tower.

One day while she wandered from room to room, she climbed all the way to the top. In a corner she noticed a worm-eaten old chest, went up to it, and pulled out its drawer. Inside, there lay a severed hand.

That moment, from heaven knows where, an eagle came screaming down upon her.

"That's my hand! That's *my* hand you're holding! Give it back! Give me back my hand!"

She saw the eagle had only one leg. Terrified, she gave it the hand.

As soon as it took hold of the hand, the eagle changed into a man. He was a magician who'd had his hand cut off by the evil fairy, and his fate was to remain in an eagle's form until he got the hand back. He thanked poor Bootface and touched her with his wand.

Instantly, abracadabra, everything in the princess straightened up. A lovely face was hers, and a lithe body.

"From now on," said the magician, "you'll be known as Radiant. "I can't take you to my home, but I'll make you a shepherdess. You'll lead a free and happy life."

Hurrah for magicians, when they turn an ugly, boot-faced creature into a lovely girl with golden eyebrows and hair! Horror though she was before, now she was a true beauty. She led her sheep down onto the plain, took care they were sheltered from storm and burning sun, and kept them from eating the little reeds that might give them flukeworms.

In the woods and pastures she often met a very pleasant shepherd, as decent as a bouquet of flowers. His name was Peerless. The king's servants, who were scouring the countryside for them, never thought to recognize in this shepherd and shepherdess Prince Crickneck and Princess Bootface. The two hadn't even recognized each other.

Together they led their sheep to graze, and Peerless kept watch against the wolf. In the heat of the day he herded the sheep into the shade, then the two of them took shelter under some green arbor and shared their hard-boiled eggs or their black bread. In fall they shared their chestnuts or their turnips baked in the ashes. And depending on the season, Peerless would bring his friend a handful of serviceberries or wild strawberries in a rush basket.

As young and fresh as water they were, and free as air. What a blessed life, all of tenderness and ease, in fine grass or ferns, among the hazels or beneath a great oak. They wore no more than homespun shifts or goatskin tunics. But compared to their life at court in their princely brocades, these shepherding days were all woven with gold.

The poor things didn't realize that someone was skulking around them, someone who'd recognized them as Crickneck and Bootface. Who? The evil fairy! The one at war with the fairy who'd changed Crickneck into Peerless, and with the magician who'd transformed Bootface into the shining Radiant. She couldn't forget that it was Crickneck and Bootface who'd broken her spells over those two.

"Yes, they played me that trick," she told herself, "but one day I'll get back at them!" She spied on them from between two hazel thickets, or stole round and round them in the sheepfold. But she had to look out for the golden twig.

How fortunate Peerless would have been had he really minded the good fairy's warning: "Never lose your golden twig. Don't forget that it protects you."

For three days now, Peerless had had his eye on a dove's nest high in the branches of an elm. Late one sunny May afternoon, it seemed to him that the chicks had grown big enough. He removed his tunic, leaving the

golden twig in its pocket, climbed the tree, and took the nest. He meant
to give it to Radiant.

She, meanwhile, was looking for him. Seeing his tunic beneath the elm,
she called him. He was just climbing down, with the nest and the dove
chicks in his shirt.

Suddenly he jumped down onto the moss before her. Speechless with
surprise, she blushed, and reddened more deeply still when he offered her
the nest.

So lovely was she just then, and so charming, that even as Peerless
offered the nest, he dared also to offer his heart. Down he went on one
knee before her and began to talk of marriage.

She only grew more speechless still. All in a fright, she barely glanced
at him, then sighed, hesitated, turned and took flight.

No doubt she knew that he wasn't making fun of her, but she remembered
having been Princess Bootface—the one Prince Crickneck had refused
before the whole court to marry.

She was fleeing wildly toward the open meadows, her hair streaming
behind her, when suddenly the evil fairy rose before her from a bush.

"Wait, wait, Princess Bootface!" she cried. "I'll give you legs to run
with!"

Now poor Radiant, touched by the wand, was changed to a green
grasshopper.

Just then Peerless dashed up. He'd been struck still more speechless
than she by her flight. Then he'd run after her, wanting to calm her and
throw himself at her feet. As he reached her he heard the evil fairy and
was thunderstruck when Radiant vanished. Then, at a touch of the wand,
he felt himself vanish too, changed into a cricket no bigger than your little
finger.

"You too, Prince Crickneck!" gloated the fairy.

Now the pair no longer knew the meaning of "good times." They lived
deep in the meadow, in the thick of the grass, shrinking into their earthen
shelter at the sight of a kite or an owl which might swallow them whole.
Their only comfort lay in sharing their miserable fate. In the depth of their
misfortune, the evil fairy's words had led them to recognize each other.
So, Peerless and Radiant were Crickneck and Bootface . . . They placed
in common all they had, their fates first as deformed children and then as
charming shepherd and shepherdess. Though now just a cricket and a
grasshopper, they were friends for life.

But an evil fate never fills *all* space. There's blue sky beyond every storm. Wandering one day among the trees, the poor cricket came across the tunic and found in the pocket the golden twig. He'd no sooner brushed against it with his tiny cricket leg than he was Peerless once more.

By the same power of the golden twig, the grasshopper turned back into Radiant.

"The king, the good fairy, the evil fairy, *everyone*," thought they to themselves, "wants us to be together. So we might as well keep each other! And since we've gotten ourselves back again, the king should get us back too."

They set out to show themselves to the king, and proved who they were by displaying the golden twig. He knew their voices and their eyes, yes, he remembered them well. But how far behind they'd left what they'd been as Crickneck and Bootface! How straight they were now, and how they'd bloomed!

Everyone cried out with wonder.

"Yes, yes," said the king, "you've had quite an adventure. But whatever you may have been through, I swore once that you'd be married, and I'm not going back on that. Such is my will, just as before!"

Of course they weren't about to complain. And so they were married.

Chirr, chirr, chirr, went all the crickets and all the grasshoppers in the meadows,

> Chirr, chirr,
> My tale's over!

9. The Picnic

There once were two brothers-in-law who'd quarreled over their inheritance. Before then they hadn't gotten along too well, and afterwards they didn't get along at all. Tienne had made himself some money, and despised Toine, who had practically none. Toine was just that much more furiously jealous of Tienne. They hated each other like cats and dogs.

One morning they each set off for the fair and met on the way out of the village. Both joined a group that took the path through the fields. They were passing the mill, down in that hollow that's always wet, when they came across a toad waddling along as best it could, dragging one leg after the other, as bloated as a pastry puff.

"Hey," said Tienne to Toine, "why don't you stick it in your pocket? You've probably got just a breadcrust with you anyway. I don't suppose your wife could find you anything else. There's your lunch."

"You saw it," answered Toine, "it's all yours. We know how tightfisted you are. It'll save you a meal at the inn."

Tienne stopped, glanced at the toad, then looked at his brother-in-law. Crushing the toad under his heel, he set about grinding Toine into the dirt, right there in front of everyone.

"You see that?" he asked.

The toad, about the color of a rotten leaf, and all warts and blisters, didn't look very appetizing.

"Yes, you see it? Well, I've got sixty crowns here, and I'm on my way to the fair to get me another cow. My sixty crowns are yours if you eat that toad."

"You heard him," said Toine to the others. "You're witnesses. Just say that again."

"Yes, I'll say it again. Eat it right there in front of us—*all* of it, head and legs too—and you win my sixty crowns."

Sixty crowns! To earn the price of a cow in five minutes, however bad those minutes might be! Toine made a sign he'd take Tienne at his word. Then he frantically grabbed the toad, tore it to bits, and fell to.

The others looked on, greener than the toad's belly and guts, their foreheads clammy and their stomachs crawling up into their throats. Toine was going wild, and well he might! Sixty crowns, not only to fill his own pocket with, but to snatch from his brother-in-law's! Sixty crowns!

He got the toad's back legs down more or less, but he knew he'd get no further. Any minute he'd throw up everything he'd eaten for days. You can't really control your body, after all. But if he gave out, his brother-in-law would have made him swallow half a toad, and he'd still keep his money and laugh. Toine was seething. He couldn't go on eating that filth of a toad, but his rage inspired him with an idea.

"All right, Tienne, I'm eating it. Your sixty crowns are mine! But I'm generous. Why not split it? You eat the other half, just the way I did, and keep your sixty crowns."

Tienne, who could already see his money—the money for his cow!— skipping off into Toine's pocket, was sweating with misery and greed, and too worried to see what was really happening. Now he'd a chance to get back his money, he jumped at it.

He too went wild. Not a pretty picture to paint, I'm sure, but he got down the other half of that toad. Unfortunately, both were now so wobbly in the knees that they had to stay where they were. No more fair! Home again they staggered, sick as dogs.

"Well," murmured the oldest of the men present, "those two certainly hate each other enough, goodness knows, but I still don't understand quite what they got out of *that*. Neither gained anything. Seems to me about the only good it did them was that they each got to lunch off half a toad."

10. The Village of the Damned

There was once a lace merchant who roamed the mountains with his wife. Both carried bundles on their backs. They'd buy in the high villages, up among the pines and rocks; then come down to sell in the low villages, among the wheat and the vines. He was a red-haired man, stocky and strong. She was as slender and slight as an ant, but she followed him everywhere, always.

One day they walked into Montbrison and went to eat at an inn. There were soldiers there smoking their pipes, and cattle traders drinking.

When the waitress brought the couple their soup, the traders struck up a conversation. They talked about that part of the country and about mutual friends. When the cheese and fruit came, the traders signaled to each other and put on strange faces.

"Yes," the youngest finally said, "I know you go everywhere looking for lace, but there's one place I'm sure you *won't* go."

"Where's that?"

"Up there in the woods, over by Deadman's Cross—the village of the damned."

"Why not?"

The young man spat silently on the ground. An older trader answered, "Because."

Perhaps the lace merchant was a bit tipsy with the wine he'd drunk. He gave the traders no more peace till he'd gotten the whole story out of them.

"The place isn't on any map, you see. Oh yes, it's quite a mystery."

Still, the young trader told them the way. The cross was gone, he said; those people had torn it down. There were streams to get over, boiling and leaping among the rocks; and pinewoods to climb through, among tangled ferns that would catch your foot and trip you up.

"But no one risks going up there," the young trader went on. "Once a band of hunters ended up nearby and the boldest decided to enter the village. He came back down faster than he'd gone up, with a pack of dogs at his heels—dogs like mad wolves. And the men and women up there are even more like wolves than their dogs."

"Those pagans up there have taken themselves out of Christendom," said another trader. "That's all there is to it."

"Some priests thought they should go there and were lucky to make it back, all pale and crossing themselves as they said, 'No, no, we won't talk about them, they've given themselves to the devil.' That's about it: the place is a village of the damned."

"You see that stick?" said the lace merchant, pointing to it as it hung on the wall. "It's never failed me. As long as I've got my stick, I don't give a hoot about their dogs or their devils! I'm going up there tomorrow!"

They could see he was hot with wine. One old fellow motioned him to be quiet. His wife signaled to him to get up from the table, but he downed another glass. Then he said, "I'm going up there tomorrow if I have to sweat blood for it."

The next day his wife saw well enough what was on his mind. "You're not going, are you?" she asked.

"Hey, am I a man, or what?"

When he had an idea in his head, well, that was that. She knew it perfectly well, and she knew she couldn't do anything about it. Anyway, she'd at least go with him, as always. She sighed as she tied her shawl under her chin. Then she shouldered her bundle and said, "All right, I can understand your wanting to face *men*. But getting mixed up with the Black Beast . . ."

"If you're afraid of the Beast," he retorted, "put both your hands on your head and tell yourself, 'I've got the Beast under me now!' All right, let's go!"

He'd no more have considered passing up a challenge than Saint Joseph would have abandoned the Holy Virgin on the road to Egypt.

As they climbed the hillside through the vines, he remarked that the wolf in people's stories is always bigger than the real one. And when they'd reached the mountain pines, he told his wife that the dogs those fellows in

Montbrison had likened to wolves were probably no more than skinny mutts better at yapping than biting.

Meanwhile their path had vanished among the gorse and weeds. You could tell no one ever went that way. Then a weasel or some such creature flashed past ahead of them. As everyone knows, that's not a good sign.

The flies were biting and the still heat was oppressive. There'd be a storm before noon. But on and up they went. The lace merchant kept climbing and his wife gamely followed.

Soon they heard a sound like a great wind rising in the distance and coming closer. No, not a wind exactly, but a rush of air such as they'd never heard before.

They exchanged glances. The lace merchant shrugged. Up on the plateau the sound followed and surrounded them. The wife had taken her rosary from her pocket and was saying Ave Maria bead by bead.

All at once, the storm swooped down in a squall that bent the trees low. Dazzling lightning exploded around them. Thunder roared in their ears. The clouds burst like great bladders and water fell in buckets. They sought shelter as best they could under the trees. When lightning struck a nearby pine and the tree crashed down, shooting splinters far and wide, they scrambled off somewhere else through the downpour, backs bent and hands over their heads.

The whole forest danced in a nightmare frenzy. Split rocks gushed torrents of yellow water while lightning bolts, an eye-burning pink, exploded in your face and their thunder shook the mountains.

Suddenly the storm was over as quickly as it had begun. They no longer knew where they were.

Then they saw the gentleman dressed half for town and half for country, all in black.

Something about him struck them, though at first they didn't know what. The lace merchant asked the way. The gentleman took three steps forward and pointed without a word to a village among the rocks. He pointed very politely, with a little gesture of greeting and a slight smile. Then he took three more steps and they couldn't see him any more.

The air smelled the way it does after lightning strikes. They were covered with gooseflesh.

"But, that man . . . !" the wife suddenly blurted out to herself. "Oh yes, now I see what struck me just then, though I couldn't put my finger on it at the time. Here we are, soaked through, covered with mud from head to foot, and everything around us—trees, ferns, trails, and clearings— is dripping wet; yet there he stood, right in front of me, as neat as a pin and perfectly dry! Holy Virgin, when I *think* about it! Where could he have come from, out here in these woods? Not a spot of mud on his shoes, not a drop of water on his hat. My God, that man! Oh my God, that man!"

She wanted to talk to her husband but her tongue was frozen. The lace merchant was walking on.

They entered the village and knocked on the first door they came to. No one asked them in. They knocked at the second door and a man came to open it for them. He was thin and swarthy, with a black mustache.

"Would you have any lace to sell?" asked the merchant.

The man shook his head in a way that gave you the feeling he had no interest in such foolishness. Then back in the shadows someone else stood up.

"I suppose we might have some."

This one had wolflike eyes in a heavily bearded face. He turned and banged on the wall with his fist. In came an old woman with lace, all linen, and so fine you could go blind examining it. A girl followed with more, all of silver thread, more luminous than a spider's web on a dewy morning.

They'd never seen lace like that. And all the designs in it were godless: curves with hooks, signs with tails, stars and planets like the ones there'll be in the sky the night the world ends.

"I have more," said the old man. "How about drinking some of my wine first?"

The two women had left. Even the older one had been as lovely as a queen in an old song, but the younger had been something else again: beautiful, but beautiful enough to make you tremble just looking at her. The black-bearded man had slipped out silently.

The old man took a bottle from the cupboard. Now the girl was back. She put three glasses on the table. The wife turned hers upside down so as not to be poured any wine, but the lace merchant let himself be served and drained the glass in one go. The dark, dark wine was so powerful that, strong as he was, he shivered the way a woman does when she swallows brandy.

"Woman, wait for us here," said the old man to the wife. "You, my man, come with me."

The old man took the lace merchant away, pushing him along in front of him. The wife wished she hadn't let her husband leave, but it was too late.

Time went by. Night was coming on. So was fear. Fear came at her from everywhere in the kitchen where she sat. At last she couldn't stand it any more. Very quietly she got up, tiptoed to the door, and stole outside. From the barn she heard feeble groans.

She peered through a crack between two boards. Later on she never understood how she had managed not to scream, or how her legs could have still carried her when she fled.

A tub stood on the ground and around it were women, each with a knife—women as swarthy as gunflints, with black hair more lustrous than a crow's wing. One was holding up by the foot a naked newborn baby. Another drove her knife into the baby's chest, under his arm.

The wife ran, stumbling over rocks in the dark. She tripped on the doorsill and at the back of the kitchen collapsed against a door—which opened.

There was her husband, sitting in a chair as though stupefied. From somewhere or other came a murmur of whispers and sinister little noises.

"Quick, quick!" she breathed in his ear. "If we don't run for it now we'll be lost forever."

He seemed not to understand, but just stared straight ahead like a baby. She pulled him up by the arm, shook him, and got him moving.

"Quick, quick!" she urged him. "They kill people here!"

At last he started walking, and once outside they ran. He followed her dully, the way an animal trots behind its master. She raced between houses and rocks, down dark passageways, along one street or another. The first rock in the meadows brought the merchant to his knees. The second laid him out full-length, but she got him up again and made him go on. At last they reached the woods.

It was twilight as they went in, but under the trees it was already night. They walked unsteadily and hadn't gotten far before they heard voices and footsteps in the forest. People were after them with lanterns.

She made her husband keep going, on and on, till at last he fell like a stone. She dragged him under a pine's low-hanging branches and he slept like a log while she crouched beside him, saying her rosary. That's how they spent the night.

As soon as light returned to the sky between the tips of the pines, she got up and explored a little to the left and right. She drank from a brook, followed it awhile, and figured out which way the slope went and which way they'd have to go.

When she got back she found her husband standing, running his hand over his face.

"So, you're up?"

"Yes, wife, I'm up, but I'm not much to look at."

"Come, let's head down toward Montbrison. We have to walk toward the dawn."

So they set off. If she'd paid any attention to how she felt she couldn't have put one foot before the other, but she wasn't going to do that. They had to keep walking!

As they crossed their first stream, the lace merchant shrugged his bundle up higher on his shoulder. At the first road they came to, he shook himself in his coat and asked, "But tell me, wife, what *did* happen yesterday evening?"

He couldn't remember a thing.

She told him the whole story.

"It must be that wine they made me drink," he said, "yes, that old man and that girl. If you hadn't gotten me out of there I'd have fallen under the devil's power."

Soon the sun was shining and they got back to the inn in town. They ate and rested themselves awhile, but said nothing about the village and left without breathing a word to anyone.

Years and years later they came back through those mountains and asked about the village up there.

"Oh, there've been storms, you know. Lightning struck it square, and when lightning starts a fire there's no way to put it out. That night a real gale was blowing, enough to strip the roof off a house. The fire spread from beam to beam and barn to barn. That village burned all night. In the morning nothing was left but ashes. And the people? Who knows what happened to them? They were made to wander the roads."

The lace merchant decided to go up there with his wife. They recognized nothing. All they saw were rocks and a litter of broken masonry, or hummocks of grass. There were barely a few bits of broken tile left, or here and there a piece of a smashed bowl.

Perhaps the damned had been mountain sorcerers who'd holed up there in times of war and high banditry. Living and hiding like cave dwellers, they'd ended up forgetting all but evil.

More likely, though, they were Gypsies who had sin in their blood and the devil's own fire deep in their eyes. Yes, lost souls from the gates of hell: in short, people who didn't belong here.

11. The Two Sisters' Gifts and Fates

There was once a prosperous country lady whose husband had died, leaving her their two daughters. The elder was just like her mother: about as good to look at as a jug with a broken spout, and as arrogant, brutal, and ill-tempered as anyone could possibly be.

But the younger one wasn't that way. She took after her father: kind to everyone, sweet in speech, and charming in every gesture. Being so fresh and innocent, she was like a flower in bloom by a spring. This made the mother, who favored her elder yet saw everyone love the younger, dislike her violently. Things had grown so bad by now that the woman couldn't stand the sight of her, and when she did see her, she all but jumped out of her skin with irritation.

Slop Girl was the only name she used for her younger daughter, and she'd managed to make her do all the dirtiest jobs about the place. "Slop Girl, go change the goats' straw," she'd order. "Go clean out the henhouse!" Or, "Slop Girl, go take the pigs their slops!"

Another of the mother's tricks was to send the girl to the spring in the woods, a good way from the house. She claimed this was the only water that really refreshed her, and so this was the only water she'd drink. Once the girl set off through the upper pasture, her mother would be rid of her for a while. Perhaps the mother actually dreamed—after all, some people really are nasty!—of being rid of her forever one day. Because it was rumored to be a bit strange around that spring. You'd hear stories by the fire about a goblin appearing there in the shape of a red colt, and about people seeing fairies. And maybe one evening—who knows?—some freakish creature would pop out of the woods and carry her off. Maybe she'd keep going for water till at last she never came back.

Once after supper, in hot and thirsty weather, Slop Girl went for water and met at the spring an ancient, ancient woman, bent nearly double over her hawthorn staff. She looked like Time's own mother and was horribly filthy. This Granny-in-Tatters was waiting by the spring, seemingly in a bad way.

"I'm so thirsty," she quavered, "but if I lean over the water I'll fall in. Would you kindly give me a drink, my daughter?"

"Certainly, mother, gladly." Slop Girl rinsed her jug, dipped from where the water was clearest over a pretty sandy bottom, then hurried to the old woman. She gave her a drink just as quickly and nicely as she could.

"Thank you, my daughter," said the old woman, wiping her mouth with her sleeve. "Thank you for all your kindness and your trouble. They've won you a gift. Since all your words are sweet, for each word you speak your mouth will let fall pearls and diamonds, rosebuds and carnations."

The old woman was a fairy in disguise, and she'd wanted to see just how sweet and kind Slop Girl really was. The awed Slop Girl curtsied to the fairy and tripped lightly home.

Her mother greeted her with curses. "What's the matter with you? What kept you so long? Why, you've been gone at least three-quarters of an hour!"

"I'm so sorry, mother, I really am, but you see, I met an old lady who asked me for a drink." Lily and rose buds poured from her mouth as she spoke, mingled with pearls more luminous than a dove's throat, and jewels sparkling brighter than dew in the rays of a May dawn. The fairy had put in flowers because she knew that for this simple girl, jasmine and carnations were just as much to be prized as pearls and diamonds.

The mother, of course, kicked away the violets, daffodils, and roses, and grabbed at the rubies, topazes, and pearls. "But, but, my girl," she blurted, "what's happened to you?"

Slop Girl had to tell her story. And no matter how modestly, no matter how sweetly and shyly she did it, gems ever more exquisite, and richly scented flowers too, tumbled from her mouth.

The mother, all adither, called her eldest daughter and told her to go for water this minute to the spring.

"That's not *my* work! I don't want to!" the girl retorted. "Send Slop Girl if she enjoys it so much!"

But for once the mother made the cross-tempered wench listen. Finally the girl picked up a silver pitcher and sauntered off to the fairy's spring.

The fairy was waiting for her. To test just how rude the elder sister could be, she'd taken the form of a prettily dressed young lady.

"I'm awfully thirsty, but I'm afraid I may slip into the spring. Would you be kind enough to pour me a drink, my dear?"

"I'm not your dear, or your maid. Help yourself, if you need help!" The girl's temper had gotten the better of her, eager as she always was to insult everyone. She roughly plunged the pitcher in, hauled it out dripping, and turned on her heel.

"You shall have a gift for that," said the fairy, smiling. "For each word you speak, since your every word grates on the ear, toads and basilisks shall issue from your mouth!"

The girl turned away, shrugged derisively, and stumped off home in a snit.

The impatient mother had come out a few steps to meet her. "Well, daughter?" she demanded as soon as she saw her.

"Well, mother?" the girl replied. For these two words, a toad and a viper shot from her mouth and plopped into the mud.

The mother, terrified of such creatures, jumped away and ran screaming into the house. Right after her came the girl, determined to justify herself. "It's your fault too, mother!" she complained. "I'm not the one who wanted to go to the spring, oh no, and if you hadn't made me . . ." Each word caused a shower of polliwogs, green lizards, blindworms, and salamanders. The horrified mother hopped around, shrieking, like a goat gone mad.

Slop Girl, who'd been heating their soup, rushed out of the kitchen.

The mother spotted her, went for her, and hit her. She cut her as she smashed the jug the girl clutched in her arms, then chased her down the path like one possessed.

"It's your fault too, you wretch! You're the one who ruined your sister! Get out! Get out! If I ever see you again I'll kill you!"

Poor Slop Girl ran and never stopped till she was far away, under the cross at a crossroads. Her lovely arms were all bloody, and her pretty cheeks wet with tears.

The king's son rode by on a charger caparisoned with gold. He halted his steed right there.

"What is it, then? Why are you crying, my beauty?"

They gazed at each other as though to read on each other's face the truth of the matter, and each discovered there the purest wonder. She recounted her troubles, and how she was rejected and alone. But she complained little, and blamed no one. All her words were as fresh as dew, and at each one there came from her lovely mouth a pearl, a rosebud, a carnation, or a diamond.

Entranced, and his heart aflame, the king's son begged the girl to take refuge in his father's castle. She knew so well what he meant that she got up behind him on his white horse. They rode through the countryside in the last rays of the setting sun, and all the birds were singing.

When the king and queen saw the girl's gift, well, they realized that they would never find for their son another bride with so rich a dowry. Perhaps they didn't care that much about the flowers—who knows? But all those pearls and jewels . . . It was a pleasure just to make her talk. Her words were worth more than all the money in the world.

As for the elder daughter, things went just the other way. Her gift disgusted one and all, so much so that even her mother couldn't stand her. The least word from her meant basilisks and vipers—just imagine! And the miserable creature was so infuriated by all this that she couldn't help scolding and shouting. One evening, for just a word too many—or perhaps not even a word, only a sigh—the mother opened the house door wide and threw her daughter out.

The dreary creature had no friends. No hearth would welcome her. She made for the woods and went to die in a far corner of the forest, less from starvation than from self-hate, among her snakes and toads.

12. The Damsel with the Long Nose

There was once a lad, a bit featherbrained, who left his house one foggy morning and never could find it again.

He didn't look too hard. He'd neither father nor mother, and he'd been wanting for ages to roam around France. So off he went, free as the air, carrying with him just thirty pennies and his cheerful good humor.

The pennies didn't last long, but he went on, picking up apples from the grass ("The apple in the ditch is the soldier's," they say) and sleeping at the sign of the twinkling star. One morning he was following a poplar-lined path when he came to a mill which wasn't turning any too strongly or quickly. In fact, it wasn't turning at all. The girl sitting nearby in a spot of shade seemed very unhappy. But her face, as freckled as a quail's egg, had in it something so good and kind, so genuine, that she was a pleasure to behold.

The boy nodded to her. "Your miller's too wide-awake," said he, "and your mill's gone to sleep!"

He'd no sooner spoken than he saw tears fall from the girl's eyes. He went to her and asked if something was wrong. She told him she'd been living alone there with her father, but her father had died, the mill's works had gone wrong, and there wasn't a soul to fix it.

"I've never studied carpentry," the lad replied, "but I'm not too bad at it, anyway. Let's have a look."

She took him into the mill. He checked the machinery and saw which part was broken. Next he went to the lumber pile to get what he needed among all the boards and planks. Then he picked up a saw and got to work.

"But I'm afraid I've no money," said the girl, blushing a fiery red to admit she was poor. "How am I going to pay you?"

He went on banging in nails, and as he had three pursed between his lips, he motioned to her that she shouldn't worry. "You see?" he said at last. "It won't take long. I'll have the job done by sundown."

After they'd eaten he finished.

"I'm so grateful," said the girl. "People will come back when they find out the mill's turning again. I'll save up some money and next time you come by I'll pay you what I owe you."

"Don't worry about owing me anything."

"But I know what I'll give you in the meantime. I found them in a little chest hidden under a stone: an empty purse, a leather belt, and a hunter's brass horn."

To humor her, the lad took the three things. He put the purse in his pocket, the belt around his waist, and the horn on a cord around his neck. Then he asked the miller girl for a kiss to top it all off before he set out again. Blushing once more, she let him kiss her, thinking no harm. Still, good though it was to look at her, he didn't look very hard.

He might have realized that it takes a man to run a mill. Yes, if he'd just opened his eyes a bit more and seen what the girl was worth, and if he'd gotten her to talk and found out how to get along with her, why would he have needed to roam further through the world? But being thickheaded, he left. The miller girl watched him go.

He was off for a country he'd heard tell of, where everyone loved good eating, where all the girls were pretty, and where the king's daughter was the best eater and the prettiest lady of all. "I'd rather like to see that girl," said he to himself. "And I'd enjoy eating off the fat of the land. Who knows, anything can happen! I started with nothing and I've already a purse. True, the purse is empty. It should be holding fifty crowns."

Just then something in his pocket seemed to get awfully heavy. He stuck in his hand, pulled out the purse, and saw silver shining through its mesh. "This must be a dream," he thought, then emptied the purse into his hand and counted the coins. There were fifty crowns.

"Why, is that all it takes?" he went on to himself. "Do you just have to say, 'I want it filled with fifty crowns'?" He tried it out, and before his eyes the purse once again filled itself. He did it yet again, almost delirious now with joy. As many times as he spoke to it, the purse filled itself with beautiful round crowns.

"The miller girl didn't know what it could do when she gave it to me," thought he. "I must take it back to her."

Of course he meant to do that, but first he could line his pockets a little since it would cost her nothing. He could make himself as rich as the king or even richer! What a blessing! He poured the crowns from one hand into the other, and never mind if a few of them got away and rolled in the dirt. He jumped around, shouted, and sang, which was all right since he was alone in the wilderness. There was nothing around him but gorse and scrub, and, in the distance, line after line of woods.

But the fool got so carried away that you could hear him a league off. Robbers have sharp ears. It *is* their trade after all. Suddenly a whole company of bandits fell on him. There he was, in the middle of nowhere, helpless and alone. For some reason it occurred to him to take up the horn and put it to his lips.

At the sound of the horn, guards seemed to rise from the bushes. There were just as many as the young man needed. They attacked the robbers, put them to flight in nothing flat, and chased them into the woods.

A little farther on, the same thing happened again. Unable to believe his eyes, the young man dipped again into his pocket to gaze ecstatically at this flood of crowns. No doubt they were glittering in the sun. Another band of robbers burst from the brush and he barely had time to sound his horn. The guards got there and did their work, but he'd had a close call.

"What a miserable country this is," he said to himself as he walked on. "I wish I were already in the king's city, waiting to see his daughter pass!"

He thought he was waking from a dream when he found himself that minute before the king's castle, in the front row of the crowd. The damsel passed in her golden carriage. And she *was* beautiful—beautiful enough to make you forget to eat or drink. And now, from head to toe, he was in love.

Though a muddlehead, he still understood that the belt was magic, like the horn and the purse. "I'll have to give them back to the girl," he thought, "but as long as I'm here, I might as well use them a bit myself."

Getting what you want is no problem when you need only dip into a bottomless purse. The lad dressed himself up like a lord, all in velvet and cloth of gold. He bought a castle and gave banquets and balls. In short, his life was all sugar cakes and champagne. Above all, he and his companions gambled. Of course *he* could lose whatever he felt like losing, and in fact was quite happy to since it cost him nothing. You can imagine how many friends he acquired that way.

People talked of nothing but this lord and his wealth, and the king's daughter herself wanted to join the game. She hoped to play cards with him and win his money, like everyone else. Oh yes, she loved well enough sugar cakes, almond tarts, sweetmeats, and ruby or golden wine, but she loved pretty money even more.

So she came, with her kittenish airs, and the new lord offered her refreshments. Then he took her to the gaming table. Even if he hadn't wanted to lose, that day his head was swimming with love and plain foolishness, and he lost game after game. But each time he pulled from his purse more fistfuls of gleaming silver, and each time he put them on the table. The damsel decided in the end that this heap of crowns couldn't possibly fit in one pocket and that there must be some mystery behind the whole thing.

When it came time to leave, she had the lord get into her golden carriage with her. That way the two of them could be alone. And there she got to work on him. Oh, she was sweet-tongued, she was, and as clever as could be. Simple as he always was, he ended up betraying his secret. He showed her the purse. He even let her hold it, so she could try it out.

Money was what she wanted, and it was money she saw coming. Though amazed, she didn't lose her head. They were just approaching her father's castle. She alighted, still holding the purse, then suddenly turned her back on her suitor, darted inside, and had the door slammed in his face.

Flabbergasted, he cried out, then pounded on the door with both fists. He made quite a racket. But the damsel sent for the king's regiment, who now marched up to the beat of their drums. The lad was roughly handled and had to run home as fast as his legs would go.

There, he tore his hair. "What?" he groaned to himself. "I let her in on the secret of the purse, and then what does she do? She throws me out and makes a fool of me! Who would have believed it of her, beautiful as she is, with her angel looks and that way she has of seeming to walk on clouds! Why, she *knows* that purse is mine! Yes, it certainly *is* mine, since the miller girl gave it to me!"

All night he tortured himself over this vixen, pacing back and forth the length of his room and delivering reproachful speeches. As though she could hear him!

But come morning he suddenly began to laugh. The horn! He only had to sound the horn! He put it to his lips and blew it over and over and over—enough to summon hundreds of guards. Then he marched on the king's castle.

His forces did wonders. They fought like fiends and demolished the king's men in no time. The young man was master of the castle.

Out came the alarmed damsel, more like a white kitty than ever. "What's the matter?" she cried. "Where's the need for all this fuss? Couldn't you lend me your purse a moment? I only wanted to show it to my father. Is that all you're so angry about?"

"Silence, you smooth-tongued cheat!"—that's what he *ought* to have answered. But her glances went straight to his heart. What an innocent! He didn't even dare seize the purse and stuff it in his pocket.

The damsel began flattering him. Why, he must certainly be a great lord, and wonderfully clever too, to have come to own this fairy purse. In fact he must be a king's son, since he'd suddenly appeared surrounded by guards and eager for war.

"You therefore have my permission," she concluded, "to go and ask my father for my hand. We'll be married this very evening!"

The muddlehead could already hear wedding bells, and they addled his wits still more. All giddy and tender now, he yielded himself wholly to her. She, meanwhile, with her keen little mind, had a good idea that there was some new mystery to discover. She started questioning him about his soldiers. How had he managed to raise such a fine army in so short a time? There must be more magic behind that! Since they were going to be husband and wife, oughtn't they to share their secrets? And he—ah, he was so young and trusting—he came right out with *his!* He drew the horn from under his coat, showed it to her, and told her all about it.

When she found out he was neither a king's son nor a great lord, and that he'd nonetheless had the nerve to wish to marry her, she practically suffocated with pride and rage. She had a fit of envy, too, when she thought about the magic horn. It wasn't just greed for money or good living that had ahold of her now, it was envy, pride, and rage. This daughter of a king wore around her neck, like a golden chain, the seven deadly sins.

But she controlled herself. She hadn't let go of the purse. As though playing a game she stretched out her hand, took hold of the horn, then sounded it once, twice, and enough times more to bring her an army stronger than the lad's. And he—well, love had made him quite stupid, in fact a man's got no right to be that stupid—he admired the sweet grace with which she blew the horn . . . until she dropped the pretense and had her soldiers attack.

Everything changed in an instant. The lad barely got out of it alive. She'd have had him killed as blithely as she'd have squashed a fly. He hid in an apple tree right at the back of the garden (he was lucky he knew how to climb), and there, perched on a branch like a squirrel, he waited for night to fall.

"My God, is it possible, the way she fooled me?" he murmured. "And I'd gladly have given my blood for her!" He kept chewing it over, beside himself with indignation. "If I had her in my hands right now, I believe I'd slit her throat with this blade of mine. Ah, if only I could be right there in her room!"

He'd hardly voiced the wish when it came true. He had on the belt, after all, though he'd forgotten it. There he was in the damsel's room, blade in hand, beside her bed. She woke up to see him right before her eyes, raging and ready to cut her throat.

"Oh dear, are you angry with me?" she cried. "I only wanted to see whether those soldiers could outfight yours. Why did you run off? Do you think I don't like you?"

Instead of taking back the purse and the horn, and disappearing again immediately, he stood there rolling his eyes around and wondering what to do. The poor fool, he still hadn't quite grasped that he should never believe anything this damsel said.

"And even if I was wrong," she went on, "can't you forgive me? Oh, I can see you don't really love me! Why, the traitor! Straight off he thought ill of me! And I only wanted those soldiers so I could be his queen, in his kingdom at the end of the world!"

That gave the young man an idea. He took her in his arms and wished, according to her own words, to be with her at the end of the world.

And there they were, where the world stops in a point like a tail, sealed off by rocks. Beyond, there was nothing at all. But the king's daughter had no intention of standing around staring at the world's end by moonlight. Though shaken, she still hadn't lost her malice. She was in the lad's arms, so there she stayed. In no time she managed first to make him feel awful about having wanted to kill her, and second to want desperately to redeem himself by proving to her that he trusted her completely. So she got the secret of the belt out of him too.

A single mistake deserves no blame. If the person does it again, well, all right. But what about the one who falls three times into the same trap? He should have a fox's tail tied to his collar and then be put out of his misery with swift kicks in the behind.

To show the lad how touched she was by his trust, the damsel kissed him sweetly. But she was curious about the belt and wanted *so* much to see it. Before you could say Jack Robinson she unbuckled it and put it around her. And since her only wish was to be back in her room, she was.

The poor young man was now alone at the end of the world, without purse, horn, or belt, without resources and without hope. Demoralized by the damsel's trick, and crushed by sorrow, he could only collapse, broken-hearted, beneath a tree and weep tears as big as peas. At last, exhausted by his labors and by his despair, he fell asleep.

He slept the rest of the night, or perhaps a whole day and a whole night more. At any rate, when he woke up it was broad day and he was famished. He could have eaten a horse. He'd have given anything in the world, even the damsel and her pretty ways, for a bowl of the soup that masons eat, so thick the spoon stands straight up in it. But he was at the end of the world and there was no soup.

He hadn't eaten a thing since he'd last played cards. He simply had to find a meal.

Then he noticed that the tree he'd slept under was full of apples—well, not apples exactly, but fruit as red as any apple could be. Briskly he knocked down five and just as briskly devoured them.

He could have sworn he'd never eaten anything so delicious. Those apples tasted better than any fruit from any orchard. He ought to have been more careful, though. He'd no sooner finished eating the apples than he felt a sort of tickling at the end of his nose. His nose began to grow. How much did it grow? A foot for each apple!

What a disaster! He had to continue on with this sausage of a nose that dragged on the ground. But you see, the damsel's treachery had so destroyed him that nothing else really mattered. He'd put five more apples in one pocket before he found out what they did, and he didn't even throw them away. Still, with this nose of his swinging from side to side, he didn't get far that day. In the evening he stopped under another tree full of sort-of-apples. These were yellower than gold.

He might have learned to watch out for fruit, out there near the end of the world, but after all, he had to eat. And anyway, now the king's daughter had played that awful trick on him, the sort-of-apples could play him whatever tricks they wanted. "They can grow me donkey's ears for all I care!" he told himself.

He picked a yellow apple and ate it. It was delicious. Then he noticed his nose was tickling again, This time it was getting smaller. It shrank a whole foot.

He ate a second apple with the same result, then a third, then a fourth. After the fifth apple the nose on his face looked its normal self. No doubt a sixth apple would have made it sink right into his head.

So now he had back his perfectly normal nose and, despite his earlier attitude, that made him very happy. Meanwhile all these adventures had opened his eyes a little. He knocked down five yellow apples and stuffed them in his other pocket. Then with nimble step he set off again for the damsel's country.

It was rather a long way, but the sort-of-apples never spoiled. They stayed as fresh as when he'd picked them. The lad was careful not to bite into them. He had something in mind, and would rather have eaten acorns than touch his little store. Instead, when he had to, he lived off nuts and berries.

Finally he made it back to the land of good eating, where he got proper meals and felt much better. But he didn't forget that he had a little score to settle.

He dressed himself up as a sort of wizard and blackened his face and hands with soot. Then one Sunday morning he put the red apples in a basket, and when high mass was over he went to hawk them where the king's daughter would pass by. He knew well enough how she liked her food.

She came to see the sort-of-apples, as curious as a cat that's just smelled a mouse. She sniffed at them. The black man showed her on his fingers that he wanted five gold pieces for them. But as soon as he'd struck his bargain, he made himself scarce. He knew the weather would shortly turn unfriendly to merchants.

Sure enough, the king's daughter ate up those dainty apples one after another and her nose started growing. It reached her waist, then her knees, and finally her slippers.

She who was always so pleased with her looks, and who so loved pretending butter wouldn't melt in her mouth, now saw herself with this nose!

Just imagine her fury! A search was made for the black man, but in vain. Then physicians and apothecaries were sent for, but not one of them could think of a cure.

The damsel, meanwhile, was all but dancing like a cat on hot coals. She'd die if they didn't rid her of this nose! The king, trying to look useful, hanged six physicians and a half-dozen apothecaries.

The third day she heard a magician was there to see her.

In came a sort of Moor, dark brown of skin and bearded like a billy-goat, wearing a vervain hat. From his shabby robe he drew an apple yellower than gold and announced that eating the apple would heal the damsel's illness.

The magician was shown a bag of silver and a rope, and told the silver was for him if his remedy worked, while the rope was to go around his neck if it didn't. He accepted that arrangement and held out the apple. The damsel plucked up her courage and ate it. Her nose—oh wonder of wonders!—instantly shrank at least a foot.

"But it should have gone back to normal," said the magician as he stepped closer. "Something must have hindered the power of the remedy. Could the damsel have upon her person some treasure which is not rightfully hers? If so, then let her entrust it to me, and we shall try another apple."

The treasure she valued above any other was after all her own beauty. She drew the magic purse from her bosom and held it out to the magician. He took it and put it in his pocket.

The second apple took effect and the nose shortened another foot.

"Surely there is some other precious thing which the damsel ought not to have appropriated."

"Heavens," she replied, "it's practically nothing—just this brass horn which I forgot to give back."

She held out the horn, got a third apple, ate it, and saw her nose shorten still another foot.

There were still two feet left, however. The magician again sang his refrain.

"Oh yes," cried the damsel, "it had slipped my mind! But it's really nothing at all—just this dirty old belt I have under my dress."

She unbuckled it and the lad put it around his waist. Ever since he'd seen the king's daughter with her nose dangling like a sausage, her red eyes, and her furious looks, he was quite freed from the bonds of love and felt only like bursting out laughing.

He watched the damsel eat the fourth apple. Having no more bitterness in him than a dove, he had the fifth all ready to give her—because, you know, the princess still had a foot of nose hanging from her face.

But just then she glanced at the magician. She didn't recognize him under his walnut stain and his billy-goat beard, but she noticed his amusement. Enraged, she decided that as soon as the remedy had done its work, she'd have the man rewarded for his services, not with the bag of silver, but with the hempen rope.

This noble thought showed a moment on her face. The impostor magician couldn't read it plainly, but he trembled. Everything came back to him and he fully saw the damsel's treachery. "How much nicer it would be," thought he, "to be with a kind and simple girl!"

It was a wish, and the magic belt did its work. The young man found himself, with his apple, at the mill next to the miller girl. He'd probably been thinking about her without realizing it, for she seemed so good and so true that it was a pleasure to look at her.

The beautiful princess was left in her castle, with that nose dangling right down to her chin for the rest of her life. So God did what the young man could never have done.

But the young man wasn't thinking of the king's daughter any more. He and the miller girl were soon married. She put purse, horn, and belt back under the stone. They lived happily without miracles and had lots of children.

And dilly-down-dale,
That's the end of my tale.

1 3. The Ill-Lodged Goat

O nce a good woman, now a widow, retired to a little cottage. She
moved in, set up house just right, and then, at the next fair in town,
bought herself a nanny-goat. Her parish priest met her that evening, as
she led the goat home on a string.

"Why, yes, Father," she said, "a little goat to give me a drop of milk
. . . Of course my cottage isn't all that roomy, you know . . ."

"So what'll you do with your nanny?"

"Well, you see, in warm weather I'll tie her up to a stake in the
garden . . ."

"And in winter, then?"

"Heavens, in winter I'll keep her in my room."

"Yes, but a goat—what about the smell?"

"Oh, the smell . . . But what can I do? The poor thing'll just have to
get used to it!"

1 4. The White Rat

T here once was a king in a land at the other end of the world. Though
married, he had no children, and being childless, he and his wife had
befriended a female white rat.

How they doted on this white rat! You should have heard them talk
about her sweetness, her airs, and her graces. Nothing in their whole
kingdom, or in all the kingdoms of the world, could surpass this white rat
of theirs.

One day at last they went off to the queen of the fairies, to beg her to
change their white rat into a real girl. The queen of the fairies no doubt
owed them a favor or two. After all, kings and fairies help each other out
from time to time. So she agreed.

Usually, fairies change the sons and daughters of kings into blue birds,
or perhaps into fabulous beasts. This time it went the other way round,
which was a fancier miracle still. Suddenly the white rat was a princess,
and such a deliciously pretty one! She just had the faintest touch of pink
in her eyes, and an ever so slightly pointed face.

Actually, the good people of that country did mutter a little, though not too loudly (the king had his police), about bitches not bearing kittens or about pinewoods always smelling of resin, and a dozen other proverbs to the effect that your origins mark you. Blood will tell.

Anyway, there came a day when the king decided that, like other kings, he should marry his daughter off in grand style. "You've got to get married, my dear, my sweet," said he. "Tell me you will!"

"Why yes, father, certainly. But what husband will you give me?"

"Whomever you want, my girl, whomever you want."

"Father, I want the most powerful husband there could ever be in the world."

Now *that's* talking.

The king thought it over for three days. Then he told his daughter he'd ask on her behalf for the hand of the sun.

The princess pouted. "The sun?" she cried. "But *he's* not the most powerful in the world! All it takes is one cloud! The cloud comes, covers the sun, puts him out, and the light's gone! Nothing's left but fog and spreading shadow. No, no, I want a better husband than that old sun."

The king left her and thought three days. Then he came back to let her know that, all things considered, he meant to ask for the hand of the cloud—the cloud which fills all space and covers kingdoms.

The princess pouted. "The cloud? But all it takes is a little wind. The wind pushes the cloud, tears it in tatters, carries it off, and melts it away in the depths of the sky. Then no more cloud! No, no, I want a better husband than that old cloud!"

The king left her and thought three days. Then he came back and told her she should have the wind which sweeps all before it and rouses the sea to fury.

The princess pouted. "The wind? It doesn't take long to get away from *his* power! All you need do is take shelter behind a wall, or behind a mountain. Even when the wind's making the hazels lean and uprooting oaks, what can it do against a mountain with all its mass of earth and rock? No, no, I've got to have a better husband than that old wind!"

The king left her and thought three days. Then he came back to tell his daughter that she should have for her very own husband the mountain, which storms batter and lightning strikes without ever weakening it.

The princess pouted. "The mountain? But there's someone more powerful than the mountain! Why, there's the one who gnaws the mountain with teeth sharper than needles, who nibbles and digs his tunnels, who's as much at home there as in a cheese, and who makes the mountain his castle! There's better than the sun, the cloud, and the wind, there's better than the mountain. There's the rat, the Mountain-Carver, Ratty with his pointed teeth, so brave and handsome, the wonder of wonders, and the most powerful of all who can be imagined in this world! Yes, in short, the rat!"

Well, now it was out. That's what the princess wanted, and she wanted it so badly that the king and queen had to go back to the queen of the fairies. They went down on their knees and begged her to turn their daughter back into a white rat.

With her wand the fairy did it, and the wedding was held. The pretty white rat lady married a scabby rat boy with a tail a foot long.

There's cockcrow,
And what do you know,
My tale is done!

15. The Flight into Egypt

O nce Mary and Saint Joseph had to take to the road with the Child, to flee the wrath of Herod: to flee his soldiers on their horses, a whole brigade behind their captain, with sword and dagger massacring the innocents. Blade in hand, all spattered with blood, they brutally scoured the countryside.

That evening the Good Lady was all tired out. But then the riders came again into view, trotting, charging, racing like fiends, striking sparks from every stone, and she had to start off once more and run. She ran and ran, the Good Lady, with her lovely Child in her arms, but she was down on the plain, and you could see her from anywhere.

She ran and ran, as hard as she could, holding Jesus tight against her, Jesus whom Herod had ordered slain. Then suddenly her breath failed and she fell as though dead to the ground. But by God's will she fell on a clump of sage.

"Sage, sage," she cried, "save my Jesus!"

Yes, the sage heard her. Quickly it shot up into a tall shrub. And there came the soldiers, glaring down from their horses, searching and prying hither and yon, rolling their big ugly heads.

And mint, the tattletale, whispered to them as loud as it could, "Under the bush, under the bush!" But with all the clatter of their trappings, the ringing bits and the clanging hooves, thank goodness, they didn't hear! So they left again empty-handed.

"Mint, mint," said Our Good Lady, "you are mint most false. Flower you shall, but never bear seed."

And to the sage she said, "Sage, sage, may God save you! Flower you shall, and bear seed too."

That's why you need sage when you feel poorly. And you shouldn't forget it when you feel well either, because sage is the hand of God.

But King Herod's soldiers were still beating the plain. From far off they spied the Lady and raised a great shout. On they came at furious speed, sparks flying, amid swirls of dust. The Good Lady with her lovely Child hid beneath an aspen tree, which started trembling, turning, parting its leaves, leaving both in full view. A hazel—such a good fellow!—that chanced to be there spread its leaves and made itself as thick as it could. And ever since, the aspen, all pale and faint, always trembles with fever, while the hazel is the most wholesome of trees. It need only touch a snake for the snake to fall dead, and it won the privilege of flowering several times yearly, on each feast day of Our Lady.

But that wasn't Egypt yet. The Lady still had a long way to go. And as she fled before those fierce, bloody riders who ever sought her, she had once more to find a hiding place. She asked the cuckoo to take the Child into its nest among the stubble. The cuckoo began to raise the cry, calling the pursuers, "Cuckoo, cuckoo, cuckoo!"

Sparks flashing, dust clouds churning, Herod's riders raced that way. Thank goodness the oriole, close by, took the Child into its own nest and hid him there. And ever since, the cuckoo is a sorry creature, grey of feather, who no longer has a nest of its own; while the oriole's feathers are all golden, a reward from the Lady. And another gift the oriole won is to warn people with its song, near sundown, that it's going to rain. Everyone loves the dear oriole, who eats cherries and leaves the stones.

The Good Lady was still fleeing, her Jesus in her arms; and Herod's captain with his cavalry was on her trail. On their great galloping horses shod with iron, amid dust and sparks, crushing and blasting all before them, they bore down. They'd sworn that this time *nothing* on the fields, no nest, tuft, or thicket, should escape their eye.

But there was a herdsman, weeping with hunger in his poor little house. He'd eaten no bread for seven days, nor had his wife or children. This was in the heart of the year's black time, past Christmas, when all is dead. "Twelfth Night, winter's bite," they say. And, dear God, how's one to manage till the next harvest comes in?

"Go, go, go to the valley!" a voice told him. "Sow the wheat!"

He obeyed, and while he was sowing, the Holy Virgin came by.

"Good day, good day, gentle herdsman. My, what fine wheat you're sowing!"

"Good day, good day, noble Lady. What a fine Child you have there!"

"Tell me, tell me, gentle herdsman, would you kindly protect him?"

"Why yes, yes, noble Lady, I'll do all I can!"

What made him so kind, you see, is that helping others filled him with joy, and that's the way people in the old days used to be.

So the Virgin had him plow a deep furrow to bury her in, with her Child in her arms. He leaned on the plowshare and made a furrow so deep that the Lady, her Child at her breast, disappeared in it from sight. Then over them he spread his cloak.

"Tell me, tell me, gentle herdsman, don't you lack the wheat you need?"

"Oh yes, yes, noble Lady, for seven days we've had nothing to eat!"

"Then go fetch your sickle, and you'll reap your wheat!"

"But how, Lady, how could that be? The wheat isn't even all sown!"

"Just go, take up your sickle, the wheat will be ready for reaping!"

And while he was gone the Lady, down at the bottom of her furrow, sang to the wheat what she had to sing:

> *Wheat, wheat, bloom and bear!*
> *Ripen now your grain so fair!*

The wheat sprang from the earth above the Lady and the Child, wheat suddenly standing, green, in ear, and ready for the sickle.

"Go, go, go to the valley," called the voice. "It's time to harvest the wheat!"

The gentle herdsman did as the voice urged, and as he worked, the riders passed.

"Good day, good day, gentle herdsman. What fine wheat you're reaping!"

"And you, captain to Herod, what a fine mount you ride!"

"Tell me, tell me, gentle herdsman, haven't you seen the Lady go by? In her arms she bears the Child we have orders to kill!"

"Yes, captain, yes, she passed by while I was sowing."

"Then turn back, men! It was last year she came by here! But health

to the king, on my soul I'll catch her, yes I will! I'll strike off her breasts, I'll cut off her arms! The Child will fall to the ground and he'll not be able to nurse any more!"

They were talking, swearing, raging, the captain and Herod's soldiers, as they raced off again in a clatter of iron and rattling weapons, like clouds of dust that disperse over the fields.

The Good Lady arose from the furrow, and the Child blessed the wheat. The wheat had come forth from the earth in a moment as though from the Child's own breast, from his flesh itself. The gentle herdsman, his wife, and his children had plenty. And from this wheat blessed by Jesus comes the flour for all man's bread, and for the bread of God. Alleluia.

16. The Boat That Went Both on Land and on Water

There was once a great kingdom whose king had a daughter to marry off. A bit proud she was, but more beautiful than any. The king was in no hurry to find her a husband. He loved to have her with him, for she was as quick as a warbler, as straight as an arrow, and as sunny as an Easter day. He didn't look forward to letting any young man have her, not even a king's son. "Anyway," thought he, "where will I ever find a real match for her? She's *my* daughter, after all, the daughter of a great king."

But in time, the queen, the dishwasher, the minister, and the cobbler, in fact everyone in the castle and in the streets, began reminding the king at every turn that this daughter of his was his only child and that he had to get her married—not to a prince, perhaps, if he couldn't think of a suitable one, but at least to a capable lad who could one day govern the kingdom.

"Is that what you want?" cried the king one morning, as his minister brought the subject up for the umpteenth time. "Is that your wish? You want a capable lad? All right, at the stroke of noon, have it announced with a flourish of trumpets that I'll give my daughter to anyone who takes wood from my forest and builds me a boat that goes both on land and on water. Yes, I'll say, to anyone who comes asking for her riding a boat like that!"

To himself he said, "A lot of water will flow under the bridges before any mother's son brings me a boat you can sail over fields and waves. These fools won't pester me any more with their nonsense about having to get my girl married!"

In the same kingdom, near the castle, lived two brothers, both country boys. The elder was so clever, I tell you, his hands could make him anything he wanted. He could have made a cat a new pair of eyes, as they say.

He knew he was clever, though. In fact, he knew it a bit too well. Self-confidence is fine, but you see, you shouldn't count too much on your own cleverness. The lad said to himself, "If anyone's to build this boat that goes both on land and on water, why, it has to be me! I'll build it and I'll win the king's daughter. If I don't, no one else around here will!"

He took up his saw, his ax, and his adze; he filled his toolbox with chisels, gouges, and hammer. Then with a light step he set off for the king's forest.

On his way over Three Beech Trees Hill he met an old woman like the ones who comb the woods for dead branches. She greeted him.

"Good day, journeyman carpenter!" she cried. "Did you wake up this morning in good spirits?"

Courtesy should have made him stop, since she'd struck up a conversation. But he strode proudly by, filled as he was that morning with self-importance—he who always seemed to have the world at his fingertips. He only nodded to her.

"Where are you off to?" she asked.

"To look after my business."

"What are you going to do with all your tools?"

"Make me some skittles!"

"Very well then, journeyman, skittles they shall be!"

When he got to work in the king's forest, everything he felled, shaped, or carved turned to skittles. He began again with elm and ash instead of beech, but it all ended up the same: skittles, nothing but skittles.

Being hot-tempered, he got angry and swore, then hurled adze, gouge, saw, and chisel through the trees. That way he labored twice: first throwing, then picking up.

In the evening he came home looking as though he'd been taken down a peg or two. "I ran into one of those old women with the evil eye," he complained to his younger brother. "Anyway, it was stupid of me to get wrapped up in the idea of building that boat. A boat that sails both on land and on water! Why, it'll be a month of Sundays before anyone builds such a contraption! The king just wanted to show everyone who's boss."

"You never know!" the younger objected. "Time is the father of miracles. You should have kept at it."

"You keep at it, then," growled the elder, angry again. "You go to the king's forest tomorrow and waste your time."

The younger didn't answer. He wouldn't have started the job on his own, but he wasn't going to turn away from it now. You have to let yourself be led and trust that you will be led.

The next morning he took the toolbox and set off for the king's forest, humming a song. On Three Beech Trees Hill he met an old woman hobbling along, bent in two, with one hand on her hip. She looked like one of the women who gather deadwood in the forest.

"Good day, journeyman carpenter," she greeted him.

"And to you, good lady."

"Where are you off to work?"

"My brother sent me to the king's forest. He wants me to see if I can build this boat the king's asking for. I don't know quite what I'll do, but sometimes ideas come when you try."

"A good thought, journeyman. Why shouldn't you succeed? Just get to work."

"Oh, don't worry, I will."

"And when you've built it, go up and show it to the king. On the way you'll meet six men-at-arms. Have them board your boat one after the other. The time will come when you'll need them."

The younger brother tipped his hat to her and took careful note of what she'd said. Then he thanked her and said good-bye.

He came to the king's forest, took off his jacket, and began felling trees.

Believe it or not, the wood he cut fell into place all by itself. One branch made an axle, another the rudder; one length made the gunwale, another the rail. The pieces joined themselves each to each by tenon and mortise, fitted themselves where they belonged, and worked out what the next piece would be. The whole design grew by itself. At last the boat the king had dreamed of, without even knowing what it might look like, took shape under the lad's fingers just as a pinecone takes shape on the tree—but a mite faster.

The journeyman sang and the work went forward. By midday the boat was finished—perfectly finished, and even rather nicely decorated with delicate carvings.

The lad went aboard to try it out. The boat rolled down to the pond, launched itself, came back to land, and sailed as well on land as on water! So he steered it toward the castle where the king lived.

Without horses or mules, this carriage-boat sailed so straight over rivers, ponds, fields, and moors that the tall poplars bent low out of its path and the whole landscape glided swiftly by. The lad rolled along, hair to the wind; but he still didn't assume, as many others would have done in his place, that he was the best in the world.

The first person he met on the way was a man-at-arms with a belly like a huge waterskin, lying flat on his stomach by the river. When someone wanted to cross, he'd swallow the river at one gulp so the person could go dry-shod.

"Ahoy, what are you doing there?" the lad cried.

"Drinking up the river!"

"That's all you do?"

"Yes, and I live very well by it!"

"Come aboard, I'll take you to the king's castle."

A little farther on he found another man-at-arms with a mouth like that of an oven, gnawing furiously at a mountain.

"Say, what are you doing there?"

"Chewing up the mountain!"

"That's all you do?"

"Yes, and I live very well by it!"

"Come aboard, I'll take you to the king's castle."

What did he see a little farther on? Another man-at-arms with a backside as round as the full moon. The fellow was lying on his back, and the wind from his behind was turning nine mills on the hill.

"Say, what are you doing there?"

"Living off my wind!"

"That's all you do?"

"Yes, and I live very well by it!"

The lad took this third man-at-arms on board his rolling boat.

Next was a fourth man-at-arms with ears like cabbage leaves. He was lying full-length on his side, with one ear to the earth, listening to dandelions grow on the other side of the world. This Sharp-Ears had no other trade and he lived very well. The lad had him come aboard, then sailed on toward the king's castle.

And next? A fifth man-at-arms, with arms like staves, who was throwing stones and knocking down larks for a hundred leagues around. That was all he did, and it gave him a good living! On board, on board! He too boarded the boat that went both on land and on water.

And last? A sixth man-at-arms, with legs like poles, who'd put on these legs to catch hares and who could outrace any hare! That was all he did, and it gave him a good living.

"Come aboard, come aboard!" cried the lad, "you too!" The man-at-arms with the long legs got in, and they sailed off to see the king.

In no time all seven reached the castle. Everyone came out to look and shouted with amazement. People rushed to the castle from all around and they couldn't believe their eyes, which they opened very wide. The grubby kitchen boy was there; and the old woman who darned the rags (she came panting up, needle in hand); and the king, the queen, and the damsel too.

The king stared and stared, with his crown askew on his head. Though amazed and frustrated, he'd given his word. He'd said what he'd said and he'd had it announced with flourishes of trumpets. Could he refuse his daughter to the one who came asking for her, quite simply and honestly, with just the boat he himself had requested—the one that went both on land and on water?

"Yes," he admitted, smoothing his beard, "the boat seems to be the one

I'd imagined. My word's a king's word and I won't take it back. But there's one little thing, a mere nothing, to look after before the wedding. The heat's rather soured the wine in my cellar. It would be wrong to throw the wine away, and it wouldn't be right, either, to serve it for my daughter's wedding. So you or one of your men," he said to the lad, "must drink it all up before nightfall. Tomorrow I want my barrels filled with good, new wine!"

The lad, hat in hand, listened respectfully. When he'd heard the king out he gave a sign to River-Drinker.

River-Drinker started in as though he hadn't drunk for nine hundred years. The job was quickly done. Of course the king's cellar was impressive. What vast stores of wine it held, what leagues of tunnels and chambers, what rows and rows of hogsheads and barrels! But River-Drinker swallowed all the wine, and he'd have swallowed the barrels too if anyone had asked him.

The amazed king wrinkled his nose. "Just one more thing," said he, "the tiniest thing. Whoever drinks up the sea should also eat the fishes. There's still the bread. It wouldn't be right to serve stale bread for my daughter's wedding, so by nightfall you or one of your men must eat up all the bread in my kitchen."

The lad gave a sign to Mountain-Cruncher. Mountain-Cruncher started crunching, and the job was quickly done! In no time he'd devoured all the buns and loaves. He'd have eaten the baskets and hampers too if anyone had asked him, and the stones of the oven as well.

The king frowned. "Well," he said, "there's one more thing, a mere trifle to look after before the wedding. My castle seems to me set a little too much toward the shade. You or one of your men must blow on it till it turns a quarter-round toward the sun."

The lad, hat in hand as always, gave a sign to Mill-Puffer. Mill-Puffer lay down on his back and drew back his folded legs, facing (so to speak) one wing of the castle. The castle turned three times around like a top.

The king frowned more and more blackly.

"I'm going up to the highest room of my highest tower," he declared, "to whisper in my daughter's ear what she must fetch for her wedding. You or one of your men must hear the secret and repeat it to me exactly as I said it."

The lad winked to Sharp-Ears, who had only to prick up his ears to hear the king's secret. The king told his daughter to fetch her wedding jewels from the treasure tower, deep in the mountains.

Off rode the damsel on her fine white horse, racing as though to clear her own mind. Perhaps she hadn't yet decided what she thought of this marriage.

The king pulled his pipe from his pocket, stuffed it, lit it, and smoked it. Everyone waited in respectful silence for the princess to come back. The lad himself was wondering whether they really were going to ring the wedding bells. He didn't yet dare believe himself in paradise.

Time went by.

"Heavens!" the king suddenly cried. "I forgot to give my daughter the key to the tower! That puts a stop to everything. We won't be able to have any wedding. The only hope," he went on, knocking out his pipe on his thumbnail, "is if you or one of your men can catch up with her on foot, just as you are, and get back here at exactly the same time she does."

The lad nodded to Long-Legs, who set off with great strides. In no time he caught up with the king's daughter, gave her the key, and went with her to the tower. She took out the wedding jewels, then turned her horse's head around and galloped rather fast toward home.

She was a bit proud, as you can tell. She had her father's tendency toward swiftness and secrecy. As far as she was concerned, why *not* marry a village boy. But she still hadn't even glanced at this lad. That's why she was driving her white horse so hard. It was running like the wind.

That was nothing for Long-Legs. He'd have been constantly passing her if he hadn't held himself back. When the king's daughter saw this, she thought of a trick. She pretended to be tired, stopped her horse, sat down on a bit of green grass under a tree, and said she was going to take a nap.

It was growing dark. Long-Legs, the runner, sat down nearby and dozed off too. His head sank onto his chest and he set off for the land of dreams.

He'd taken care to sit on the end of the damsel's train, but being clever she very gently got it out from under him. Next she jumped into the saddle, walked her mount ever so softly over the grass, then spurred it on and headed for home at a full gallop. Long-Legs was still asleep by the path.

The lad, meanwhile, was thinking about the damsel. Yes, he wanted her, though she still hadn't even looked at him! He was watching for her return, and it bothered him terribly not to see her or Long-Legs coming.

"Sharp-Ears!" he called, "listen carefully and tell me what's happening!"

"What's happening," replied Sharp-Ears, "is that your runner is snoring. He's fallen asleep somewhere and the king's daughter is coming home all alone."

"Your turn, Stone-Slinger, quickly! Wake him up with a pebble on the tip of his nose!"

Long-Legs jumped up when the pebble hit him.

Here came the princess in a cloud of dust. You could see her yonder, at the last turn in the road. Her white horse was going like a whirlwind, striking sparks in the midst of the cloud with his iron shoes.

But Long-Legs too rushed into view, his feet hardly touching the ground, leaping along like lightning. Though the horse galloped, he still came on. Now he was three strides ahead, and he had to slow down to get there at exactly the same time as the princess, right in front of the king and everyone else.

This time the king just *had* to give his daughter to the younger brother who'd built the boat.

The evening after their wedding, the bride told her husband they should take Sharp-Ears along with them on their honeymoon.

The king wouldn't let them take the boat that went both on land and on water, and anyway, the lad had spotted two or three very black looks shot their way. There was a plot brewing, as far as he could tell, and trouble was coming. But he was full of love for the king's daughter, and since she'd sworn to love him too, nothing bad could happen to them.

After all, the girl had finally looked at him when she came home to the castle on her white horse. She'd wanted to see what he was like, this boy who'd so cleverly overcome all the impossible obstacles willfully put between her and him by the king. She'd seen a village lad whose eyes after all spoke her own language, a lad who'd won out after all these tests, yet who wasn't strutting or boasting. Hat in hand, straight as a poplar tree, cheerful and smiling, he told very simply how the fairy had done everything for him and how she'd appeared to him on Three Beech Trees Hill.

The princess was clever. Since she knew the ways of the court, the evening after her wedding she had Sharp-Ears listen to what people there were saying.

"Madam," said Sharp-Ears, "they've told your father so many awful things that he's furious about your marriage. He's just ordered three thousand men to pursue you. They're to get rid of your husband and bring you back to the castle!"

"Well then!" she cried. "It's just as well to keep informed! But we certainly are in trouble now!"

That minute they started preparing for war. Sharp-Ears took up his post on a knoll to listen. He kept the young couple constantly up-to-date on what was happening at court and in the army's camp. Long-Legs dashed everywhere, carrying orders. Stone-Slinger struck the first blow in the battle with a barrage of baked apples. Meanwhile Mountain-Cruncher crunched up a mountain so that the young couple could get away, and River-Drinker drank up a river so they could cross dry-shod. Then when the king's army appeared, River-Drinker spat the river out again and the army was stopped by the water.

Finally, Mill-Puffer lay in wait. He lay on his back, tucked up his legs, and let go. What a storm struck then! Hats, plumes, capes, and belts flew left and right in the fearful gale. Chariots too, and teams of horses, cannons, battalions, and squadrons—everything flew like oat chaff. In less than two minutes the battlefield was cleared.

The lad had carried all before him by good white magic, over land and water, before the wedding and after. The king had gotten nowhere at all. And at last his anger subsided.

He told himself that his son-in-law had the fairies on his side and that he might as well get along with a fellow like that. The two of them made up. Now life rolled on in a friendly way for young and old, in good seasons and bad, just like that famous boat that rolled so nicely over land and water.

17. The Finch in May

Once in the old, old days there was a finch that had been wise enough to nest in the linden tree of a convent.

Wise enough? No doubt the idea was an inspiration from on high. God watches over all things, even the life of a finch.

Providence wakes each morning
An hour or two before the sun.

So there's the finch in its tree, among the new May leaves. It was May, you know, Mary's month, when narcissus bloom in the high meadows— the flowers they call the white gloves of Our Lady. Eight times a day, from its nest in the middle of the cloister, the finch heard the nuns at their prayers, and from prime to terce to compline the same two words kept coming back. It heard them, listened, then tried them out with its own little bird throat. The dear thing didn't know it was an angel from Heaven who'd brought those two words down to mankind when he came to proclaim our salvation. The leaves swayed, and the sunbeams through them swung like censers. There in the green, moving light and the gentle breezes, the finch repeated over and over those two words: *Ave Maria, Ave Maria!*

The convent stood under steep, forested slopes and towering spires of rock, beneath a spur of the mountains. One evening the finch had ventured up into those piney, stony wilds when suddenly it felt a presence hovering above it, under the clouds. With all the speed of its wings it fled for the convent roof and home.

But a kite's eyes are more piercing than hell. The one slowly circling up there, round and round in the streaming clouds and wind, stopped like a spider hanging from its thread. The white bands on the finch's wings had given it away.

The kite dropped and gripped the finch in its talons.

Nearly fainting, the little bird cried out. It cried out the two words that had so gotten into its head that it had said them over and over all day long: *Ave Maria, Ave Maria.*

So great is the power of Mary's name that the name alone—just one call to Our Lady—loosened the kite's grip. Up again into the clouds it flew, not daring now to touch its prey.

The terrified finch raced and dove straight into the heart of its linden tree. Among the sweet flowers again, saved, comforted, and overjoyed, it fairly nestled into her hands who is the Flower and Queen of the World.

18. Endless Wishes

There once was a girl so sweet and pretty that a little drop of oil, as they say, could have rolled right down her smooth golden hair to the straps of her wooden shoes.

Late one summer afternoon, while the sun was still high in the sky, she was coming home to the village along the path through the spruces. She went by way of the wood so she could gather hazelnuts. Me, I see her taking the Gayre road to Daragon, on the mountainside. And she came to a spot that must have been just like the pool behind Germaine's, near the fairy cave. There's an arch there too, a stream, a stone, and a big, twisty old tree.

An old woman was huddled on the stone, so old she must have been born two days before the world.

"Hello, my dear," said the old woman. "Where are you going?"

"To pick hazelnuts, ma'am. Won't you come too?"

"Ma'am," the little girl had said, though the old woman wasn't at all like other women. She looked as though she surely knew the secret of the fern seeds. As for the little girl, she hardly knew what she was saying. No doubt she'd never had an experience like this one in her life.

"No hurry, my daughter. Sit yourself down here."

The old woman made room for her on the stone.

"My mother's expecting me, ma'am. She told me not to stop on the way."

"The way's not something your mother decides. Sit down a moment, you'll only walk better for it later."

The little girl sat down, not daring to disobey. It all seemed a dream.

"Tell me, my dear, your wooden shoes are pretty enough, but they still must pinch your feet. Wouldn't you like some proper shoes, ones with buckles on them?"

"Ma'am, I'll have leather shoes on the day of my first communion. My mother promised."

"But why not right now, my dear?"

"Right now? Oh no, ma'am."

"My dear, tell me what your heart desires. Whatever it is, hazelnut bread or striped silk ribbon, you shall have it this minute."

"Oh ma'am, would you let me have two or three wishes?"

"Two or two dozen, all you want!"

> Tell me what you wish, my dear:
> This old woman in return
> Asks only a single hair.

"Only a single hair! Why then, ma'am, I can make thousands of wishes!"

My dear, as many as you please,
And for each wish, you see,
It's just one hair you'll give to me.

"First then, ma'am, I'd like the pretty shoes."

She got them right then, and they were astonishingly pretty—in fact so pretty she felt no tingle at all when the old woman pulled out a hair.

There was so much to think up and wish for. Marzipan cakes! They came next. Third, she wished that her little sister, whose leg wasn't right and who could only limp, could be able to walk like other girls. Next, a lovely red petticoat, then a starched bonnet, a damask coat, a satin apron . . .

The ideas came freely now, and her heart was dancing with pleasure. She hardly felt the hairs go. She wished for candy sugar, a dozen oranges, raisins, nougat white and brown, the fruit-and-nut mix called "the four beggars," three pomegranates . . .

Then her desires took wing and she wished without end: a mirror, a gilded belt, a pink brocade dress, a silver-embroidered Holland hanky, a grey donkey with a red velvet saddle, gold-plated scissors on a chain . . .

Wishes popped into her mind all fat and lively, crowding each other like bubbles in a fizzy-water spring that wells up from a bottom of rust-colored mud. There *are* springs like that up there in the mountains. Their water's so light it tickles, but later it feels much heavier than regular water and gives you a headache.

The hairs kept vanishing. A wish, a hair, a wish, a hair. The old woman's hand clutched a whole bundle of golden hairs. The little girl noticed nothing, she just wished and wished and wished: a garnet pendant to go around her neck with earrings to match, a canary in a brass-wire cage to sing in her room . . .

Suddenly she thought of glass slippers, like Cinderella's in the story; and three dresses, star-colored, moon-colored, and sun-colored like Peau d'Ane's . . .

To be helpful, and also to make things go faster, she decided to pull out each hair herself. Twice, then three times she put her hand to her head, then looked at herself in the pool and saw her face. She was bald! Like a scalded rat she was, one with a mad, sad look on its face and a pointed little skull as smooth-peeled as an egg.

The pretty dresses and the gilded belt, the silver bracelets and the pearl necklace—how they mocked her now, in the state she was in!

When she came to in the cool of the evening, nothing was left of the old woman's gifts—no jewelry, no singing canary, no sweets or velvet-saddled donkey. Nothing but three brown leaves dancing with two yellow ones in a little whirl of wind.

There she was, bald and fit for everyone to laugh at—bald just as they warned her would happen when she wanted to stay up in the evening with the grownups instead of going to bed.

> Yes indeed, here comes a bat:
> He'll pee upon your little head
> And make you bald, so go to bed!

She was starting home, all weak and fainting, when she opened her eyes a little wider and saw a lady before her. The lady was wondrously beautiful, and her kind eyes fairly melted your heart.

"What's the matter, little girl? Why are you crying so?"

"Oh ma'am, I'm sad because my hair's all gone, and I just can't stop crying!"

"I see your wishes didn't work. But if you could keep just one, among all the wishes you made, which would it be?"

"The one about my sister, ma'am. The wish that her leg would get better."

"That's a good wish, little girl. And since you must pay for everything fortune gives you, that wish will cost you only a single one of your hairs!"

The little girl felt a tingle and put her hand to her head. How lovely! Her fingers touched golden hair. It was back!

She wanted to cry out her thanks, but the lady was gone. Instead her little sister came running toward her through the wood, and her bad leg was healed. She dashed past bushes and trees the way little girls have done ever since the world began, shouting aloud that she was all better!

> Fiddle-dee-dee,
> My tale's over,
> And I've planted a tree
> To grow us another!

19. The Secret of the Ferns

Once the ferns held a secret. Fern roots are black and form letters, as you can see if you dig them up carefully enough. But in the earth the letters run on and on, and break and crumble away. You can never get them all out. And you have to have them *all*, you have to find all their branchings, because then the letters spell a word: the word of happiness.

Who's going to find that word now, the way the world is going?

Once upon a time—a long, long time ago it was, before they began ringing the angelus—there were wild men back up there in the endless woods. Evenings, they'd come down to the houses and spy on people through cracks in the shutters, by the glow of the fire. No one had glass windows then. Three families shared one hearth, under the same roof, and simmered their dinner in common.

The people knew the wild men came spying, though they were always ready to run off. Yes, they were as wild as wild could be, far beyond reason. Still, they got what they could out of life, in their own way. You might say they did their poor best to mimic Christian ways.

One evening when the people knew they were out there peering through the leaves, they put on their wooden clogs, right in front so the wild men could see them, then walked and danced around with the shoes on.

The next morning they left a nice new pair of wooden shoes before the door, still tied together, as though they'd just forgotten them there.

One wild man comes stealing up, step by step, very carefully. He gets to the clogs, puts them on the way he's seen it done, then tries a bit of dancing. But dancing hobbled like that . . .

They jump him from three sides at once. He struggles like a trapped animal and smashes the clogs on the rocks, but it's too late, they've got him, they've really got him.

Now he's a prisoner in this dark house, groaning and crying.

At night his woman, as wild as he, comes calling through the door, "Wild man, O wild man, my love, whatever you do, don't tell them the secret of the ferns!"

Some say she cried, "Don't tell the secret of the sage!" But it must have been ferns, because ferns bloom only once a year, on Saint John's Eve—at night, I believe, so you have to really open your eyes to see them. Their flowers have a wonderful power. But people nowadays have lost all that, all those great secrets . . .

If only we knew how to see green things, see them as though in bloom, in their wonder. How their power could help us then!

2 0. The Man with the Bean

There was once a poor man who'd brought up twelve children. His land was so small that two foxes fighting in the middle of it would have had their tails sticking out into the neighbors' fields. Who could have fed a family from land like that? As soon as the children grew up a bit they hired themselves out to work. One watched geese, another herded sheep; one became a mill hand, another a kitchen boy. One by one they went off till that fine day their mother and father were at last left alone.

Now, the father had gotten old. His arms and legs were rusty. He could see the time coming when he wouldn't even be able to go and cut wood in the forest.

"Well," he'd say to himself, evenings, staring into the fire with his elbows on his knees and his head in his hands, "well, what I need now is a nicely spread table and a little donkey to carry me to the woods. Otherwise I'll have to take up begging."

Yes, a father may feed twelve children, but twelve children don't feed a father.

One day he was dragging himself painfully home from the forest, with a great bundle of wood on his back, when he saw a man with a white beard coming his way. The man stopped, wished him good evening, then slipped a bean into his hand.

"Here, poor fellow," said he, "you shall plant this bean. When the bean plant has grown, take the road the beanstalk makes for you. Climb up to see me from branch to branch. I've something up there for you."

Then the nice old man with the white beard vanished at a turn of the path.

Good gracious! The woodcutter went home clutching the bean, and quickly told his wife what had happened.

"See?" he said. "You see this bean? But, my poor dear wife, where are we to plant it? We haven't an inch of ground that doesn't already have something growing in it."

"Well, husband, if you want to plant it, plant it all the same, by the hearth."

"A good idea, wife. It'll be warm, and it'll always get a bit of water when you put up the cooking pot."

He poked a hole with his thumb and dropped the bean in, then refilled it with his clog and tamped the earth down. The two of them ate and went to bed.

What a surprise the next morning! Overnight the bean had grown. The plant, thick with green branches, had shot up the chimney and you got a crick in your neck, you had to lean back so far to see how high it went.

I tell you, if the man had any aches and pains that morning, he didn't feel them. He took hold of the plant and started climbing. Yes, off he went.

"But husband, where are you going?" cried his wife. "Are you mad? Tell me, where do you think you're going?"

And as he climbed from branch to branch up the blackness of the chimney you could hear him singing:

> *Branch by branch, one by one,*
> *Up I go to my whitebeard friend.*

Then from over the roof, from up in the clouds, and from up over the clouds you could still hear him singing:

> *Branch by branch, one by one,*
> *Up I go to my whitebeard friend.*

You know where he finally got to? Paradise. And guess who was the first person he met before the gate? The fellow with the white beard who'd given him the bean.

"Good day to you, Mister Saint Peter," said the woodcutter. "I've come as you told me to."

"Good day, good day, my friend. Wait a minute, I have something for you."

Saint Peter went off and came right back with a table. It looked like a nice ordinary table from an inn, made of cherry wood reddened with limewater.

"Here you are, my friend," said he, "here's the table you wished for. All you have to do is say:

> Table, table,
> Give as you're able!

The table will cover itself with everything you and your wife need. Watch over it and use it well."

The woodcutter thanked him all he could and heartily, then loaded the table on his head with its legs in the air and started home—not by the beanstalk this time (that was the shortcut) but by the road, the great road.

That's a long way, though. Imagine! There are an awful lot of brushy and rocky places between this earth and paradise. By nightfall the woodcutter still wasn't home.

Far off he saw a light. It was a sort of inn by the roadside, in a hollow of the mountains. The place didn't look too inviting, but after all, there wasn't anywhere else to seek shelter.

In he went and said he wanted to spend the night. "All I ask for," he went on, "is a room where I can keep my table by me. There's no table like this in all the world, you see. I'm taking it back to my wife, and it'd be too bad if someone other than she or I came to the table and said:

> Table, table,
> Give as you're able!

"Oh, don't worry," replied the innkeeper. "The maid will show you all the rooms, and you'll be able to choose the one you think best for your table. Go have a look, and never fear. I'll look after your table myself in the meantime."

The woodcutter went off, so honest and good-hearted that no thought of suspicion entered his head.

As for the innkeeper, he quickly carried the table into his most secret room and replaced it with another, practically the same, for the woodcutter's table seemed perfectly ordinary. "Ah," said the innkeeper to himself, "but we shall see. Perhaps I'm about to have a surprise."

He got back to the main room of the inn just before the woodcutter entered by another door; for the woodcutter was not particular, and the first room he'd seen had looked quite good enough to him.

"Good night, good people!" he called. "Wake me up early tomorrow. I'm anxious to be home."

"By all means," answered the innkeeper. "Sleep well next to your table." And the simple woodcutter did.

As soon as the innkeeper heard him snoring, he hurried back to his secret room, bursting with impatience. There he shut himself up with his servant and his maid, stood before the stolen table, and recited the words he'd remembered:

> Table, table,
> Give as you're able!

He'd no sooner spoken than the table, as at the stroke of a magic wand, covered itself with a hearty supper: steaming soup, a quarter of a roast goose with chestnuts, a loaf, and a good jug of white wine. There were trimmings too, like a dish of nuts and a bunch or two of grapes.

Flushed with excitement and delight, the innkeeper and his companions had only to sit down. They were such scoundrels that their dinner weighed nothing on their conscience, and after eating, they too had a good night.

In the morning the woodcutter got up, paid the innkeeper, loaded on his head this table which was only one from the inn, and made his way home by the shortest path, through the broom, the woods, and the meadows.

"Ah, dear wife, Saint Peter's a good fellow, he is. If you only knew what a gift he's given us! But you'll soon see what this table can do."

He set the table firmly on its four legs in the place of honor, before the fire. His wife stood by with her eyes as round as saucers, not knowing what to expect.

Said he:

> *Table, table,*
> *Give as you're able!*

But the table just stood there. It gave nothing, not even a scrap of bread.

The poor woodcutter felt miserable. "What sort of swindle is that?" he cried. "Saint Peter can't have tricked me. Well, I'm going back to heaven." With these words he took hold of the beanstalk:

> *Branch to branch, one by one,*
> *Up I go to my whitebeard friend.*

He came to the gate of paradise, politely announced himself, and told his sad tale.

Saint Peter listened with a smile. "Very well, my poor friend," he said, "just wait there a moment. I've another thing for you."

Off went Saint Peter, and was soon back leading a grey donkey with a cross mark on its back. "Here you are, my friend," he said, "this is the donkey you wished for. Take it. All you have to say is:

> Donkey, donkey,
> Pop cork and disendonkey!

and as many crowns as you and your wife need will tumble from under his tail. Look after this donkey and take good care of it."

The delighted woodcutter thanked the saint, then started on his way, driving the donkey along as quickly as he could. He was so eager to get home, you know, and to amaze his wife with the donkey's gift!

But whatever your hurry, you can't go too fast on loose stones, among thorns. Night overtook him on his way—a black, black night. He had no choice but to stop again in the same mountain inn. There was no other shelter for leagues around. Anyway, he was so trusting and simple that he wasn't on his guard.

In he went, and said he wanted to spend the night. "All I ask for," he went on, "is a corner in the stable where I can keep my donkey near me. There's no other donkey like this one in all the world, you see. I'm taking it back to my wife, and it would be too bad if someone other than she or I should come to the donkey and say:

> Donkey, donkey,
> Pop cork and disendonkey!

"Fine," replied the innkeeper, "the servant will show you the stables, and you can choose whatever corner seems best. Meanwhile I'll just go outside here and keep the donkey safe myself."

Oh yes, he'd keep it all right, he'd keep it for *himself*. He just happened to have (what a coincidence!) another donkey exactly like the woodcutter's, in a shed behind the inn. In a flash he made the switch. He quivered with anticipation over the surprise he was sure he'd soon have—when, with the woodcutter asleep beside *his* donkey, he'd go to the woodcutter's donkey and say the special words.

As soon as the traveler was safely out of the way, he rushed to the new donkey.

> Donkey, donkey,
> Pop cork and disendonkey!

The donkey slowly turned around, lifted its tail, and let go a flood of gold coins. How sweetly they rang on the flagstones, and how warmly they glowed! The innkeeper, his servant, and his maid scurried left and right, reveling in the task of picking up the gold. How nicely the table and the donkey were taking care of these good people, yes indeed. It had taken only a little wit to get ahold of them, and there they were, a real blessing from heaven!

In the morning the woodcutter started off again, even earlier than last time because he so longed to show the donkey to his wife. He didn't know the donkey was only one from the inn. He took the shortest path he could through the dewy meadows, under the rising, singing larks.

He got home as the sun rose.

"Come, my dear wife!" he called. "Bring our best sheet and spread it on the ground behind this donkey. No, no, I'm not crazy! Just see what'll fall as soon as I've spoken!"

He drew himself up, all proud and happy.

"Now, wife, look!"

> *Donkey, donkey,*
> *Pop cork and disendonkey!*

The donkey didn't just stand there like the table, but what fell was a pile of donkey dung, in clumps like big, smoking chestnuts.

"Oh but you *are* crazy, surely you are this time! You just had to go and soil our very best sheet! Now get out of the way, you lummox, you big fool, or I'll sweep you up with the rest!"

The poor woodcutter felt so miserable he could have cried. Then suddenly he grabbed the beanstalk and started climbing up through the greenery like a madman.

> *Branch to branch, one by one,*
> *Up I go to my whitebeard friend.*

Up and up he went, so desperate that he hadn't even taken off his wooden shoes. The last two times, he'd taken the trouble to hang them around his neck.

"Saint Peter can't have tricked me!" he told himself. "Saint Peter just can't have played me false! There must be some devilry behind all this! But good Saint Peter will take care of it."

Quickly he clambered up before the gate, took a moment to dust himself off, and knocked politely three times.

"Good health and good day to you, noble Saint Peter! Yes, it's me again." Humbly he told how the donkey hadn't had the gift. Or maybe—he suggested—it was he who hadn't known quite the right words.

"Well then, my poor friend," said the smiling Saint Peter, "wait right there a minute. I've something else for you."

Off went Saint Peter, and soon came back with a big stick.

"Here you are, my friend," said he. "Take this. All you need do is say:

> *Stick, stick,*
> *Slap, whack, and kick!*

The woodcutter thanked him ever so gratefully. Then, holding his stick like a candle in a church procession, he wasted no time starting home.

Night had only begun to fall when he reached the inn, but he stopped there anyway. In he went and asked for a bed. "I need a room like the other day," he said, "and I'll just put my stick in there right now. No one must go and say to the stick:

> *Stick, stick,*
> *Slap, whack, and kick!*

No, no, that would never do!"

"Come, come, my good man, first come and eat!" cried the innkeeper. "You're a friend by now. Dinner's on the house." His eyes gleamed at the thought of this new, heaven-sent windfall. "Put your stick right there! I'll look after it, never fear! Oh yes, I promise I'll keep it safe!"

The innkeeper fairly danced with the sheer pleasure of not needing to do anything, for he'd only to pick up the woodcutter's dinner from the famous table. And soon he'd be dancing with even greater delight! In the meantime he served butter and sausage; left the woodcutter at work on a roast guinea fowl; slipped out; made his little switch; came back; and served a pear and another bottle. Finally he took the woodcutter to his room, having returned to him an ordinary stick which of course wasn't the one from Saint Peter.

The woodcutter lay down and went to sleep. But he'd hardly dropped off when he was waked up by squeals and screams worse than from a stuck pig! The inn might as well have been on fire, roasting the innkeeper and his servants.

He jumped out of bed and into his trousers, and dashed into the inn's main room where the howls were coming from. There, oh good heavens, he found only a whirl and a blur. The innkeeper, his servant, and the maid were all racing around, screaming, twisting, dodging, straining desperately to escape the stick. But the stick gave them no rest and chased them mercilessly.

As soon as the innkeeper had heard the woodcutter snore, he'd run to the stick and said:

> Stick, stick,
> Slap, whack, and kick!

The order given, the stick had swung into action. It slapped and whacked and kicked the ribs of the thief, the servant, and the maid, dealing them such a drubbing from ankles to ears that in no time their hide was thoroughly tanned. They jumped very nicely this way and that; they ducked and squinched down into corners, sweating, hooting, crying for mercy; but the flying stick stung them everywhere.

"Traveler, oh good traveler, get this stick to stop!"

He, in the doorway, rubbed his eyes without understanding the hullabaloo.

"Mercy, oh mercy, please!" the innkeeper howled to him. "You'll have back your table, you'll have back your donkey!"

The stick itself, with great thumps and whacks, turned the thief in the right direction, driving him first to the room where the table was, then to the shed with the donkey. It beat and drummed away till the wicked innkeeper had brought both back. Only then did it stop. The innkeeper, the servant, and the maid were as green, white, and blue as cheese plates.

By now the moon was rising. By its light the woodcutter put on his coat, loaded the table on the donkey, and so long! He went straight home in the moonlight.

This time, oh, what a blessing! He only needed to say the words:

> Table, table,
> Give as you're able!

Then:

> *Donkey, donkey,*
> *Pop cork and disendonkey!*

The table no longer just stood there in front of his wife. Neither did the donkey, which did its business in a flood of gold coins. No more nasty tricks for the old couple, thank God and Saint Peter! Hand in hand, they gave thanks with all their heart.

> *Me, I gave mousie's tail a tweak,*
> *Mousie let out a squeak, squeak, squeak,*
> *And my tale's done.*

21. The Insult Redeemed

There once was a farmer who quarreled on the market square in town with the wife of one of the local gentry. He had a point, but unfortunately he insisted on calling her an old bag.

She raised a fuss and called the police, because if he was a bit of a rustic, she was a bit stuck-up. Finally, she had him dragged before the judge.

The judge scolded and fined him.

"So," fumed the farmer as he counted out the money, "so, I'm not to call this lady an old bag?"

"No indeed, and I warn you, if you do it again it'll cost you a good deal more!"

"But Your Honor, if I meet an old bag, may I call her a most esteemed lady?"

"If you wish. I have no objection."

The farmer withdrew politely from the courtroom. On the way out he passed his adversary. "I look forward to meeting you sometime again," said he, "most esteemed lady."

2 2. The Miller's Three Sons

There was once a miller in the little valley over by Forie. Eel Mill— you know the place. This miller wasn't all that rich. He lived his life bravely with his three sons.

But there came a year just like the one two or three years ago, you remember, when we got so much rain. It was the March moon that did it. That March moon is terrible. Snow fell four days straight and buried everything under four feet of snow. Then the wind suddenly turned, the snow began melting, and it rained cats and dogs. Meltwater came hurtling down the mountains from up there beyond Le Bégonin.

How the waters boiled, tumbled, and roared through the valley! They'd hang up here or there for a moment, at a bend in the streambed, then crash on down like a wall. They smashed the mill and carried off the miller who, poor fellow, had stayed behind a second too long to snatch up his scarf, his boots, and his purse. The three boys only just got out. All they managed to save was the donkey, the cat, and the cock.

The disaster left them penniless, with nothing but the three animals and the clothes on their backs. The rest was gone forever, even the three plum trees in their garden. The garden itself, their two pastures, and their three little fields were just rocks and mud.

"We'll have to go and seek our fortune. Who knows what we'll find?"

"Yes, who knows?"

"Maybe we'll do well and rebuild our house."

They had guts, those three. Me, if I were ever penniless, I wouldn't count too much on my luck.

They packed up their things quickly enough and shared out the animals. The eldest got the donkey, the second brother got the cat, and the youngest got the cock.

"All right, brothers, good luck and good going! And let's agree on one thing: the first who fills his purse comes back here and waits for the others."

So off they went. They meant to cross over the mountains, the way the ragmen do, to hit Saint-Etienne-en-Forez and all those towns where there's work—who knows, maybe Lyon, Franche-Comté, even Switzerland out there at the end of the world!

The elder got to Pèges with his donkey and went up to Grangettes. There are plenty of houses around there, but at the time no one could sleep in them. People were too busy taking their wheat down to the mills, then taking the flour back up. They had to carry the sacks on their backs because they had no animals to do it for them. That whole area's more for squirrels than for people, and the paths are awful.

On one of those paths the elder brother came up beside a fellow burdened like a mule and struggling up the slope, stubbing his toe on every stone and bumping into all the outcrops. Sweat was pouring down his face.

"You're having a terrible time, aren't you, my friend?" the elder brother asked.

"My boy, by evening I can't even stand up. I can't wait to go to bed, but I'm so done in I can't even sleep."

"Put your sack on my donkey's back and take a load off your feet."

"On that pretty creature, with its fine ears? What do you call it? A donkey? What if the load crushes it?"

"Go ahead, go ahead! Don't be afraid!"

The fellow obeyed. Soon he was amazed. Before his eyes the donkey scrambled on, hardly noticing the sack, up this path good only for goats and steeper than a washboard.

"You must sell me your donkey," said he. "But what does it eat?"

"Everything and nothing—a handful of hay and some thistles."

"Oh, do *please* sell it to me!"

"But you see . . ."

"Come, my boy, I'll be in your debt. This creature could do wonders for all of us here!"

"Yes, but unfortunately . . ."

"Your price is my price. I won't haggle."

"Well then, my friend, three thousand francs."

Three thousand francs! Do you realize that when all this happened, a man worked a whole day for perhaps ten pennies? Three thousand francs for a donkey! *I* wouldn't ever like to pull off a trick like that. I had this red cow, you know, and one time I didn't have enough hay to feed her over the winter. Well, I'd be embarrassed to tell you what I got for her at the Saint-Anthême fair!

"Three thousand francs, you say? Let's go drink on that! I'll count you out your three thousand francs in good silver."

Fine. The second of the three brothers came to Valcivières. In those days the people there had forgotten how to sleep.

He asked for a bed.

"Won't you be kind enough to lodge me and my animal?" he said.

"My boy, we'd be glad to, but you wouldn't get much rest. The rats are eating us alive. We're helpless against them now, and they don't let us sleep a wink."

"The rats? Oh, don't worry, my animal will keep them off me."

"Your animal, you say? What *is* that furry creature?"

"It's called a cat. Tomorrow morning you'll see what it'll have done."

The next morning they did see. The floor was covered with enough bloody rat corpses to fertilize the fields of the whole parish.

"What a blessing that cat is!" they cried. "My boy, you must sell it to us."

"Ah, but my friends, I'm not anxious to part with it. You can see yourselves how nicely it protects me from rats."

But all the people of Valcivières were after him now, pleading so hard that an hour later the bargain was struck. The price? Six thousand francs.

Six thousand francs for a cat! I tell you, I'd be glad to get my hands on a cat worth just a third of *three* thousand! I like cats, though many people don't. They're pretty in the house, and they teach cooks to keep their cupboards closed. But a cat for six thousand francs—well, I declare!

All right. The third brother had gone higher still, up toward Thiolerette, Le Puy, and Le Suq; in fact, right to the top, up into the deepest shadows of the great forest, to a dark and lonely spot. In those days no one around there could sleep any more.

"Won't you be kind enough to give me lodging, me and my bird?"

"My boy, we'd be glad to, but with all the work going on here you'll never even get to close your eyes. You see, around here the sun wouldn't come up unless we took a cart up onto the ridge to fetch it."

"Well, you won't need to do that tonight. This bird I have with me will call up the sun."

"But my boy, how can it do that?"

"It'll call from your stable. I guarantee you'll see dawn that minute."

"You guarantee it, you say?"

"Indeed I do. With my bird—it's called a cock—you won't need to go and fetch the sun up there any more."

"Well, we'd just like to see *that!*"

"You will."

And they did. The cock sang cockadoodledoo and the sun rose right away. What a wonder! The day had come, and they hadn't needed to go fetch the sun with their cart.

"My boy, you must sell us this cock—you say the creature's called a cock? We don't care what it costs."

"Good people of the mountains, I wouldn't sell you this cock for silver or gold."

"We can't stand going up there any more after the sun. Give us a price, my boy, and we'll pay what you ask."

So, well, in the end he did tell them they could have the cock for nine thousand francs.

A cock for nine thousand francs! Oh, I tell you, I could take *all* my cocks to the market and I'd get nowhere near that kind of money. But that was when people in the towns and villages around here didn't have donkeys or cats or cocks. Old people used to talk about those days. Cats? A mill's the only place you'd find one. And there weren't any chickens. Just think what a help chickens are to a household! Without eggs . . . Why, on Easter Monday people are so glad to have the red eggs!

There was once a time around here when people lived three families to a house. They were so poor it took three to make a fire and a stew for dinner. And they say you could still see fairies and wild men. People could trap those wild men by leaving a pair of wooden shoes out somewhere by a bush. The wild men'd put them on so as to do like the people, but then they couldn't get out of them in time . . .

Well, to get back to the story. All three brothers returned to Eel Mill. The mill hadn't grown back, in fact there wasn't any mill at all. So they built a little higher up, by the side of the road. They put up a nice new place, and they even hung a juniper branch over the door to show they served food and drink. Those three brothers had once been millers, but they were innkeepers now. Go on in, you'll see them there!

> The other day I dropped in too,
> Had me a glass of the local brew,
> And that's it for my story.

2 3. The Fairy's Gown

There was once a lad who used to go and watch his cows on the high pasture, between the mountain peaks. He and his mother had their house beneath a cliff. The mother would put the milk to clabber, make the cheeses, and set them to cure in the cellar. All that needs care. The lad, he'd let the cows out each morning as soon as the dew was off the grass, then follow them up into the wilds. At noon he'd cry, "To water, to water!" the way herdsmen do, and lead them to drink at a pond hidden behind scrubby willows and mountain ash. Then they'd graze again till the evening, when he'd bring them home.

With his chin on his hands and his hands on the head of his staff, he'd spend the whole day gazing at the clouds drifting between heaven and earth, there at the end of the world. At home in the evening, he'd sit down beside his mother to eat. That's how they lived, just the two of them.

Everything else was far away. No one ever came near. They were more alone than two stones at the bottom of a pool. "How'll I ever find myself a wife?" the herdsman wondered. "My mother knows lots of secrets, but I don't suppose she knows *that* one. Oh, that's a secret that troubles me, it surely does!"

Leading his cows to water one midday, he saw three girls flying through the air in gowns as white as hawthorn flowers in April. They came down by the pond, took off their gowns, and went into the water. He, meanwhile, left the bushes where he'd been sitting on a rock, drew closer, and watched. His heart was pounding.

Suddenly they saw him. Quicker than startled thrushes they leaped from the water, put on their gowns, and soared, all white, into the air. In a flash they were gone.

But eyes need only meet sometimes, just long enough to say, "Who are *you?*" He'd seen one of the girls' eyes gazing into his. Up there, you know, the air is light, the waters shine, and there are wildflowers between the rocks: the flower of Saint Laurence like a rosy star, the devilsbane, all radiant gold, the johnny-jump-up, and the gentian—tiny, miraculous beauties. And the herdsman had seen in the girl's eyes a world just like that: a world of wonder, a world not of grass and wild creatures but of human glances. A world of things that dwell in the heart. The words for them don't come easily. He couldn't tell his mother about it that evening.

The next morning he didn't wait for the last of the dew to bring out his herd and drive them back up there. Before noon he was at the pond, dying with impatience. And the three girls came again, flying through the air like white doves—whiter than doves, in fact, though doves' downy feathers are ever so soft. They were coming back to bathe. Off came their gowns and into the crystal water they plunged. He couldn't help it, he had to go nearer. He was too enthralled to stay hidden. Then they saw him, caught up their gowns, and flew away.

The next day he was terrified they wouldn't return, but they did. The clear water brought them. As clear as air it was, so that the waterweeds and stones at the bottom gleamed—a clump of waving cress, perhaps, or some sparkling pebble. And it was the place, too, so far from everything, so high up there by itself above the villages. Once again he saw them, though not for long, because he just couldn't control himself enough to keep out of sight.

Nor could he keep his mother from seeing that he wasn't the same any more. His eyes stared into space over his bowl and his thoughts wandered even farther. All at once he sighed.

They were both sitting on stumps before their door, eating supper. The moon was shining bright. His mother knew he wouldn't talk while the sun was up, and you can't talk in the dark. But after all, words don't say everything. You can talk with your eyes too, or with a nod of the head or a gesture. Anyway, she started drawing him out. She knew there must be a girl at the bottom of this. Sharp as she was, almost like a fairy, she managed to lead him from one thing to another till she knew everything she wanted to know.

Then he fell silent, as embarrassed as any boy. He nudged a stone around with the toe of his clog, then another stone, and still didn't dare look up. "Well, mother," he said, "you who know everything, do you know what these girls are?"

"Oh yes, only too well," she replied. "These girls who fly through the air and bathe in the pond, why, they're fairies. They're creatures, yes, but not really girls. Listen, son, don't go back to the pond. Don't take the cows there any more. Take them to the spring to drink."

He didn't answer, but his bowl fell and shattered on a stone. He fell too, in a faint.

"Son," said the old woman after she'd dashed water in his face, "son, I'd like to spare you many troubles. Forget this fairy of yours!"

"Fine, if I could do it, but she's all my eyes will ever see. No, I'll either marry her or jump off the cliff up there." He was almost himself again now.

Both rested a bit in the moonlight. For a while they were silent.

"What shall we do?" sighed the mother. "Well then, son, listen to me. Up in the pasture tomorrow, keep the cows from grazing. They won't be thirsty at noon, but drive them to the water anyway. And you, watch where the fairies leave their gowns. Tell me, do you really want what you want?"

"Yes, mother, I do."

"Then here's what you have to do. Pretend to be very busy watering your cows. They won't be thirsty, so they'll move nice and slowly while you, from bush to bush and from rock to rock, steal closer and closer. Be very careful, take your time. Then, in a flash, seize the fairy's gown. When you have the gown, you'll have the fairy herself. She'll beg you, she'll implore you to give it back, but you won't."

"No, mother, I won't."

"And if you don't, you'll see her give in to you. She'll have to follow you."

His mother whispered in his ear all he needed to know, there under the pale moon. Of course this was in the old days, before people got in the habit of ringing the angelus three times a day. Fairies used to come and play here then, and shepherds and hunters would meet them in the fields or woods. The shepherds and hunters didn't always fare so well in the encounters, either.

Anyway, the next day, up in the high pasture, he did everything as his mother had told him. He stole from clump to clump of rushes, and from willow to willow. The cows he hadn't let graze wandered around looking for grass instead of heading straight for the water, and he hid behind them as he guided them, slowly, toward the bush where the fairy—the one whose eyes he'd looked into—had hung her white gown. Quicker than the wind, he dove for her gown and clutched it with both hands. Nothing could have torn it from him.

The three fairies cried out. The two who were able slipped on their gowns and were gone. In the twinkling of an eye they'd vanished into the depths of the sky.

"O man," said the third, the lovely young one, "give me back my white gown! I'll let you have all the hoards of treasure hidden in these mountains. I know where there's gold and silver! It'll all be yours, if you just return my gown! Oh, you must!"

He so wanted to do as she begged, to bend his knee to her and serve her. She was crying, and she pressed her palms together beseechingly. But he remembered his mother's words.

"I've got your gown and I must keep it!"

"I'll give you green stones, purple stones, more than the greatest merchants have in their ships! I'll give you the fairies' gifts!"

"I've got your gown, and you're mine. All I want is you!"

"All right, all right, then I must follow you. I have no choice. But I won't have to stay, if I can get away. I'll go with you to your human world, O man, but fairyland is where I'm from!"

And she followed him home.

The lad's mother took the white gown from him, quickly put it in their chest, then locked the chest and hung the key around her neck.

So long as we've her gown in there,
She'll no more take to the air!

The herdsman and the fairy were married with two gold rings at the parish church till death should them part.

"We're going to have children," he told his mother. "I can see them already." And by the time a year was out they had pretty, curly-headed twins, a boy and a girl. They went on living with his mother, in the house in the mountains. He stayed a herdsman. His fairy wife never gave him the slightest trouble.

Two years later his mother died. But before she did, she put the cord with the key to their chest around his neck. "Never open the chest, my son," she said, "never take out the white gown.

So long as we've her gown in there,
She'll no more take to the air!

And never, never give the fairy gown back to your wife!" Then she breathed her last.

When they came out of mourning, at the end of the third year, the couple wanted to go to the great gathering, the one for Saint John's Eve. She asked him for her gown. He wouldn't give her the key, but she talked, she begged, and she wept.

"If you don't believe I belong here now, can't you at least see that my two little ones keep me here? How could I leave them, with their dear curly heads? You *know* I couldn't!"

He felt it was true, but he still hesitated. He fingered the key on its string.

"Give me back my gown!" she cried. "How can you still mistrust me? I want to be as pretty as I was when you first saw me up there, flying your way through the air."

He slipped the string off over his head and held out the key to her.

She drew the gown from the chest and put it on, leaving her old clothes where she stood. In a moment she had the boy on her right arm, the girl on her left, and in three leaps bounded, like a goat, to the top of the rock.

"Good-bye, my husband! Good-bye to you! I have to go to fairyland, I have to go to the Magic Mountain! You'll come for me there, you'll come and find me!" Then she soared from the rock like a bird and rose through the air with the babies in her arms.

Now he was alone in the house, which was suddenly all dark.

"Oh mother," he lamented, "you knew, you knew!

> *So long as we've her gown in there,*
> *She'll no more take to the air!*

If only I could punish myself enough for not having done as you said!"

He beat his fists against that head of his that had gone so wrong; he bit till it bled that hand of his that had given up the key to the chest. But

moaning and crying never help. "Perhaps," he thought, "it's all because of the gown's enchantment. Perhaps she does still love me. I've got to go to that mountain she talked about!"

So off he went wherever the road might lead him—after all, where would *you* look for the Magic Mountain? And after a long, long way over hill and dale he came to a land which certainly didn't seem Christian. By now, though, nothing could stop him. He wanted to find his wife and get her back.

One morning as he was walking along he came upon two men who were quarreling loudly. They had three things to divide between them: a staff, a pair of shoes, and a coat. But the staff, you see, was more powerful than that of Jean de l'Ourse, the mighty strongman, and *his* could fell an oak. The shoes had more power than the ogre's boots, because whoever wore them could fly like a lark. And the coat had more power than those rings you just turn a little and then you disappear, for whoever wore it was invisible to all.

The men told him the whole story. How were they to divide these three things, when there were only two of them?

"There's only one way," said the herdsman, "but it'll solve the whole problem. Do you see that tall elm, a couple of hundred yards down the road there, at the bend? Go stand under it. When I raise my hand, start running, and the first one here gets shoes, coat, and staff."

They thought that was a fine idea. But . . . well, they never reached the herdsman. As soon as their backs were turned, he put on the coat which made him invisible, took up the staff, stepped into the shoes, and took off through the air. Maybe those two are still waiting for him under the elm.

"That must be the way fate wanted it!" he thought. "Fate's decided to help me! All right, I'm going to get my wife back! This coat, these shoes, and this staff aren't all I've got now! I have hope!"

Still, for all his soaring and sailing through the sky, he had no idea where he was going. Where was he to look for the Magic Mountain? It might as well have been toward the night as toward the day, toward the west as toward the east.

Well, he came to where the king of those parts lived. This king was in the thick of a great war which was not going well for him. His enemies had him besieged in his city. He was out of gunpowder and out of flour. His soldiers had no strength left nor anything to defend themselves with, and the enemy was just about to attack.

"I can tell you what their plans are," said the herdsman. Wearing his coat he went to the enemy camp, and no one, captain or foot soldier, could see him. He entered the tent with the generals, he listened to all their talk and heard their plans.

An hour later he was back with the king. "At dawn tomorrow," he said, "you'll see them coming to do battle with you, from the mountain down to the river."

"What's the use of knowing all this?" asked the king. "My army can't fight any longer."

"Don't worry," said the herdsman. "My staff will fight for you."

At dawn the staff did its work. Horsemen and foot soldiers, rank on rank, battalion after battalion—he beat them back, crushed them, and swept them away. Those soldiers had been about to overrun everything, but nothing was left of them now except a bit of cloak here and there, or a bit of plume tossed along with the dust by the wind.

"Herdsman, herdsman," cried the king, "how can we thank you enough? What would you have us give you?"

"All I want," answered the herdsman, "is to know where to find the Magic Mountain."

Right away the king summoned all the most learned men of his kingdom: those who wore the tallest hats and who climbed the highest towers to tell the king whether or not it was raining. They said yes, of course, they'd *heard* of this mountain. It was in Fairyland, and in fact was the most famous of all the mountains there. But giving directions there wasn't their business.

"So who'll tell me?"

"Perhaps the birds will."

The king summoned the birds: every one of them, from the kinglet to the eagle! Straight off he gave them all the grain the enemy had brought in their wagons. Then he asked them where to find the Magic Mountain.

"Dear birds," he said, "surely *one* of you has been there? If that one will tell me the way, I'll give him my crown."

They looked at each other, cheeping and twittering. None of them seemed to know.

Finally the magpie, who's always cackling, said surely the lark must go often to fairyland; *she* ought to be able to show the way there. They looked for the lark, and the king realized he'd forgotten her because her color blends in so well with everything, and because she's always out in the fields, lurking on hilltops, or out of sight high in the air. The herdsman, like all herdsmen, had a powerful voice that carried far. He called her right away. But being a bit miffed that she hadn't been invited to the feast, she stayed where she was and wouldn't come. They had to promise her the king's crown.

At last she appeared and said that yes, she could take the herdsman to the Magic Mountain. The king crowned her right away, and it's since then that she has her crest. She's very proud of it.

The herdsman was so anxious to find his wife that they set off that very minute through the high country, above the mists and the wisps of fog, up where the wind blows free, among the pathways of the clouds. They passed over the Mount of the Thirteen Winds, and over the Heavenly Wood. But the eager herdsman flew before her like a swallow, and the lark twittered with all her might to call him back. "Da-myoo, da-myoo, da-myoo!" she cried like a real pagan, then dropped exhausted into the hollows below. But what she'd said so mortified her that she promised in her own language to stop talking that way:

I'll not swear any more, dear God,
I'll not swear any more!

After that she regained her strength and launched herself again into the sky. The journey put her in the habit of crying out and praying that way, of falling and rising again, and she's done the same ever since.

It's a fact, though, that the herdsman did fly too fast for her. He had to take off one of his shoes, which fell into the sea. After that she could keep up.

They still had a long way to go and it seemed they'd never get there! But they reached the Magic Mountain. The lark told the herdsman to land near a spring at the foot of a knoll, under a wild apple tree. Then she left again for the heaths and moors where she has the whole landscape to herself.

The herdsman hadn't been sitting by the spring a minute when he saw a little girl coming, her head all curls, carrying a green earthenware jar. He thought he recognized her, though he wasn't sure.

"Little girl with the green jar," he said, "tell me, where's your brother?"

"In the wood behind our house, picking strawberries."

"Little girl with the green jar, tell me, where's your mother?"

"At home kneading dough. She sent me for water."

He was sure now he was very close to his wife.

"Little girl with the green jar, would you give me a drink?"

As he drank, bent over the jar, he dropped in his golden ring. And when the fairy poured water for her dough, she found the ring in the bottom.

"Ah, I know that ring! It's my husband's!"

She questioned her daughter and heard about the man who'd asked after the girl's brother and mother, and who'd drunk from the jar. Then she dropped everything and ran to him.

When they met they kissed as though they'd never kissed before. But she soon tore herself from his arms.

"Oh husband," she cried, "you've come to the Magic Mountain! No human has ever been here!"

"Didn't you tell me to come and find you?"

"Yes, but dear, dear husband, the fairies will soon be by! It's the time when they pass through here on their way to the land of the humans. What would they do if they found you in *their* land? They have cruel fingers and sharp nails. Go, go away, quickly!"

"I'll only leave with my wife—with my wife and children."

"I promise, I *swear* I'll follow you. But it's time for them to come, you see. They'll tear you to pieces with their nails! Oh, please don't wait for me! Go!"

"No, no, I'll wait. Run and fetch the children!"

She ran, she flew, and was back in a moment with her children, the boy and the girl, in her arms. He put his shoe back on (he just had one!) and they soared away together.

The fairies felt it right away. Fairies don't just have eyes and ears, they *feel* things. They hurled themselves after the fugitives. The herdsman had only one shoe, and his wife had the two children to carry, so the fairies gained on them as they raced through the clouds. They were catching up! Fortunately, though, the herdsman had the coat. When he covered his family with it, the fairies could no longer see them.

They got back to their house and their cows, in the land of the Christians. The herdsman built a big fire on the mountain, just like the one on Saint John's Eve, and on it he burned the gown. His wife never, never left again.

They lived in their home then, worked hard, and were very happy. And since by then people had begun ringing the angelus, no more fairies were seen flying through the air.

Part
Two

THE DEVIL

24. The Devil and the Farmer

There was once a man—a farmer—who wasn't all that rich. He had strong arms, though, and a stout heart, and an honest turn of mind. Once he got a chance to buy a farm for little more than a song; and that farm wasn't the worst you ever saw, either. Talk about luck! You could grow anything there except vines, because it was, after all, pretty high. High enough up among woods and pastures, in fact, to be a bit off by itself—one of those spots where, as they say, God's been by only twice: once to make it, and once to forget it. Actually, there were rumors going around about the place, but he paid them no heed. It was a good farm, and he'd gotten it dirt cheap! All he asked was to live there, on his own land, and with God's help he'd know how to rid himself of anything that got in his way. And he'd have a family there, too!

All right, then. He pays his money, up he goes, and in he moves with his wife. He had to have a wife, of course. As the proverb says, "It's the wife who makes the home." His was just right: plump but perky, quick as a partridge, and as brave as a bee.

This was summertime, a little before Our Lady's day in August. He stepped out, that first morning, sturdy and bold and full of zip, ready to tear into his work. Then off he strode through the brush to look over his property.

He'd hardly been out a minute when a crackle—or maybe not even that, maybe just some thought in his head—made him look around. There, two paces off, stood a tall gentleman, staring at him with eyes shining like candle flames.

"Well, my boy," began the gentleman (that was the way landowners talked to their tenants in those days), "well, my boy, what are you going to be planting for me here?"

"Sir," replied the astonished farmer, "I only bought the place yesterday evening, but as it belongs to *me*"—he stressed the *me*—"I plan to do my best."

"Belongs to *you*! To *you*! Maybe you were sold the place on that understanding, but if so, the seller lied. There's only one landowner around here, and that's me."

That was some warning, my friends. You should have heard it! The words exploded like pistol shots. And those eyes! That face! The air all around smelled of brimstone.

"But all right," he went on, "you seem to know something about farming. I'll take you on as my tenant. You'll have no trouble with storms or hail, and when the time comes, we'll just split the crop."

The farmer didn't lose his head. "Fine," he replied, "but before we get started, we'd better get a few things settled. Which share do you want for yourself—what's above, or what's below?"

"What's above," answered Old Nick.

All right. The farmer sowed just what the season called for: turnips. When it came time to pull them up, he set off with his wagon to do it. The devil came too. They had their agreement. The farmer pulled out his knife, and in no time had all the green tops off. Each got his due: the farmer his pile of turnips, and the devil his pile of greens.

Devil and farmer went to market to sell their wares. By evening, one had a pocketful of good coins. The other got nothing but laughter. He could have filled a sack with it if he'd wanted to.

"You took me that time," declared Old Nick to the farmer, "but you won't take me again. Next year, you get what's above, and I'll take what's below."

All right. The farmer sowed barley. The weather gave him no trouble at all, and the devil was there for the harvest. The farmer got the barley sheaves, as they'd agreed, and the devil got the stubble.

Back they went to the market. You can imagine how it went. Old Nick, with his heap of stubble for sale, got laughed at all day long. By evening he was bursting with rage.

"You scoundrel, ah, you scoundrel!" he bellowed. "You've tricked me again! But I'll get you, just you wait! Next year, I'll have what's above *and* what's below, both!"

Fine. That year, the farmer planted pole beans. He collected the beans. The devil, when he came, got for his very own the roots and the stalks all twined around the poles.

Back from the market that evening, he was choking with fury, snorting and cursing, and red as a hot coal.

"Listen," said he to the farmer, "we can't go on sharing this way. We must settle who owns the farm. So let's agree on one thing: at sunrise tomorrow we meet at Devil's Bridge."

"Yes? And then?"

"Each will be riding an animal, whichever one he chooses. If I guess yours, I get the whole crop and you get all the work. If you guess mine, you'll be the sole owner. I'll leave it all to you, free of storm or hail."

All right. There wasn't much choice, after all. The farmer had to go along with Old Nick.

The next morning before dawn, the farmer roused his wife, had her take off her nightshirt, and smeared her all over with honey, from top to toe. Next, he rolled her over and over in the down from a comforter, a dozen times or two, whatever it took. I tell you, that woman was properly honeyed and feathered. She looked like a huge feather ball. Then he tied a donkey's tail under her nose, put a bridle on her, and set off for Devil's Bridge.

He took care to be there before sunup. The two of them went to hide under the bridge, behind the reeds and the alder clumps. Then they waited, with a sharp eye out for the devil and his mount.

At last he came, trotting out of the woods on his beast.

What did it look like? Well, you know the dahu with horse's hooves, that climbs trees? You know the chabirou, that has shorter legs on one side so it can run on mountainsides? This creature was more amazing than either of *them*!

The devil on its back had his legs dangling on either side, and to make a slightly more impressive entrance, he decided to make it gallop—never mind the upward slope and the humpbacked bridge. So he dug his heels into the thing's belly and shouted, "Giddyap, giddyap, ricalon of Bigorne!"

Instantly, across the river, the farmer straddled his wife and capered off.

The two riders met on the hump of the bridge.

"Morning! I've just made it myself, you see!"

"Ah, so you're here, are you? Morning, my man!"

The sun was coming up. Now they'd find out who was to have the farm.

"Well," the farmer began, hardly glancing at Old Nick's mount, "didn't you have anything rarer than *that* in your stable? My poor gentleman, you're about to lose!"

"I am? You've bought and sold a few of these, then?"

"Why, good heavens, around here, even the children just learning to talk have seen as many of these as they've seen donkeys at the fair, or even pigs—with all due respect, of course—at the market!"

"And you could name it for me?"

"Any child could name it. It's a ricalon of Bigorne. Now, your turn. See if you can guess what *I'm* riding."

The devil couldn't have been more amazed if he'd found horns sprouting from his backside. He got down from his mount, circled the farmer's, stared, sniffed, poked, and circled it again.

"What *is* this impossible beast? It's got no head and no rear end either—it's got a donkey's tail where the nose ought to be. The thing's feathered like a goose and it's got four legs. Who ever saw the like? Bah, keep the farm. You won't catch *me* again in a county with weirder sights than the whole rest of the world!"

The crestfallen devil turned on his heel, climbed back on his beast, and galloped off. In no time he was out of sight. And, just as he'd promised, he was not seen again in those parts.

25. The Fifth Cow

Up in the high country, there was once a man who had four work cows: Marcade, Fromente, Sardeire, and Pige. Powerful cows they were, as red as chestnuts fresh from the shell, and as brave as fire.

In late fall it was time to plow, because up there the crop must be sown by Saint Martin's Day, or the fields will grow more blue flowers than wheat. He'd yoke them up four times to the plow, two by two. Yes, that made four teams a day.

In the evening, when the plowing was done, he'd take them down by the barn, to the hedged pasture watered by all the drainage from the stable. There the good fresh grass grew as thick as a fox's pelt, and the cows could rest all night, grazing, sleeping, and chewing their cud. He'd be back for them at first light, then yoke up one pair and leave the other in the stable.

One fine morning he found in his pasture—the one that was hedged good and tight—five cows, not four. He couldn't have been more amazed if he'd seen himself in the pond as a cow, not a man.

"Must belong to someone around here. Why yes, it has to be a lost cow."

Looking more closely, he noticed that two of the cows were the same— as alike as two peas in a pod. He just couldn't tell which was Pige and which was the other.

He yoked up Fromente and Sardeire. The three others he left in the barn, where he tied them as usual.

"No doubt Look-Alike Pige's owner will soon be by looking for her," thought he to himself.

So off he went to the fields, where he strode behind the plow, in the cool of the morning, singing "When the Herdsman." Others on the same slope were plowing too, and singing as they plowed.

> *Found his wife there by the fire*
> *All downcast, alas,*
> *Yes, all downcast!*

The women and children were gathering chestnuts. All was well and in its place, from the fields nearby beneath the slanting rays of the new-risen sun, to the mountains yonder across the valley, their sharp blue peaks still caught among the clouds.

> *If you die, we'll bury you,*
> *Sing you mass and vespers too,*
> *Yes, mass and vespers too!*

He wasn't going to worry his head about this mysterious cow.

Bit by bit the work got done. When the team's stint was over, he unyoked Fromente and Sardeire, and led them back to the stable. There were only two cows. The new one had left without stopping to say good-bye. Not that she hadn't been properly tied up.

Why, her owner must have come by and found her. He'd just taken her away.

The next morning, the same thing happened. Five cows in the pasture. Look-Alike Pige was back. He led her to the stable with two of his own and tied her to the feed rack. When the first team's stint was up, she was gone.

"That brute's owner has some nerve," he muttered. "He sends her over to rest at my place, I give her pasture and shelter, and he doesn't even come to thank me or say he's sorry. But if she's back tomorrow for the third time, I'll make her earn her keep."

That evening he thought things over some more, drew his knife, and marked each of his cows on the right horn—with a cross, mind you. Then he shut them in the pasture and went to bed, commending himself to God's care.

Down in the pasture the next morning, he found five cows again. This time, though, he could tell the stranger. He took Pige to the stable with Sardeire and Fromente, then came back to yoke up Marcade—the strongest of his cows, for he had a plan—with Look-Alike Pige.

And off to the hardest of all his fields, with its earth as thick and heavy as tar. Then to work! A whole day turning up that field!

When his own cow was weary—Marcade first, then Fromente, then Pige, then Sardeire—he'd take her back to the stable. But he left Look-Alike Pige yoked up from morning to night, and no one ever came for her.

When it was too dark to plow any more, he took his team back home. He unyoked them before the stable door.

As soon as that foreign cow was free, she lifted her tail, skipped aside, took three jumps, and put herself out of reach—just like an excited cow in May, when you let her out after a whole winter in the stable and she's spooked by the sight of all the green. Then in a flash she was off through the fields, and from far, far away she shouted back:

"You pig! Oh, you worked me, didn't you! But you won't catch me again soon!"

At last he understood something he didn't want to know. Still, there was no doubt about it, *he* was the one who'd tricked the fiend.

"So you wanted to pass yourself off as Pige, did you? All right, now you know what it means to pull a plow all day!"

He felt so happy, remembering how he'd driven that fiend, and how he'd pricked it in the behind over and over with his goad, that he fairly split his sides laughing.

He laughed all alone there before his door, laughed for the birds and the angels, till he could laugh all over again with his wife.

26. The Devil's Three Golden Hairs

There was once a man—a king, maybe? He was filthy rich, like a king! Cows by the dozen. And proud. How he drove his people!

And he had a daughter. Oh, the queen of all daughters, she was! One look at her eyes, and you'd fall in love. It was high time, in fact, to marry her off. But that rich man let it be known that he'd give her only to the man who'd bring him—you know what?—the devil's three golden hairs.

Now, there was a lad, handsome and brave, who'd caught sight of that girl. He couldn't get her out of his head. She'd seen him too. They'd both blushed at the sight of each other. But what were they to do? They weren't crackbrain simpletons, and they weren't crafty, either, like those sneaks who can teach the Fiend himself new tricks. All they had were clear heads and good red blood.

"Who in the world will ever go pick those three golden hairs from the devil's head? I've got to try, though. Now the rich man's said it, I've no choice but to try."

He was polishing his shoes and packing his travel bag.

"Maybe, just maybe, his daughter likes you. That's got to bring you luck! Oh, just the idea of being her friend makes my heart leap so!"

Early the next morning he got up and took down his staff. And off he went through forests, over mountains, far across wide moors and river fords, always straight ahead till he reached the depths of the wilderness. And still he went on, and on, and on!

Under a rock he found a spring, and nearby a whole crowd of men and women groaning and crying on the green grass, as though that was the one thing they knew how to do.

"What is it, good people, why are you crying?"

"Why, my lad, you see, the spring used to give us wine . . ."

"And now?"

"It won't even give us water! My lad, since you're passing by, tell us what we must do to make the spring give us wine again!"

"All right, good people, since you're so sad, I'll look after your problem with mine. I can't answer now, but I'm on my way to a place where you can learn whatever you want to know. I'll answer you on my way back."

So he kept walking by hill and dale, bluff and vale, rough and trail, till far, far from here he saw a pear tree on the terraced side of a mountain spur. On the green grass all around, men and women were groaning and crying as though that was the one thing they could remember how to do.

"What is it, good people, why are you crying?"

"Well, you see, this pear tree . . ."

"What's the matter with it?"

"It used to bear golden pears, and now it doesn't even bear green ones. How can we stop it from withering? We do believe it's going to die. My lad, you who are passing by, tell us what we must do to have the tree give us golden pears again!"

"Very well, good people, since you're so sad, I'll look after your problem with mine. I can't answer now, but I'm on my way to a place where you can learn whatever you want to know. I'll answer you on my way back."

On he walked, through green spruce forests, in a land of red cliffs and hairy beasts. Straight ahead he went, and on, and on, and on!

Suddenly he came out by a river as wide as a sea. Fortunately a boat glided up, with a boatman; he was there to take people across.

"My lad," said the boatman as he poled his boat, "if only you knew how tired I am of being here! Always sailing back and forth, back and forth, from bank to bank! And I'd so love to see the world! But *somebody* has to man this boat and ferry people across! Tell me, my lad, what am I to do?"

"Very well, boatman, I'll look after your problem with mine. I can't answer now, but I'm on my way to a place where you can learn whatever you want to know. I'll answer you on my way back."

He got out on the other side, where the road turned to cotton wool. The clumps of broom were like morning clouds, the trees like evening clouds.

But straight ahead he went, and on, and on, and on!

At last he got to the devil's place, and managed to find the right door. The devil's wife was home alone. They exchanged greetings, compliments, and politenesses.

"What do you want, my fine young lad? What can I do for you?"

"A great deal, ma'am. I'm here to fetch the devil's three golden hairs."

"His golden hairs! Well, lad! His three golden hairs!"

That's it, you see. The way the story has it, the devil had three golden hairs. Maybe they were in that black mane of his, up against his horns, left over from when he was an archangel—from the time when our ancestors were still in their innocence, and when everything was still fresh from the hands of God.

"Why, that's quite something to want, dear boy," simpered the devil's wife. "Do you mean to leave him only his horns? But we'll see, we'll see. His three golden hairs! And what else?"

"I've three questions, and I must have the three answers."

He repeated, in order, the three questions he'd been asked by the boatman, the people by the pear tree, and the people by the spring.

"Well, I don't know," the devil's wife answered. "I'm sure my husband does, though. I'll comb his hair, as I do every evening, and try to lead him on. Yes, I'll do that for you. Oh, I hear him coming! Slip under the bed. Keep your nose out of sight and open your ears! But as for taking his three golden hairs . . . Do you know he treasures them more than his own dainty innards?"

In came the devil and sat down at the table. He swore at his wife, who hadn't made him the tripe with mustard he'd called for. He claimed the calf's head with green sauce was no good, but gobbled it down as though it were delicious.

All that meat, though, all that cheese, and all those cakes! And, to top it all off, so many gulps of wine! He finally slumped, nose first, to the table. Now he was snoring. His wife seized her chance and started combing him— not with her pretty silver comb, no, but squarely with her nails.

Suddenly she pinched one of those golden hairs, tweaked it out, and threw it under the bed.

The devil jerked awake.

"What? You're pulling my hair out now? What is it, wife, what's gotten into you?"

"Oh, dear husband, what got into me, you see is a dream. I was fighting that dream, you just can't imagine! Yes, I dreamed of a boatman who wanted so much to leave his boat and go roam the world. So I was rushing to you, I took you by a hair and asked you what he should do!"

"He's not too smart, your ferryman. Why, the first passenger he gets, all he has to do is hand the fellow his oars and jump out on the bank."

Chattering and muttering, the devil scratched his head, then slumped again, nose first, to the table. He fell back asleep between bottle and plate.

He was no sooner snoring than his wife started in again with the combing. She picked her moment, pinched a second golden hair, tweaked it out with a jerk, and threw it under the bed.

"*Now* what? Will you pull out all my hair? What's gotten into you, wife?"

"Oh, dear husband, I'm so sorry! What got into me, you see, is that I had another dream."

"Stop dreaming so much, it'll bring you bad luck. And what did you dream this time?"

"There was a pear tree, a big pear tree which bore golden pears. But it was dying. A whole crowd of people were crying over it, and they didn't know how to bring it back to life. They were coming at me, so I rushed to *you.*"

"If only those fools would look at the roots of the tree, they'd find a rat there, gnawing away. Let them just kill the rat, and the pear tree will start bearing golden pears again. Come, wife! Give me some peace! I'm going to have me the best nap I ever had in my life. Don't go pulling me out of it, especially by the hair!"

He'd hardly finished talking when his nose slumped again into the breadcrumbs and cheese rinds. Instantly he was back to snoring.

But as soon as her good old devil was snorting and snoring away, the wife crept up on him. She picked her moment and, with a tweak, snitched the third golden hair.

The devil jumped to his feet, and without knowing it, dashed his glass against the wall. He knew perfectly well what he was doing, though, when he sent his plate sailing at his wife's head.

"*Again?* You've been at me *again?* Is all this dreaming of yours going to leave me bald?"

"I'm sorry, dear husband, I'm so sorry! But I dreamed again, you see, and in the dream I needed you so badly!"

"What for, then, devil-wife, what for? What was the trouble in your dream?"

"There was a spring under a rock below a green meadow. Everyone from round about was there, crying, because their spring, which used to run with good wine, wouldn't even give them clear water any more."

"If the fools looked under the stone, they'd see a toad is plugging the outlet of the spring. Let them kill the toad, and the spring will give them wine again. But look out, now, devil-wife. One more dream, and I'll brain you!"

"Yes, yes, dear husband, I promise. I won't dream any more. Have a nice snooze!"

His nose dropped back among the crumbs, the gnawed bones, and the circles left by the wineglass. When his snoring rose like thunder, she signaled to the boy, who wriggled out from under the bed. In his hand were the three golden hairs. Safely stored in a corner of his brain, he also had the three answers.

"Did you hear them? And you've got them?"

"Oh yes, ma'am, devil-wife! You got them so cleverly out of your good devil-husband! Thank you, thank you a thousand times! I'll take the answers right away to those who need them, and I'll remind them to be grateful to you."

More greetings, compliments, and politenesses. They congratulated each other and gave each other their best. "Good-bye, my fine young lad!" It could have gone on forever, but he slipped out the door.

For a long, long time he walked through that land of fog and cloud, where the path sank under his feet. Then he reached the great river.

"Well, lad, did you bring me the answer?"

"Take me across, boatman, and you shall have it."

He waited till he'd jumped out on the far bank. Then, before going on:

"Boatman," said he, "look for the first passenger who comes your way. When you're about to let him out on the far side, hand him the oars and get out yourself, instead."

"What a good idea! Thank you, lad, thank you very much!"

The boatman, eager now for his first passenger, held out to the lad a sack of gold.

The lad took it and hurried on through the land of spruces till he reached the terraced mountainside, and came to the pear tree.

"My lad," they asked him, "what answer have you brought us? Tell us what to do."

"Dig down to the roots of the tree, and you'll find there's a rat down there, gnawing on them. Kill the rat, and the pear tree will bear golden pears."

They'd no sooner killed the rat than the pear tree burst into bloom and put forth golden pears. The people lifted their hands high to bless the lad. They gave him a sack of gold, not to mention several dozen of the pears.

He kept walking by hill and dale, bluff and vale, rough and trail, till he reached the green meadow, and the spring under the rock.

"My lad," the people asked him, "what answer have you brought us? Tell us what to do."

"Move the rock aside. You'll find a toad plugging the outlet of the spring. Kill it, and your spring will give you wine."

They'd no sooner killed the toad than the wine flowed free. The people danced and sang, and they gave the lad a sack of gold. Back then, people weren't stingy with gold. It wasn't worth as much as nowadays.

Three bags of gold, golden pears, and the devil's three golden hairs— the lad staggered under his burden. Those three hairs, especially! He nearly tripped over a stone, and all but tumbled into the road's deep ruts. But there was that girl at the end of his journey, the rich man's daughter, so young and so pretty, who'd blushed at the sight of him. His legs were done for, but his heart bore him on, and he kept going.

At last he reached the girl's father's house. It was quite a shock for the rich man to see him back. "But I'd sent you to the devil," the fellow muttered. He was even more amazed to find that the lad had brought him those three golden hairs.

"But what are those three sacks, my boy? What have you got in those three sacks?"

When the rich man saw all the gold the lad had brought back, he cried, "Very well, then! I'm off to see that land myself! You two don't need *me* to get married!"

He gave them his blessing, if he happened to think of it; then pulled on his boots, took down his staff, and set out.

He found no one on the way—no one at the spring, no one around the pear tree. And when he reached the other side of the river, the boatman thrust the oars into his hands, sprang out, and kicked the boat back out into the stream.

"Till I get back," cried he, "row if you're able, and if you're not, then learn!"

> *"What next, friends—do you know?"*
> *"Oh, the boatman's still roaming high and low."*
> *"And the other, the rich man: where'd he go?"*
> *"Still in the boat, he is, learning to row.*
> *Never made it back for the wedding."*
> *"And the bride and groom, how are they doing?"*
> *"Why, they're at home, you see,*
> *Still just as happy as can be!"*

27. The Devil Who Was a Hog Dealer

There was once a boy whose father had sold him to the devil. The man was desperate, and that year it took so much to buy a loaf of brown bread! He's a great trader, the devil. He does as much buying and selling as he can—quite a business, in fact! And his religion is money. So he turned to dealing hogs. He made the boy his swineherd, to serve and follow him to the fairs.

But it was slavery, to be in the devil's service! He'd be rushing hither and yon, herding the hogs back from the mountains where all the trails are awful; and, what's worse, dragging his lord and master back through thickets and sinkholes, the fellow being blind drunk and unable even to see the ground before him. After those fairs where his master had eaten and drunk to bursting, the little servant would gladly have wielded his fork himself. Instead he got nothing but blows of the pitchfork.

What you have to put up with, sometimes! But you make do with what you've got. That life made the poor boy nimbler than three squirrels, more alert than a whole basket of rats, and quite beyond fear.

One day they'd gone to a fair over by La Chaulme, or Estivareilles, maybe—anyway, some village up there among the high pastures. And the devil was doing fine. He'd bought fifteen hogs (no disrespect to the creatures intended)—yes, big, fat, meaty ones. No doubt he was in some inn, boozing it up and carrying on, trying to attract still more business. His servant, meanwhile, was waiting on the fairground, full in the wind, and from time to time tossing a fistful of grain down in front of the hogs' snouts to keep them quiet.

Suddenly, here comes the devil, red in the face and hat askew.

"Get along, boy, get along! You'll drive our friends here home for me. I'll be along myself in a while. I've got one or two more deals coming. You and the hogs, go on ahead. But just you watch out! Lose me the tail off a single one, and you'll find out what I'm made of!"

The servant touched his switch to the hogs and set out. He'd have been glad of a go at the bottle before he went, but he wasn't allowed any wine— even less, in fact, than dogs are allowed sausages. It was too hard! "What a master I got myself!" he thought. "And when I've driven all his hogs back home, with all their tails, what'll I get for it this evening? Well, too bad! One day I'll give *him* something to think about!"

Other dealers were heading home too, and they hadn't forgotten to stop by the inns. They and their animals hogged the whole road. There were voices, shouts, laughter, and songs! Hog dealers are wonderful people as long as they're asleep. Each wanted to show himself off as smarter than his neighbor, and as having brought the best hogs from the fair. They argued, quarreled, laid bets, and cut deals. One especially, a big hothead, was the most persuasive of all. He carried on so loudly and aggressively, swearing and whacking his palm with his fist, that by the time they'd gone a quarter of a league, he'd bought all his colleagues' hogs—except for the devil's, and they weren't the worst of the lot, either.

"A word, boy: I want yours too. What'll you take for them?"

"Nothing. They're my master's, and my master already has a customer."

"Customer or not, my money's as good as anyone's."

"Maybe, but I can't sell them."

"Anything can be for sale, dummy. It all depends on the price. You have to be a pretty poor fool not to think of your master's own interest."

The master had bought the hogs for fifteen francs apiece (prices then were a long way from ours, these days), and the dealer was offering sixteen.

"Come on! Sixteen a head! How about it? And a good round crown just for you!"

"Listen, my master told me that if I so much as lost the tail off a single one . . ."

"Is *that* all you're worried about? Their *tails*? All right, you can keep 'em! Done! There's your crown!"

The boy felt suddenly bold and brave. He could treat himself to a bottle of red wine, to end this Lent he'd been in for maybe four hundred days! Above all, he could send his master packing. Yes, when all was said and done, he'd enjoy a little freedom!

The dealer had already pulled his knife out of his pocket and whetted it on his palm. In a flash he'd cut the fifteen tails off the fifteen hogs, flush with their behinds.

How they squealed, and what chaos broke loose then on the road! But the best company must always part. Everyone went his own way. The boy at last was alone, clutching a handful of hog tails. Oh, what would his master do to him now? He could see himself heading for very big trouble. Well, bold moves would get him through it. All by himself he felt as cool and clever as all the assembled devils in Hell.

That was when he noticed, just off the road, one of those green and quivering bogs you find up in the high country. They look almost like pastures, with little puddles, and moss, and nice smooth grass. But the sod wobbles under your feet, and if you go in you're lucky to get out.

The sight of that bog gave our boy an idea. He was crazy, too, that evening. Maybe it was the wind. He kicked off his wooden clogs and took off lightly across that sort of squishy pillow. Darting, all but flying, he planted his hog tails here and there the way he might have transplanted lettuce shoots into a vegetable bed. He had no fat to weigh him down. All his fat was *under* his ribs, like a goat's. He flitted like a new-fledged partridge. Every step over that muck risked getting him stuck forever. He had to be quick and he had to be light. Even so, it can only have been God's grace that got him out of there alive.

He'd hardly finished when he heard a massive tread and heavy puffing. Here came the devil, leaning into his strides and making time, but also lurching to right and left, and not keeping terribly straight. He'd trip over any bit of rock sticking up. But when he saw his servant running about frantically, howling and tearing his hair, he stopped short.

"Oh, master, master, come quickly! The hogs! The hogs!"

"What about the hogs? Why, yes—where are the hogs?"

"They ran into the bog, all fifteen of them! Look, master, all you can see are their tails sticking out!"

"The tails are sticking out? Then it's nothing! Right, I see. Just you watch!"

The devil stripped off his coat and shirt, and with two swipes rolled up his sleeves like a man faced with heavy work. Then he spat bravely in his hands and charged forward.

He caught the first tail, near the bog's edge, twisted it into his fingers for a good grip, and heaved away as though uprooting a turnip. The tail flew out, dripping blood, and over he went, backwards, arms and legs waving in the air.

"Master, master, not so hard! You're pulling the poor pigs' tails off! Not so hard!"

The devil got up again, shook himself like a wet dog, and ran for the second tail. The same thing happened, and the same with the third, the fourth, and the fifth.

The devil, befuddled with food and wine, was getting madder and madder—and heavier, too, there in nature's own gravy, as he paddled, splashed, jerked himself free, and swore oaths to split the hills. The whole bog shook like a mound of toad eggs on mud. Every step sank him in a bit deeper, but, furious at losing his money, he still insisted on pulling out some hogs. All he got, though, was tails—the twelfth, the thirteenth, the fourteenth . . .

And the fifteenth! Who knows how the boy had managed to plant it right smack in the middle of the bog? The boy, meanwhile, was getting more and more frightened. His eyes were glued on his master, as the devil leaped from clod to clod and waxed in fury. If his master made it back, there'd be one awful account to settle.

Drunk though the devil was, that last tail gave him pause. But how could he bear to lose so much? All weighed down and wobbly himself, he charged more grimly than ever into the quivering bog.

This time he didn't come back. A clod tipped under his weight, and the ground folded like piled-up hay on a hay wagon when you climb aboard—folded, collapsed, and sank. Into that sudden hollow the bog gulped the lurching devil. There was a sort of *shlup*—the noise a great maw might make before it swallows—then the devil was gone.

He was never seen again, at least not around those mountains. Still, everything goes right on, just as though the devil's hand was in it. So who's really going to believe the devil took the trouble to let himself die?

2 8. The Black Mountain

There was once a lad as brave as a bee. Jeantou, they called him. He was so lively, he'd have hurled himself bodily, anytime, through a hundred feet of mustard.

But he hadn't had much luck yet. Twenty-two years old, and he still had no money, land, wife, or intended bride. He so longed for a field of his own to hoe, for a house to come home to in the evening and smell supper all ready, and especially for a wife! He'd tell her about his work that day, and she'd tell him the dream she'd had the night before.

Anyway, house or no, wife or no, you have to get your work done. And that's what he tried to do: to keep on going and see what would come next.

One evening at twilight, he happened to be passing a crossroads when he caught sight of a big, ugly figure standing there—a man, perhaps, but all bearded and horned.

"Where are you going?" the figure asked.

"Where the wind takes me, everywhere and nowhere," answered Jeantou.

"Would you like to make your fortune?"

"My fortune? Oh, I might."

"Then let's play cards. Win, and I'll give you fourteen barrels full of gold. Lose, and you belong to me."

"But I'd still like a chance even if I lose."

"All right, I'll leave you one. In a year and a day you'll have to go to the Black Mountain and be my servant. I'll give you three things to do. If you do them, you'll have your freedom back. I'll also give you my purse, my daughter, and anything else you want. Agreed?"

"Agreed, Old Hornbeard."

They played cards all night. Hornbeard had pulled a pack from his pocket, and then from somewhere behind his coattails—Jeantou never figured out where—he'd drawn a spark. They'd made a fire with dead branches, and its light was as bright as day.

> Spades and hearts,
> Power and courage;
> Clubs and diamonds,
> Money and pleasure.

But the fellow always had the cards he needed and more. Jeantou watched his fingers like a hawk, but never caught him cheating. At cockcrow, he'd lost everything he had to lose. He had nothing left to his name but himself and his shirt.

"You're mine," said his opponent with a little laugh.

"One last game," replied Jeantou. "All right, Hornbeard? Double or nothing!"

He took the pack and shuffled. They were playing écarté. His opponent got the king and made a slam.

"I've still got that chance I wanted," declared Jeantou as he stood up.

"Then in a year and a day," snickered Hornbeard, "be at the Black Mountain."

"But where *is* the Black Mountain?"

"Over where the wind comes from. Find the way yourself. If you don't I'll come for you, and you'll be mine forever."

And with that the devil vanished.

A year went by—quickly, too, what with that prospect at the end of it. Jeantou set out on the morning of the last day. He strode along into the wind, staff in hand, like the wandering Jew. Over hill and dale he went, over moor and meadow, on and on and on, with never a glimpse of any Black Mountain against the horizon.

It was nearly evening when he came at last to a poor mud-and-straw cottage. He stopped and knocked three times.

An ancient, tottery woman opened what passed for a door.

"Good evening, ma'am. Could you please tell me the way to the Black Mountain?"

"The Black Mountain, my boy? Oh, I'm not old enough to know that. But look way over yonder, where I'm pointing. Do you see, right at the edge of the clouds, a little house even older than mine? That's where my sister lives. She's nearly a hundred years older than I am."

He almost ran there, because the day was fading like the light of a dying candle. He practically wore his legs off in his hurry.

At the door of the second cottage he stopped and knocked three times.

An ancient woman, even more tottery than the first, came to the door.

"Good evening, ma'am. Could you please tell me the way to the Black Mountain?"

"The Black Mountain, my boy? Oh, I'm not old enough to know that. Go ask my sister over yonder. She's nearly two hundred years older than I am!"

So he went. He had no choice! And that third sister finally told him what he wanted to know.

"The Black Mountain, my boy? Go if you want, come back if you can. Myself, I've never seen anyone come back from there."

"If I can only get there," replied Jeantou, "then, God willing, I'll come back. I promised. I have to be there by midnight."

The old woman stepped out her door and clapped her hands. Clouds of birds gathered from far and wide.

"Birds, how long would it take you to get to the Black Mountain?"

"I know the way," the crow replied. "It'd take me three days."

The old woman went back into her cottage, and came out again with a little pot of butter. Jeantou, burning with impatience, was waiting. She gave him the butter.

"Listen, my boy," said she. "Climb on the crow's back and give him a beakful of this butter. Keep the other two beakfuls, if you can, for the way back. But if the crow drops low, look out! Give him another beakful, or he'll send you hurtling to the ground. You *must* hold back the third, though, if you want to return. Boy, do you understand?"

"Perfectly, ma'am."

"Listen, boy: here are three eggs, too. Break the red one first, then the blue one, then the white. When that's done, you'll find on the mountaintop three girls, taking a bath in the pond around the castle. Ask one very nicely for some water."

She explained it all to him, carefully.

"Kiss the youngest," she said at last. "Kiss her and say, 'Where I come from, a kiss means you're married.' "

So he climbed on the crow's back, gave the crow the first beakful of butter, and sailed up into the sky.

What vast reaches of space stretched above the land! The crow flew with great flaps of his wings, while earth and clouds streamed by. But the vastness went on and on, and time passed. Night came, and Jeantou could tell the crow was losing strength. He had to give the crow that second beakful, he just had to. Then it flapped on again, and made good time.

What a long way there was to go! You could just barely make out the Black Mountain, as far off as the eye could see, under the rising moon.

"I'll have nothing to come back with, but I must get there first. Never mind! I'll take whatever comes!"

And Jeantou gave the crow the third beakful. The crow left him at the foot of the Black Mountain.

The mountain was as slick as a bottle. The nimblest little climber would have just broken his nails on it. But Jeantou broke the red egg, and a great ladder rose before him.

At the top of the ladder, he broke the blue egg, and a broad path stretched before him.

At the end of the path, he broke the white egg, and a great pond spread out before him. In the middle of the pond stood a moonlit castle. Three fairies were bathing in the pond.

"Oh, miss, if it's not too much trouble, would you be so kind as to pass me some water?" said Jeantou, hat in hand, to the first of the bathing fairies.

"Keep going, boy," she answered. "You need more nerve than that to succeed."

He stepped up to the second.

"Miss, would you be kind enough to pass me some water, if it's not too much trouble?"

"Keep going, boy! Success here takes more nerve than that!"

"They don't have that much to be so stuck-up about," thought Jeantou. "Those two goat-girls are blacker than that crow I was riding. All right, let's try the third. She doesn't look the same at all. And let's show a bit more nerve!"

His heart was beating, though, because *that* fairy was as white as a moonlit birch tree.

"You there, the white girl, give me some water, would you?"

"Would I? And if I said no?"

"All right, then just do it. That's an order. Give me some water. Now!"

"You've got some nerve! But that's what you need here, and I can't say I mind."

She tossed her long golden hair before her to the far shore, like a light, waving bridge. Jeantou crossed over the bridge, and as he did so, glanced to one side.

He saw the two black girls hurrying out of the water and carefully looking themselves over. For all their washing, their skins were still blacker than ravens. In their vexation they swore like troopers, spouting oaths and curses. At the same time, though, they were keeping a close and malicious eye on their sister and the boy. Jeantou saw that, and he saw them make their move when their sister's back was turned, by hiding her blue dress among the lilies.

When the white girl knew the boy had crossed the water on her hair, she stood up and started out of the pond. But her dress was gone! She didn't know what to do.

"White girl," said Jeantou, "I can give you back your blue dress. I'll trade your dress for a promise to help me whenever I need it."

"Give me the dress," the girl answered, "you have my promise. It's agreed. Yes, I promise to help you."

He fetched the blue dress from among the lilies and flags, then went back to wait on the shore for the girl. Dressed now, she soon came to join him. She was doing up her hair.

"My name's Bélélalie," she said. "Those two black goats are just my half-sisters. *I'm* the daughter of a queen our father deceived. She was a magician, and her wand passed on to me. My two sisters are jealous, and they play terrible tricks on me. If you could only get me out of the castle!"

Suddenly, he knew that from now on that would be his only purpose in life. She didn't need to hear him say it; she saw it clearly enough in his eyes.

"I don't know whether you'll manage or not," she said, "but do the opposite of everything my father suggests. You must be very careful here about what you eat or drink, and about where you sleep."

They exchanged glances, then made an "iron lock" to seal their pact: you link little fingers, each pull out a hair, and send the hair sailing away with a puff of breath.

Next, he remembered what the old woman had told him—the oldest of the old women: "Tell her, 'Where I come from, a kiss means you're married.' "

There they were, each other's forever.

And he thought, "She's the devil's daughter. But she's been baptized, so she's not already damned. We'll escape from the devil's own hands since she wants to so much—since *we* want to so much. Oh, she and I are going to want so many things!"

"I'll leave you now," she said at the castle door. "We mustn't let my father suspect anything, though my sisters will tell him far too much."

Jeantou entered without even knocking and went straight on into the sitting room, which was all done up in red.

"Hey, Hornbeard, are you here?"

The devil rose before him like a viper when you've trod on his tail.

"Aha, my fine cardplayer! So you've made our appointment? You're just in time! Another minute, and midnight would have struck. Then you'd have been all mine. I'll give you your task tomorrow. If you can do it, you'll have another the day after. If you can do that one too, then you'll have still another the following day. One failure, and you lose your last chance. You'll be my servant forever."

He sat Jeantou down across from him at the table. "Now then," said he, "let's have supper."

One of his daughters brought in a pear and the other an apple.

"Eat the pear, won't you?"

"No, I'll eat the apple."

The pear was poisoned, and the devil spat with vexation.

One of the daughters served white wine, the other served red.

"Have some white wine, won't you?"

"No, I'll have red."

The white wine was poisoned. Again the devil spat with vexation.

At last it was time to sleep. The daughters set up two beds: one wooden, one iron.

"Sleep in the wooden bed," said Hornbeard.

"I'll sleep in the iron bed," thought Jeantou, though he didn't say so.

The wooden bed was meant to become a bed of fire. Bélélalie took the bed of fire for herself.

Bright and early the next morning, Hornbeard came to wake up his servant.

"Did you sleep well, servant?"

"Very well, master. I'm at your service."

"I order you to make a spring. This evening at suppertime you're to put a bottle of its water on the table."

He gave Jeantou a spade and a hoe. Jeantou set off to work.

The spade and hoe fell to pieces as soon as he tried to use them. They were made of bark and pumpkin. All Jeantou's work that morning was for nothing. You couldn't even tell he'd been there.

Round about noon, Bélélalie said to her father, "I'd like to take your servant his meal."

"*We'll* go!" cried the sisters.

"No, no, *I'm* going, I tell you! I *want* to!"

"We'll go, we'll go!"

"Go ahead, Bélélalie, if it means so much to you," said the devil, who loved his white daughter better than the other two.

So she went. She saw right off how things stood.

"Good day, Jeantou."

"Good day, Bélélalie."

"You seem troubled. What's the matter?"

"What's the matter? My tools are made of pumpkin. I couldn't do a thing with them."

"Just eat your meal and keep up your courage."

Jeantou ate his meal like lightning, trusting his sole friend to manage what had to be done. She wanted to make this spring, so she'd certainly know how to do it. She, meanwhile, watched him eat, laughing with pleasure at his appetite.

When she took back the bowl, she drew a wand from her sleeve:

> By the power of my wand,
> Let my father's will be done.

It was all over. The spring was dug and running. Jeantou had only to fill a bottle and put it that evening on the table.

Then he shouted to Hornbeard. The devil came, and his black daughters with him.

"Father, I tell you Bélélalie gave him help!"

"That's right! Bélélalie, I see your hand in this!"

"*I*, father? *I* helped him?" Bélélalie shrugged her shoulders.

They sat down to supper. Jeantou's love signaled to him with her eyes to refuse what he was offered, and to take what he wasn't.

"Daughters," said the devil, "take the servant to the bed in the little bedroom."

So they took him. It was a bed of fire. But Bélélalie managed to slip through the door before Jeantou lay down on it.

"Go and sleep in my room," said she.

And she slept in the bed of fire.

The next morning, Jeantou came to greet Hornbeard.

"Did you sleep well, servant?"

"Very well. I'm at your service."

"I order you to plant a vine, and I want this evening, on this table, a bunch of its grapes."

Hornbeard gave Jeantou a pruning hook and a pick, and Jeantou set off to start work.

Yes, well and good, but as soon as he tried to use the hook and pick, they flew to pieces. They, too, were made of pumpkin. You could hardly see that Jeantou had been working at all.

At noon, in the castle, Bélélalie said, "I'll take the servant his meal."

"No, no, *we'll* go," cried the sisters.

"But I *want* to go, I tell you."

"Go ahead, Bélélalie, if it means so much to you," said the devil.

So she went. Right off, she saw that Jeantou had gotten nowhere.

"Good day, Jeantou."

"Good day, Bélélalie."

"What's the matter? You seem troubled."

"It's just that the tools are made of pumpkin. I couldn't do a thing with them."

"Eat your meal and keep up your courage. You'll see how the vine gets planted."

Jeantou ate like lightning. Bélélalie watched him empty his bowl, and laughed with delight. Next, she drew the wand from her sleeve:

> By the power of my wand,
> Let my father's will be done.

The vine was planted. Soon it budded, then covered itself with leaves and bunches of grapes. Jeantou had only to pick a dishful, and put the dish that evening on the table.

Then he shouted to Hornbeard. The devil came, pulling at his little beard. The black daughters came too, their noses in the air.

"Father, I tell you, Bélélalie's helping him!"

"Yes indeed, Bélélalie, I see your hand in this, sure enough!"

"*I*, father? I'm supposed to have *helped* him?" said Bélélalie, wide-eyed.

They sat down to supper. Jeantou, as always, watched for his love's winks, and was very careful about what he ate and drank.

She made sure he slept well, too.

The next morning, the devil was surprised to see Jeantou come in, as fresh as a daisy.

"It's that white daughter of mine who's helping him," thought he. "But anyway, I'll get rid of him this evening."

"I want you to go and level that mountain for me," said he to Jeantou. "Plant a garden of white carnations there, and in the middle a beautiful rosebush covered with silvery buds. That way we'll have flowers on the table tonight."

Those white flowers for the table were the most difficult of all, because nothing white would grow on Hornbeard's Black Mountain.

Of course, Jeantou hardly got anywhere with his pumpkin tools. But Bélélalie came with his noon meal, because she'd wanted to so badly. Her wand was in her sleeve.

> By the power of my wand,
> Let my father's will be done.

The white girl managed far more than her father would have thought possible.

That evening, when Hornbeard saw those flowers, whiter than snow, in the middle of the table, his face twisted up with rage. Those flowers made him much angrier than the bottle of water or the dish of grapes!

"Hornbeard," announced Jeantou, "I've done all three things you asked me to."

"So I see. Well, you're free. I'll give you three purses full of gold. Then get out of here and go to the devil!"

"I'll gladly take the gold," Jeantou went on, "but that's not enough for me to leave with. You must give me Bélélalie for my wife, with three white roses at her breast!"

"I'll give you one of my daughters," roared Hornbeard, "but you will first have to bring me the dove, with her three eggs in her pretty nest— the dove that's nesting way up there on the topmost point of that tower!"

The tower, straight as a reed and as smooth as oil, was the tallest of the whole castle. There was no way up it. Not even a squirrel could have climbed it, not even an ant. The order was impossible, simply impossible.

But Jeantou was determined not to lose courage. He trusted his white love, his true and only friend. He could tell, though, that Hornbeard meant to watch him more closely from now on. Something in the air had changed. Father devil, steaming with rage, was with his goat-daughters; while poor

Bélélalie hadn't quite the power that he, the devil, had in this black-magic castle.

"Get out of here!" roared Hornbeard. "Go to bed! Get up tomorrow when I ring for you."

Hornbeard watched Jeantou go. Then he jerked his chin imperiously.

"Daughters," said he to his black girls, "put a cauldron of oil on the fire. We'll boil that servant in it."

They didn't have to be told twice.

But deep in the castle, where the nights were like war between red cocks and black, Bélélalie heard everything, divined everything, and arranged everything with her own white hands. Quietly, quietly, she stole to the little bedroom and spoke to her Jeantou.

"I'll sleep on the bed of fire, and you'll sleep in my bed. But now, you really must look out. This is your real test. Will you be as brave as you'll need to be? Swear you'll be pure boldness and courage!"

He raised his hand and swore.

"You must put me to boil in the cauldron of oil . . ."

"Bélélalie, my darling, my love, dearest Bélélalie, I'll do anything, but I'd rather die myself than kill you, and put you in oil to boil . . ."

"You're not going to die. You'll do what I tell you. You'll do what you must do tonight. When I've boiled so long in the oil that the flesh falls off my bones, take the white bones and set them end to end. You'll be able to climb them up to the point of the tower. Take down the dove's nest, the dove, and her eggs. Next, gather up my bones, and make sure you have them *all*. Then, put my bones back in the cauldron. You'll see me come out of it alive again, and in fact more lively than ever."

Bélélalie lay down on the bed of fire, in Jeantou's place. And for her Jeantou, she entered the cauldron of boiling oil. Oh, she knew it's the woman who must take the worst. Perhaps a woman's heart is more alive, if less bold, and perhaps with this heart of hers she can endure whatever comes her way.

> *Sorrow kills men,*
> *Gives life to women.*

Anyway, they settled what had to be done. Jeantou trembled and wept, but he laid the white bones end to end and climbed far, far up to the point of the tower, to fetch the dove's nest, the dove, and her pretty eggs.

But poor Jeantou wasn't quite himself, and when gathering up the bones he left out one, the very smallest, that belonged to a little toe. By the time he noticed it was missing, it was too late for him to go groping for it again under the tower, in the pitch-black of night.

"Never mind," he sighed, "never mind! With or without her little toe, she'll always be my love, my Bélélalie, the fairest of all white ladies, and the whitest of the fair!"

He had to hurry. Dawn would soon be breaking.

At dawn's first light, Jeantou called for Hornbeard. Hornbeard couldn't believe his eyes. He'd been so sure it was his servant boiling in the cauldron of oil!

And when he saw his servant handing him the dove, her eggs, and her nest, his rage boiled up so that he'd have been glad to beat his head, as wasps do, against the wall.

"Hornbeard, I've done what you ordered. Give me your daughter for my wife."

"Yes, I said it, I won't deny it. But what I said was, *one* of my daughters. I'll have you choose one this evening. You'll come down with me to the cellar. All three will be under a cloth, and you'll choose with the end of a stick."

And that's what happened that evening. The devil took Jeantou down into the depths of the cellar. It was darker down there than in a wolf's belly. There the three daughters were, but even a cat's eyes couldn't have told the white one from the two others. Anyway, a cloth, as thick as a cook's apron, covered them all up.

Jeantou was shaking, nearly fainting. Still, he felt that one had her foot a bit forward. He felt at the foot with the end of his stick. The little toe was missing.

"That's the one," said he.

It was Bélélalie.

Dear God, what strange things we sometimes have to do in this life!

"There's no chaplain here in the castle," said Hornbeard, "but I'll look after arranging the wedding tomorrow."

Oh, he'd look after everything, all right. Bélélalie knew him well enough.

"He wants to make sure he kills you with his own hand," she whispered to Jeantou. "And who knows what he plans to do with *me?* We must leave tonight. At midnight, he'll ask you which cock is crowing. Answer, the red one. A little later, he'll ask you again which cock is crowing, and you'll say, the black one. Then it'll be time for us to go."

At midnight, the devil spoke up, sure enough.

"Servant, which cock is crowing?"

"The red one," answered Jeantou.

An hour later, the devil bellowed again, "Servant, which cock is crowing?"

"The black one," replied Jeantou.

He and Bélélalie got up in haste. Bélélalie put the distaff in her bed—the bed of fire—to take her place; and in Jeantou's place she put the spindle.

"Hurry, my Jeantou, hurry! Run to the stable! You'll see there two horses—Big Horse and Little Horse. Take the little one and bring him, quickly, quickly!"

Jeantou jumped out the window—he'd no wish to linger!—and ran to the stable. There he saw two horses, and one was small and skinny, like a kid. "That *can't* be the one," thought Jeantou. He took the big one.

But nothing in that land worked as it would have elsewhere.

"Ah, what have you done?" cried Bélélalie when he brought her the horse. "But it's too late now. My father would find us. Let's go, let's go!"

They unbarred the door, jumped in the saddle, and were off like the wind.

An hour later the devil bellowed, "Bélélalie, get up!"

"Yes, I'm getting up!" answered the distaff.

The devil listened, and let a moment pass. Then he bellowed again, "Bélélalie, get up!"

"Yes, I'm getting up!" the distaff replied right away.

"You too, servant, get up!"

"Yes, I'm getting up!" the spindle answered.

The devil waited some more, still listening. He sat up in bed. He couldn't hear a thing.

Suddenly he jumped to the floor, dashed to Bélélalie's bed, and found there only the distaff. Next he dashed to the servant's bed, and found only the spindle.

"Daughters, daughters! The servant's gone! He's run away, and your sister with him!"

"No, father, surely not?"

"Oh yes, daughters, I tell you, it's true!"

Now they were all up, racing down to the stable.

"Daughters, they took Big Horse!"

"Father, father, take Little Horse! He goes three times as fast! You'll catch up with them in no time!"

The pair, meanwhile, were urging their horse across what seemed an endless plain. On and on they galloped. And as long as they didn't fall off, why, at least they didn't have to pick themselves up!

Dawn came, all red. Bélélalie told her Jeantou to look around and see whether the day would be fine.

"There's a storm coming. I see a huge cloud bearing down on us."

"Oh, it's my father, he's after us!"

"He certainly is. We're lost!"

"Jeantou, don't lose heart!"

They were galloping past a pond.

> By this magic wand I shake,
> I'll be a duck and you a drake!

That instant, they were changed into a duck and a drake. Into the pond they plopped, and swam about.

Shortly, the devil came up.

> Duck and drake, good day, good day!
> A girl and boy—have they come your way?

"Quack, quack, quack!"

> *Duck and drake, hear what I say!*
> *Have a girl and boy come your way?*

"Quack, quack, quack, quack, quack!"

"Confound you, you can't even understand me! Confound you, and my daughter, and that servant! Confound this whole land, and its ponds, and its wind!"

The devil spat with vexation, turned bridle, and rode home like a whirlwind to his Black Mountain.

"Why, father, my father, haven't you brought them back?"

"I saw nothing, and found nothing throughout the whole land. All I met was a duck and a drake swimming in the pond. I asked them what they'd seen go by, but the only answer I got was their quack, quack, quack!"

"Oh, father, why didn't you understand? That was the pair of them, the duck and the drake! Turn round, turn round! Start after them again, and this time bring them back!"

Little Horse, who goes like lightning, reared at the touch of the whip, and turned round on his hind legs.

As soon as the devil had gone, Bélélalie and Jeantou became themselves again. They galloped on, on Big Horse.

But Big Horse only goes like the wind. Jeantou soon saw that cloud again. Hornbeard was coming!

"Your father! Here comes your father! We're lost, Bélélalie!"

"Jeantou, don't lose heart!"

They were galloping by a thornbush.

> *By my wand's magic power,*
> *Be you a finch, and I a warbler!*

Instantly, they turned into a finch and a warbler, chirruping in the bush. In a moment the devil came up.

> *Warbler and finch, good day, good day!*
> *A girl and boy—have they come your way?*

"Twitter, twitter, tweet!"

Finch and warbler, hear what I say!
Have a girl and boy come your way?

"Twitter, twitter, chirrup, chirp, tweet, tweet, chrrr, chirrup, tweet!"

"Confound you, you can't even understand me! Confound you, and my daughter, and that servant! Confound this whole land, and its thornbushes, and its wind!"

The devil spat with vexation, turned bridle, and rode home like a black whirlwind to his Black Mountain.

His goat-daughters were watching for him from the doorway.

"Why, father, my father, haven't you brought them back?"

"I saw nothing, and found nothing throughout the whole land. All I met was a pair of little birds flitting about in a green bush. I asked them what they'd seen go by, but the only answer I got was their tweet, tweet, tweet!"

"Oh, father, why didn't you understand? That was the two of them, the pair of little birds! Turn round, turn round! Start after them again, and this time bring them back!"

"Again? My back's killing me! This chase has worn me out!"

"No, no, you *must*. This time, you'll get them!"

"All right, I'll go, if it means so much to you!"

Yonder, on the green plain, Bélélalie and her Jeantou were fleeing again on Big Horse. But Big Horse only goes like the wind. Suddenly, Jeantou saw the great cloud again. It was he, Hornbeard!

"Your father! Your father's coming! Bélélalie, we're lost!"

"Jeantou, don't lose heart!"

They were galloping along a brook, among the mint and rushes.

By my wand, without fail,
Be I a plank and you a rail!

But the devil was looking a little more closely, now his black daughters had given him such a bad time. And he knew the brook had no plank over it at that spot.

"Aha, Bélélalie, I see your hand in this! But this time, you and that servant won't get away from me!"

He hurled himself at the plank and rail, to smash and burn them.

That instant—

By my wand so powerful,
Be I a frog and you a bull!

The railing changed into a bull, which leaped into the meadow among thirty other bulls; while the plank changed into a frog, which leaped into the brook among three hundred other frogs.

The wand, however, stayed a wand, drifting on down the stream. The devil seized it.

Servant, servant, you are a bull,
And six years shall be one.
Bélélalie, you are a frog,
And seven years shall stay one.

Jeantou had to stay on as a bull among the green meadows. Every morning and evening he came to drink from the brook where his Bélélalie lived, in her frog shape. This was the only way the poor things could see each other at all.

After six years, Jeantou turned back into a boy, just as he'd been on the morning of the great chase. But so much had happened since then that he'd lost his memory and forgotten his Bélélalie.

So he set off to earn his living. He hired himself out to a mill as a miller's boy.

After seven years, Bélélalie stopped being a green frog. She turned back into a white girl. But Jeantou wasn't there any more.

She looked for him everywhere, desperately.

The first day, she found neither hide nor hair of him.

The second day, behind a certain mill, she heard the washerwomen beating their washing and talking about one Jeantou.

The third day, she saw a wedding start out from the mill toward the church. The bride was the miller's daughter; and the groom, why, he was Jeantou himself.

Bélélalie ran to the village, to the baker woman's house.

"Good woman, wouldn't you have a bit of dough to give me?"

"No, dear, I'm afraid not. I've baked so much for the wedding that I've no dough left at all."

"Are you sure? All I need is a tiny bit, the size of a little toe, or the head of a pin."

The baker woman searched her dough trough and found a lump as big as a pea. She gave it to Bélélalie.

Bélélalie kneaded the dough till, in a moment, it rose. She made it into two pigeons, a girl pigeon and a boy pigeon, and gave them life and speech. The pigeons flew to perch above the church door, just as the bride and groom were going in to be married.

The boy pigeon began saying to the girl pigeon, "Coo, coo, coo, O pigeon my love, give me a kiss!"

"You'll have no kiss from *me!* You'd be just like Jeantou. He saved Bélélalie from her father's castle, then forgot her and wandered off to another land!"

Jeantou heard that. And then . . . Oh, and *then* . . . !

He turned around in one jump, went out to the church door, and found the white girl there.

At the mere sight of Bélélalie, all his love for her came back. He remembered every last thing.

He threw his arms around her neck. She hugged him to her and took him away, and they were never parted again.

The cock's crowed,
And the tale's over!

29. The Old Woman in Red Slippers

There was once an old woman—oh, she had those seven secret, evil folds deep in her heart. For ages and ages now she'd already been working on her damnation.

She kept company with the devil, on equal terms, and in fact could have shown the devil himself a few tricks.

When the devil steps out to dance,
The woman's already far in advance.

And it was true enough of that old woman: when any business came along she could stick her nose into, she'd imagined all the harm she could do long before the devil had.

Well, one day she and Satan were together when she heard him start in complaining.

"Everyone who lies dying these days, why, people just get 'em confessed and given the unction, and they set out on their great journey all spick-and-span. They never make it to *my* place."

"I'll send you *two* souls if you like, unconfessed and unblessed," said the old woman. "All I ask for my trouble is a pair of red slippers."

"It's a deal," grunted the devil.

The old woman knew a good young wife whose husband was jealous— more jealous than any Christian ever had a right to be. And she knew this husband had just left an hour before to go hunting hare. She went straight to their house (after all, she felt as much at home everywhere as a ladle in a pot), and found the young wife kneading dough.

"You're baking, friend?" said she. "Well, I was just going to ask you for a bit of flour. I'll give it back as soon as I've had some ground."

The wife went to the sack and gave her some. She ought to have been wary, though, because she brushed the scissors off the table as she went by, and they stuck point-first in the floor. That's always a sign of betrayal.

Now she had the flour, the old woman lingered a moment to gossip about the news from the village. The wife, meanwhile, had gone back to kneading.

"I'm in a hurry. I have to take the bread this evening to bake at the village bakehouse."

Poor thing, she didn't know what was in the oven now for *her.*

At just the right moment the old woman laid her hand in the flour, then pressed it more gently than a cat's paw to the waist of her bent-over neighbor. That was all, and the young wife never noticed a thing.

Next, the old woman went into the forest and pretended to pick up firewood; but she never left the path.

At last, she saw the hunter coming back. She gave him a sly look with her rheumy eyes.

"Some chase after hare in the woods," she cackled, "while at the bake-house the baker chases after their wife."

"Old woman, you've said too much or not enough!"

"The baker chases after their wife. Oh, I saw him, taking her by the waist!"

While the hunter stood, thunderstruck, in the path, the woman slipped behind a bush, then into the thickets and away.

The hunter knew his wife had meant to take the bread to the bakehouse that evening. The old woman's words struck deep. He gripped his rifle hard, ran home, and burst in in a rage. The first thing he saw from the door was the handprint in flour on his wife's waist.

That's all a jealous man needs. He fired questions at her, reproached her bitterly, and stormed and threatened.

She had no idea what was going on, but, like too many women, she had a temper of her own—and quickly lost it. She told him a few of those things that may flash across your mind but that you must never say, because the one who hears them will never forget them, and you'll never get along with that person again. She said she was sorry she'd married him, and that she'd have done a lot better to marry So-and-so. To him it was clear: it was all over, they were through. His gun was there in his hand. Madness boiled up, as a stream floods after a storm. He cocked the gun and fired without even aiming.

The first shot killed his wife. With the second he killed the baker, just coming up then with a wheelbarrow of bread fresh from the oven. Then he opened his knife and cut his own throat.

Three souls, unconfessed, left for the afterworld: one more than the old woman had promised. The murderer's surely belonged to the devil, no doubt about that. But what of the other two, who'd been taken unawares? Who can say?

That very evening the old woman went to claim her due from the devil, at the gates of Hell. She looked like the cat that ate the canary.

They say the devil himself shook to see her, purring and blinking her little snake eyes. He wouldn't let her set foot in his house.

"Quick," he hissed, "bring me the slippers!"

"You see," explained the old woman, "I did even better than I predicted. I asked for red slippers, but now I'd like pompoms on them!"

Half frightened (because he can tell old women like that are even worse than he is), and half desperate simply to get her off his doorstep, the devil wasted no time letting her have her scarlet, pompom slippers. Yes: he held them out to her at the tip of his longest pitchfork.

30. The Little Grey Bird

There was once a poor, poor family whose daily diet was the opposite of a dog's: dogs eat their meat without bread, while these people ate their bread without meat. And I'll tell you, they didn't even get bread every day, either!

Their boy would be sixteen in March. What were they going to do with him? They couldn't have him forever looking after their goat. Those who don't grow their own bread have no choice but to find themselves a master. Hunger rules—almost as much as God himself.

March is the season when a master takes on a servant. In the winter he'd just have the fellow lazing around the place, warming his legs at the fire while it snows outside. Nothing to do! But in March, all the work shows up.

The father—they called him Chichourle—decided to go hire out his son, Chichourlou, at the big hiring fair.

Early on the day of the fair, both took a crust of bread, an onion, and a pinch of salt. And as the father was heading out the door, the mother pulled him back.

"Say, Chichourle, you'll look out for him, won't you? It's so hard to see my dear boy, my Chichourlou, go off to someone else's."

"Oh, there are some who aren't strong, but he's not like them," the father replied. "And he already knows more than the devil himself."

"It makes my heart bleed to see him leave. Try and find him a good master."

From the path outside the boy heard her. "Why, mother," he said, "God willing, I'll get by, even if I fall into a hundred feet of mustard!"

So off they went. At the first hedge they came to, the boy broke off a green twig and stuck it in his hat, to show he was for hire. Just short of the brook they saw an old woman coming toward them; they greeted her as they crossed the bridge.

"Good morning, Chichourle and Chichourlou," said she. "Good morning!"

"Good morning to you, good woman. But you—you know our names, then?"

"I suppose I do. And you're off to the fair?"

"As you say. But I'm not singing as I go. We've got to send the boy to work for others. His mother feels awful about it, and maybe I do too."

"Feeling bad never helps. Listen. You'll find at the fair a man as tall as a wagon tongue, with crookedy eyes. He'll want to hire your boy. Ask him for wages three times higher than you'd ask from anyone else. Don't say ten crowns, say thirty. That man wants the boy. He'll accept. The work's worth it, though. Don't come down on the price."

Everything went as the old woman had said. They saw the man coming toward them, taller than a wagon tongue, with crookedy eyes all black and red. He looked the boy over—this alert boy, as smart as a weasel.

"What wage are you asking, good man?"

"Thirty crowns, not less."

"Thirty crowns!" cried the other. "The boy knows nothing, I'll have to teach him everything. It does a boy no good at all not to have been to school."

"Perhaps, but it's thirty crowns. Otherwise, no deal."

The father wasn't a bit happy, despite the high wage, to let his son go to this fellow. But the boy himself was all set to plunge into something new, and to charge head-first through anything that might come his way. That spring morning, he was determined to look on the bright side of everything.

So the bargain was made.

"In a year," said the man, "come back to the fairground. You'll have your boy back, with the thirty crowns."

The father started home, scratching his head. When he got there, he stood his staff behind the door, sat down, and stared at the fire.

"Well," said he, "it's done. We'll have to get used to it. The boy's hired out to a tall man with a crooked eye—hired out at a very high wage. Thirty crowns. The man's going to teach him things and push him hard. How it'll turn out, I have no idea."

"Oh, it's terrible!" the mother cried. "And he's all we have!"

"Maybe he'll learn a lot and come back ready to make his fortune. But maybe . . ."

"Well, all I want is to have him back! If we didn't see him a year from now, my God, what would we do?"

Slowly, slowly, the year passed by: the working season, the season for haying, harvesttime, the sowing, the vigils for the end of the year, and again the high season for work. The hiring fair came back again. The man took his staff and set off.

"He went off to hire as he might have skipped off to supper! I can still see him with that green twig in his hat, that Chichourlou of mine, my boy . . . But how's he been faring with that big devil of a man? How will I ever find him again?"

When he got near the brook he again saw an old woman approaching— yes, the same old woman as last year.

"Good morning to you, Chichourle," said she. "Good morning!"

"Good morning to *you*, good woman. But what, you're still around here?"

"Not always, no, not always. If I'm here this morning, it's because I knew you'd be passing by. So, you're off to the fair?"

"As you say, good woman. I'm going for my boy. Do you know how I'm to find him?"

"Listen, and remember what I tell you. If you don't, oh, you'll never see your boy again. That tall man will take you home with him. Don't you accept food from him, or drink either. Don't take a thing from him, whether he offers it to you or not. No refreshments at all. He'll take you through the rooms of the house, he'll show you barrels full of silver, and he'll invite you to fill your pockets. But you, take only your thirty crowns. And keep asking him, over and over again, to give you your boy back. Because look out! All that man wants is to keep him. In the end he'll lead you through a garden to a tall tree full of birds, and he'll tell you to take whatever bird you wish. Take only the littlest and greyest one singing away on the highest branch."

"Thank you, good woman. That's the one I'll take."

"That one and no other. Be firm, now. Insist that's the one you want."

"It's so easy to make a mistake when you just don't know! Ah, good woman, what would I have done without you?"

So he went to the fair. The tall man was waiting in the middle of the fairground, legs apart and hands behind his back, like a hog dealer.

"Come home with me, my good man. You'll get your boy there, and your money."

He took the father home to his own place. It didn't take long.

"Sit yourself down now, and we'll have something to eat."

"No, no, sir, thank you, but I can't stop to eat. It's the boy I want."

"Don't worry, the boy's all right. We'll just have a drink."

"No, no, sir, no drink for me. I want the boy. It's the boy I've come for."

"All right, then. First, you must have your money."

The tall man took him through the rooms of the house. There were barrels and barrels full of silver crowns.

"There you are, help yourself. I don't count change. Help yourself and fill your pockets."

"We agreed on thirty crowns, sir, and it's thirty crowns I'll take."

He counted out his thirty crowns. Not twenty-nine, not thirty-one, but thirty.

"And now I want my boy. I hired him out for a year, the year's over, and I must have him back."

The tall man took him into the garden. A tall tree was growing there, and it was full of birds: pink ones, red ones, green ones, with crests or with sweeping tails.

"Take whichever one you wish!"

"I'll have that grey one up there, sir, the little grey one that's singing."

The tall man looked sullen—what a wooden face he had! But he'd made his offer, and he had to stick to it.

Chichourle and Chichourlou started home again. Chichourlou was the little grey bird on his father's shoulder.

"Never fear, father," said he, "I know a lot of things. Forget all your worries. When's the horse race?"

"A week from Sunday, in Four Winds Town."

"I'll turn myself into a horse. Take me there and watch what happens."

So on that day, Chichourlou changed himself into a horse—an old nag, head hanging like a sheep with a goiter, hardly able to stir more than one foot at a time. Both knees were shot, and covered with scabs, scrapes, and flies.

The father rode her to the town, and down to the meadow along the river where the race was to be run.

The sleepy old nag was embarrassed even to stand with the other horses. Everyone nearby laughed and cracked jokes. People were shouting at Chichourle to keep that mare on a close rein.

"Rein 'er in there, rein 'er in, that beauty of yours, or she'll shoot off and spirit you away God only knows where!"

They were making up songs, stamping their feet, and roaring with mirth.

At last came the starting signal.

The nag didn't even seem to want to start the race, but at last she made up her mind. The others, meanwhile, were far away, racing flat-out along the river, at least halfway to the finish. Suddenly the nag took off like a rifle shot. In a moment she'd caught up with the others, and passed them, and left them behind. The eye could hardly follow her. She reached the finish line first by a mile. Chichourle got a big bunch of ribbons and a purse full of gold.

Up stepped a big country gentleman.

"I'll buy that horse," said he.

"If I do sell her, sir, I'll be selling her dear. And the bridle's not for sale."

The boy had carefully told his father, "If you sell me, don't sell the bridle, or I'd never be able to come back!"

"What do I care about the bridle? I've plenty of bridles at home! How much do you want for the horse?"

"Two hundred pistoles, sir."

That was ten times the price of a perfectly good horse.

"Two hundred pistoles? Fine. Two hundred. It's a deal."

The fellow took Chichourle at his word. He counted out the money, one foot propped on a milestone, borrowed a bridle, and led off the nag with all her scabs and flies.

"But, sir," cried his servant, "what on earth do you want with this wreck of a mare? You'd think she'd swallowed a barrel, with all those ribs sticking up under her skin!"

"This wreck of a mare, as you call her, can overtake any hare in full flight. I saw her run myself, down by the river."

The servant spat down between his feet, shrugged his shoulders, and kept quiet. But as soon as his master's back was turned, he gave the beast a savage kick in the ribs.

"You stinking carcass! You want to have all the boys laughing at me when I take you to water? Well, don't worry, I'll see you dead before three months are out!"

He never had to take the trouble. The old horse changed into a little bird and sailed up into the sky. Neither master nor servant ever saw her again.

Back home again, Chichourlou told his father, "You can bring me to fairs and sell me to traders or gentlemen. Ask the very best price you can, and never back down! But never let go of that bridle! Remember, when you strike that deal, always keep the bridle or the rope for yourself!"

As the seasons turned there'd be donkey fairs, hog fairs, or cattle fairs, so Chichourle would change himself into a donkey, a fat pig, or an ox. Oh, he knew his tricks! Gentlemen would come, look him over, and buy—big gentlemen, serious gentlemen, maybe even somewhat cross-eyed gentlemen.

The father would head home with the rope. Then the boy would turn back into a bird, and fly home again from the buyer's.

On Saint John's Day there was going to be a big horse fair in the town where the boy had once been hired.

"You'll take me there, won't you? I'll turn myself into a pretty horse this time."

"And what if the tall man comes to buy you?"

"Oh, I'll be all right. I'll get myself out of it if you just don't let go of that bridle."

So off they went to the fair. What a pretty, prancing horse he made, that Chichourlou! Sparks seemed to shoot from his nostrils and eyes.

The tall man came. He walked up and looked the horse over.

"Why, Chichourle, it's you! Good day, good day!"

"Good day, sir."

"And what do you want for this horse?"

"Five hundred crowns, sir."

"I'll take him, with his bridle."

"I'm sorry, sir, but I must keep the bridle."

"All right, a hundred crowns for the bridle."

A hundred crowns for a bridle! Chichourle let it go.

The man didn't waste a minute. He took hold of the horse and led it straight off to the nearest inn, then hailed the stableboy.

"Listen, boy, I want you to tie this horse up high on the rack, just as short as you can. Then get me a pitchfork handle, and let's dance! Beat him till he sticks his tongue out."

"But he's a beautiful horse, sir!"

"Yes, yes, he's got too much fire. I've got to break him if I'm to take him home."

"All right, sir, at your service."

The tall man winked and went back to the fairground to continue his trading.

So there was poor Chichourlou, tied up high and short, with his head raised so far that he couldn't rear. He couldn't run: the bridle held him. For his sins, no doubt, he caught from that stableboy an awful volley of blows. That was quite enough. He stuck a foot of tongue out right away, and the stableboy left him there. What with the fair that morning, work was piling in from everywhere. There were horses to feed, a filly to water, tips to pocket, a mare to unhitch, a carriage to put away—and, best of all, whenever luck smiled, glasses of red wine to down.

"Why, oh why did I ever turn myself into a horse?" groaned Chichourlou, still shaking. "But what I just got are but tender caresses next to what's coming!"

Oh, he knew, all right. As soon as that man got him home, he'd have him stunned, brained, and bled. "He'll kill me this evening, and tomorrow he'll eat me! Ah, poor father, what did you do when you sold him the bridle as well!"

Each minute he thought he saw the tall man coming, and couldn't help shivering all over.

Finally he heard the man's voice in the courtyard, shouting to the stableboy.

"How about that horse? Did you give him something to remember? All right! But I'll give him something else again, that'll carry a bit more weight!"

Terrified, Chichourlou tugged on the bridle, but all he got for his pains was to nearly strangle himself. That bridle was tough. It wouldn't break. And that was the spell, anyway, in this story of magic: Chichourlou was caught.

Never sell your luck short, that's what they say. Just as the man appeared in the doorway, rolling up his sleeves, the innkeeper's son happened by. Pocket knife in hand, he was peeling a willow wand.

He noticed that pretty little horse, tugging away with all his might and shivering with mad terror.

Just a slip of a boy! How could he resist the pleasure of helping the horse and playing a trick on that stableboy? Up on tiptoe he went, and cut the bridle with his knife.

Chichourlou was free! Oh, he wasted no time turning himself into a bird.

The tall man in the doorway just caught sight of the little bird flitting over his head and racing off. He wasted no time, either, turning himself into a hawk, and dove at the little grey bird. What a chase, through the town, from yard to yard, all in sudden turns, dives, and climbs!

But can a sparrow escape a hawk? The poor grey bird was about to be caught, stripped, and torn to pieces.

All at once he changed into a golden ring, and fell into a garden at a young lady's feet—oh, a young, young lady, who was wandering there and looking carefully about. She was gathering herbs to nurse her sick father. She heard the ring clink on the gravel, saw it, picked it up, and slipped it on her finger. The hawk, which had been diving at the ring, wheeled up and away, disappointed, into the clouds.

That evening the young lady retired to her room. She took off the ring she hadn't yet even glanced at, so worried was she by her father's illness; turned it round and round; bounced it up and down in her hands as she sang a golden-ring song; and set it on the table. Then she lay down and fell asleep.

In the night a moonbeam woke her. She opened her eyes and thought she saw before her a beautiful boy.

"I had to turn into a golden ring, miss," said he. "I'm the golden ring which fell at your feet on the garden gravel. Don't be afraid. But tomorrow a tall man will come to speak with you. He'll offer to heal your father, who's so ill, and he'll ask you first for the golden ring which fell to earth before you. Oh, miss, when you give him the ring, please, please be kind: don't put it straight in his hand! Instead, let it fall to the ground."

She fell back to sleep, unsure whether or not she'd been dreaming.

But the next day, everything went as the boy had said it would.

The tall man came to the house, found the young lady walking in the garden, and bowed.

"I have come, miss," said he, "to place myself entirely at your service. If you will allow me, I shall heal your father."

"But sir, all the doctors have come and left without being able to tell what his illness is."

"I know what it is, therefore I can dispel it. All you need do is give me the ring which fell to earth yesterday before you."

"The ring is yours, sir."

In haste the tall man seized the young lady's hand and began to pull off the golden ring. But she remembered her dream, and made sure the ring fell to the ground. It changed as it reached the earth into a millet seed.

That same instant the tall man, intent on swallowing the seed, turned himself into a red cock. Magic upon magic, spell upon spell, the seed made itself a fox, a beast of prey. Jaws gaping, the fox leaped on the cock and took care of him in two crunches! Chichourlou had beaten the tall man. The crafty little servant had eaten his master.

Oh, he managed well enough to turn himself back into a boy. The old woman of the bridge, the river fairy, would have helped him anyway, if he'd had any trouble. But he knew all the tricks! He'd studied at that tall man's school and become cleverer than his teacher. Then he'd outsmarted his teacher again, and eaten him.

After that, he healed the young lady's father. The two had been born in the same year, and one day they were married. She was so well brought up, and so sweet by nature, that she never, ever (so the story goes) made a donkey of him; and that, after all, is something that befalls a good many men in this world.

Part
Three

BANDITS

31. Red Eyes

There was once a girl, a country merchant's pretty young daughter. Her father had to go off to a great, splendid fair—a fair he couldn't possibly miss.

"I'll be back Tuesday," said he, "or at latest Wednesday, or Thursday for sure. Go fetch your cousin from the village. She'll keep you company."

He was a widower, you see, and the girl was his only child. Their house stood all alone in a pasture by a spring, in a little grove of rowan trees alive with thrushes. Nearby, where the landscape opened out, rose a blue mountain spur. Everywhere else was woods, woods, woods.

The merchant's daughter went for her cousin, which made her late for the milking. Then the two dawdled in the house and had to struggle to finish their work in the stable. When they got back to the hearth the fire was out. They had to go for fire to the nearest neighbor's, five hundred long paces away.

They ran off, thinking they'd closed all the doors. But there were so many, many doors! Back they rushed with some live coals in a broken clog. When they'd left the light had been fading and the marsh hawks crying. It was night when they got home, amid the hooting of owls.

From a bend in the path the cousin saw a shadow slip past the house, and from the spring she thought she saw a hay-barn door pull shut. This was dusk, though, when you no longer know what you're seeing, or what you can believe. Anyway, the merchant's daughter, walking with her head lowered against the wind, hadn't seen a thing.

"I won't tell her," thought her cousin. "People these days are talking about a robber in a fox-skin cap and a russet cloak: the famous Jean de Bort. Maybe he's lurking in the woods with his gang. She'll be frightened if I talk. No, it's my own eye made that shadow—a fleck in my eye. And the door, why, we must simply have forgotten to close it, and the wind blew it shut."

Actually, she went straight to the window as soon as they'd gotten inside and barred the door. Yonder, at the edge of the hay, she noticed a pair of shoes. She told herself they were her uncle's.

The two girls ate and drank a little wine. The wind was howling in the chimney and whistling at all the windows. The blazing fire they lit did nothing to lighten the blackness of the night.

"The best thing we can do is go to bed," said the cousin, bending down to take off her stockings. In the shadows under the bed, she saw two red eyes watching her. The face was a man's, but the eyes a brute beast's. They were shining, and staring straight at her.

Shivering, she put her stockings back on. "Oh!" she cried, "my nightcap! I'll never be able to sleep without my nightcap! I'll have to go get it!"

"But you can have mine, my prettiest one! You'd be mad to go at night, in this storm!"

"No, no, I must, I must!" She opened the door as she spoke, drew her cloak around her, and ran down the steps.

"You're crazy, cousin, you're crazy!" shouted the merchant's daughter behind her. But the girl had disappeared into the night.

The merchant's daughter went to bed, but couldn't sleep. She didn't dare even turn over. "It's eleven now, and there goes midnight," thought she. "Dear God, take me under your holy care! How long, how very long a whole night can be!"

Suddenly she heard something stir beneath her, and that instant felt a prick from below, as though a pin had been stuck up through the mattress. But she was brave, and didn't cry out.

Out crawled the man and stood up, then leaned over her in the dark. She saw his red eyes but pretended to be asleep.

He understood she would stay as still as a log. And what good would it have done her to struggle or cry out? There was no ear to hear her, and no arm to give her help. The man felt himself the master of the place, and master too of the whole countryside and of the night. He was in no hurry. He went to the fire, lit the lantern, and brought the light to the girl's face, close enough to singe her eyelashes. She went on sleeping.

But she stole a peek at him while his back was turned, and recognized Jean de Bort, the robber captain: there was his fox-fur cap with the fox's tail and his russet cloak. He, meanwhile, made himself at home. He laid his big pistols down on the table, and his cutlass beside them. Then, humming a tune, he poured himself some wine, which he drank as he gazed around the room. Next he went to the door, drew from his shirt a little silver whistle, and blew into it from the doorway, as though to call in all his companions skulking through the woods in the depths of the night. He even took three steps down to whistle again, so the sound should carry properly.

All at once he jumped. The door! The door had slammed behind him, as though caught by a gust of wind.

He hurled himself against it, only to hear the bolt shoot home on the other side. The only answer he got when he shook it was a sigh and a laugh. Then he thundered threats.

"Take care, my pretty, take care, you'd better not laugh at Jean de Bort! I'll smash down the wall! I'll take off your head!" That's how he roared at first, battering at the door with his fists. Then he caught his breath and ran his hand over his face.

"Listen, girl," he went on in a very different tone, "I'll go away. But first you must give me back my weapons. You'll be a thief, girl, if you don't. I'll leave if you give them back, I promise, I swear! Now, crack open the door, and we'll shake on it!"

"No, I won't. If you want to shake on it, put your hand in under the door."

He did so. "Once I've got your little white hand in mine, my dear," said he to himself, "nothing will ever make me let it go!"

Then he screamed. All he retrieved from under the door was his wrist, spurting blood like a fountain. She'd chopped off his hand with the cutlass.

"You swine!" he howled. "You'll regret this, I swear! The day will come when you'll beg for mercy, you merchant's wench, and mercy's the last thing you'll get!"

He wrapped his wrist in his russet cloak and staggered down the steps as though drunk. At the bottom, he sank to the ground. His robber companions, who were just running up to the house, made him a chair with their hands and carried him off into the woods. They were no doubt camping there in the depths of some cave.

"I swear it!" he thundered again in a terrifying voice as he went. "You'll remember Jean de Bort!"

On the third day the merchant rode home. Below the hill he slowed his horse to a walk, then stopped on the village square. He'd spotted the cousin on her way to the well, carrying a green pitcher.

"Hey!" he cried. "Aren't you with my daughter?"

"Your daughter!" she retorted. "Your daughter has more welcome company than mine! When we got back to the house that evening I saw her lover steal inside; and that night, when I took off my stockings, I saw him hiding under the bed. So I made myself scarce. Yes, good-bye to the likes of her! I went home."

"Do you know what you're saying, girl?"

"I'm saying what I saw right there before me. I saw the man's eyes under the bed, shining red like a hare's, or like those of the Beast himself!"

The merchant galloped off like one possessed, like a storm of thunder and hail. He leaped up the steps in three bounds and burst through the door.

His daughter lifted her skirt, as always, to greet her father with three curtsies. But with one blow he stretched her out on the ground, then raised his boot to smash its heel into her face.

"You wretch!" he cried. "Is it true, what your cousin says? A lover came and hid under the bed?"

"Oh yes, it's true, father, a lover came . . ."

"You've shamed me, and you're shamed as well! Everyone in the village will be talking about it. Not a single young man will ask for your hand."

"Very well, I'll give you my lover's hand!"

She took the bloody hand from the table, and with it the pistols and the cutlass.

"You do me wrong, father," she said.

When he grasped the truth, he begged her forgiveness and swore a great oath that to guard her from Jean de Bort, he'd never leave her alone again till she was married.

Months crept by, then a year, then two. No one around wanted to get mixed up with the robber band. The young men of the village feared Jean de Bort, and none would have dared ask to marry the merchant's daughter.

The awful threat weighed upon her. Everyone said the robber captain would surely be back one night to take revenge. Though the nicer neighbors felt sorry for the merchant and his daughter, they wouldn't have done anything for them. Others kept out of their way and were quite ready to betray them.

The merchant kept one eye open all night, every night; and during the day he opened both eyes. But his caution cost the girl dearly, though he never quite realized it. This life of watching and waiting wasn't a life at all.

There came one evening another merchant, who'd lost his way in the meadows and ended up wandering through the forest—a merchant, yes, but dressed all in black with a feather in his hat and wearing gloves like a lord. On his horse's croup rode a great chest.

Having asked for a bit of bread and a glass of water, he got a saddle of hare and a bottle of wine. Then he wanted to know the way and when the moon would rise. The father told him there would be no moon, and offered to let him stay the night. What with his staff of servants, he felt strong enough. Besides, his pistols were never out of his belt, and he watched over his daughter every minute he breathed.

Anyway, this merchant didn't look at all like a cutpurse or a highwayman. He got up, ate his breakfast, and before leaving drank with his host to the new day and the road before him. He'd opened his chest, and now had a gift for each: for the father a belt of buffalo hide, and for the daughter a pair of scissors damascened with gold.

The scissors fell and stuck point-down in the floor—a sign of betrayal. As far as the girl was concerned, the man's company oppressed her; but he kept after her till she had to accept a silver chain and a gilded thimble as well. He promised he'd be back.

He did return, with his chest more richly filled than ever. He unpacked it on the table. It wasn't just ribbons or satins this time, but jewelry, precious stones, garnets, and amethysts.

"Do you see these earrings," he asked, "and these necklaces? I've a fine selection of laces, too. Take some, pretty miss, take all you want!"

He drank to the father's health, and spread out his wealth; he drank to the daughter's and asked to marry her.

"Give me her hand!" he said. "I promise I'll make her happy."

The girl hardly knew what to say. Her heart was not singing.

"You might as well marry him as another," her father advised. "He's rich—filthy rich!"

"Yes," she replied, "too rich for us. Why doesn't he ever take off his gloves?"

"That's the way fancy people are. And what a match for you! I don't want to marry you off in the village, and *he's* worth a hundred times any of our local boys."

"Well," she told herself, "it's true I'm afraid, but I might as well go to meet whatever's coming. At least father won't have to live this way any more. And as for me, who knows? I'll see what's in store."

Her father kept pressing her, and in a trice it was done: on Friday evening the engagement, and on Saturday morning the wedding.

Down the path strolled the newlyweds, the bride and groom. He told her he'd had letters from his home far away. Urgent business called him there.

"Bridle my horse," he cried as soon as the wedding feast was over. "I'll saddle him myself! My wife will ride behind me. We're off this minute."

They set out over the mountain. She sighed as they entered the woods, and wept as the thickets closed around them. "Good-bye, good-bye, O house of my father! Good-bye, good-bye, O place where I was born!"

"What is it, my dear? What's troubling you? Why are you so sad?"

"It's just, it's just . . . that I want to know why you never take the glove off your right hand, not even here, deep in the woods!"

"I never take it off because I don't want you to see what my hand looks like. But now, in these woods, yes, I'll take it off for you!"

He did so, and lifted his hand. It was iron. He struck her in the face with it, twice.

"*Now* do you recognize Jean de Bort? Ah, you wretch, my hour has come: the hour for my revenge!"

He laid hands on her. When she struggled to escape, he stunned her with a blow of his iron hand and threw her unconscious on the ground. Then he stripped her of everything she had on: dress, petticoat, and

underwear. She was left clothed, like Geneviève de Brabant, in nothing but her hair. Then he tied her hands together with a rope he had in his pocket, winding it around her wrists many times, and hung her by the arms from the main branch of an oak.

"I was taking you to my cave," he muttered, "but here it'll be better still. I'll go and get my band, and they'll begin torturing you. Whoever makes you suffer the most will please me best. You'll beg them to let you die, but there'll be no death for you, or at least not so soon!"

He left her hanging from the tree, knees sagging, head sunk on her chest, and hair in a tangle. Then he galloped away.

The pain in her wrists brought her at last to her senses—the pain and her mad fear. There was no one in these woods to hear her screams and shrieks, except for wolves, foxes, and the robbers themselves. No one came hunting there. People avoided the place for fear of Jean de Bort.

God heard her, though. Through the wood came riding a young cavalry officer, on his way home from the wars. At the first sight of her he thought he was dreaming. When he looked again, his heart leaped in his chest. He drew his sword and cut the rope. She was trembling so violently that she could hardly get on her petticoat or her lovely flowered dress.

"Take me away, take me away!" she cried. "There's not a moment to lose! Jean de Bort got me and he'll be back! Oh save me, save me, please!"

The officer took her in his arms and galloped away with her on his white horse, at breakneck speed.

Jean de Bort came back with his band to find the victim gone, and went pale with rage. Foaming at the mouth like a monster gone mad, he hurled insults after the unhappy girl, and his eyes burned redder still than they had under the bed.

High and low the band of robbers hunted, from thicket to thicket, but found no trace of her.

"I swear," roared Jean de Bort, "I swear I'll know neither peace nor rest till I have my hands on her! She'll pay for this more dearly still!"

But the cavalry officer had carried her off. By a spring she redid her hair, and when they reached the first town he let her rest.

"Eat, my dear," said he, "and sleep in peace. I'll take you far from here, to my father's castle. No one will know you there, and no one will wish you ill."

At the castle late that afternoon, in the orchard, under God's own sun, she told him the whole terrible story: that she'd been married in church, married to the robber captain Jean de Bort.

He looked down at the ground.

Three days later he went off again to the wars. "I'll leave you here, my dear," he said, "with my mother and father. They'll treat you as their daughter; and I, if you'll allow me, will have you for my sister. I leave you here as in a safe refuge."

Once more he mounted his white horse and set out. Months crept by, then a year, then two.

One evening the lady was at her window, lost in her thoughts. The officer's father had died at Christmas, and since Easter his mother had been ill. For herself, she kept gazing at the road which ran off over hill and dale toward her own woods and her own home. Farther still, the road ran on toward the army and the war. People were saying the war would soon be over. The lady, as she sat sewing, could not hold back her sighs.

"Lady at the window, come and open the door! We've a chest for you, from the gentlemen at the wars! It's full of goods and jewels. He himself will bring you the key before three days are out. You'll soon be surprised to see him whom you least expected!" The speakers were two mule drivers, tanned and scarred, leading a mule with a chest on its back.

The lady ran happily to open. Her maid was out on the heath, and her valet working among the vines. She herself helped the drivers to unload the chest, and poured them wine. They left the chest in the castle hall, then went their way.

She hurried to tell the gentleman's poor, sick mother, then came back to see what he'd sent her. Her faithful little dog, as she quickly noticed, was now circling the chest, growling, sniffing, and barking. He wouldn't calm down, but kept starting in again, sniffing and growling.

She shivered as fear swept through her. Next she knelt down and tried to peer in through a crack. Though she saw nothing, she caught a sort of billy-goat smell. She heard nothing, either, when she pressed her ear to the chest; but it seemed to her that someone was in there, breathing. Pale as death, she stood up again, and backed away to the door. Then, at a loss for what to do, she went out onto the road.

God was with her, for just then the town marshal came by. He saw she was whiter than the lace at her throat.

"What's the matter, lady?" said he. "What's troubling you?"

In the castle, he saw the dog and the chest.

"They told you it was goods, did they?"

Suddenly he drew his sword and thrust it between the planks. A scream rang out, and blood ran red on the flagstones. When the marshal's men broke open the chest with axes, they found in it Jean de Bort, pierced through, just then giving up the ghost.

They arrested the two mule drivers that evening, and the next day caught the whole band. Within the week, the judges had sentenced them in the king's name, and the executioner had sent them to settle accounts with God.

Meanwhile, the war was over. The rumor ran through the countryside, and soldiers began passing along the road. The young gentleman returned, this time for good. He heard in town about Jean de Bort's death, and at the castle found the lady. They exchanged glances and took each other's hands. Soon, he'd made her his wife.

Jean de Bort was buried in his chest, at the back of the cemetery, under a nameless stone. No one spoke of him any more, save the little children who made up this song, to sing when they went for hazelnuts:

> *Fee, fie, fiddly, fum!*
> *Who's done for?*
> *Jean de Bort!*
> *Who's mourning him?*
> *The white hen.*
> *Who has to laugh?*
> *The little calf!*
> *Who's crying like a friend so fond?*
> *The green frog in the pond.*
> *And who's gone and dressed in black?*
> *Fiddle, faddle, fuddle, fettle,*
> *It's the bottom*
> *Of the kettle!*

3 2. The Hundred Pistoles

There was once a good country fellow who one year had no luck at all. An epidemic finished off his whole herd in two weeks. All his steers and cows ended up in a trench.

What was he to do without his cattle? He sold off his standing timber, scrounged up money wherever he could, and even borrowed from a cousin. Finally he got together a sum of two hundred pistoles. With this capital tied securely around his waist, he set off for the big three-day fair at Brion.

"Look out!" warned his wife. "Those fairs get pretty lively."

"What do you mean, woman?"

"I mean that thieves swarm there like maggots in a cheese. Don't let your purse be stolen out of your pocket. That's all we need, after you lost your herd that way. Not that that disaster was your fault, but do be careful!"

Well, he *was* careful. He even pinned his breast pocket shut. Then off he went into the mountains, to Brion.

As soon as he'd gotten there and taken a room at the inn, he had a bright idea. The innkeeper looked like a jolly sort, all roly-poly and pink. The fellow took him aside.

"I'm here to stock up on cattle," he explained. "I'd better not hang around the fairground with too much money in my pocket, as I'm sure you'll agree. So I'm going to leave a hundred pistoles with you."

He counted them out on the table, gave them to the innkeeper, and went straight off to the fair.

There he soon noticed a dealer with a whole herd of cows that might well be just what he was looking for. He looked around a little more, came back, got a price, protested, argued, pretended to leave—well, the whole process of haggling. Finally the two agreed, then shook and drank on it. It all took only half an hour. The final price? One hundred and ninety pistoles. The fellow put down the hundred he had with him as a deposit, then went to get the rest at the inn.

A moment later he was back, as pale as clabbered milk, and shivering like a cat born after midsummer. The dealer stared at him, with his ghastly expression and his lopsided jacket.

"Say, my friend, what's happened to you? You've even buttoned your jacket all crooked."

"Have I? I must have done it when I put my purse back in my pocket. I went to the inn and asked for my money, but the innkeeper told me he had no idea what I was talking about. 'You never gave me a hundred pistoles,' he said, 'never! Not even a franc; not even a penny! Besides, do you have a witness?' And there it is. He wouldn't even listen to me. He just told me to get lost."

The dealer looked him over, shrugged his shoulders, spat down between his feet, then looked at him again with narrowed eyes.

"All right, I believe you. So what are you going to do?"

"Go home. I can't think straight. And since I don't have enough money any more, our deal is off. Give me back my hundred pistoles, please. I'm going back where I came from."

"And what if I talked to you like your innkeeper? What if I asked you for your witness? You'd be dead, right? But here they are, your hundred pistoles. Will you treat me to dinner if I get the others back for you too?"

"Get them back for me? How? You'll have to tell me, because I don't understand."

"Then listen. Take these hundred pistoles I'm giving you, and go deposit them at the inn."

"Like the first hundred? All that money? But you're crazy!"

"And apologize for having made that claim just now. Talk politely to the innkeeper. Anyway, it'll be in my presence. I'll go there with you, then I'll come back here. After that, you come out after me. All right, let's go."

On the way, the dealer explained it all. The fellow scratched behind his ear. Still, once they got to the inn, he went in.

"Listen," said he to the innkeeper, "are you certain, quite certain that I didn't leave a hundred pistoles with you a while ago? I was so sure . . . But ever since last winter I've gotten so muddleheaded. Someone must have stolen them from me on the fairground."

"Yes," the innkeeper replied, "we do have some very nimble-fingered thieves."

"So," the fellow continued, "I'd just as soon leave these hundred pistoles I have in my pocket with you. Here, count them." He gave the innkeeper the money, then looked toward the dealer and, in a low voice, took him to witness: "You see, I'm giving the innkeeper a hundred pistoles."

The dealer nodded assent, accepted a drink, then hurried away. The fellow paid for the drink, then went to join the dealer on the fairground.

"Now," said the dealer, "go back to the inn, pick your moment, and when you see the innkeeper all alone, tell him you've just made a deal and ask for your hundred pistoles."

He went, picked his moment, and asked for the money back.

"If I don't give it to him this time," thought the innkeeper to himself, "he'll just bring me his witness. I'd better not try to pull anything." So he returned the hundred pistoles.

The fellow was very happy just to get that much back, because with nothing at all in his pocket he'd felt half dead. Then back he went to the cattle dealer.

"Fine, that's *one*," said the dealer. "Now, let's both go. You'll ask him, in front of me, to return the hundred pistoles I saw you give him."

The innkeeper paled at this request. Though he hesitated a bit, he could

see he was caught like a sparrow in a snare. At last he returned those
hundred pistoles, too.

What the devil gives, the devil knows how to get back.

"Well, my friend," whispered the dealer once they were outside. "What
do you say? Did I earn that dinner?"

"You certainly did!" replied the fellow, as happy as a little prince. "I'll
be delighted to treat you. But we're going to eat at another inn."

33. The Master Thief

There was once a good woman—oh, *so* good, the very cream of all
good women—but a bit too good, perhaps, and as harmless as a jug
of milk: in short, an awful bore. Maybe it was boredom that did it, but
anyway, for whatever reason, her husband died.

And she with a new baby! Now she gave her whole life to the child,
watching over him, looking after him, and catering to his every whim. She
promised herself she'd feed him so well that he'd grow up into the finest
lad thereabouts.

One day she'd just washed and combed him, covered his head with a
pretty bonnet, and then begun playing with his tiny fingers: "This little
hen laid the egg, this one put it on to boil . . ." Suddenly she saw that his
nails really were rather long. She took up the scissors which hung from
her apron on a chain and without further thought set about cutting them.

Just then, in came her aunt—a good woman too, who knew every old
wives' tale as well as you know your Our Father.

"Jesus and Mary!" she cried. "You're cutting his nails? But is he a year
old?"

"A year? No, not quite. He'll be a year old when the plums ripen."

"God save us! Didn't you know, then? If you cut a baby's nails before he's a year old, you make him turn out a thief."

"A thief! Oh, dear Lord, how awful!"

The mother collapsed, almost fainting, on the bench. Her aunt slapped her palms and rubbed her temples with vinegar till she was more or less herself again.

"A thief! Well, I've done a good job! To think that my son could become a thief!"

"Listen, dear niece: God made thieves, too. Each parish needs one, you see, to teach people not to leave things lying around—just the way each household needs a cat to teach the housewife to keep her cupboards closed!"

"But aunt, I just don't know. I'd rather see my own liver frying in a pan than watch my son turn out a criminal!"

"Ah, but my poor dear, it takes all kinds to make a world."

And it's true: in those days there was one thief per parish, just as there was one blacksmith, one tailor, one carpenter, and one mole catcher. That was his trade. It gave him an honest living and kept him out of trouble.

Still, the poor mother now really had a bee in her bonnet. All she could think of was how her son was now bound to turn out a thief. But by and by she thought of it less. In the end she forgot about it altogether.

The boy grew up nice and straight, a fine lad. In time he was old enough to work in the fields, at the plow, and to sit around the inn on Sundays. He seemed well on his way to being a lad his mother could be proud of.

"My boy," she told him one evening, "you need a trade. Have you thought about one?"

"Yes, mother, and I've made my choice. I'm going to be a master thief."

"Oh, but my boy! You, a thief? It's done me such good to see you grow up so well. Tell me I heard you wrong!"

"No, no, mother, I didn't say just thief, I said *master* thief. You have to be clever all over, sure-footed and sharp-eyed, always quick and alert. You need sense and strength and courage, and all sorts of things like that."

"Oh, but my boy, I don't know! For myself, I'd want nothing to do with such a frightening trade!"

Weeping now, she wiped her eyes on a corner of her apron. Then she went to complain to her aunt and the other village women.

"What an awful day that was, when I cut his nails before he was a year old! Now he wants to be a thief! What saint can I turn to?"

"I know," her aunt replied, "that Saint Spiridion had something to do with thieves—they stole some of his flock. But there's no image of him in our church. Maybe you should appeal instead to Saint Dismas, the Good Thief . . . No, listen, go and talk to our own parish saint: he can handle any problem."

The unhappy mother went to the church, still weeping. "Oh great saint," she prayed, "I have to talk to you about my son. He wants to follow a trade. What trade should he choose?"

"That of master thief, good woman, that of master thief!"

She went home dumbfounded, unable to believe her own ears.

The lad was waiting for her at the door. "So, mother," he greeted her, "what have you got to say? I'll wager you've just been talking to our parish saint. And I already know perfectly well what he told you: I'm to be a master thief!"

Oh yes, he knew, he did! It was he, hidden behind a pillar, who'd taken the trouble to answer for the saint. He'd seen his mother go off to his aunt's, though he never let on. He'd managed to overhear some of their talk. Wherever he went, he always had his eyes and ears about him. And with silent steps he'd slipped into the church. Why, he knew his trade before ever learning it.

"My poor boy," his mother sighed, "you're going to put yourself to such trouble, to end up worth nothing at all!"

But she had to resign herself after all. Her only comfort for now was that he'd not be a thief, but a *master* thief.

It all started when the innkeeper, one of their old neighbors, had to prepare a wedding banquet. Needing a sheep, he remembered that the widow and her son had a very fine herd: fat, pure-bred, and the best for miles around.

When the innkeeper came around, the lad insisted he was in no hurry to sell one of his sheep. Still, the innkeeper offered a good price. They talked it over, bargained, and finally struck a deal. Having counted out the money, the innkeeper had a drink and led the sheep away on a rope.

Out in the woods, he found he had to stop a moment, so he tied the sheep to a tree and went behind a bush. But the lad had trailed him. Up he stole now (oh, he knew how not to make any noise), untied the rope, and made off with the sheep.

When the innkeeper came back for the sheep, it was gone.

"I thought I'd tied it up well enough," he thought to himself. "It must have gotten loose in the woods."

Still, he couldn't prepare that banquet without a sheep. He went back to the widow's.

"Yes, yes, it's me again. You never know what'll happen next. The sheep got away. My boy, you're going to have to sell me another."

"Another? There'll be nothing left of my herd!"

"You can see yourself I've no choice."

"All right, on one condition: if you ever find the first, I'll take it back and refund your money."

So the lad sold him the first sheep again, the very same one, and this time, in fact, got six pennies more. They drank on it and put a rope around the sheep's neck, then the innkeeper led the animal away.

Back in the woods, where he'd stopped before, he suddenly heard a sheep bleating.

"Good heavens, that's my sheep!"

He tied to a tree the one he'd just bought—with a double knot this time—and went looking for the one he'd lost.

Not that he was going to find it, of course, since the bleating came from the lad himself. He chased after the bleats, deeper and deeper into the wood, eagerly looking everywhere. Meanwhile the lad got back to the sheep, untied it, and led it home.

After hunting, searching, rummaging, and beating every bush, the empty-handed innkeeper decided to go back to the tree where he thought the second sheep was waiting.

No more sheep.

"But it was a double knot I tied!" he muttered to himself. "These creatures must be enchanted. Come, I simply can't go home without a sheep!"

Back he went to the widow's.

"Oh no, no," cried the lad, "I'll have no herd left! You're going to lose as many as our priest could bless on the Sunday after Saint-Roch! No, I just don't have any more to sell you!"

The innkeeper put another six pennies into the bargain, and after insisting awhile, got away with his sheep—the same one as always, bought for the third time.

When he reached the same area of the woods, he heard the sound of a struggle, and dull blows.

"It must be my two sheep!" thought he. "They met, and now they're butting their heads together."

Actually, it was the lad. He'd wrapped his wooden shoes in bark, and was hitting them one against the other.

The innkeeper lost no time tying his sheep to a tree, but with three knots this time, and tight ones. Then off he went into the woods, toward the noise. It seemed to keep moving from place to place.

In short, when he got back to the tree, the sheep was gone.

"Well, this time the sheep *can't* have gotten away. There's some devil behind all this. I believe I see who's playing these tricks."

This time he didn't go back to the widow's, but to the prior's.

"Father Prior," he announced, "you have a parishioner who's going to make himself quite a reputation. He'll end up on the gallows if you can't get him to mend his ways."

Father Prior was the local squire's brother: a heavy, gouty man with bulging eyes, who mumbled and wheezed like a bellows. He called the lad before him.

"Well now, what's this I hear? What's this all about? Good news indeed! There's the best of all our women, and her son turns to thieving? So! We can't even trust our families any more? Oh, we're bound for perdition!"

No more alarmed than a sparrow, the lad stood there, turning his hat round and round in his hands.

"Come, Father Prior," he replied, "I'm only going to steal from the rich! And anyway, what can I do? Thievery is my calling!"

The prior went on roughly reproving him.

"Thief! A fine trade! For pity's sake! So, you mean to . . . ? A perfect way to get on in the world! Ah, no, no, no, you rascal!"

His words tumbled out faster and faster.

"Nice work, oh, very nice work! And he thinks he's a master, does he, a master in his line, because he filched what? Some mangy sheep! Big talk, big talk! As though he really *had* pulled off something—as though he'd stolen a wagon, for example, with the two oxen hitched to it!"

"Your wagon and oxen, Father Prior? Fine! It's a challenge I won't forget. I accept!"

Light-hearted as a nestful of finches, he saluted the prior and withdrew without waiting to hear more.

This prior was rich. He had cattle and woods. Not that he gathered his firewood himself. He was too important, too fat, and too ill to do that. Instead he sent his servants. And just then it happened to be time to lay in a store of firewood for the winter.

The lad went to hang himself from a stout branch, so he could be seen from the road—to hang himself carefully, of course, so as not to get hurt. But he certainly *looked* hanged.

Perhaps lots of people had been hanged that year. At least, the two thickheaded, dull-witted servants didn't pay much attention to the body when they noticed it. They just goaded the oxen on.

The lad got himself down and in a trice went to hang himself higher, in a more obvious spot, from a particularly tall tree by a rather steep rock.

"Another one hung! Another one!"

This time they went for a look, walking in under the leafy cover. They had a little trouble getting through. When they came again in sight of the rock, the body was gone.

First they thought they'd gone wrong, and lost the big tree. But no, there was the rock . . .

"Damn, we didn't dream it! We both saw him!"

The lad, meanwhile, was slowly leading away the oxen and the wagon, by one forest path and another. To challenge well given, challenge well met! Bold, lively, and high-spirited as he was, he was always ready to try something new.

"Father Prior will say that was easy, in fact hardly anything. I'll have to do better. I'll have to steal his lard."

All alone there on the path, he laughed just to think about it. His laughter was so cheerful that anyone who'd seen him would have laughed too, without even knowing why.

Father Prior's lard was in his larder. The only way in was through the room where Father Prior always sat. On those rare occasions when he was absent, there was always a manservant in the room, or perhaps his house-keeper. Moreover, this lard was no little chunk you could slip in your sleeve, but a whole carcass' worth, heavy enough to weigh down a big strong man.

For the lad, this was no problem.

For several nights now, the beadle had been hearing noises in the cemetery: sounds of slabs being lifted, and a clatter of coffins.

"Father Prior," he cried, "the demons are up to mischief! They're opening the graves and removing the dead!"

"What? What's this you're saying? Here I'm stuck with this devilish gout, and you're going to start rattling off cock-and-bull stories to me? If I could just go myself I'd show you, I certainly would. Demons? In our cemetery? Not likely! There are no horns or demons out there! There's nothing at all!"

"Nothing at all? I can see well enough how the gravestones are all topsy-turvy! There are demons out there, I tell you, coming to fetch the dead!"

"Yes, yes, yes, and why not the living too, while you're at it? You're just afraid, that's all, afraid. Fear's scrambled your brains!"

The next morning before dawn, after the angelus, the beadle dashed into the priory. He lifted Father Prior in his arms, all the while protesting his humble respect—lifted him and carried him off.

"No, no," cried he, "I won't have it said that I've been telling you cock-and-bull stories! You're going to see, Father Prior, whether or not I've misled you! Since your own feet can't carry you there, let mine do it for you!"

Off he staggered with his burden, among the crosses, the rosebushes, and the nettles. The prior pricked up his ears because there was quite a racket going on: a sound as of bumped coffins and falling gravestones.

Suddenly there was a cackle of laughter in the dark, and a strange falsetto voice cried out, "Aha, you've brought me a living one! Is he nice and fat?"

"Fat or thin, take him!" stammered the beadle. He dropped Father Prior among the thorns and ivy, and took to his heels as though all the demons in Hell were after him.

The prior didn't mean to be afraid. It was his gout that made him think how much nicer it would have been to be sitting now at home, by the fire. His feet caught in all those heaved-up slabs, those leaning crosses, those creeping ivy tendrils and hummocks of grass. He tried to hurry, got up, stumbled again, then thought he was being seized and carried away. His screams for help brought his servants and housekeeper running.

Meanwhile, the lad got into the priory, loaded the lard on his back, and made off.

After that he became a master thief from head to toe, just as sly as he was saucy. Salamis and jars of oil, fat geese and fine shirts, clothes and sheep, mules and wagons—nothing was too hot for him, or too heavy. The rascal got his hands on everything, thinking up more tricks than there are days in the year.

Once, he laid a bet with the richest commoner in the county that he'd steal all the bread from the fellow's bakehouse, right out of the oven. The man had his cowherds stand guard, rifle in hand, before the iron door. Our hero, meanwhile, slipped behind the building, dislodged two stones, and raked out the loaves with a hay hook.

It would take a century of Sundays to tell all his exploits!

"My poor boy," said his mother, "if you used to good purpose a quarter of what you put into your escapades—yes, a quarter of your bright ideas and your trouble, your labor, and your cudgeling of your brains—you'd now be the richest man in the parish. Don't you at least realize that ill-gotten gains bring no profit? If you don't, then look: what do you do with the things you steal from hither and yon? You drink them up at the tavern, so as to strut and look big, with hangers-on who aren't even grateful. Or else you give them away to beggars who drink them up the same way. Everything slips away. In the end, all this pretty money you work so hard to get just goes down the drain."

She tried to bring him back to the straight and narrow with her talk. She'd make him a sermon like that any evening she managed to back him into some corner, to sew a button back on his pants. But he ran from her homilies as a cat runs from water. He just laid on his mischief thicker than ever.

The village squire had taken all this foolishness quite lightly. The tricks amused him, especially the ones that had been played on his brother the prior. So when his own bread, pigs, calves, wine, geese, and furnishings started disappearing, he didn't want to look angry right away.

He summoned the lad and looked him over.

"So," he said, "now you're going to steal from *me*? You'll say you're a thief, and that that's your trade. All right. But are you really the master thief I hear you are? Listen, if you manage to make off with my horse, the horse is yours, and a thousand crowns too. Pull it off any way you want, it's up to you. But the horse will be guarded. I give you fair warning. If you fail, I'll make a man of you! That's it. Do you understand me?"

"Yes, sir," said the lad, laughing. "I understand you. And I give you fair warning too. Tomorrow's the day of Saint Spiridion: a good day for good work. So I'll make off with your horse tonight. Yes, this very night."

He bowed and took his leave.

At nightfall, the squire went to his stable and gave all the orders needed. He thought a lot of that horse, with its glossy coat and its proud bearing—a horse more spirited than a falcon, and gentler than a white, woolly lamb. He didn't think he'd find another like him from here to Paris.

"Tie a rope to his tail, and another to each side of his bridle!"

All three of his manservants were dancing attendance on him, open-mouthed, awaiting his instructions.

"There! Each of you is to hold on to the horse by one of these ropes, and myself, I'll sit astride him. Now let your master thief come!"

The squire got up and settled himself in the saddle, sword at his side and pistols in his belt.

Midnight passed, and the wee hours came. After all that time, the squire twice nearly tumbled to the ground. His head kept dropping onto his horse's neck.

A little before three o'clock he dismounted, so as to make sure that the third time, he didn't simply fall all the way off.

"Our master thief won't come," he declared. "And anyway, if he does, I want to be fresh to receive him. I'll take a nap in the straw. Just five minutes! Then it'll be your turn. Meanwhile, look sharp! There are three of you to keep your eyes open, and I daresay that'll be enough!"

He stretched out full length on the straw, and instantly fell asleep.

"Keep your eyes open!"—that's easy enough to say. The three servants' eyes kept closing in spite of all their efforts. The candle was smoking in the horn lantern, but none of them could even get up the energy to go and snuff it. The cock didn't seem ready yet to crow in the new day, and the squire's five minutes went on and on and on. Apparently he was not about to relieve their confounded watch.

Finally the servant on the tail rope felt someone take him by the arm.

"I've had my nap," the squire whispered to him. "I'll get back up in the saddle. It's your turn to sleep. For safety's sake I'll let out the rope a bit. Keep it wrapped around your wrist."

Next came the turn of the servant on the right to be allowed to sleep, then of the servant on the left. All three slept with a clear conscience, as soundly as badgers. The ropes were wound dutifully around their arms.

Actually, though, the ropes were tied only to a bar of the feed rack, because the so-called squire, who'd just spoken to them in their master's clothing, was none other than the thief himself.

Quieter than a fly on a windowpane, and more agile than a cat, the crafty lad led the horse very, very gently out into the courtyard, then mounted it and galloped off into the night. Just try and catch him now!

Suddenly the lantern went out, and the squire woke up.

"Are you awake, my men?" he thundered.

"Yes, master, we're awake, of course we are!" cried all three after a pause.

"Have you still got hold of the horse?"

"Yes, master, we do!" Each one pulled on his rope. The horse couldn't possibly have moved!

"Very good! Anyway, dawn can't be far off. Let's all stay awake, and I'll get back in the saddle with my pair of double-barreled pistols. Aha, let him come, the master thief! We'll wash his hair for him with lead!"

He tried to get back on, but instead got all tangled up in the ropes. He bumped his shoulder on the side of the stall and his head on the feed rack, and swore, and spouted fire—because, in truth, he couldn't find the horse.

"Master, master!" called his servants. "The horse can't possibly be gone! We can feel it perfectly well when we pull on the ropes! All you have to do is find the stirrup!"

But the squire could find neither stirrup nor horse. He gripped his pistols, and nearly fired them at random into the darkness. He had to strike the flint and light the lantern again.

Then they untangled the ropes, and untangled too, pretty well, the trick the thief had played on them. But the horse and his rider were far away, and galloping still.

The squire decided to laugh it off and to pay the thousand crowns. That was the agreement.

"Yes, yes," said he to the lad, "you got away with it because we fell asleep. But I won't say you're a master thief till you wake me up as you do it! Come and take the sheet out from under us, my wife and me, while we're lying in bed. I warn you, she's a light sleeper. You'll have a thousand crowns if you pull it off, and the gallows if you don't. I'll have you hanged from the elm in the village square!"

"And I warn you too, sir," replied the lad respectfully, smiling as always. "A challenge is a challenge. If that's your pleasure, I'll steal your sheet tonight. Yes, this very night."

They bowed to each other. Then, to be in better shape for his vigil, the squire plopped down on a bed and went straight to sleep. He could sleep in peace. After all, what did he have to lose? Just a sheet and a thousand crowns.

The master thief, though, didn't sleep. He had his *life* to lose. Maybe his throat was even a little dry. Stealing the sheet out from under a couple is quite a trick. He had a boy's high spirits, though, and was as daring and mischievous as he could be.

"God willing," thought he, "perhaps I'll manage it after all! I see more or less the right gambit. The trouble is, though, that I don't quite know how these lords talk to their wives. I'll say, 'Move over, my lady,' and I'll push her toward the wall while I pull the sheet toward me. But what if those aren't the right words? Well, whatever will be, will be. You can never foresee everything. You have to know how to plan and plan, and then seize your chance as best you can."

Evening came, and then night. The squire got in bed next to his wife, but stayed sitting up. Now and again he felt the pair of double-barreled pistols that lay before him on the counterpane.

The moon was almost full, and hardly a cloud dimmed its light.

"He insisted on tonight, just to show off. Now the moon's going to hinder him. For myself, I'm fresh and well rested. The only way he can come in is by the window, and I'm sure to spot him. How could he possibly get this sheet away from me? Oh well, that's his problem. If he doesn't, then tomorrow he'll hang!"

All at once the squire saw him. There was a head at the window, nodding from left to right. It was only a glimpse. The head instantly disappeared.

It would be back, though. The squire could hear him: he'd climbed the wall and was now getting ready. He cocked his pistols. Then the head reappeared, this time for good.

The squire fired twice from each hand: four shots that made just one clap of thunder. The windowpanes shattered. There were sounds of glass and a body falling, and an awful scream.

No doubt it stuns you for a while, to actually kill someone.

"I'd much rather have had him hanged," said the horrified squire aloud. "But I got him with four bullets in the head. He can't have suffered.

"He wasn't a scoundrel, really, just a braggart," the squire went on, jumping out of bed. "I'm going to look after the body, my dear."

He lit the candle, put on his trousers, and dashed down the stairs. His wife, meanwhile, ever since those four pistol shots, was trembing all over, at the bottom of their still-shaking bed.

Hardly a minute later the squire rushed back in, his nightshirt and trousers pale in the moonlight.

"I killed him, all right! He asked for it, the poor fellow! The best thing is for me to bury him myself at the bottom of the garden. Quick, my lady, give me that sheet."

He spoke in a sort of stifled voice, came to the bedside, busied himself frantically like someone quite out of his mind, grabbed the sheet, and pulled.

"But dear," his wife protested, "I'll have you brought another! I'll call the maid."

"Absolutely not! You won't call anyone. We'll keep it a secret. He's dead, and I'm burying him. Not a word!"

He threw the sheet over his arm and vanished down the stairs. Hardly had he reached the bottom when his wife heard him charging up again. In he burst, so fast that the candle flame was flickering hither and yon, though he was sheltering it with his hand.

"A fake body, my dear, a fake body!"

"What, dear? What on earth do you mean?"

"I mean that body wasn't real, it was just stuck up in front of the window on the end of a pole. The thing was only clothes and straw. What do you suppose he's up to?"

"But the sheet, dear! What did you do with the sheet?"

"What sheet? What sheet are you talking about?"

"Why, the one you just took!"

Finally she understood: the squire who'd come a moment ago, and who'd taken away the sheet, was not really the squire at all, but the master thief.

"So I won't be able to have him hanged after all! And I owe him another thousand crowns. Well, I'm not playing any more games with *him*."

The squire would have liked to keep this latest mishap a secret, but the four pistol shots had made too much noise. That very dawn, people began asking each other what had happened. And the master thief, with his sheet flapping in the wind like a flag, was hardly going to be discreet about his exploit.

The squire was eating his breakfast soup, bowl in hand before the kitchen hearth, when he saw his brother, the big fat prior, waddle heavily in.

"Well, there you are!" snapped the prior. "And having breakfast, too! Swallowing your losses, perhaps? What's this I hear, brother? What have you got to say for yourself? Here you're our village squire, and you let yourself be bamboozled by a local burglar? Congratulations! You certainly know how to uphold the honor of our house!"

"Very kind of you, brother, I'm sure, to read me a sermon," the squire replied. "But it seems to me I've heard stories of pilfered lard, and of a wagon stolen along with its oxen."

"What's this about a wagon and lard? That was my men and my housekeeper! As for myself, for heaven's sake," the prior continued, almost incoherent with rage, "as for myself, I look after my things! Yes, my money's in my ironbound chest, with a lock so strong that the only way to open it is to use my key! And just look: here the key is, around my neck on a chain, and I have it on me night and day. That's how to secure what you have! Master thief, bah! The rascal's no threat to *me!*"

"Look out, brother! He may get you one day!"

"Let him try! And you, brother, if you'd followed my example, you wouldn't be the laughingstock of the whole countryside!"

The squire went back to his breakfast, poured a glass of wine into the soup, and drank it without a word.

But when Father Prior had gone, and a few moments later the master thief himself was announced, the squire shook himself like a dog stepping out of a stream.

"Here are your thousand crowns," said he. "Let's not talk any more about tonight. But you never get two without a third. We'll have to have a third test. My brother the prior has all his money in a chest, and the key to the chest hangs on a chain around his neck. He's not like me: he loves that money about as much as his own salvation. And I'm warning you. You know what to expect if you fail. You'll hang from that tree on the square, and that'll be the end of you!"

"I give you fair warning too, sir," replied the lad as he took his leave, livelier than ever. And he added with a little laugh, "I'll take all your brother's money tonight. And I mean *all!* This very night!"

Perhaps he could tell the weather would favor his little maneuver. Or perhaps it's just that luck was with him. Yes, luck! Some are lucky, others not.

Anyway, that evening the weather turned blackly threatening, and the storm which followed during the night was worse than anyone had expected. Thunderclaps shook the earth. In fact this same night another thief got himself into trouble—not a master thief, just a poor country burglar who thought he had the weather on his side. Off he ran to steal the wool off the squire's sheep. But all the thunder frightened him so badly that he lost his head, got into the pigsty, and, groping around with his big scissors, sheared the porkers' back hair instead: a pretty skimpy take. As the thunder roared louder than ever, he sighed, "So much noise for so little wool!"

But to get back to the story. It was all bolts of dazzling lightning and crashes of deafening thunder—a witches' Sabbath where God himself couldn't get in a word edgewise, and a worse rumpus than at Babel, the time the tower fell down. Father Prior couldn't sleep any more than anyone else.

Suddenly, in the midst of this frightful racket, he heard the bells. There are bells people ring during a storm, because of their bright sound which parts the clouds and wards off hail and lightning. But these bells were never used for anything like that. So who was ringing them?

Father Prior was so curious and alarmed that, despite his gout, he got up, put on his cassock, and, puffing and groaning, shuffled off to the chapel.

He was hardly inside when a voice addressed him from on high. Up in the gallery appeared a figure with a long beard, and a cassock just like his.

"Prior, prior, I was once, like you, the prior of this priory, oh, so long, long ago! Do you hear the thunder? The end of the world is at hand. And it's only proper, since you're the prior, that you should be let into paradise before the rabble from all these parishes round about. I've been allowed to come and get you. There's just one little thing to settle first."

"I'm much obliged to you, good prior, and very grateful for your kindness! The end of the world! Paradise! But what is there to settle first? What can it be?"

"A little offering, and a little penance. Are you prepared to follow me?"

"Oh yes, good prior, certainly! Quite prepared! Thank you so much for your trouble!"

"Gather up what you need, then, and go quickly to fetch your offering."

Puffing louder than ever, the prior struggled back to his house. His housekeeper too was up, her hands clasped in prayer.

"Oh, Father Prior, it's like the end of the world!"

"It *is* the end of the world! Why, Jeannette, one of my predecessors has come for me. I'm getting my money, and in a minute I'll be off with him to Paradise."

"But then, Father Prior, you ought surely to give me my wages. All these years I've been with you, and asked for nothing!"

"Your wages! But you see . . . Good heavens, they add up to quite a bit. Well, all right, since the world's ending, come and count out what I owe you!"

Once the housekeeper had her wages, the prior plopped the other moneybags into his skirts like a girl gathering apples.

"Prior, prior, what are you doing?" cried the predecessor, now suddenly in the room. "I see the gold isn't all there! Put all the bags, including that one you gave the housekeeper, straight back into the chest! I can't take you you-know-where if you don't."

Father Prior went back to Jeannette.

"*Now*, Jeannette!" he urged her. "Because, you see, Saint Peter won't let me by if all the money in the priory isn't in the chest. You *will* give the money back, won't you?"

"If I have to so you can get into Paradise, well, all right, Father Prior, I will!"

She put the bag back with the others.

"Leave it all in the chest," ordered the former prior. "Just give me the key. Then quickly, quickly, let's be off! You'll do your penance on the way. It'll be taken off your time in Purgatory. Now, hurry! Get into this sack!"

The former prior—you know who he was—hustled Father Prior into the sack and dragged him off up slopes, through the courtyard, by shortcuts, and down the road! The worst part was getting to the dovecote at the top of the castle tower, bump, bump, up the stairs. Ouch, my head, my butt, my poor, poor back! Father Prior couldn't help moaning and groaning.

"Yes, yes, it's your penance! Well, here we are. But you still—it's the rest of the penance, you see—you still have to spend the night in the sack."

"The whole night? And then I'll be free?"

"Yes, free tomorrow morning. Meanwhile, listen to all these winged beings fluttering around you!"

You really have to be thick, you know, you really do . . .

"My poor boy," cried the lad's mother when she found out, "the more you do, the deeper the hole you dig for yourself. Your tongue's going to rot, with all your lies."

She put on her spectacles, looked him in the eye, nodded three times, and began her sermon.

"Live well, my poor boy, and you'll *be* well. Keep to the straight path, and just walk on, straight before you . . ."

Next came the warning, the complaints, and the laments. "The police

. . . Oh, the time is coming . . . You'll get yourself killed . . . What you really ought to do is get married . . ." She knew *such* a nice girl . . .

But he was already out the door.

So the mischief and escapades went on, but not very long. One day the word spread that the master thief had been killed by the taxmen:

> *Going through the toll one day,*
> *The taxmen laid their hands on me . . .*

Killed, or all but killed. People said they'd brought him back to his mother that night with three bullets in him. He died Sunday evening, and was buried on Monday.

The villagers were rather surprised at how well his mother took his death. But perhaps, in a way, she could rest easy now. As long as her boy was alive, *she* was half dead, wondering whether he'd be ambushed one night and shot, or hung high from the gallows one day in the village square. At any rate, he was bound to come to a bad end. So what kind of life was it for her, to live in terror like a pig that feels Christmas coming? I ask you. She may have mourned, but perhaps his death was her deliverance.

Still, what a blow . . .

Then the rumor started up: the master thief was dead only for the benefit of the police. His coffin, out in the cemetery, had nothing in it but a log and some straw. The bullets hadn't killed him forever. He'd get over it in the end, and his mother's prayers would do him good.

But even when he was better, he had to get out of the village, and that's certainly a kind of death.

Later on, it turned out he was married. That was the last anyone heard. A married man and a hanged man are much the same: there's nothing to say about either. He mended his ways.

People did say, though, much, much later, that after his good kind mother died, he—now good and kind himself, and a warden of his parish—founded a confraternity: the Confraternity of the Good Thief.

> *The sun's sinking,*
> *The devil's choking:*
> *God be blessed,*
> *And the devil cursed!*

34. The Fat Mistress of the Inn

There was once a girl who'd have liked to get married—not that she was the only one in France who wished that! She wanted to get married and run an inn. That was her dream.

One Christmas Eve, in cold weather but without snow, she happened to go into the woods—yes, into the woods, all alone, to pick up wood for the fire. This was over by Planfoy, that famous hill near Saint-Etienne. There was a forest there in those days. So there she was, all bent over, working from thicket to thicket, busily putting together her bundle of wood.

Suddenly she heard a great crashing of branches, and voices, and screams! It was robbers attacking a traveler. They fell on him and in a flash had seized his bag, beaten him, and driven him off. The poor fellow fled as best he could.

The girl, as quiet as a mouse, was cowering behind some spruce trees. As long as she heard cries, she didn't dare peek out; but eventually she sneaked a look. The robbers were examining their booty. They knelt before a spread-out coat, and emptied onto it a bag of silver coins! Then they counted and recounted, talked and argued, till they got into a fight and drew their knives. One wanted to share out the money, but another insisted it would be too dangerous to carry that much silver around on them. Finally, they lifted a clump of moss under an oak tree, dug a hole with their knives, stuffed in the bag, trampled the earth down, and put back the moss. You couldn't see a thing.

Next, they gathered up their things and went away to seek another fortune. Perhaps they took care to mark a tree from time to time, with a secret mark known to them alone.

For a good while the girl didn't even look up. Then she made her decision. She was clever, that one.

"What if one of the robbers comes back," she wondered, "to rob the other two? Oh well, nothing ventured, nothing gained!"

She dug at the earth with the toe of her clog, and got away quickly with the bag. When the three robbers came back for it, they must have murdered each other on the spot.

Anyway, the girl got married. A girl has only to go to seven weddings. After the seventh she finds a husband—unless she's *really* unlucky. But when she's got a dowry of thirty thousand francs, just one wedding may do. You make friends, with that much money! Enthusiastic and determined as this girl was, her luck stayed with her. So she got married, and built an inn by the road, at the very spot where the robbers had stopped the traveler. The wagon and cattle drivers found there the refreshment they needed on their way up the hill. And in those days there were big fairs. That was the age of the cattle dealer. Those folk liked good service. The inn became famous, and got as big as the hostess grew fat. She'd always been as plump and pink as an apple, anyway. With time, she became as round as a demijohn and as ruddy as a peony; but she still loved a good time, good company, laughter, fine food, and witty talk.

One Christmas Eve she was peeling chestnuts into her apron, to go with the turkey for the feast to follow the midnight mass, when a traveler came in and sat down by the fire—a merchant of some sort, with big twill gaiters. He looked like a good man, but not a rich one. The two chatted about weather and business.

"It was just twenty-five years ago," the man said, "that I last came by this way. I'm glad to find your inn here now. Yes indeed, my good mistress, I was dealing in lace then. I was on my way to stock up in the mountains. And would you believe it? Right on this spot I was stopped by robbers. Oh, I remember it well enough! They took everything I had: a bag full of thirty thousand francs!"

The woman looked up, stared at him, nearly spoke, then hesitated. She looked back down at the chestnuts for the feast. Then, suddenly, she made her decision, and looked him straight in the eye.

"And if you got your money back, would you demand the interest?"

This time it was his turn to stare at her, dumbfounded.

"Goodness, no! Those thirty thousand francs . . . I never managed to get back on my feet after that. And now I'm getting old, it would be so wonderful to recover that money that I'd gladly give half to whoever brought me the bag!"

Then she told him the whole story: what she'd seen and what she'd done. And right there she gave him back his thirty thousand francs—not the same coins, obviously, but thirty thousand francs in gold louis. She kept nothing for herself. And there he was, almost an old man, nearly destitute, seeing his thirty thousand francs fall on him like that, out of the sky! He'd be comfortable now, and have all he needed for his old age! Imagine! Just imagine!

"Whenever you come through here," she promised him, "you'll have your room and board, and it won't cost you a penny. Even if it's in October

or November that you come by, I'll always have a fat goose with chestnuts for you!"

They say that inn is still there on the Planfoy hill.

What? You seem to be tickled by what the innkeeper woman said first—about the interest she didn't want getting in the way of her nicely returning the whole amount. She must have been one of those impressive women who know how to sail their own ship . . .

Now what? You think she should have looked a bit earlier for the owner of the bag? But in those days, long ago, she couldn't advertise it in the papers! And the police! Oh, everyone knows about the police! Those thirty thousand francs would have all gone for costs and legal fees. You say she took it a bit far, keeping that money herself for twenty-five years. The polite name *you'd* give that is theft.

Well, later on, the fat innkeeper woman told how tempted she'd been to keep her mouth shut! But it was Christmas Eve, and the weather was just the same as twenty-five years earlier—cold, but without snow. The bells were about to ring for the midnight mass. "If you don't speak up," she told herself, "you'll be no better than those robbers!" So she did speak up. She went and got the bag, and counted out the gold louis.

She said she'd never had such a wonderful Christmas feast.

But you still blame her for having used the money, and then for having given it back only because it was Christmas and the bells were ringing? Go on! Why be so fussy? So what if it *was* theft? Our Lord on Calvary never had a word of respect or comfort from anyone there—not the judges, the lawyers, the bailiffs, the scribes, or anyone else great or small, on foot or on horseback—except from a thief.

Here I'm telling you all this, but I'm with you in believing that you're rich if you're honest and disapprove of underhandedness in others!

35. Tarnagas and His Priest

There lived at Combegrasse, long, long ago, a fellow named Tarnagas. He was no saint. The priest must have put a grain too much salt on his tongue the day he was baptized. And after that, what a drinker! A pillar of the pub, he was, a party-chaser, and a lush to gulp down a whole kingdom—one of those fellows who, as they say, would empty a whole house out the window. On top of that he was as sly as a fox, as mean as an old witch, and as great a scamp as the devil in person.

All he had was an old cow called Pije, so skinny her ribs stood out under her skin like the rings on a barrel. Her manger was out of hay, and his cupboard was out of bread for the children.

"I wouldn't mind selling our Pije," said he one evening to his wife, scratching his ear. "What bothers me, though, is the idea of leading her to the fair. She's so old, skinny, and broken-down that people'll just laugh."

"Well, the first thing, you see . . ." began his wife, a good, pious woman. "Come, since you can't feed Pije any longer, give her to the poor."

"Give her away? You're crazy!"

"It'd make up for what you've taken a bit too lightly, here and there. Why just last Sunday, our priest was saying, 'Who gives to the poor, lends to God.' "

"Yes, but when does God make good on your loan? I'd like to see the priest put a due date on it!"

He twisted his hat around, shrugged his shoulders, and went back to the stable for another look at Pije. No, she certainly wasn't fat! Then he headed for the tavern.

His wife stared at the fire, sighed, and gave the children one last crust she'd saved. Then she too went to the stable for a look at Pije, tied up there by one horn. Next, well, she led Pije away, straight to a pauper woman called Catinou. Catinou lived behind the tangle of willows and grasses along the pond. You have to realize that Tarnagas' wife was a bit upset—enough that she didn't realize she'd left the stable door open.

Back home again, she put the children to bed, then sat down by the fire to say her prayers and wait for her husband. Shivers ran up and down her back at the thought of what Tarnagas would do when he found out she'd given the cow away.

Hour after hour went by. The weather turned threatening. Far off, you could hear the distant rumble of thunder.

At last, flushed and swaggering, Tarnagas came home.

"Done!" he shouted from the door. "I've sold our Pije—sold her to the village butcher. He'll be here for her tomorrow morning."

He clinked the coins together in his pocket.

Oh heavens! Oh sweet Mother Mary! The poor woman, crouching by the fire, squinched down a little further on her heels. How was she going to tell him? And she just couldn't go and take the cow back from Catinou over by the pond.

> You give it first,
> Then take it back:
> Why, you're accursed,
> And your heart is black!

"Now, woman, to bed! There's a storm coming, and from a bad direction, too. Who knows what this weather'll bring? Let's go to sleep and let tomorrow come."

"You go to bed, Tarnagas. I must finish saying my prayers."

So off he went. She stayed by the fire, shivering, mumbling, dozing off, then starting awake, fretting even in her dreams about what would happen the next morning when the butcher came and Tarnagas found the stable empty.

Meanwhile the storm broke. Thunder crashed, rain fell in sheets, and the winds warred with each other, as though all the devils from hell were roaming about, turning the countryside upside down. And there she was, poor thing, still shaking and praying. She almost wished a bolt from the sky would blast the house, Tarnagas, the children, and herself.

Just before dawn, cowering there against the side of the fireplace, she at last slumped forward and fell sound asleep.

Laughter suddenly woke her. She opened her eyes wide. There was Tarnagas right in front of her, apparently bubbling over with good humor. In fact, he was doubled up with mirth.

"Well, God's played a good one on us this time! Pije is gone!"

Yes, he was as merry as an oriole that's found a cherry. His wife just stared at him, speechless. For all she knew she was still dreaming.

"That's right, wife, Pije is gone! But in her place we've two new cows—fat ones."

"Two fat cows?" she murmured, getting up. "Whose are they?"

"Whose do you *think* they are? They're ours, of course! Didn't you tell me God would repay us if we gave Pije away? Our Pije took off to Catinou by the pond—people saw her there this morning—and God repaid us by sending us these two cows!"

All at once he turned around and stopped short. The village priest was coming.

"Good day, my friends. Tarnagas, I'm looking for my cows. Last night lightning struck my big poplar tree. They got frightened and jumped the fence. You haven't seen them, by any chance?"

"Your cows, Father?"

"They can't be far away."

"All we've got here is the cattle God gave us."

"Fine, I'll look somewhere else. See you later, Tarnagas."

Out the door he went, with his little dog behind him.

"Listen, Tarnagas," said the wife from her bit of shade, "you're setting out down a bad path. Those two cows in the stable are Father's. Take them back to him this minute."

"Those cows are the ones God sent us. It'd be an insult to Him not to keep them."

"You should shrivel up with pure shame! Club me over the head if you want, but I'm going over to tell Father the truth!"

"What in the world? God's obviously gotten mixed up in this business, and now you want to go against Him? There's no more faith in this world! Nothing but pettiness, everywhere! Ah, it's true, as my uncle used to say:

> A stirrup, this morality
> Each gets to fit his foot so neatly!

"Twist things however you want. I'm going straight to Father's house."

"Go ahead, woman, go ahead! But the cows are in *my* stable, and that makes them mine. This stool can stab me to death before I'll give them back! The butcher's coming this morning, or one of these mornings. It wouldn't be right of me not to let him have one, since he's already paid me a deposit. But just a minute: these two cows are both fatter than Pije. He'll have to pay me extra!"

His wife said nothing more, but she did go to find the priest; and she told him quite frankly what was going on. That very day, the priest wrote a letter of complaint to the bailiff. The bailiff summoned Tarnagas to court the following Monday.

On Sunday morning, on the way out of church, Father spotted Tarnagas and drew him aside.

"Come, Tarnagas, my friend," said he, "you know perfectly well those cows are mine. Make Satan blush now, and admit it!"

"Father, you've put this affair in the judge's hands. He'll judge it."

"But it's not very nice to see one good Christian suing another."

"You're right there, Father. More right than you think, in fact. Tomorrow you're going to embarrass me. Look at this old smock of mine, the way it's falling to pieces. And my breeches, patched with bits from every parish for miles around. How could I not be embarrassed in town, before the lord bailiff? Say, *you're* the one who's dragging me there. How about at least lending me your late father's suit?"

"All right, Tarnagas, come and get it. And I hope tomorrow you'll give me back my cows!"

The next day Tarnagas went to court, as cocky as a newlywed, in the priest's father's suit.

The priest made his complaint, and the bailiff asked Tarnagas what he had to say.

"Well, you see, Your Honor, our priest is a good fellow and all, but he always claims everything belong to *him*. Look," said he, lowering his voice and speaking into the bailiff's ear, "let's make a wager. Ask him if this suit I have on isn't his, and see what he says."

The bailiff asked the question.

"Absolutely, absolutely," replied the priest. "That suit certainly *is* mine. It came down to me from my late father," he added, not quite so loudly. "I lent it to Tarnagas for the day."

"That will be all," said the bailiff, without waiting to hear more. "Case dismissed."

Now Tarnagas was saucier than ever. Still, he couldn't take possession of the priest's cows right out in front of everyone in the village, or lead them to his pasture, or hitch them up to his wagon. Besides, he had a mind to celebrate his victory in court. So, ready as he always was to fry up any meat or fish, he didn't even wait for the butcher. He killed one of the cows and began feasting.

Word gets around in a village. The priest found out about it. He soon learned too that the Tarnagas children were reciting a certain prayer their father had taught them. That same day he met the youngest running about on the square with a paper pinwheel.

"Well, my boy," said the priest, "I hear your father's taught you a nice little prayer to recite after dinner by way of grace. You'd have had some hazelnuts if you'd recited it for me, but I'm sure you're too little to know it."

"I know the prayer just as well as my brothers and sisters."

"Well then, you'll have your hazelnuts after all. How does it go?"

> We give thanks, Lord, each lad and lass,
> To our priest of Combegrasse:
> Having now downed quite a few
> Bowls of broth and good rich stew,
> Praise God and His cow!

"Oh, you *do* say it nicely, and what a clever prayer it is! Why, I'd like *everyone* to hear you. On Sunday (now, don't tell anyone) you'll come up into the pulpit with me and recite it for the edification of the whole parish. Yes, you will, my boy! And I'll give you a franc."

Delighted, the little boy ran off. He couldn't keep this to himself, though. He went out to his father in the yard, and told him everything.

"Aha," thought Tarnagas, running his hand over his hair, "our priest has it in for me, no doubt about it. Just look at that! And my wife *did* take him back the other cow. The first, well, yes, the first is eaten, and he oughtn't to keep on bringing her up. As for his late father's suit, as far as I can see, the judge recognized it as belonging to me. And now he wants to shame me in front of the whole parish! But I'll make him up a pretty little posy that'll teach him some manners."

The boy was tugging at his jacket. "Can I, daddy, can I? He promised me a franc!"

"Why, you snippet, he'll give you *two* francs if you do it nicely. Let's hear you say it."

"Well, it goes like this."

> *We give thanks, Lord, each lad and lass,*
> *To our priest of Combegrasse:*
> *Having now downed quite a few*
> *Bowls of broth and good rich stew,*
> *Praise God and His cow!*

"Right. But just think about it, now. You don't talk about broth and stew from the pulpit, except in the pastoral letter for Lent. Why, you'd have the whole parish laughing! No, no, we'll fix up this prayer better, so everyone likes it."

On Sunday, the priest climbed up into the pulpit hand-in-hand with the little boy.

"My brothers," he declared, "you certainly know what's been going on lately in the parish. I wouldn't dare even speak of it myself. But listen now to the boy. Listen carefully! For truth issues from the mouths of babes; and in the end, you see, the truth will out!"

Then the little scamp, perched on a stool, recited in ringing tones:

> *We give thanks, Lord, each lad and lass,*
> *To our priest of Combegrasse.*
> *The women went and told him this:*
> *"Come, Father, now give us a kiss!*
> *After Easter, the plump, sleek ones,*
> *And before, the ugly, thin ones!"*

Of course everyone was all ears, after what the priest had said. People were wondering what it was that he didn't dare say himself, and that the boy was going to say for him. When the women heard what Father was accusing them of, and what he was asking their husbands to believe, well, they rose up in revolt, with cries of rage!

Father only just escaped to the sacristy before they hurled themselves against the door, shaking it, battering at it, and egging each other on to ever fiercer attacks. Their anger was mounting. The poor priest could already see himself torn to pieces by the maddened women of his parish.

Somehow or other he'd taken the boy along on his flight.

"Quick, quick, boy, out this little window! Run to your dad! He's the only one—the scoundrel!—who can get me out of here. Tell him he can have my second cow if he'll just come and save me from these women!"

Tarnagas got there right away, and scrambled in through the window to join the priest. They struck their deal.

"The cow's mine, right? Fine. Shake on it."

They shook. He took the priest on his back, and opened the door.

The women charged. Each was brandishing some sort of stick, or at least her wooden clog.

"Here he is!" cried Tarnagas. "Let the most fickle strike first!"

Goton, who already had her clog raised, fell back a step.

"All right, then, Madelon, come on up! He's all yours!"

"You gutter-mouth, who are *you*, you filth, to dare insult me?"

"Oh, don't I know you, you floozy, you painted woman!"

Nanon and Nicole, Perrette and Catin got and gave the same. The frenzied women fought under the square's three elm trees, with shrieks and insults, flying sticks, and a hail of stones. They were grabbing at each other's hair, ripping and scratching. As the cats fled, the dogs dashed up, yapping, then howling through the din of battle when they too got hit.

Meanwhile Tarnagas managed to sneak away, so that Father escaped more or less safe and sound. That evening, however, Father went to ask Monsignor for another parish.

So Tarnagas got the priest's second cow, and ate her as he had the first. Just to make the party complete, he emptied so many bottles that he ended up under the table.

His wife put him to bed, then gazed a long time at him. Suddenly she had an idea.

While he was snoring, dead-drunk, she sewed him into the sheet the way they do a corpse. Next, she took hold of the broom and beat him. She whaled away at him just as she might have pounded a dirty shirt on the laundry stone by the pond.

"You black pig," she cried, "you disgusting pig! You're going to mind me for once!"

Yes, that day she collected everything Tarnagas owed her. And from that day on, she was on top. She got him to listen to her, and obey her.

They say that after that he was always on his best behavior around her. Not that she changed him, of course. He was the same as ever: as greedy as a piglet and as lazy as a slug. But the years quieted him down a bit, with the help of some whacks from the broom. It wasn't as much fun for him, perhaps, but at least he saw old age.

36. Just the Time to Pay Back a Debt

There were once three merchants—cloth merchants, that is—named Eatmorn, Goodpocket, and Whitefat. They planned to buy tow at Auzelles. The hemp there isn't as fine as in Limagne, but it's cheaper; and they felt they needed some in their cloth, the way you need a basket of wild apples in your cider. They started out all together, so as to feel more secure on the way.

But the robbers must have been tipped off by their spies. Down below the hill, the merchants suddenly saw four strong, bearded men burst out in front of them and seize their horses' bridles. There were others in the brush, drawing a bead on them with their rifles. Resistance was out of the question. Obediently, the three merchants dismounted and put their hands in the air. Eatmorn and Goodpocket were robbed forthwith. They had their pockets turned inside out and every seam of their clothing felt through.

Meanwhile Whitefat, poor old Whitefat, was trembling all over, waving his arms, and groaning miserably.

"Oh please," said he finally, "please! It's my rheumatism, you know . . . Do let me put my arms down! I just can't bear it."

The chief robber looked him over and decided the fellow wasn't going to make any trouble.

"Oh, all right, put 'em down if you want, you old wreck. Go ahead, put down your arms."

Whitefat did so, took his purse from his pocket, and went to put it in Goodpocket's hand.

"Here you are, Goodpocket, here you are! You remember I borrowed a hundred crowns off you at the big fair in Clermont? Well, I'm returning them with interest. Now we're even. And I've got witnesses!"

37. Dad, Hanged

There was once a boy up in the hills there, a pretty thickheaded sort. Oh yes, very clever he was—clever enough to bury a donkey and leave its tail sticking out.

In winter, he hired himself out down on the plain, carding hemp.

The first Sunday in Advent, on the way out from mass, he met a neighbor of his from home—an almanac peddler named Ambroise.

"Good thing I ran into you," said Ambroise. "I've got some news. The police have been up to your place. Lately they've been finding travelers face down in the grass, at the edge of the wood. The police got all excited—you know how they are. They came sniffing and prying, and figured it must have been your dad who bludgeoned those people. So they went after him and, in short, they hanged him."

"They hung dad? Incredible! Where?"

"From the big pear tree in the yard."

"But what about the cabbages under it? They must've trampled the cabbages! Tell me, Ambroise, tell me: did they hang him high?"

"Oh yes, just the way the judge told them to: high and short."

"*Really* high?"

"Well, yes, pretty high, I'd say."

"Poor man! How awful!"

All upset now, he wondered what to do. He thought of the judge, his father, and the cabbages. At last he set off, head low like a sheep with a goiter, for his mountain.

As long as there was no snow on the ground, he went barefoot, with his wooden clogs around his neck. Then, higher up, he found snow, and put them on. But it was cold on those paths, even with his clogs.

"I'd really go for some good hot soup . . ."

He got to the yard and opened the gate.

"Well, well, at least the cabbages look all right."

Then he glanced up and saw dad swinging in the wind, frozen stiff as a board, clunking now and again against the tree-trunk.

"What's that Ambroise was telling me? That he'd been hung so high? He's not too high and he's not too low. No, he's just right. They did a good job."

He cut off the biggest cabbage and went to fix himself some soup.

AROUND THE

VILLAGE

38. The Reopened Knife

There was once a rich countryman with six farms. Every year on Saint Martin's Day the farmers would bring him their rent, and he, in return, would naturally have them that evening to dinner. During the dinner they would complain, quite naturally too, about how bad the year had been, in hopes of getting a tenth off their rent. "Ah, what a year!" they'd groan. "Even worse than last!"

It was the same again that Saint Martin's Day. One of the farmers, especially, went on and on about the rye, which had failed completely. So had the spring wheat. The oats had never come into head and the turnips hadn't come up. Even the carrots were a loss. The bugs had gotten at them as soon as the shoots broke the earth, and had eaten the tiny leaves.

Dinner ended amid these lamentations. So, at least, the farmer thought, since the servant girl wasn't bringing in any more dishes, and since, in any case, he'd eaten four times more than usual. So he closed his clasp knife with a loud snap, the better to punctuate his speech.

The master woke up, as it were, sat up straight, and glanced at the table. "Heavens!" he exclaimed. "I forgot the turkey! There's a roast turkey. Jeannette, bring in the turkey!"

That farmer, closed knife in hand, was in a proper pickle. Closing your knife means you can't eat any more. When a master closed his (some even lifted it above their heads to snap it shut), the meal was over. Everyone, sons and servants, had to close theirs in turn and get up from the table.

Only a real pig would have opened his knife again. But a turkey! Just think, a turkey!

It's good to have a little wit. If that farmer had none, the turkey gave him a bit.

"On the other hand," he now went on, "I should be fair. The wheat up on the hillside made superb ears—long ones." He showed the knife he was holding. "As long as . . . No, the handle's not long enough." He opened the knife again, held it up by the point, and marked the place with his thumb. "That's it," he said. "*That* long."

He'd managed to open his knife again without offending good manners. And he made proper use of it, too!

39. The Poacher, the Gamekeeper, and the Squire

There was once a man who lived in a countryside alive with hare and partridge, and whose sole pleasure was hunting. All his thoughts went to hare and snares, to crossbows and game birds. In the old days of the lords, when people blew their noses on their sleeves and had to make do with just bow and arrow, hunting was free. Later, it wasn't free any more, and it was no joke when the nobles caught someone breaking the rules. But this fellow couldn't help poaching. He was a clever companion and a fine hunter, but he was a bit rash, too. When he started something, he never quite managed to consider how it might end. Forgetting to do that is a mistake which can cost one dear.

One day the man was checking his snares among the ferns, and in fact was just lifting a hare by its ears out of the underbrush, when the gamekeeper caught him.

"Aha, there you are! I've finally got you! You've made quite enough fun of me, in front of your friends in the village. You've been telling them I'd never catch up with you, but now I have you!"

"Isn't your taking the hare enough?"

"I'll take it, and I'll take the one who caught it."

"Listen, what are you going to get out of making trouble for me?"

"My living, that's what I'll get out of it. That's what I get from this gamekeeper's pouch of mine. I'm just doing my job."

"Well, don't be so fussy, for once. I'll send you all the hare I can, you know!"

"Oh yes, by all means! If the squire or any of his men saw you handing me a hare . . ."

"Why, dummy, I didn't say I'd hand it to you, I said I'd *send* it to you!"

"I see. Well, in that case, perhaps . . . But watch out! You'd better not forget your promise!"

"I won't."

"Fine. Get out of here."

One headed one way and one the other, through the green ferns. Neither had done or seen a thing.

Still, each was thinking about that promise during the days ahead.

Less than a week later, on his way to sow rye in his highest field, the man startled a magnificent hare from a pile of stones under a thornbush.

Hare play dead if you come straight onto their nest. They crouch there with that big, rounded eye of theirs on you—it's quite a sight. They don't move a muscle, they just blend with the clumps of dead grass and the heath. But if they hear you coming up *behind* them, then they really fly!

That one had his little tuft of a tail turned the man's way, and he took off at top speed. The man had his seeder and his bag of rye, but not his crossbow. He didn't lose his head, though.

"Hare," he shouted after it, "run to the gamekeeper as fast as you can! Tell him I sent you, and I wish him a good day!"

"Fine," thought he, "I'm keeping my promise. When I think of a man like me keeping a promise like that, it makes me feel pretty good!"

By the following Sunday, he'd kept his promise twice more.

The first time, he did have his crossbow, and was stealing along a hedge. He shot at the hare but missed. It happens sometimes, all too often in fact, however good a shot you may be.

But he didn't forget! He gave that hare just the same instructions to run and greet the gamekeeper for him.

The second time was three days later, and near the end of the month there was a third. He did the same with all the hare that he shot and missed, or saw but couldn't shoot at, in the woods and meadows. He sent every one of them to the squire's gamekeeper.

Being a discreet fellow, however, and knowing how embarrassed he'd have felt to be thanked, he fled the gamekeeper's company as he'd have fled the Black Beast's.

Nevertheless, the pair ran into each other much sooner than two mountains might have done. One fine, dewy morning, out among the bracken, the gamekeeper stumbled upon the fellow again.

It was time for some fast talk.

"I've sent you thirteen, I tell you!"

"Is *that* what you call sending me hare! Well, those thirteen aren't going to bring you any luck. All right, enough. Follow me!"

He took the fellow to the squire—a squire who didn't fiddle around when it came to hunting.

"You're either going to pay thirty silver crowns—" said the squire.

"But I don't have them!"

"—or you're going to eat thirty heads of garlic, or you're going to get thirty blows with an apple switch."

"I'll take the garlic," the poacher replied.

Perhaps he spoke a bit rashly, without thinking whether he could actually go through with it.

By the tenth head, his mouth was already on fire. So were his stomach and his guts. He never would have believed garlic could do that to him.

He made it to the twentieth head.

"Ah, I give up. I'll take the switch."

But those blows from the apple switch, vigorously applied by the squire's groom (and he an old friend from the tavern!) were something else. After the twelfth he couldn't bear any more.

"Higher, higher! No, not there any more! Lower, lower! Oh no!" he bellowed to the groom. "Up higher—no, lower down!"

The groom swore and whaled away with all his strength.

"I'm doing my best," he answered, "but you know, old boy, you're not easy to please!"

Then there'd be more cries, piercing enough to split the castle door.

After the nineteenth, the man gave up again.

"I'll take the crowns!"

Pulling a wry face, he paid his thirty silver crowns. But he'd eaten nineteen heads of garlic and taken nineteen blows of the switch as well. That cured him of his taste for hunting—for at least three weeks.

Later on, they say, he learned to look to the consequences of what he did, and especially to work things out with the gamekeeper in some better way than just sending him the hare he'd missed.

40. The Nail

There was once a poor countryman who'd heard in his youth, from his father and grandfather, that anything may prove useful for a household, and that it's important never to waste a thing.

Skinny nail
May yield fat purse.

The winter had been long and hard. Loft and larder were pretty bare. Now spring was coming with its new grass, wild daffodils, and open lanes. But those are the hardest months of all to get through, when the flour sack is empty, and the purse, too.

One morning, the man set off for town, telling himself he'd surely find some sort of work. Then he'd bring back a big round loaf and a chunk of bacon for his wife and children.

He was striding along the road when a rider passed him: a young blade on his way to join the army, nicely mounted on a horse as shiny as a silk ribbon. On trotted the charger, all four hooves striking sparks in the morning gloom, while his rider sat up there as proudly as Saint George.

Suddenly the farmer saw something bright drop onto the road. He ran to the place, leaned down, and picked up a nail that had come loose from one of the horse's shoes.

"Sir, oh sir! Your horse has lost a nail!"

"A nail?" thought the fine gentleman. "Am I going to stop for a nail? That's nothing. I'll soon be through that big wood and at the camp. Why, he can have it."

"Keep it, keep it, my good man!" he shouted, waving good-bye. Then he spurred his horse into the shortcut and forgot all about that nail the farmer was holding aloft between two fingers.

The farmer remembered that proverb of his elders:

Skinny nail
May yield fat purse.

He put the nail in his satchel and continued on his way.

A little farther along the highroad he saw a carriage on its side against the embankment. One of its wheels had rolled on another ten paces. The traveler himself seemed exceedingly vexed and impatient. He rushed up to the farmer.

"Good man, I'll reward you well if you'll just help me make some repairs. I have to be twenty leagues from here by this evening!"

The farmer went for a look. Nothing was broken. But the road was in very poor condition, the cannon from the camp having rutted and pitted it, and one of the bumps must have knocked out the pin which held the wheel on the axle.

"If you happen to have on you any old bit of iron to replace it with, I'll gladly give you a louis. Sometimes a piece of iron is worth more than gold."

The farmer took the nail from his satchel. Then he helped the traveler put the wheel back in place, pinned it with the nail—a good strong one, made by a blacksmith, with a well-forged head—and bent the nail with a stone to make sure it wouldn't drop out again. The repair was done, the carriage was back on its four wheels, and the gold louis was in the farmer's hand. It seemed like magic. But perhaps he was even happier to see the traveler so pleased to be able to continue his journey.

"If you're going to town, good man, then get in! I'll drop you off."

The rider, meanwhile, was trotting his horse along. Soon he had to slow down. With a nail gone, a shoe jiggles, and up there on the plateau it was all rocks. The shortcut was more like a mountain streambed than a path. The horse kept tripping on the stones, till at last the shoe came off. The young blade had to jump off and lead his horse the rest of the way.

Cursing, he came to a hamlet of three houses and asked for the blacksmith. There wasn't any. All he could find was a hammer and tongs. He'd have put the shoe back on himself, more or less effectively, if only he'd had that nail he'd lost on the way. There wasn't a single nail in the whole miserable hamlet.

As they say, what you kick away with your foot one minute, you may go after with your teeth the next.

Not a nail in sight. He had to do without it. Bridle in hand, he kept walking in his heavy boots, beside his limping horse.

Nothing looks sillier than a horseman on foot. This one pushed on, thoroughly out of sorts, dragging his horse along, and cursing and swearing some more to pass the time.

All at once he found himself surrounded by a band of those youths—deserters, smugglers, robbers, what have you—who earn their money out in the woods. He charged them, eyes glinting and sword in hand. Those in front avoided him, but one of the riff-raff farther back got him in the legs with a pole and brought him down. They all fell on him, clubbed him, beat him savagely, stripped him stark naked, and tied him to a tree. And there they left him, half fainting, in the thickest part of the forest.

As for the farmer, once the carriage had left him off in town, he went straight to do his shopping. A whole louis! Twenty-four pounds! The kind of days he worked, it would have taken him two months to earn that much. (A man got just ten pennies a day, before the days of the Revolution and that worthless paper money.) As he wanted to treat his family, he bought four round loaves, smoked bacon, dry salami, and some nice ripe pears. What next? A big ham, salt herring, and plums. All he took for himself was the crust of bread he'd put in his satchel that morning, along with a raw onion and a few coarse grains of salt. He ate knife in hand, sitting on a milestone in a deserted street lined with gardens and monasteries. He napped a moment beneath a wall, his head pillowed on his bag, then started home again about two o'clock, rested and fresh, with his bag over his shoulder.

"Robbers?" thought he. "Well, I'll just have to keep my eyes open and not get caught. Robbers or no robbers, I'm taking the shortcut through the woods. The road goes too far around."

He was in a hurry to get home, and could just imagine how happy his family would be. That's all he thought of, in fact, as he walked along.

Quite deep in among the trees, he started to prick up his ears. No, there was no mistake: some way off he heard cries and shouts.

He stopped and listened, then headed for where the shouts were coming from—cautiously, though, because he knew there might be robbers nearby. Still, something made him feel it was all right. He hid his satchel under a bush, noting the place carefully, then opened his clasp knife and left it open in his pocket. Now he walked on more boldly.

In two minutes he came on the people who were shouting. He hadn't been wrong: those *had* been the voices of women and children. That's what had reassured him. But he was still afraid it might all be a trick. He saw before him a lady and a whole troop of girls and boys—seven or eight of them—from five to sixteen years old. Pale, lost, and starving, they could barely stand.

The lady, who was from a castle nearby, told him what had happened. They'd all left the castle early the day before, to see the new green of spring and to picnic on the grass. The children had picked bunches of daffodils and dashed from grove to grove, following the warbler's song. They'd gone into the forest, where they'd played tag and all sorts of games. By the time they realized they no longer knew quite where they were, a wind came up and they were enveloped by fog. She'd immediately gotten worried and had wanted to take the shortest path home. They'd lost their way.

They'd been going round and round in the woods since yesterday. At first they hadn't dared call, for fear that bad men might find them, but at last they just had to risk it. Desperate by that time, they'd been afraid they might simply die of hunger and exhaustion.

"There's no need to die, madam," said the farmer. "I'll have you back under the cross at the crossroads in a quarter of an hour."

"Ah," replied the lady, "but they can't walk a step more without fainting from weakness! It's been a whole day, and many hours more, since we last ate or drank."

"If that's all that's the matter," said the farmer, "come with me! I've everything you need to make you feel better."

It was such a pleasure, in the old days, to do someone a good turn! You couldn't bear knowing your neighbor was in trouble. People were happy to help each other. Why, that was the very spice of life, for those who'd been properly brought up by their mother and father.

He ran ahead and came right back with his satchel.

The children could hardly believe their eyes when they saw him unpack all those good things for them on the grass. They were in luck, the poor things, starving as they were. It was all they could do to keep from hurling themselves at the fresh loaves, the smoked fish, the bacon, and the sausages. Never in all their lives had they enjoyed such a feast. Laughing and crying, their mother tried to make them behave, though she constantly interrupted her efforts to thank the farmer, who was laughing as gaily as she. Because it's true, you know: for really good country people, there's no greater pleasure or pride than helping someone out of a scrape. That's what it means to be a Christian. There's nothing finer on this earth.

The children ate so hungrily that the lady was a little embarrassed. And they'd have shriveled up with thirst if the farmer, who knew the forest, hadn't taken them to a spring down in a hollow, behind a clump of March willows.

> We've drunk well and eaten well:
> Jesus, we thank you well!

Now they felt better. The farmer showed them the way to the cross at the crossroads, and even to the edge of the forest and to the castle itself, for fear they might meet bad people.

How they thanked him! He was practically walking on air. But his satchel, too, was a good deal lighter. The lady insisted he take her purse (with half-a-dozen or more gold pieces shining through the mesh), and she did it so graciously that he just had to accept.

Toward sundown he was on his way again, striding along through the woods—and anxious to get home, with that gold in his pocket—when once more he thought he heard distant cries.

"Seems like the shouters are after me today!" said he to himself. "Let's go have a look."

Not that he didn't peer very cautiously all around him, or take special care once he'd spied through the branches, a naked man tied to a tree. But he soon recognized that morning's gallant blade.

He untied the fellow, revived him, covered him with his coat, and gave him something to eat.

Finally the young lord, seated under a tree, found his mind beginning to work again.

"Yes," he mused, "it's true. I turned up my nose at a nail, and that's what got me into all this trouble."

The farmer was so eager to get home that he offered to take the gentleman with him. He'd have the young gentleman for the night, and the next day would lend him his Sunday suit. He might even advance him a little money for a new horse . . .

Three-quarters of an hour later, the two men sat on either side of the fire, in a cramped old living room blackened with woodsmoke. All the children were huddled before them, and if they didn't dare open their mouths, their eyes at least were open wide. The wind from the forest sighed outside, the cauldron was singing, and the cat by the hearth was purring away. The fellow who'd lost the nail, and the fellow who'd found him, smiled at each other through the steam from the cabbage soup. Both felt a little lightheaded at the end of this day that had been as strange as a dream.

Suddenly the young lord sat up straight.

"I've been thinking," he said. "I'm afraid my whole property may end up slipping through my fingers, just like the nail, the horseshoe, and the horse. I need a careful, thoughtful man to look after my woods, my lands, and my castle. You're very capable. Would you like to be my steward?

You'd do me an even greater favor than you've already done me today."

"Me, sir? Your steward?"

"Please accept. You'll oblige me, and you'll be set for life."

Well, the dream wasn't over yet. In a daze, the farmer said yes.

"That crazy nail," thought he, "had a whole new life for me hanging from it. I don't think I'll have to teach my children that proverb. They'll never forget that

Skinny nail
May yield fat purse.

41. The Pair of Masons

There were once two masons, good friends and tireless workers. On the other hand, they did, of course, have a few small faults.

One was a sincere, practicing Christian. As he drank only moderately, his bottle lasted him two days. But he had a passion for gambling. Once he had his hand on the cards, he was another man. Even sitting smack in a puddle, he'd still have kept on gambling! And it might have been all right if he'd ever won, but there he was out of luck! No doubt he had a good wife who never meant to reproach him. The only ones with any luck are those poor husbands . . . Well, at any rate, believe it or not, he always lost. Yet he kept right on. It was a mania with him. People called him Ace of Spades.

The other . . . Ah, him. All he cared about, besides his trade, was drinking. Well, don't worry, there was also swearing, smoking, and beating his wife. Above all, though, he loved draining bottles. People called him Booze.

These two friends liked working together. They'd keep up each other's spirits, and give each other good tips.

"The devil take your cards," said Booze to Ace of Spades. "You'll eat up everything you've got: your money, your fields, your house, and even your bowl!"

"All right, but they won't weigh on my stomach. You, though—you just *drink* all yours. And those bottles are making a fool of you."

"I'll see you with a satchel over your shoulder, begging your bread from door to door."

"I'll see you die in the ditch, where the devil will come to fetch you."

Each warned the other, but neither could deny what the other said of *him*.

This didn't keep Ace of Spades from pulling the cards from his pocket and inviting his friend to play; and it didn't keep Booze from having the woman at the inn bring on another bottle, either! Naturally, Ace of Spades would go home without a penny in his pocket, his purse empty enough for spiders to spin webs in; while Booze would do the same with a head so full that he saw only rats and flies before him.

One evening, a fine May evening, as Ace of Spades was setting off to gamble at the tavern nearby, he saw an old traveler—no doubt a pilgrim—coming his way. The traveler's beard and curly hair were grey, and he looked like a thoroughly honorable man.

"A good evening to you," said the pilgrim. "Would you mind someone sleeping in your hay?"

"Yes, pilgrim to Saint James, we'll make you a bed in the hay. And whether or not you have food with you, you'll dine with us."

"Thank you, my friend! God will reward you. But I'm not alone."

"Bring your companion here, too. There's room for two in the hay, and soup for two in the pot."

"No doubt there is, but you see, I'm talking about twelve."

"Twelve! Heavens! That's a lot! But if you leave our larder bare, well, bare it'll be."

The curly-headed old man (you might as well know right away he was Saint Peter) went to fetch Our Lord and the apostles. Ace of Spades greeted them. His wife served them their soup and poured them a spot of wine. Then he led them to the hayloft and arranged beds for them as best he could.

In the morning, the pilgrims came to say thank you. Ace of Spades offered them breakfast. The highroad stretched away toward chapels, towns, woods, and the brightness of dawn.

"We're leaving right now," said the one to whom all the others turned. "My Father will reward you one day for the kindness you've shown us. In the meantime, is there anything troubling you—any special anxiety or worry?"

"There's just this problem," began Ace of Spades, who'd taken his cap off now and was holding it in his hand; "there's just this problem that, be it plain bad luck or the Other's malice, I can never win at cards."

"If that's all, then you'll always win."

And it was true. After that morning with the pilgrims, Ace of Spades always won. He could in fact have lived without working, just from his winnings at écarté, beggar-my-neighbor, and basset. But gambling, though his passion, was not to be his trade. He wanted to go on earning his living in the sun, beside Booze, building houses, not in the shadows at the back of the tavern, emptying Pierre or Paul's purse.

Booze couldn't warn him any more that the cards were eating up all he had; but he, more than ever, had to tell Booze that the bottle was turning him into a sot. Booze got drunk every evening God gave him. He'd rage and swear, batter the walls on his way home, and then, once in the door, beat his wife.

"It'll end badly!" Ace of Spades kept harping at him. "You'll see, it'll end badly!"

And Booze did see.

In fact, though, he hardly had time to see it. They were both up on some scaffolding, repairing a church tower. A rope broke, the scaffolding tipped, and both masons tumbled all the way down onto the town square. They landed on the pile of cut stone, between the heap of mortar and the wheelbarrow of sand.

"That's it," breathed Ace of Spades. "I'm dead and done for. There's nothing left now but to head for Heaven. How about you, Booze?"

"Oh, I'm done for too. And where will I be heading for?"

Just then Ace of Spades heard a snicker. Whom did he see, right next to them? A horned, forked, pointy, hairy character who seemed part billy-goat and part wolf. The fellow's piercing eyes drilled right through you, like knives.

"Tell me, friend," Ace of Spades barely managed to ask, "what do you want with us?"

"Hardly anything," came the reply. "Just the soul of brother Booze."

"He's not dead yet, not completely. So sorry he's keeping you waiting. In the meantime, would you be good enough to join me in a game of cards?"

"A game? Why not? I used to think you'd be coming to my place, to play a few where it's good and warm. And you would have, if Someone hadn't stuck his oar in. Well, never mind. But what about the stakes?"

"Yes, what'll we play for? Money?"

"Money? I get gold louis just by spitting. No, if I win, I win your soul."

"And if you lose, you lose Booze's soul. He and I stuck together in this world, and we'll stick together in the next."

"Soul for soul, then? All right, we'll play for Booze's soul!"

So right there on the work site, they started a game of écarté. Ace of Spades dealt, turned up the king, and the round was over. In no time he'd won the second, and quicker still the third.

The devil threw down the cards, picked up his pitchfork, and made himself scarce, spitting like a cat.

The three rounds hadn't taken four minutes. It was early in the morning. The crash had waked everyone up, but the men needed time to get on their trousers. No one was there yet.

Ace of Spades turned to his friend Booze.

"Try not to die right away! Give our priest time to get here!"

"Oh, I'd have too much to tell him!"

"But surely, if you got to start your life over, there must be a few little mistakes you'd like not to repeat?"

"No doubt about *that*."

"I'm sure our priest will like your answer. You won't do it any more?"

"What do you mean, do it any more? I'm *dead!*"

"That's right. We're both dead. But we'll stick together, Booze! All we have to do now is set out together for Heaven."

"Go ahead. I don't dare. Saint Peter would never open the gate for me."

"Oh, come on! Follow me. Maybe it'll help to talk to him."

Off they went. Ace of Spades stepped up to Saint Peter.

"Ah yes, there you are," said Saint Peter. "You're the mason who lodged the twelve pilgrims. But all you asked for, you know, was to win at cards. So you got your reward on earth itself. Well, anyway, you did observe your religion. Perhaps I might let you in, despite everything, as a special favor. But who's that with you?"

"My mason friend, Booze. Yes, great Saint Peter, we always stick together."

"Oh, Booze, he can go and booze it up somewhere else. This place isn't for *him*."

"Your goodness, though, might well . . . After all, I could have been strict about things, too, that evening you came asking to sleep in the hay."

"Yes, but *Booze*, for pity's sake! A fellow who dragged around in every ditch and who never set foot in church! Beating his wife wasn't enough for him, he had to take the Lord's name in vain as well. Come now, how could he possibly get into Heaven?"

"But he repented at the last minute! And anyway, he was a tremendous mason and a tremendous worker!"

Silent, head low, Booze was making himself very small nearby. The argument heated up and got louder. Ace of Spades was waving his arms, while Saint Peter had an answer for everything and refused to listen.

Just then, God happened by. He stopped and asked what was going on.

Ace of Spades took his cap in his hand, as when the twelve pilgrims had set out on the highroad at dawn. Now he hardly dared say a word. Still, he murmured a greeting and an apology.

"Don't you recognize me, Lord?"

"When you argue so loudly, you don't look the same at all. Well, what is it? Speak up!"

"This Saint Peter of yours doesn't want to let in my brother mason. I'm sure Booze drank and sinned a lot in his life, but when he died he repented. Anyway, we promised to stick together, and I practiced my religion."

"You practiced your religion. But there at your house, all you asked me for was to win at cards. It's true, though, that you played a last game just now to save your friend's soul. That game saved many others as well."

God glanced at Saint Peter, and Saint Peter threw wide the gates of Heaven.

42. The Donkey Dealer

There was once a donkey dealer. He wasn't one of those major dealers who go as far away as Poitou for their donkeys, to restock the whole countryside with mules. No, he stuck to the counties right around here, buying, selling, striking his little bargains, wearing a blue smock trimmed with white thread, and trying to be a prosperous man. His only fault was coming home late when there'd been a fair. Those nights, the road wasn't wide enough for him any more. He'd get his feet tangled up in his staff, and all the bushes would catch on his smock.

One year just like all the others, he'd gone to the great donkey fair— never mind where, since around here there are donkeys wherever you go. And he just didn't come home. His wife was forever peering out the door, one hand to her forehead, but she didn't see him coming.

Twilight came, night fell, and he still wasn't back.

Finally at eleven o'clock, or perhaps midnight, he returned with his donkeys. She was as furious as any stock dealer's wife the night after a fair.

"Well," she snapped, "you think this is a decent time to come home? Where were you? What were you doing? Ah, what you have to put up with when you've had the misfortune to marry one of these drunks!"

There she was, even before he'd dismounted (because he was riding), calling him a wastrel and a lush!

"You always know when I've been drinking, and you never know when I'm thirsty. But, wife," said he, raising his arms, "this evening it's something else. I've lost one of my donkeys."

"You've lost a donkey?"

"I'm afraid so. I've been all over, looking. I bought three, and I'm only bringing back two!"

"Three, you say?"

"Why, yes! One black, one grey, and one white. Here's the white one and here's the grey one. In all this darkness, I lost the black one. I'll have to go out again and look for it."

He started working with his knees and tugging on the bridle.

"Look for it?"

"Well yes, for goodness' sake! Take the others to the stable. I'm going back out again."

"Just a minute, you clown, you stuffed buffoon! You've brought back two donkeys? But I see no fewer than four. The white is one; the grey makes two; the black one you're riding—because your head was so heavy you couldn't walk—the black one makes three; and you, who're more of a donkey than all the rest put together, you're the fourth!"

43. The Sick Vine Grower

There was a vine grower from Saint-Hippolyte, near Riom, who, for his sins, ended up burdened with a belly the size of a barrel.

He went to see the doctor.

"It's dropsy, my friend."

"Dropsy? What in the world is *that?*"

"Well, water on the stomach, you know."

Flabbergasted, the fellow headed home from Riom, ruminating all the way. When he got there he told his wife all about it. But going over it again just flabbergasted him even more. How could he possibly have water on the stomach, he who'd never drunk a drop of frog-juice in his life, and who'd never even washed his glass, to keep it from tasting of water?

Suddenly the light dawned.

"Say, woman, I've got it!" cried he, slapping the table. "Why, it must be that confounded soup of yours!"

44. The Woman Who Wasn't Herself Any More

There was once a good old girl they called Julie. Her husband was a poor thresher. They hadn't much in their pockets, those two, but still, they got along one way or another.

To earn a few pennies, she'd gather an apronful of grass, evenings, on the hillside. That way her goats gave her a little more milk. Then she'd make cheeses, which she'd go to sell in town, down among the vines, where the people, being rich, were fond of good eating.

One day at the fair she had a whole basket of cheeses to sell and did quite well. Seeing herself so prosperous, she first bought herself a bowl (the cat having broken her last one), then a nice little loaf of white bread. And then, and then . . . she wanted the nicest of all nice things, the one that never reached her own godforsaken corner of the world. She marched into a tavern and had her bowl filled with wine.

After that, she went to sit in a dead-end street, under a wall. All around were orchards and gardens. She lunched at ease in a spot of shade, among the milkweeds and dandelions, dipping her bread at each mouthful into the wine. At last the bowl was empty, and she still hadn't finished her loaf.

"Well," said she to the bit of loaf she still had in her hand, "you took a whole bowlful of wine! Now you've drunk yours up, I might as well drink mine!"

Up she got, went back to the tavern, and had her bowl refilled. This time it wasn't the bread that drank it. *She* did. She went off into a corner (it's never very nice to see a woman in a tavern), stuck her nose in the bowl, and in four gulps found out what it had in the bottom. Then she popped the bowl into her basket, clapped her hat on her head, and left.

The path twisted and climbed as soon as it got out of town. Julie lit into the trip like a girl on her way to a wedding. But the sun was beating down, and buzzing worse than a hundred hornets. The people who'd built the path had put far too many curves and bends in it. Why, struggling that way from rock to rock through the broom, you just never seemed to get anywhere. Your head got all muddled up, and your legs, too. Besides, the legs seemed to be getting all rubbery.

All at once, under a chestnut tree, on one of those hairpin bends, Julie tripped and tumbled into a grassy hollow. She dropped her basket, off rolled her hat, even her cap caught on a dead shrub, and her bun came all undone. She didn't even notice. In no time she was snoring like mad.

A little later, along came an old fellow whose trade it was to supply wigmakers with girls' hair he'd buy at fairs. He'd swap the hair for a piece of cloth or a calico apron, adding sometimes a silver coin.

Things must have gone well that day. He was only a little drunk. Stopping in front of Julie, he considered her grey braid. On the fairground he wouldn't have given ten pennies for it.

"Never mind," thought he. "I'll pay her the compliment, just as though she were young."

Out came his scissors, and in two swipes, snip-snap, he cut off her hair. Backing up now a step to admire his work, he took two more he hadn't planned, stumbled, stepped on the basket, and heard something break. It was the bowl. With a single kick he sent that basket, patched as it was with corduroy squares, sailing into the bushes. The braid, which he still had in his hand, flew right behind it. Then he pricked on his donkey.

Still, he'd hardly gotten going again when he started to feel scruples. "I've got to give her *something!*" he thought. So he took his last calico apron (a pretty blue one with little flowers on it), put it around Julie, and even knotted the strings. Then off he went, singing the evensong of the wild.

Julie only opened her eyes toward evening, as night was falling. She was quite confused to find herself among the broom and the rocks. There was a cap. "Must be mine!" said she, and quickly put it on, all embarrassed. There's no worse shame than being seen with your hair undone. But as she did so, she found she was missing her hair. Next she saw a hat. It was hers, but not hers—it was too big, and wouldn't stay on her head.

"And my bowl?"

Yes, where was the bowl she'd bought? It was gone. So was the basket. And around her waist was this blue apron with little green flowers that she'd never seen before.

"Perhaps I'm somebody else."

Was she Julie or another? The thought whirled around in her head, but never seemed to stop anywhere.

"That's it, all right! You aren't yourself any more! You're never outside at this hour. If you were you, you'd be at home, in the house. So who do you suppose you are?"

She looked again at this apron which confused her so, felt her head—no, no hair—and then, hat in hand in lieu of the basket, started again up the hill.

But this idea that she wasn't herself any more went on making her feel weak.

Finally, at the last bend, she paused. Perhaps she'd find she had no husband and no home. What if she got home only to find Julie there already, the real Julie?

There was Toine, in front of the barn, splitting wood. He turned and peered through the gathering dusk, uncomprehending, at this woman striding up—this woman without a hat, and wearing a bright apron, like a girl.

"Toine! Is Julie back?"

"Julie? No, I'm still expecting her."

Thank goodness! She came on straight toward him and her home.

"If Julie's not back yet, I must be Julie after all! I'm still me!"

45. A Household Can Use Anything

There was once a nine-year-old boy as bright as a new penny, and in fact a bit of a rascal. When it came to mischief, laughter, and tricks, he was always there. But that was his nature: he was born to it and couldn't help it.

One day at school, the old teacher taught them that everything's useful to a household, and that a good householder should never go home empty-handed.

"You can always take home a bundle of deadwood, or a handful of straw from a rut in the road, or a few tufts of wool caught on a bush. Pick up everything, even old nails or bits of string. A household can use anything."

This was a fine lesson for a boy who loved ransacking the hedges for blackberries, or the pear tree for its pears. It stuck in his head.

His good, kind mother, a poor widow who had just one goat, kept telling him every day to mind the teacher.

"So I've got to show I *do* mind the teacher," thought the boy. "Today, it's a promise. Anything I find out there, I'll take home! Mother'll find it there this evening, when *she* gets home."

Determined now, he set out on his way.

A few steps from the school, he picked up a big stick, practically a log, as thick as his leg.

"Stick, come with me!"

On the way out of town he met a mangy, skinny cur. The day before, he'd have greeted the creature with a hail of stones, but now he spoke gently to it and got it to follow him.

"Dog, come with me!"

At a bend in the path, he saw the gleam of a pin, one as long as his finger. All right, the pin, too! He stuck it in his jacket.

"Pin, come with me!"

The path wound through the fields, then dipped down to the river. There, in a shallow pool, the boy spotted the blue back of a pike stranded by a flood.

"Pike, come with me!"

He swept it up by the gills, not even bothering to be afraid of the terrible, tooth-filled mouth, and took it along.

He'd promised! *Everything* would come with him!

Then he met with more than he'd bargained for. There he was, hurrying along with log, dog, pin, and pike, when just short of his door he stepped straight into a fresh cowpat.

Well, if that was the way fate would have it! So be it, for good luck! "Cowpat, come with me!"

In he went, took two big steps to scrape the dung off his clog on the stove door, threw the pike into the water bucket, and stuck the pin in a towel.

Night was falling. Just then he heard a footstep by the window. He glanced outside, and there was a dirty, ragged, bearded character with a satchel over his shoulder—one of those marauders who frighten the chickens. He was sniffing around, looking for the way in.

Instead of sneaking out the back door, the boy, more full of mischief than ever, quickly put the log up over the door, caught the dog by the scruff of the neck and slipped in a flash with him under the bed.

But the thief, afraid to be seen from the road, didn't try to open the door. Instead, he broke the window. And here he came, filling the window frame with his beard, his rags, and his satchel. He looked like the bogeyman himself. Then down he jumped, with a fearful crash, into the room. He went straight to the stove. Perhaps he was after a coal to light his pipe, but more likely he'd caught a hen on the way and wanted to do some roasting.

He opened the stove to reach into the ashes, but instead put his hand into you-know-what.

"Blast! It's *that!*"

Catching sight of the water bucket, he plunged his hand in—a hand like a flail, but blacker and harder than a billy-goat's hooves. To the pike, though, it was just meat. The glutton sank his teeth into it and tried to gulp it down.

"Blast and blast!"

The house nearly turned upside down. The marauder grabbed at the towel and stuffed it into his hand to stop the blood. The pin went right through two of his fingers.

"Blast and blast and double blast!"

What a devil of a house! More panicked now than a bumblebee caught in a morning-glory's throat, he struggled and swore, danced from one foot to the other, and bumped into the stove and the walls.

Amid all the racket, the dog felt his moment had arrived. He sprang like a demon from under the bed, leaped at the burglar's breeches, and tore out the seat before the fellow ever knew what had hit him—the seat and a piece of behind as well!

Now *that* was a decisive blow!

The marauder dove at the door with a howl, and the log tumbled from the lintel onto his head.

Nearly stunned, he dropped his satchel and zigzagged on down the hill, half rolling and half staggering, right to the bottom!

At the bottom was the river, and a deep pool. In he went, head first . . . and never came out again.

The boy and his mother inherited the satchel. Under the crusts and trash they found a purse. With it they bought three cows and a farm.

> *Down the row of wheat I've run,*
> *And now my story's done.*

46. The Smart Servant

On a riverbank there once lived a poor but honest woman, a widow with three sons. The sons themselves were good enough boys, who got through a good deal of work in a day. Still, the family barely managed to make ends meet. The two older boys had lively ideas, but the youngest— Snot-Nose, they called him—had only one idea at a time. He was squat, dark, coarse, and quick to anger.

He hadn't even been able to learn his prayers. In the morning, he'd rattle off, "Lord, your little servant's getting up."

At noon, it'd be, "Lord, your little servant's having lunch."

And in the evening, "Lord, your little servant's going to bed."

But these three prayers stood him very well.

One year, in March, it snowed a whole week, with heavy flakes as big as leaves. Then the wind shifted to the south, bringing torrents of rain. The river rose and rose. Rolling and rumbling, it carried off the fields in a single night, and very nearly took the house as well. They had absolutely nothing left but a little wheat in the attic.

Now, *that* was a disaster. What could they say? What were they going to do?

One evening at the very beginning of April, as the cuckoo sang his first song, there appeared at the door a big man, well mounted on a large, powerful horse. His red face, framed by his black mane of hair, was broader than a barrel's end, and his heavy belly jutted before him. He and his horse were both fitted out in scarlet leather with silver rivets, and at his belt he had a great big knife.

He considered the mother and her boys with his little piggy eyes.

"Look," he said, without the least word of greeting, "I need a servant. I'll take your eldest. If he doesn't do, I'll bring him back and take the second. And if *he* doesn't work out, then the youngest."

How could she refuse? It was their only chance to survive. But the poor woman shrank from giving this man her boy.

"All right," he went on, "let's get things straight between us, so they're settled once and for all. I'll hire him a year, at thirty crowns per year, until the cuckoo's first song. I'll lodge him, clothe him, and feed him. He gets an egg a day, and all the bread he can spread it on. But he'll have to feed my bitch, who'll go to work with him. And he won't come back from work until my bitch does. Do you understand?"

"I understand," said the boy.

"Fine," answered the big man. "I keep my promises, and I don't want any complaints. Look out! Look out! Anyone, master or servant, who says he's not happy gets his pockets emptied and a strip of skin three inches wide peeled off him, from his neck down to the small of his back. That's our way, where I live, and it keeps things rolling along very smoothly."

Now the bargain was struck, the boy got up behind the saddle, and rode off by the red, dusty light of the setting sun. His mother and brothers stood in the doorway and watched him go.

"Dear God, dear God," sighed the poor mother, "I should never have let him go with that big, ruddy, hot-tempered man, who looked like some cousin of the devil!"

She didn't realize how near she was to the truth. This fellow with the pig's snout, wily as a badger and lumpish as a bear, was the ogre from the lowlands. That's where he had his property and his vines, at the end of a poplar-lined lane. He lived there with his ogress wife—an awful woman, vast of girth, redder and a still worse rascal than he. She had just one tooth in her mouth, reddish, and bigger than the tooth of a rake. It came down to the middle of her chin.

Leaving with the ogre meant taking off for the land of the absurd and the insane: a land of raw, bloody meat and of horned, madly flying visions— a land people no longer imagine, but such as used to exist back then. Ah, if the eldest of those boys had only known what he was heading for . . .

"Here we are," declared the gentleman, dismounting heavily at the end of a certain lane. "It's tomorrow you'll get your food, since you'll be working tomorrow. For tonight, go to bed. Your dinner's your sleep."

The next day, the woman gave the boy an egg, hard-boiled. You can't spread much bread with a hard-boiled egg. All the boy could get was a crust.

Then the gentleman appeared.

"Here's your job. Today you're going to be plowing the big field on the hillside. And remember what we agreed: you'll take my bitch, you'll feed her, and you'll come back only when she wants to."

The boy hitched up the oxen and went to the field. He had little heart for singing behind the plow, which he steered as well as he could by keeping his eyes on a willow pole he'd planted at the field's edge. That nasty red bitch kept coming back for more bread. She have eaten him up if he hadn't given it to her.

"A nice mess you're in!" he told himself. "So little bread and so much work! And those faces the master and mistress have! And this red bitch you've got to feed with your crust! And this filthy countryside, without a tree or a spring! Who could possibly stand it?"

The bitch didn't want to go home till nightfall.

By the time the boy reached the house, his legs would hardly hold him. The gentleman was waiting for him at the door.

"All right! And you'll be back at it tomorrow. But what's the matter? You don't look too lively."

"The matter is that you can't work if you're not fed."

"Well then? You're not happy?"

"No, that's exactly what you could call it. I'm not happy."

The miserable lad had hardly spoken when the gentleman pounced on him. So did the woman who'd been watching from behind the door, the way a spider in the middle of her web watches for a fly.

They seized him, lifted him up, and slapped him face down on their dining table.

"So, you're not happy? Aha! But we have our little agreement, right? We're going to skin your back, my friend!"

The poor boy was screaming so loud his mother might almost have heard him. And well he might. As pitiless as a hunk of iron, the ogre was ripping off his clothes. Then, with his horrible knife, he set about stripping off a three-inch band of skin, from his victim's neck to the small of his back.

The ogress leaned over the boy with bared teeth and greedy nails, as though she too meant to join in. Meanwhile the ogre was pulling the skin off in little tugs, to make the pleasure last longer. Both of them were purring, with shining eyes, like a pussy-cat playing with a fresh-caught mouse.

"Are you having a good time, my boy, are you having a good time? How does that little back of yours like it? And what's that little mother of yours going to say?"

The boy screamed, howled, and begged for mercy. But the ogre and ogress just laughed and licked their chops.

In the morning, the ogre emptied his servant's pockets, then loaded him like a suitcase across his horse's back. He took the boy back to his mother.

The poor woman wept tears of blood when she saw him in that condition, but she had to give up her second son. That was the bargain, and she had to stick to it.

The gentleman blinked his little eyes, got the second boy up behind him, and rode away. Off went the boy to ogreland.

As soon as the sun was up, the ogre issued his orders for the day. Everything went exactly as with the boy's older brother: the hard-boiled egg, the crust, the field to plow, the nasty red bitch to watch and feed, and the return to the house only when the bitch was ready to go.

The boy came back so hungry and exhausted that he'd forgotten all about the agreement. Thoughtlessly, he blurted that he wasn't at all happy either.

That did it! The gentleman and his wife laid him out flat on the table. Then, with as much enjoyment as a polecat bleeding a chicken, they peeled three inches of skin off him, from his neck down to the small of his back.

Ah, what a night he had! In the morning, the ogre emptied his pockets, packed him up, loaded him on the horse, and took him back to his mother. When the good woman saw her poor dear come home this way, she collapsed before her door.

"There you are," said the gentleman. "I keep my promises, so you keep yours! That servant didn't work out either. I want the third."

"All right, master," replied Snot-Nose. "Let's go!"

He took advantage of his mother's having fainted. She'd never have let him go, good Christian soul that she was! But he, why, by thunder, he was mad! Those were his brothers that he'd grown up with, the brothers he went with to gather hazelnuts and watch the sheep—his brothers and his mother, all the family he had to huddle with evenings around the fire, and who were closer to him than his own heart! His blood boiled when he saw what that couple had done to them. Snot-Nose's head could hold only one idea at a time, but that idea was in there to stay. His eyes sparkled so brightly that you'd have thought the devil was going to jump out his windows.

"Just you wait, you fine gentleman!" said he to himself. "You're looking for a good servant? Well, you've found him! I don't know what I'm going to do, but I'm sure I'm going to make you pay for what you've done to my family."

The gentleman would have trembled, had he looked him carefully in the face. But ogres are dumb. That one was full of himself for having skinned those two boys. "Now for the third!" thought he. "Let's make him writhe! What a pleasure for us, to listen to this midget bawl!"

He meant to seize the boy by the collar, lift him up, and plop him down behind the saddle; but Snot-Nose didn't wait for that. Up he hopped so resolutely that the gentleman stared. But the gentleman was too pleased with himself, with his stupid wiles and his ogre ways, to fear this slip of a boy.

The mother came to in time to see the horse disappear in a cloud of red dust, taking her Snot-Nose away! She'd have wished herself at the bottom of the river, but no, she had to get up, look after her skinned sons, and, as always, take care of the household.

Snot-Nose went to bed at his masters' house without his dinner, but also jumped out of bed the next morning at cockcrow, without having been called. He took an egg in the henhouse, then a feather. Next, he cut the top off the egg, dipped in the feather, and with it painted a whole loaf. The couple appeared as he was arranging his modest breakfast.

"As much bread as he can spread with one egg": that was what they'd agreed. But they were puffing with rage.

Grumbling, the gentleman gave his orders. Snot-Nose listened, took the loaf, ran the ox goad through it, put it over his shoulder, and set off leading the oxen. The red bitch followed him. That was the routine.

Snot-Nose had no sooner reached the field than he caught that horrible bitch. "That bread you'll be getting from me," he said: "you're going to earn it first."

He hitched the bitch up in front of the oxen, then started in plowing, singing at the top of his voice.

The sun rose higher and the morning passed. At noon, Snot-Nose unhitched his team. Free at last, the bitch scampered down the path like a rat, she was so anxious not to be put back on that plow.

Snot-Nose ate in peace and led his oxen home.

"You're back a bit early, boy," said the gentleman, coming out under the vine arbor.

"Your bitch gave me the sign, master. What's agreed is agreed. Perhaps you're not satisfied?"

The snippet spoke so forcefully that the gentleman ducked back under the arbor, as red as though he'd been smacked in the face.

"Yes, yes, boy, I'm satisfied."

If he was, though, his looks didn't show it.

He paced around a bit, sat down, got up again, and finally went into the kitchen to talk to his wife.

"We've got a servant here who's not going to be easy to manage. A loaf every morning, not to mention the new-laid egg . . . Did you see him? He's back from plowing at midday. Wife, what are we going to do?"

"Why, you big red donkey, get rid of him as soon as you can!"

"But it's agreed, he has to stay on till the cuckoo first sings."

"Well, use your head a bit, you lummox! Order him to do something he can't. When he comes and tells you he hasn't done it, you throw him out."

"Pretty smart, my turtledove, pretty smart! I'll come up with something for tomorrow."

He took a bottle back with him under the arbor, and settled down to some serious thinking and drinking. Inspiration didn't come. Feeling a bit heavy, he paced up and down between his poplars.

"Thirty years from now they'll be giving me some shade," he reflected. "But in the meantime, I'd better think up an idea."

A whole month went by, or perhaps a week or two more. Finally he got that idea.

One morning like the others, Snot-Nose came for his orders, still with a gleam in his eye. "That's all right, sir," he was thinking, "go ahead and wait! You'll get yours in the end. You skinned my poor brothers! I'll take the price of that from your own skin!"

The gentleman was sitting solemnly in his wooden chair. He crossed his legs. "Aha," thought Snot-Nose, "the old bogeyman's got a trick for me. Well, I'm no genius, but I'll just tear straight into what's coming, like a cannonball. Then we'll see what we shall see."

He already had the goad through the loaf, and over his shoulder.

"No," said the gentleman. "You're not going plowing. You're going to cut wood: two bundles of wood, one of straight branches and one of crooked. As straight as you can find, and as crooked as you can find. Two bundles, both bigger than you. And it's all to be done in a hour! Do you understand, boy?"

"Yes, master, I understand."

Down went the bogeyman to the cellar to report to his wife, who was clotting cheeses.

"And I told him to have it all done in an hour. The only place to get wood around here is our own forest up on the mountain. The trip there

and back will take him two hours, and then he'll still have to sort the branches and make the bundles. You see what I mean, my turtledove?"

He was so proud that he rewarded himself with a gulp of brandy.

Just as he was licking the last drop, why, there was his servant again.

"What? You're back? And what about my order? Where are your two bundles? Ah, you can't have, you certainly can't have . . . No, no, my boy, you're going to smart for this!"

"It's all done, master: two bundles, bigger than me, one of nice straight branches and one of nice crooked ones. They're right there. Come and see!"

That brought the gentleman to his feet. Off he went to look in front of the house. The sight almost popped his eyes from his head. Snot-Nose had cut down the whole avenue of poplars, and all the vines as well.

"My vines! My poplars! My arbor that gave me such good wine! The avenue I was so proud of! Why, you miserable, misbegotten scamp!"

"You gave the order. If you don't like it, what am *I* supposed to do?"

"If I don't like it? You dare ask me whether I like it, you wretched ragamuffin? Why, by thunder . . ."

Snot-Nose nearly had the word which would let him collect what the gentleman owed him. His eyes were already sparkling with pleasure. But he pulled his knife from his pocket just a moment too soon.

"Yes, yes, boy," the gentleman cried, "I like it very well! I only said you shouldn't ask me whether I did or not," he added in a strangled voice, purple with rage. "For today, go wherever you want."

The ogre watched Snot-Nose go as far as the place where his avenue and his vines had been. If his eyes had been pistols, the boy would have been dead on the spot. Then he turned on his heel and went to complain furiously to his wife.

"Who in all his life has ever seen a servant like that! So, he's going to get the better of me? How am I to find him work that'll be too much for him?"

"Oh, you're just too simple-minded, you big red donkey, with your two bundles of crooked branches and straight branches! Give him some work that isn't a riddle but a real task, one too hard for him. I don't know . . . How about a nice white path a whole league long, from our wood to our own door?"

"There you are, turtledove! I'll find him something. Wit I've got aplenty, more than I need, but my ideas just don't come too fast."

A month went by—a month and more.

At last one morning, when Snot-Nose appeared with the ox goad over his shoulder and the loaf speared on it, the gentleman announced: "All right, boy, you're to make a white path from our front door here up to my wood. Nice and smooth and white, I want it. And have it ready this evening. Understood?"

"Understood, master."

"Aha," thought the boy, "you skinned my brothers. The devil will have to skin *you*, or I'll do it myself!"

Just that past March, when the yellow and white butterflies were fluttering about, Snot-Nose had gone around as though following them, with wandering glances and half-open mouth. But since getting mixed up with the ogre, oh, he knew how to keep his lips together and look straight ahead! So he took that order very straight indeed.

"A white path? Very well, you'll have it! You'll walk that path, my fine gentleman, or others that I'll make for you, and I'll never let you go!"

He hitched up his trousers, took a deep breath, and off he went around the whole estate, from farm to farm, rolling wagon and cart, loading the horse, goading the oxen, flying from courtyard to mill and from wood to front door.

By evening. "Your path is ready, master. Come and see!"

The gentleman went, and nearly burst a blood vessel. That white path, well, Snot-Nose had made it with flour. All his wheat! All the wheat of his whole estate! The poor folk were already running in from everywhere, like sparrows to the vines. Scraping and raking, they were salvaging what they could. It was a sin to waste so much wheat! But after all, wasn't that wheat for the ogre and his ogress? They'd have just gobbled it down in the end, or spoiled it and let it rot.

Besides, Snot-Nose had something else at stake. The fire in him burned too hot, every time he thought of his brothers and his mother. And he thought of them always. In his heart, he had nothing else.

The gentleman shouted in a choking voice for his wife. She came, she saw, but at first she didn't understand. Then the truth dawned on her.

Now both were purple with rage, like apoplectics. Their wheat, their whole store, was gone to the beggars, to the little birds, and to the winds!

Louder than any lowland she-ass, the wife set in to braying, "Ruined, fleeced, cleaned out! This'll cost us a thousand crowns!"

"Mistress," said Snot-Nose, "I did as you ordered. Could you possibly be dissatisfied?"

Dissatisfied! She was frothing at the mouth!

Luckily for her, her husband had just remembered that agreement. He quickly clapped his hand over her mouth.

"Look out, turtledove!" he warned. "Oh yes, yes, we're quite satisfied!"

So satisfied were they, that they'd have gladly bashed their heads against a wall.

"You did it all wrong, you double donkey!" the ogress scolded.

"But, my turtledove, I did what you told me to do!"

"You've got to give him an order he can't possibly carry out!"

"You're smart, turtledove, you're smart! That's it! Something absolutely impossible! This time, we'll get him!"

A month went by, or a little more.

At last, one morning, the gentleman called his servant. Snot-Nose appeared with his loaf over his shoulder.

Every day Snot-Nose had been getting up more determined than the day before. The air was light that morning, and there was even some wind. The paths were dry, the weather fine, and the view was beautifully clear. There stood the boy, a wheat stalk between his teeth, well planted in his wooden clogs. He'd charge straight through all their cheats and tricks. He'd catch up with them and he'd get them. He'd lay hands on them and carve a nice strip out of their hide.

Eyeball to eyeball with them now, he didn't blink. They were the ones blinking their beady little eyes.

"All right, boy. You're going to take the cows out of the barn without opening the door; and then, without opening the gate, you're going to put them in the walled pasture. And no holes in the barn wall, either. Do you hear me? Do you understand?"

"Yes, master, I understand."

And he did, too. Everything came straight to him, very big and plain, with the power of a thunderclap.

An hour later (oh, they had him this time!) the gentleman and his wife went to the walled pasture. They found Snot-Nose sitting on a stump outside, by the gate, enjoying his bread.

"Did you do what I asked, boy?"

"Yes, master, it's done. Your cows are in the pasture. They're taking care of themselves."

Astonished, the gentleman took out the key and opened the gate.

Yes, there were the cows. Snot-Nose had clubbed them, cut them in quarters, put the quarters out through the little window (how else was he to do it?), then thrown them into the pasture over the wall.

The gentleman and his wife were black with fury! They seemed as cut up as their cattle, and they started in bawling so loudly that their song would have drowned out any bull's for miles around.

"Well, master? Mistress? Aren't you satisfied?"

The poor things just had to swallow their sobs or get their backs skinned!

Snot-Nose can't have been used to those cows yet. If he had been, could he really have clubbed them that way? Whether an ogre's or another's, wheat and cows are still good wheat and good cows. But war makes savages of us all. And the boy knew nothing any more but his war with the ogre and ogress. On and on he'd drive through ogreland, through this contempt and these cruel fantasies, till he had those two laid out flat on their table. Such a passion for vengeance was burning in him that his blood was boiling. He no longer knew himself.

As for his master and mistress, they knew him all too well. They could stand him no more than the devil can stand holy water.

They went to their room without their dinner—ogres skipping dinner! But they had troubles! They couldn't have swallowed a single cracker. No, they shut themselves up. Everything, they blamed on their servant. How they insulted him! They called him every nasty name they knew.

And it was true: the miserable ragamuffin, the little hellion, was devastating their whole estate. He'd managed to fell the poplars, to cut down the vines, and to cast their flour to the winds and their cows to the nettles. About all he'd left them were their eyes, to cry with.

"The rotten little toad!" grumbled the ogre, pacing up and down in his nightshirt before the bed, with his cotton nightcap on his head. "How was I supposed to know? The first time I laid eyes on him, he looked as innocent as you please, with his mouth agape like a gudgeon out of water."

"You ought to have looked more carefully, you double donkey, you! And now what are you going to do?"

"Well, I . . . That is . . . All right, turtledove, what *are* we going to do?"

"The little brute's got you beat. So we've got to find someone who can beat *him*. About the only one I can think of, you know, is cousin Babouane. She's an ogress, a sorceress, and everything else. I'll send her a note. She'll take care of that Snot-Nose. He'll hardly make a mouthful for *her*. To-morrow, send him to mind our pigs in her wood."

"Why, my turtledove, that's it! After all, we *do* still have our herd of pigs!"

"No one's gone into Babouane's woods and come out again. She's skinned, cooked, and eaten them all. However much of a menace that Snot-Nose may be, she'll take care of him."

She wrote the letter by candlelight, her tooth chewing at her chin (scritch-scratch went the quill, she leaned so on every word), then sent it straight off with their bitch—who, like her masters and their cousin Babouane, was a bit of a sorceress too. Then they went to bed, hugely relieved, and snored in chorus.

Snot-Nose knew quite well that things were getting serious now. But he'd still fix that gentleman, with a little help from the Almighty. Yes indeed, with his mind as much as ever on his mother and brothers, he felt wide awake and as strong as an ox. The wind rushed by with a sweet smell of grass. Three white pigeons flew overhead. It was morning yonder, on the mountain. He clenched his teeth and looked fearlessly at whatever might come his way.

"Here's your job, boy," said the ogre. "This time you're going to mind the pigs. Take all sixty to forage for acorns in Babouane's wood. Follow the bitch, if you don't know the way. She'll take you there. Understood, boy?"

"I understand, master."

He picked up his cloak and set off, striding along as though he might have been heading home for dinner.

Climbing behind the red bitch, he reached a forest of oaks. Then he saw, in a green meadow, a shepherdess watching her flock.

"Where are you off to, my boy?"

"To Babouane's wood."

"If you go, you won't come back. Babouane will eat you!"

"Perhaps she won't, if you'll give me a cheese."

"A cheese? Of course! Here you are, poor boy!"

A little farther on he came to a pasture where he found a herder watching his goats.

"Where are you off to, my boy?"

"To Babouane's wood."

"If you go, you won't come back. Babouane will eat you!"

"Perhaps she won't, if you'll let me pick this puffball."

"This puffball? Oh, go ahead, my boy, pick it!"

It was a mushroom, as round as a river stone, and weathered all brown.

A little farther on, Snot-Nose met a hunter, a bearded fellow out for hare.

"Where are you off to, my boy?"

"To Babouane's wood."

"If you go, you won't come back. Babouane will eat you!"

"Perhaps she won't, if you'll lend me your gun."

"My gun? Certainly I'll lend it to you. If you rid us of Babouane, my boy, I'll *give* it to you!"

"Well, why not, God willing?"

Snot-Nose winked, stuffed the gun under his cloak, stuck the sheep's-milk cheese on his sleeve, then drove the sixty pigs before him into the wood.

He hadn't gone four strides before he spotted mother Babouane. She looked like the ogress, but bigger, redder, and meaner. As tall as a tower she was—like the tower at Montpeyroux—and the pigs she was watching were bigger than houses.

"Well now! In my wood! Boy, what do you want?"

"Pasture for my pigs."

"I'll eat you, you and your pigs, if I'm stronger than you. If you're the stronger, my pigs are yours. Tell me, though: aren't you Snot-Nose?"

"Yes, Babouane, that's me."

"And you're supposed to be so strong?"

She stared at him with her rheumy eyes that age was beginning to dim. But her neck was thicker than a great oak's trunk, and her arms stouter than an oak's branches. With her hands on her stomach (those big red washerwoman's hands!), massive, heavy-jowled, scarlet-faced, and as solid as a rock in her colossal strength, she looked more powerful than twelve oxen pulling together.

Snot-Nose didn't flinch.

"Say," she went on, "what's that you've got on your arm there—that round white thing that looks like a cheese?"

"Well, mother Babouane, you know how they call me Snot-Nose. I don't always blow my nose too neatly, down between my feet. I may have gotten a bit on my sleeve."

"Really? Then, when you spit . . . Here, spit in front of you. Let's see how you do."

Snot-Nose pretended to clear his throat. Then from under his cloak, he fired a double charge of buckshot straight into her face.

"God Almighty! When you spit, you *spit!* Yes, you're strong. They weren't fooling me. But here, can you do what I do? Look!"

She bent down, searched left and right in the grass till she found a stone, then stood up again and squeezed the stone. When she opened her hand, out fell a shower of gravel.

Snot-Nose shrugged his shoulders, bent down in turn, pretended to look, came up with the puffball, then squeezed it in his hand. A reddish sort of smoke spurted from his fist.

Breathless with wonder, Babouane stared at him with eyes bigger than a barn door. Then she somehow settled into herself, as though trying to look small among all these great oaks as thick as castle towers.

"Yes, Snot-Nose," said she after a pause, "listen: I admit it, you're stronger than I am. You've beaten me the way you beat cousin ogre and cousin ogress. The wood's yours. I leave it to you; and I leave you my pigs, too, the poor things. Good-bye, and stand tall!"

She cleared out, scuffing her clogs through the dead leaves, shoulders stooped and head low, more ashamed than the red bitch when Snot-Nose unhitched her and she scampered home, her tail between her legs.

Snot-Nose collected the pigs and drove them to town, to the fair. Such animals had never been seen before, with their black patches and short snouts. Round as barrels they were, and their ears were like cabbage leaves. As the ears flapped and flopped before, the little corkscrew tails wiggled behind. Trotting onto the fairground, they looked like little scamps off for a lick of mustard. People gathered around just for the fun of watching. The dealers fought over them.

"They're crossed with English, I tell you!"

"No, as far as I'm concerned, they're Périgord."

"Anyway, they're fine pigs!"

Snot-Nose sold them like hotcakes, at six louis each. He sold the gentleman's, too, while he was at it. "Well," thought he, "I'm that much ahead! I won't have to bother to empty his pockets."

Stuffing a big purse full of gold into his own pocket, he set off for the gentleman's house, his gun across his back.

The gentleman and his wife were out for a stroll before their door, enjoying the cool where once they'd had their arbor and the avenue of poplars. At the sight of Snot-Nose they turned as white as sheets. That boy made them turn every color of the rainbow.

"What?" cried the wife, her tooth sticking straight out. "Cousin Babouane didn't take care of you?"

"There you are again, you estate-eater, you wrecker of kingdoms!" the ogre blurted. "What have you done with my pigs?"

"Your pigs, master and mistress? They went the way of Babouane's. Babouane and I chatted at the edge of the wood. Then she left and I came back. She gave me her pigs. I took them to the fair. And as you'd told me to mind your pigs, well, considering the prices I was getting, I sold them, too. Are you by any chance dissatisfied?"

The gentleman had no intention of not being satisfied. He was so satisfied, in fact, that he was completely speechless. He and his wife stood there as though bewitched.

"We've got ourselves in a pretty fix," said she at last, an hour later, when she managed to catch her breath. "Everything we've done to him has fallen on *us*. What are we going to do this time?"

"That's right, my turtledove, that's the question: what are we going to do?"

They thought and thought till their heads were steaming like buckets of laundry.

"Our pigs! Our poor pigs! They were our last resource!" groaned the gentleman that evening, when they'd retired to the safety of their room and closed all the doors. Even then, he kept his voice low. "I'm getting thinner every day. Soon I'll be hardly more than a beanpole."

"And my dresses, then! Just look at the weight I've lost!"

"The worst of it all is that we simply have to keep him till spring, till the cuckoo first sings."

"Till the cuckoo sings! Well then, I know what I'll do. Yes, that's it! Tomorrow morning, bring me some tar and a sack of feathers."

The next day, Snot-Nose had hardly got on his trousers and stepped into his clogs when he heard a cuckoo sing: cuckoo, cuckoo, cuckoo!

"Hmm, that's funny. We're nowhere near spring. Why, autumn's hardly here. What kind of crazy cuckoo is that?"

He picked up his gun and went down into the garden. There, how he stared! Back among the black currants, the wild quinces, and the nettles was a feathered object, a flying creature of some sort, but bigger than Babouane's pigs. A pretty bird, yes indeed! It was a cuckoo, apparently, since it was singing cuckoo, cuckoo, cuckoo at the top of its voice.

"Sing, cuckoo, sing! I'll teach you to sing in April so early!"

Snot-Nose took a few steps forward on the grass, brought the gun to his shoulder without aiming further, and favored the cuckoo with a dose of shot in the posterior.

What a howl! The wife—for it was she who'd rubbed herself with tar and rolled in feathers—the wife toppled onto the bitch and flattened her.

Not only that, but in falling on her behind she managed somehow to break her big reddish tooth.

The gentleman rushed up, howling too.

"Disaster and perdition!" he cried. "He's blown my wife's brains out!"

"Goodness!" Snot-Nose exclaimed. "I had no idea that's where she kept her brains!" He was getting clever. "Well, master, did my shot displease you?"

Right then and there the gentleman finally burst like a puffball. "The devil take you, you cutthroat!" he roared. "No, I'm not pleased, you murderer, you bloodthirsty cannibal!"

The whirlwind struck him.

That grubby little slip of a Snot-Nose jumped on him, caught him, rolled him over, cleaned out his pockets, carried him off, laid him out on the table, and ripped off his coat and shirt. Then, his little knife between his teeth, he mashed him down with one hand against the table.

"Just you wait, now," he gritted. "This one's for *you*, you monster! It's your turn to taste that nasty trick you played on my poor brothers!"

He'd kept his knife very, very keen in anticipation of this moment, sharpening it on a stone and polishing it on his palm. He was so eager as he did it! But you see, when he actually began peeling that strip of skin off the ogre, from the base of the neck down toward the small of the back, he soon lost his enthusiasm. He'd had to learn to clench his teeth, ever since his family had suffered such cruelty, but that made no difference. He just wasn't a brute or an ogre. To be really cruel, you have to be stupid and stubborn like an animal, or worse, since animals still have some innocence. You have to be crackbrained and vicious, with poison in your blood. He dropped the knife, loaded the ogre on his back, and went to throw him under the wild quince tree, among the nettles, beside his ogress wife.

Who would have missed them if they'd died? Only their eating bowls. But those two weren't about to die. Ogres, like cats, have nine lives. When their backs and their butts stopped hurting so much, they clambered up on their horse (which was all they had left) and went off to join cousin Babouane.

Snot-Nose picked up the broken tooth as a souvenir, to make himself a knife handle. That's all he took away—that and the purse full of gold.

By breakfasttime he was gone from the ogre's house. By noon he was at his mother's.

Ah, the poor woman, when she saw him, she was as amazed as the ogre and ogress rolled into one, though a lot happier! She'd been half dead ever since he'd gone, expecting the worst. Surely that big red man would be back on his big horse to throw at her feet, like a bloody sack, the last and least-favored of her boys.

And now, there he was, the stocky little fellow, twirling the ogress' tooth on an ogreskin lanyard. And he had a hatful of gold louis. If his two older brothers weren't quite better yet, they recovered right then.

All four began keeping house together again. Meanwhile, Snot-Nose told them all his adventures, and I've told them to you exactly as he did.

So you can be sure the whole story's true from beginning to end. Still, you didn't see it happen yourself, and neither did I.

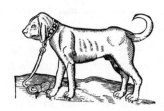

47. Dearth and Poverty

There was once a blacksmith people called Dearth; and their name for his dog, who followed him everywhere, was Poverty. This dog's coat, once silky, was now matted, dirty, and mangy. His master was the same— as thin as a rail, and all rags and tatters. The man only combed his hair on Sunday, with Father Adam's own comb: on the way into church he'd dip his fingers in the holy water and run them three times through his mop. That was it for the week.

When it came to food, he and his dog were opposites. The dog, if he could, would have eaten his meat without bread, while the master ate his bread without meat.

But he didn't even always have bread. Mornings, he'd give his ears a shake and go off to eat wherever he could find a bite. His credit was no longer good anywhere.

He had no iron for his forge, either. Dearth had laid him too low.

One day, God and Saint Peter happened past his door. They were on their way to Spain, like pilgrims to Saint James. When God's donkey lost a shoe, they stopped.

"Would you shoe my donkey for me?" God asked the blacksmith.

"Certainly," he replied.

But a hunt through his whole shop turned up not a scrap of iron. Finally he spotted the big silver buckle on one of his best shoes. He took it off, and with three clangs on his anvil, forged the shoe the donkey needed.

"What are you doing with that silver?" God inquired.

"Making a shoe for your donkey. I can't just leave you like that on the road."

He nailed the shoe onto the donkey's hoof.

"How much do you want for shoeing my donkey, then?" God asked Dearth.

"Nothing, nothing—not a thing," answered Dearth, shaking his head and sucking at his pipe.

"If you don't want money," God replied, "then make three wishes. Whatever you wish for will be yours."

Saint Peter touched Dearth's arm. "Ask him for Heaven!" he whispered in his ear.

"I've plenty of time to get to Heaven," answered Dearth. "Here's what I want. All the neighbors and old boys come and sit in my wooden chair to chat while I'm hammering my iron. Then when I want my place back, I'm out of luck. So I wish that anyone who sits in my chair should be unable to get up again unless I let him."

"Fine," said God. "You have two more wishes."

"Hurry!" whispered Saint Peter. "Wish for Heaven!"

"Well," said Dearth, "I've still got time to think about Heaven. Oh, I'm a patient fellow. But here's the thing. The boys I get to work the bellows for me, why, as soon as my back is turned, they climb up into my walnut tree—the one right there by the door—and filch the nuts. So I wish that anyone who climbs into my walnut tree should be unable to come down unless I let him."

"Fine," said God. "You have one last wish left."

"Ask for Heaven, just ask for Heaven," groaned Saint Peter, tugging at his sleeve.

"Stop pestering me with this Heaven of yours!" snapped Dearth. "What do I care about Heaven? You see," he went on, knocking out his pipe on his thumbnail, "I keep forgetting my tobacco pouch on the windowsill, or on the anvil. One fellow snitches a pinch out of it, and so does the next. So I wish that anyone who gets into my tobacco pouch should be unable to get out again till I let him."

"Fine," said God, "you'll have what you've asked for in your three wishes."

He and Saint Peter got back on their donkeys and rode away.

No one stole Dearth's seat any more, no one filched his walnuts, and no one snitched his tobacco. But his three gifts still didn't make him any richer than his dog, Poverty. Though he never bothered his head about anything, he still wondered about that. "I just didn't seize my chance," he told himself. "I never even thought about it. How dumb! I really had to be an idiot, to have asked only for fun and foolishness, and not wealth. For two pennies, I'd let the devil take me."

Sure enough, a gentleman soon rode past the forge. He stopped, dismounted, and came in.

"Why beat around the bush?" he declared. "You said you'd gladly sell your soul? Well, I'll buy it. I'll expect delivery in twenty years. Till then, you'll always have your pocket well lined with silver and gold."

Dearth had no scruples about concluding the deal. He sold his soul, and began living high. Everything he wanted he made his own, and he feasted every day as though the Three Kings themselves had come to stay with him. But his eating was nothing compared to his drinking. He went from tavern to tavern, his dog Poverty beside him, and still much preferred the drinker's mass to the priest's.

Twenty years slip by quickly when you live them that way, among dishes and glasses. Then one day, Death came calling.

"Yes, yes," said Dearth, "I'm all yours. Just let me put on my best suit, and we'll be off."

It's true he still looked just the same: unkempt and as grubby as the backside of his stove.

"Don't be long," answered Death.

"Oh no. Just have a seat."

He drew that chair of his up to the fire. Death sat down. Dearth washed up with a bit of handkerchief dipped in the water for his forge. The washing didn't make too much difference, but it was over soon enough. Then he was back, ready to go, with Poverty at his heels.

"Here I am," he announced. "Let's be off! Well? Aren't you coming?"

"I can't get up," said Death.

"No, you can't—not without permission from me. I'll let you if you'll give me twenty years more."

Twenty years! To Dearth, that seemed like years without end. What a parade of weeks and days! Still, he saw the end of it after all. Those twenty years flew by amid songs and the clinking of bottles. One day, Death was back at his door.

"I'm not coming in this time," said Death. "You won't catch me again, sitting in your chair. But your hour has rung. Come!"

"I'm coming," Dearth replied, "I'm coming! I'll just put on a clean shirt."

In fact, his shirt was blacker than chimney soot. He started bending over to slip it off.

"Don't come in if you don't want to," he went on. "But in the meantime, you might enjoy climbing up in my nut tree, there by the door. You can crack yourself a few walnuts. There are none better around here."

Poor, innocent Death did just that. When it was time to leave, with Dearth now all clean and white, and with Poverty still right behind him, Death couldn't get out of the tree. He just couldn't.

At first Death absolutely refused to compromise and give Dearth twenty more years. But all he could do then was stay perched up in the tree, like a hen on a stick. Can you imagine the world when no one was dying? No more funerals, no more inheritances, no more taking over one's elders' jobs or positions. Gravediggers, lawyers, and priests couldn't make their living. Soon things were in such a mess! And what howls of distress began mounting to Heaven! Death had to swallow Dearth's pill, and give him twenty more years.

Those twenty years, too, went by in a flash. In this world of ours, he who has plenty of money and cares for nothing but fun will hardly find time hanging heavy on his hands. Sooner than Dearth could have imagined, the hour came when his account was due.

But this time it wasn't Death who came for him. It was the devil in person, with all his little subdevils from hell.

In he strode, with a glance at the chair and the nut tree.

"You'll not catch *me* with your tricks," said he. "No, no, you'll not escape me and mine. No more excuses, no more delays. We have you now, my friend. Follow us."

"I'll follow you," replied Dearth. "Here, Poverty! Come with me! Ah," he went on, "if only I'd kept my door shut!"

"Your door!" laughed the devil. "I don't give a hoot for your door! We can get in anywhere!"

"Really?" said Dearth. "Could you get through a keyhole?"

"Of course. That's nothing."

"A likely story. I don't suppose you could all get into my tobacco pouch."

He pointed to the pouch, a well-worn pig's bladder which kept his tobacco nice and cool. It lay on the anvil.

"Then look!" the devil proudly replied.

He and his subdevils shrank and shrank till they were no bigger than ants. They climbed onto the anvil and marched into the pouch. Dearth pulled its drawstrings tight.

They weren't going to get out of *there*. Very pleased with his trick, Dearth felt like having a little fun. He picked up his big hammer, and treated himself to the pleasure of pounding away at those devils the way he might have pounded red-hot iron. Not for ages had he gone at it with such enthusiasm. The tobacco pouch hopped and sizzled under his blows like a live coal in water. Dearth kept on till he'd worked up a sweat. Then it occurred to him that he'd earned a drink. He went off to the tavern.

But devils are a bit like death: our confounded world doesn't work without them. No more quarrels, no more lawsuits, no more wars. The quibblers, lawyers, and attorneys were dying of hunger. They all went to beg Dearth for relief; and he, like a good fellow, let the whole crowd out of his tobacco pouch, after giving them another good drubbing.

And then? At last the time came for him to really be off. Dearth finally died. With his dog Poverty at his heels, he set out on the road to Hell. But the devils barred the gate as soon as they saw him coming. They wanted nothing to do with him any more.

Dearth hung his head, and with faithful Poverty still beside him, took the road to Heaven.

Saint Peter came to open the gate.

"Is that you, Dearth? I thought you didn't care for Heaven. You didn't wish for it that day when you could have, so it's not for you now."

Heaven wouldn't take him, and neither would Hell or Purgatory. He and his dog came back to earth. And that's why we always have Dearth and Poverty in the world.

48. The New Medicine

There was once, in some town, a man who was very sick. Maybe it was his heart or his lungs. Anyway, he was terribly ill. When he heard of a new doctor in town, one who was becoming more and more famous, he had the fellow come over.

The doctor looked him over for a long time, tapping and feeling in silence. Finally, he stood up and nodded.

"My friend, I must tell you the truth. You're in bad shape. It'll be hard to pull you through. But it so happens I've invented a remedy which may cure you. We'll try it if you like. But will you promise me that if I do cure you, you'll let everyone know I'm the one who saved you?"

"Fine," replied the sick man weakly. "But doctor, what if you *don't* cure me?"

"In that case, my friend, I won't ask you to tell anyone anything. We'll just keep it between you and me."

49. The Blanket

There was once a merchant who'd managed to sail his ship so profitably that he'd become rich. But he'd grown old as well. The only thing he now cared for in life was his son. He indulged the lad's every whim.

Nothing was too beautiful or too expensive for him, whether gilded sword or golden chain, silken cloak or silky-coated horse.

Now, this son fell in love with a lord's daughter. He knew neither peace nor rest till his father had gone to ask for the girl's hand in marriage.

This lord loved luxury, and had spent all his wealth at the court of the king. He let the merchant speak, then for a good while remained silent.

"Master Jacques," said he finally, crossing his legs, "if I understand you correctly, you and your son wish to enter a great and noble house. If so, you must at least do what one does before entering a monastery: one gives the monastery all one's worldly goods. Make me this gift, and then we shall see."

They say, and the merchant himself had said it dozens of times, that it's madness to let your worth go before you die, and that the only time to undress is when you're going to bed. But Master Jacques could no longer see except through his son's eyes. All he wanted now was what pleased his son. So he agreed.

The request was made on Monday, and on Tuesday the marriage contract was signed.

She was proud, that girl, and she wrinkled up her nose before this father-in-law who, for her, still stank of lucre. The servants and maids saw it well enough, and soon they too had lost all respect for their former master. In this house that had once been his, he could barely get himself served some toast in the morning, or, at four o'clock, a glass of his own white wine.

Then he had to learn to ask for nothing at all, to make himself very small, and as we say, to step aside. He'd go to sun himself in the courtyard, sitting in a corner, his chin on his hands and his hands on the head of his stick.

Year after dreary year went by, and his troubles aged him still more. He'd once enjoyed telling his grandson stories about his sea voyages, when he went to buy cargoes of spices or stock up on amber and pink coral. But now the boy was over seven, and they'd sent him to school.

Late one fall, the old man was pondering all that—the grandson he hardly saw any more, the son he never saw at all, this house that was his no longer, and the keyless house, the coffin, that awaited him—when suddenly, from his courtyard corner, he saw his son coming, abrupt of gesture and dark of brow.

"It's time," the son began, "that I made it clear . . . In my wife's opinion . . . And anyway, *you* can hardly be feeling at ease here in this house. Don't you think you'd better go and live elsewhere?"

"But my son, you're surely not going to tell me I should leave our home?"

"My wife spoke to me last night, and she insisted again this morning, angrily and in tears. When her friends go to see her, they run into you on the steps, looking like a broken-down old beggar, nodding your head, and with a drop dangling from your nose."

"Surely I'm not much in the way, in this corner of the courtyard."

The old man began shaking and choking.

"But from her room she can hear you coughing and spitting. She just can't stand it any more."

"She won't have to hear me much longer. My death isn't far off."

"Your death? Why bring *that* up? But there's nothing I can do. Father, you're going to have to leave this house."

"And where will I go, my son? Who in this city will welcome me, if my own son will not have me?"

"We're just wasting time, with this talk. I'm saying all this because it has to be said. We've lodged you here seven years and more. The time has come for us to part."

"Very well, my son. I'll go. For the winter I only ask for a blanket— the blanket from one of your horses. In my own father's day, you always put a satchel in someone's kit, to remind him that he who does not save will have to beg. I'll do without the satchel, but I do ask for a blanket."

The boy, just back from school, had stopped a few paces away. He could tell something serious was going on. Stock-still, he stared at them wide-eyed.

"My boy," said his father, "go fetch my horse's blanket, the big roan's, and bring it right back to your grandfather."

The boy ran to the stable and was soon back with the blanket. He opened it out, folded it in two, nicked its edge with his pocket knife, and tore it in half from top to bottom.

"Oh, my boy, my boy," sighed the old man as he took the half-blanket with a trembling hand, "I'd never have believed you were twice as cruel even as your father."

"What'll you do with the other half?" asked the father in a low voice. Too surprised to stop the boy, he was now watching him fold his half of the blanket like a woman folding a sheet to put it away.

"This half's for you. I'll give it to you on the day I send *you* away."

The father suddenly turned a fiery red.

"Father," said he to the old man, "will you forgive me? Now I see what

I've done. I went wrong. I'll get my wife, and all our maids and servants here, to mind me. This house is your house. From this day on, and forever, you'll have here the place which is yours."

5 o. Cricket

There was once a family people called the Crickets, perhaps because the father was stocky and dark like a cricket. Good people they were, but they didn't get much of a living out of their bit of soil that had more rocks in it than earth, and their few skimpy pastures where you could *see* the crickets scampering between the tufts of grass. The family's six or eight children didn't often spread their bread with lard, and it was only during weeks with four Thursdays that they got to whiten their soup with cream.

They kept the eldest to take over the farm. But as soon as the next son was old enough, they explained to him that he'd have to go elsewhere to seek his fortune.

He sought his fortune wherever he could. He had no fat to weigh him down, poor fellow. He was like a goat, that keeps its fat under its ribs. And he could run like a goat, too. He ran and ran, and looked and looked, but he didn't soon find his fortune. All over the countryside he worked, as a thresher here, a hemp carder there, or elsewhere as a ragman. He ended up peddling thread and almanacs. Dozens of trades, dozens of troubles. He dined whenever he found food, and lunched off a nice cool cup of water.

The poor boy was as thin as a rail. It seemed to him he'd been hungry ever since he was born. The only thought he had in his head was being able one day to eat, and I mean *eat*, till he was completely stuffed. His mind always came back to that at night, when he'd try to fall asleep on an empty stomach, behind a bush or in the hollow of a rick of wheat.

"If only I could eat and sleep, eat and sleep at ease, all I want, for three days together, I wouldn't care if they hung me afterwards. I might as well die swinging in midair, as starve to death in the mud of a ditch. And I'd at least have had three days of good times in this dog's life of mine!"

The idea of eating three royal meals, at any cost, bored into his brain like a worm into an apple. One day he was pondering it again as he peddled his almanacs from house to house, when he noticed the people he met were talking of nothing but what had just happened in the biggest castle thereabouts.

Just that morning, the lady had had it cried abroad that she'd lost her gold and diamond ring. This was a ring she treasured as she treasured her own eyes. She promised a fine reward to anyone who helped her find it.

Somehow this prospect of a reward, and the desperate desire at last to eat a good dinner, hooked themselves up in the younger Cricket boy's head.

"What if this were the chance you've been looking for? Look sharp now, Cricket, you've got to jump at it. It'll be too bad for you if you can't catch it somehow or other."

On the way out of the village, he sat down in a little wood. There he thought over the business a moment, then set out resolutely for the castle.

A maid opened the door. He showed his almanacs, then managed to let out that he was a bit of a diviner. Divining was a gift that ran in his family. If the lady liked, he might well be able to help her find that diamond ring. Oh yes, he'd find it for her, no doubt about it, if he could just eat for three days at the castle.

The maid listened to his patter, signaled him to follow her, then rushed (that's how worried everyone was) to the lady. From the hall outside, even before she opened the door, she cried, "Madam, there's a magician here who's going to find you your diamond!"

"Yes, madam," added Cricket, "all I need is to dine here three times."

That was indeed all the poor fellow needed or wanted. After that, he'd just see what happened.

Anxious as the lady was to get back her diamond, she agreed right away. Three dinners? Fine. And they'd be real dinners. The magician would be served both fish and meat. He'd spend three days and three nights in the castle, eating like a great lord during the day, and sleeping at night in a feather bed. The lady asked just one thing: that on the fourth day he should tell her where she might find her lost ring.

For the moment, Cricket cared no more about that ring than about his first pair of pants. If it was lost, let it turn up again. His own business during those three days was to be cleaning off dishes and emptying bottles. That hunger of his was so big and so old that he'd have gobbled up a whole Christian, as long as the Christian was cooked.

The first day, they sat him down at table with the castle people. It wasn't a Christian they brought him, but a whole suckling pig, crispy and golden brown; and after that, everything you could imagine in the way of meats roasted, boiled, or cured, of game, and of stews or skewered morsels. You

can be sure he didn't leave his share of these dishes to the dogs. It was
magic, the way he tucked it all away—he who hardly had a stomach left
at all. He ate everything they offered him, and all he said was, "Bring on
more!"

The astonished valet who served him goggled at him in disbelief. Finally,
the new magician got up from table the last of all, and happily patted his
stomach. The valet, just behind him, heard him say, "That's one I've got,
of the three!"

The next day, the second, he appeared again, looking like a man who
had thoroughly digested last night's dinner. Another valet brought him
different dishes, and he did them equal honor. Nothing was too salty or
too hot. He ate like a horse, he drank to match, and since even the best
things come to an end, he got up from table and patted his stomach again
as he had the evening before.

"That's two I've got now, of the three!"

The third day, at dinnertime, he got to work again blessing the cook's
labors. Poor fellow! How could he have ever imagined himself enjoying
such a feast? Still another valet brought him still other dishes, as delicious
as ever. A good life indeed! Twelve months out of the year like that, and
he'd have been happy enough to see the thirteenth come round!

At last he arose from the table and patted his stomach expansively.

"Now I've got all three of them!"

But that evening, in his feather bed, he didn't fall asleep too quickly.
He couldn't help thinking about what awaited him the next day. What was
he going to say to the lady, unless the ring happened that night to fall out
of thin air onto his counterpane?

"Well," he told himself, "I've had three good days, and I'll have one
more good night under the care of my guardian angel. Tomorrow, my
guardian angel will help me."

Then he fell asleep.

Suddenly he woke up. Someone was tugging at his arm. By the moonlight
pouring into his room, he recognized the three valets who'd served him
those dinners.

His first thought was that the lady had sent them to seize him, and he
began shaking all over.

But the valets fell on their knees.

"As you have all three of us, sir, we implore your mercy. It's true, you
are a great magician. You've discovered everything. Have pity, please, and
don't ruin us! We've brought you the diamond ring."

Actually, they'd found the ring on the tablecloth, where the lady had left it when she washed her hands upon sitting down to eat, the way people in castles do. They knew the magician had asked for three meals there in order to solve the mystery. Hearing him say, after the first meal, "That's one I've got, of the three," the first valet had thought he'd seen through everything and had recognized him for one of the thieves. After that, the valet hadn't dared go near the magician again. On hearing, "That's two I've got now, of the three," the colleague who'd replaced him the next day had ended up equally convinced of the magician's powers. And the third valet was still more convinced when he heard the magician say, "Now I've got all three of them!" So they'd put their heads together and decided to appeal that very night to the magician's kindness. There they were, kneeling before him on the floor, begging him to keep it all quiet.

"Oh, don't betray us! We'll pay you, sir! Oh, please! We each have here two fat crowns."

"Two crowns! Go hang! I'll have you hanged tomorrow before the castle gate!"

They went as white as plates.

"Four crowns each we'll give you, magician, sir!"

"Four crowns? No! It's hanged you'll be, my fine friends, hung! Everyone knows you can make a mistake, or filch some little thing, or take advantage of someone else. But to betray one's master's confidence like that! Why, that's sick! And *you*: the ring, your lady's ring! A hemp necktie, that's what all three of you deserve."

The valets, still kneeling, began shivering with cold chills, there in the moonlight.

"Oh, pity, sir, pity! We'll never do it again in all our lives!"

"All right, then. I'll have six good crowns from each. A man has to be Christian and forgive others' sins. Enough, my rascals. And walk straight, now, or *I'll* keep you straight! But what am I going to tell the lady? Hmm, I think I have an idea. Give me my trousers and take me down to the barnyard."

Early the next morning the lady, who'd hardly slept (she burned so at the thought of getting back her ring), summoned the magician.

He came before her, hat in hand, and announced that he thought he knew where the diamond ring was to be found. They should simply parade before him all the livestock from the poultry yard, and he'd speak more precisely.

The lady led the way with her maid. Next came the valets, then the

swineherd and the turkey girl, then the scullery boys and the kitchenmaids. Down they all trooped and lined up in the poultry yard, together with the chickens, the guinea fowl, the ducks and drakes, and the geese and ganders. Every one of them had to parade past the magician. He never moved. Finally, a great big goose came waddling along—a goose as fat as the mother of all geese. The magician stopped her with his hazel switch.

"There you are, madam," he said. "I'll be much mistaken if you don't find your diamond in this goose's gizzard. Didn't you come down here one evening last week and throw the poultry some feed?"

"Certainly, I come here every evening."

"Well then, madam, your ring slipped into the feed, and when you tossed it out, your ring went with it. This greedy goose gulped it down. Have the goose opened up. The ring will be in her."

He was quite sure of that, because he'd forced the ring down that goose's throat himself the night before, with the help of the valets. He'd even reminded himself, "When the goose is killed, she'll have to be eaten, and I'll be there again."

The cook slit the goose open that minute. There the diamond ring was in the gizzard, just as the magician had said.

The lady was so happy that she had no words to thank him. She pulled out her purse, took a fistful of perhaps sixty crowns, and dropped them into the diviner's hands. Not a word did she say meanwhile, but sixty crowns do quite enough talking!

At this point a great clamor arose, and there was a great stir at the castle gate. Everyone hurried, shouting, from the courtyard. The lord of the castle was back from Paris.

The lady rushed to him. After they'd kissed and asked after each other's health, she took him straight to the garden, and there she told him all that had happened.

The lord listened, twirling his mustache.

"A diviner, is he?" said he. "Aha! I'd like to see what he looks like!"

"I swear, dear husband, that he worked wonders!"

"Well, you know, I just don't believe it."

"Oh, but I tell you . . ."

"It doesn't take much to addle a woman's wits. At any rate, since he's a diviner, I'd like to see him do some divining. Now, now, run after him and bring him back! We'll see what happens."

Cricket was on his way home with the crowns in his pocket, just as pleased as a king. They ran after him.

"Come, come! Our master wants you!"

"So, you're the diviner?" said the lord. "Well, you're going to tell me what I have in my fist. Sixty crowns are yours if you can do it. If you can't, you'll have sixty blows of the rod."

Poor Cricket suddenly wanted very much to confess that he was just like anyone else, and that to divine anything, he had to know the answer beforehand. Head swimming and mind reeling, he stared at this fist with the mystery in it. He could already feel the rod on his back.

"Oh sir," he blurted, "what you're holding out there looks to me very bitter!"

The lord opened his palm. There was a bitter plum that he'd picked off the nearest branch.

What the devil! He silently counted out sixty crowns and gave them to the magician.

You can imagine Cricket's relief. But he was just making a quick exit when he heard himself called back again.

"Perhaps you were just lucky," said the lord. "I'm still not quite convinced. Let's double the stakes. If you divine what I have in my fist, you'll have a hundred and twenty crowns. If not, my servants will take you out and hang you."

What I've got in my fist! *You* try guessing it! How was Cricket supposed to answer? He twisted his tongue till it was all in a knot. Finally, he gave up and cried out desperately, in an all but expiring voice, "Poor Cricket, they've got you now!"

The lord opened his hand. There was a cricket that he'd just caught in a flowerbed.

"Well divined, my friend!"

Now it rained crowns, with an invitation to stay for dinner and eat the fat goose.

Armed with all those crowns, Cricket asked to marry the chambermaid—she was easily the nicest girl for twenty parishes around. And luck was with him. The wedding was celebrated the next day.

He was no sooner married than (well, you can imagine!) he let it be known that he'd lost the gift. Never in all his life did he regain it, and he never played diviner again. But he had pastures and farmland, plenty of cows, and more children than he knew what to do with. Finally, people gave him the name of the property where he'd settled, and called him Master de Cricket of Cricketon.

51. The Foster Brothers

Once a castle and a cottage stood right next to each other. The man who lived in the cottage was the castle hunter. He kept the lord well provided with game.

It happened that the lady of the castle gave her son out to be nursed by the woman of the cottage. The lord's son and the hunter's son nursed at the same breast and grew up before the same hearth. They roamed the fields, hedgerows, and woods together, as foster brothers will, hunting birds' nests, laying traps, and generally having a good time.

Then the lord decided to put a stop to all that. But they'd still get together by the moat and talk things over.

"Jean, I saw you take off yesterday evening. You were after nests?"

"Yes, my little lord."

You can spot a nest in a tree right away when you've an eye for it—

or *feel* one, rather. Jean could feel them. The little lord wasn't quite so good at it.

"So? Did you find any?"

"I found a nest of blackbirds."

"How many babies were there?"

Jean held up a hand with the fingers spread.

"Five! I see. Tell me, are they ready?"

"They'll need a week or ten days yet."

"And where *is* the nest?"

"Oh, down Spruce Lane, in the fork of the beech tree."

So the young hunter had a week or ten days. But on the evening of the seventh day he saw the young lord coming back from Spruce Lane with the nestful of baby blackbirds.

What good would it have done to get angry, shout, or accuse anyone? Jean just tucked the incident away in his head, where he wouldn't forget it.

Life went on quietly enough. Seven or eight years went by. Whenever the foster brothers met, they'd chat.

"Jean, I saw you take off yesterday evening. They say you're seeing a girl nearby?"

"I'll tell you no lie. Yes, I've found a shoe that fits."

"Is she sweet and pretty?"

"Yes, my lord, as much so as you please."

"So you're getting married soon?"

"A week from tomorrow."

"And, may I ask, where *is* this bride of yours? Where does she live?"

Jean ran his hand over his face.

"Well, my lord, down Spruce Lane, in the fork of the beech tree—right where there used to be that nestful of baby blackbirds."

52. Pimpon d'Or and the Three Ogres

Once in the land of sheep and rocks—yonder beyond the Aubrac range, you know, among the wild box and the blue thistles, on the sunny side—there lived a king and a queen and their little daughter. Every evening that God gave them, they'd go for a stroll in the cool air.

The little girl loved country things, which to her felt sweet and smelled good. That was because of the name she'd been given, the name of Violette.

So they'd gone out one evening in lambing time, when the grass is beginning to grow, and Violette saw a lamb. Not that lambs are rare, then, in the pastures. But that one! Its leaps were so agile, its dances so graceful, and it came so nicely to be petted, with its eloquent eyes.

A six-year-old loses her heart to whatever she sees. Violette couldn't be parted from her dear, soft, lovely lamb. All the king could do was bring out his purse and give the shepherd a gold crown. That was four times too much, but a king doesn't count change. The lamb followed Violette home.

Oh, they were in love, those two!

Children grow up by and by. The lamb became a sheep, and twice had lambs herself. Then her lambs grew up and they had lambs, till there was a whole flock.

The king's daughter took her flock to pasture daily, as soon as the heat was no longer too much for them. Sheep's heads swell up if they don't go out. She knew how to treat their wounds, how to draw thorns from their feet, how to heal viper bites, and how to keep them free of mange or staggers. All her thoughts and all her pleasures went to her dear sheep.

But one day (she was thirteen or fourteen, about marrying age), her father the king noticed three freckles on the end of her little nose.

"The sun's ruining her complexion," he cried, "the sun and the weather! She'll turn into a village shepherd girl, as dried up as a dead thistle, she who was once as fresh as a flower! I don't want her out in the fields any more watching . . . And what's to become of her flock? Well, we'll eat it—I, my minister, and my servants!"

The girl hardly dared say a word. Instead she resorted to her eyes, which were as large as her whole face. Soon she was all in tears.

"Very well," said the king, frowning, "it's not that I no longer want a sheepfold. I might leave you your flock, my daughter, but on one condition."

"What condition, father?"

"That we hire a shepherd. He'll watch them and take them to pasture. You, Violette, will go out only in the late afternoon, when it's cool, white gloves in hand. You'll go to meet your flock, since you love them so. That's my condition, and I don't intend to discuss it further."

All that remained was to find the shepherd. It wasn't the season to hire one, but sometimes luck favors us.

The king, the queen, and their daughter went out among the pastures, and came to the road which drops down toward Spain. There they met a shepherd, young and fresh, with sun-colored hair. Over his shoulder he carried a bundle, in a kerchief with the corners knotted together. The oak leaf in his cap was a sign he was free to be hired.

"Aha," said the king, "there's our man. "He's young, he looks honest, and he has that air of gentleness and reserve that does well for a flock. Give them some busy, clever boy for their shepherd, and you'll find the flock will do you little good."

With his scepter the king barred the lad's path.

"Good day, my boy. Listen, I'm looking for a shepherd. I'm the king of this land. I'll give you ten gold crowns per year, two pairs of clogs, and a goathair coat. You'll have your food every day, and a measure of wine in a china bottle."

"In that case, Your Majesty, we might well strike a bargain."

"What's your name?"

"I'm called Pimpon, in fact Pimpon the Golden, Pimpon d'Or."

"I think you'll serve us well," said the king's daughter. "Do you promise you'll take good care of my dear sheep?"

"My lady," he replied, "I'll do the best I possibly can."

The king didn't go back on what he'd told Violette. He liked the new shepherd too much. Every morning and evening he let Violette go out into the cool with her flock.

> Pimpon d'Or!
> Sweet Violette, sweet Violette,
> Pimpon d'Or!
> Sweet Violette shall step out her door!

In a week she'd shown her shepherd all the pastures. Around there the grass is far from thick, but it's very fine and tasty. She taught him to protect himself from snakes and wild bees.

"Above all, don't go near that heap of rocks that looks like the ruins of some giant's castle. It's dangerous! They say there are chasms, and ogres, too. Young shepherds have gone there, and never been seen again."

The shepherd seldom spoke. He didn't answer. Or, if he ever did answer, it was to say:

> Honor, service, reverence,
> With all due obedience.

But the next day, once the shepherd had seen the king's daughter leave—she who came every morning and evening to greet her dear flock—he stood up straight. Deep in his pocket he opened his sharp little Laguiole knife, and started boldly toward the rocks.

For the king's daughter he'd have gone, as we say around here, straight to the serpent's nest.

"God will help me, as he so well knows how to do."

He went deliberately into the ruins, those heaps and spires of stone. He heard nothing at first but a humming as the sun busily drew strong odors from the box, the pines, and the oaks. Then he heard the sound of footfalls—like a bear's, crashing through the tangled bushes and branches.

And here came the ogre, rolling his head and shoulders along like an ax without a handle. As tall as an oak he was, and as ugly as yellowed lard. The mere sight of him would have made the bread drop from your hand.

On he came like a beast, without a word. Then, with one hand to his eyes for shade, he looked the shepherd up and down.

"Small fry, I'm going to eat you. You'll hardly fill my hollow tooth. I'm going to eat you and your sheep!"

"Those sheep belong to the king's daughter."

"And won't she be coming, so I can eat her, too? What have you got in your basket?"

"My dinner: bread and a bit of meat."

"Give it here!"

In a flash, the ogre gobbled it down. But he had no intention of eating like a donkey, without a drink.

"What have you got in your bottle?"

"A measure of wine."

"Give! Give it here!"

In one gulp the brute drained the bottle.

But the ogres up in that wilderness aren't used to the fruit of the vine. That drink started bells ringing in his head, and the big lump had to sit down, then stretch out under an oak for a comfy little snooze. In a moment he was snoring so loudly that his breath stripped leaves from the branches and sent them sailing through the air.

In a fury, the shepherd cut the ogre's neck vein with his little Laguiole knife. He bled him swiftly and thoroughly.

> If the good Lord won't take him up there,
> Let the devil haul him off by the hair!

Then the shepherd went exploring. In a hazel thicket he found the entrance to a chasm. Down he went, underground, for a look. There was the ogre's castle, all of polished iron, and hanging in the hall, the shield that wards off all blows.

That evening Violette came for her flock, to see how they were doing. She found them in the middle of the pasture, quiet, nose to nose, like when the weather's too hot.

"Shepherd, my shepherd, take good care of them! And you didn't go over by those rocks, did you? Keep clear of them as you would of sin!"

"I did my best, lady, but today was so hot. The wine in my bottle didn't last long."

"Don't ask my father for more. I'll bring you another bottle tomorrow."

The next day she brought the bottle, but warned him again to stay away from those rocky ruins that looked like the tower of Babylon, or the end of the world.

"They say three ogres lurk there, each more evil than the last. They're all of a size to devour whatever they can catch."

That day, it all went just as it had gone the day before. An ogre appeared among the rocks, as ugly as anything, his head bigger than a cauldron.

He'd no sooner set eyes on the shepherd than he promised to eat him, and the sheep, and the king's daughter—because he too seemed to be all hatefulness. First he swallowed what there was in the basket, and drained the two bottles.

But that lummox wasn't used to good Christian wine either; and anyway, he was too stupid not to indulge himself. He stretched out for a little nap from which he never awoke.

Underground, the shepherd found his castle. It was made all of silver. In the middle of the hall lay the ax that cleaves all things.

"I did my best," was all he said, come evening. "But it was so hot! Both bottles were empty in no time."

"Shepherd, don't ask my father for any. Tomorrow, apart from the bottle he'll give you, I'll bring you two more."

Everything went as it had the day before, and the day before that. The ogre among the rocks was as ugly as sin, and *he* didn't seem very kindly, either.

He drained the three bottles, then lay down innocently for a nap. But not being made of solid stone, he woke up, like his fellows, in the other world. There'll always be too many brutes of that stamp in this world of ours.

The shepherd started underground, from among the rowans, the shad-
bushes, and the oaks. He found a castle all of gold, and in the middle of
the hall, the sword that pierces all things.

"And what if I now joined the joust?"

The truth is that Violette still had those three freckles on her nose, and
they bothered her father terribly. He'd decided, once and for all, to marry
his daughter off before she turned into a shepherdess.

A great joust was to be held, and all the fine gentlemen would be there.
The prize for the first day's winner was to be a branch of red flowers; the
second day the flowers would be blue, and the third day, white. The three
winners would then joust with each other, and he who came at last before
the king with all three branches in hand would have the king's own daughter
for his wife.

The day after the golden castle adventure, the king's daughter came to
visit her flock. First she stayed at the edge of the pasture, knitting a stocking
for her father. She sat, silent, under an oak, her eyes on her work.

"Shepherd, my shepherd," she at last began, "you must have heard
there's a joust starting soon. But do you know—I asked it of my father,
and he was willing—that *any* lad can enter?"

"Lady, shall a shepherd who watches the flocks, joust against princes
and knights?"

"Why should he turn from this chance before he's even tried? Come
to the joust, three days hence."

Each day, for three days, she asked him again, but got no clear promise from him.

"Shepherd, my shepherd," she finally cried, "why didn't you come? We saw an unknown knight appear, clad all in polished iron. He fought so bravely, he took the branch of red flowers. But the outcome is far from decided yet. Come yourself, tomorrow."

This time she gave him so resolute a command that he promised after all.

"Shepherd, my shepherd," she asked the next day, hurt and sorrowing, "why didn't you come? You who speak so little, answer me for once!"

"A storm was threatening, lady, and I wanted to get the sheep back to the fold."

"Ah, it's not of storms and sheep I'm talking! We saw appear a knight whom no one knew, clad all in silver. He fought so bravely, he took the branch of blue flowers. But the outcome is not decided yet. Come yourself, tomorrow."

"Lady, shall a shepherd who watches the flocks, joust against princes and knights?"

"Don't turn from this chance! What words must I use to ask you? Don't you understand? Shepherd, my shepherd, it's *you* I want to see triumph over the others. Be there tomorrow at the joust, without fail!"

The next evening she came back in despair. "The joust is over, and my happiness, too. Shepherd, my shepherd, why didn't you come?"

"Lady, the sun beat so on my head that it made me sick."

"We saw appear a knight unknown to all, a knight clad all in gold. He fought so bravely, he took the branch of white flowers; and now he'll have my hand as well, for he'll bring all three branches to my father. Shepherd, my shepherd, have you nothing in your heart to tell me?"

> *Nightingale in the grove,*
> *Go now, tell my love:*
> *Over my castles three*
> *Shall she reign right royally.*
> *One is of polished iron,*
> *One of silver, one of gold.*
> *All shine beneath the earth*
> *And in my heart still more,*
> *Yet I dare not speak to her*
> *Whom I adore!*

Then the shepherd dared to take the girl's hand, and led her to the three ogres' castles underground. In the golden castle's hall stood the three flowering branches: the red, the blue, and the white.

"Shepherd, my shepherd, then he was *you*, that knight whom no one knew, clad in iron, silver, and gold, to whom my father so wished to give his daughter?"

And she spoke again: "But now I see you're richer than my father with all his lands. Will you still have me for your wife?"

All my silver, all my gold,
Dearest, are yours to hold!
And of love my whole store
Is your own forever more.

They returned to the pasture with heaven on their faces, then went straight to speak to the king.

A splendid wedding was held without delay.

All the birds on roof or field,
Nesting or on the wing,
Trumpeted their happy song
For the high feast of the king!

53. The Big Mower

Once, on the way out of Ambert, there lived a wealthy farmer. His field, called Le Taboulet, stretched from the riverbank to the La Masse road. Around there the major crop is hay, and this farmer was known far and wide as a mower. No one would have boasted he could keep up, scythe in hand, with him or his three sons.

Being a brave, powerful worker is the most wonderful thing of all, but these men's strength made them prouder than the Ambert church steeple is tall. And they were so hard! God knows how they drove the laborers at haying time! The men they hired had to keep right up with them, every minute. Keep moving!—that was the word, and never mind if you drop dead. Not everyone's made of iron. But that's just what they enjoyed: seeing the laborers break down and practically die of exhaustion before their eyes.

An old beggar passing on the road had watched them awhile, and he remarked (for people remembered it later), "Yes, they're masters, all right. But masters though they may be, someone will come one day who's a greater master than they."

Someone told the father what the beggar had said. "I don't care who comes," he replied. "The boys and I will beat him every time."

That year, on the Sunday before the haying, this rich farmer went out into the square. There were the laborers, on Lazybones Bridge, come looking to be hired. But they all knew what to expect at *his* place. The minute they saw him, they left. Not that they made any show of it, mind you, because people said the fellow might put a hex on you if he thought you'd failed him. He might give you colic on the spot.

The farmer hailed two or three. One shouted back that he'd already been hired, while another pretended he hadn't heard.

Still, he needed a laborer. And one stepped up: a tall man with a grey beard.

"Do you think I'll do?"

"Do you know how to mow—really mow? And where are you from, anyway? From up in the hills somewhere? You're not dressed like people around here."

"That's right, I'm from up there."

"From Viverrols or Sauvessanges?"

"Maybe a bit higher."

"Chamboite or Chambonie, then?"

"No, no, higher than that. I'm sure you don't know the place."

"Well, as long as you know how to hold your scythe. Is its handle solid? You understand me, I'm sure. I mean, do you have strong arms?"

"I think so. You'll see."

They agreed on the wage. The man wasn't one to bargain it up. The master told him where to find the field. "Follow the road to Marsac," he said, "till you get to three poplars on the right, just past the houses. I'll see you tomorrow, then, at cockcrow."

Fine. The next morning at the first touch of dawn, the master and his three sons set off for their field. Mowing feels fine when the grass is all damp and tender from the night, and still bent with dew.

"Let's have a good look at the job!"

They started mowing. Though they seemed in no hurry, the scythes flew and the green hay fell; while they, rolling their hips and shoulders, pushed the swath ever forward.

> *Along the river, down below,*
> *Lies a broad field to mow.*
> *It's brave young mowers three*
> *Who've chosen it to mow, you see:*
> *Yonder, yonder in the shade*
> *A green willow tree has made.*

Dawn turned all pink, then the light grew and grew toward full day.

"Say, dad, that's quite a worker you hired! Must be one more of those fellows who like work done better than work yet to do!"

The boys, up at the end of their swath, teased their father about the laborer who wasn't coming.

"The sun's too hot now. He'll get here in time for lunch!"

Just then the greybeard turned up.

"I was expecting you earlier," said the master with a dark look.

"Earlier? Why, it isn't late. We can get through plenty of work by nightfall."

"We'll see what you get through. But the grass'll toughen when the sun's burned off the dew. Go hack away at it, then!"

"Oh I'll hack at it well enough, you'll see. But where am I going to get me a scythe?"

"What? You came without your scythe? A laborer here brings his own. That's our way."

"Oh, wait, I saw one in the cherry tree. It'll do fine."

Into the cherry tree he climbed. Up there in the branches was a scarecrow made all of rags that had been there so long, the rains had turned them the color of ashes. The scarecrow's scythe handle, long since rotten, broke in three at the man's touch. And the blade! Snaggle-toothed and eaten away, it was rustier than an old nail.

"Well, if you can make yourself a scythe out of that junk . . . !"

"Oh, a scythe's a scythe. The main thing's to give it a good handle, as you say."

The greybeard went to a woodpile beyond the ditch, pulled out a branch, and fitted it to the blade. Then he picked up the first stone he came across, and started in honing the edge.

The boys watched as they'd have watched a comic on stage, laughing fit to bust. Then they glanced at their father.

"Well, *now* we're up to strength!"

"Say, dad, is this man of yours right in the head?"

"Poor dad, you've hired the cream of the Lazybones Bridge crop!"

Frowning, the master gripped his scythe.

"Get on with it," said he. "Hurry! The job's waiting!"

Off he went, and his sons followed.

Behind them, the man, too, got to work.

At the field's end, the master turned around for a look at the greybeard's swath. It was unbelievable. The swath was as wide as his and the boys' put together.

He spat and set off once more. At the end of the next swath he turned around as before for a look.

"Well, master, will I do?"

"It's all very well, but you still lost a two good hours just now. You're that many swaths behind!"

"If that's all that's bothering you, I'll just make them up."

He mowed his way on that minute, looking like a daddy-longlegs. What strides, what sweeps of the arms! His swath, as wide as three ordinary ones, moved forward like a mountain torrent, or flood waters tumbling down a hillside.

The master and his sons lost no time getting back to work, but it was no good. The man was already right behind them, and moving two or three times as fast. Here he came, they could feel him, here he came . . .

He caught them up, leaned on his scythe, considered them patiently, let them get a good head start, then went back to mowing. In no time they heard him at their heels. Now he was up with them.

"Say, friends, you don't seem to be keeping up much of a pace. Why not let me by? I'll just go on ahead!"

Breathless and dripping with sweat, the master and his sons were shamed and bewildered as well.

It hurts to know you're not up to it any more, especially when you've always been the best. There they were, their humor getting blacker and blacker . . .

One of the sons spotted a chunk of rock by the road. He picked it up and set it down in the grass. A scythe hitting a rock at full speed feels it a bit. You have to pound the blade awhile, on an anvil, to straighten it. But the man saw the rock, and without even slowing down kicked it aside with his clog.

So the second son took their little anvil and left it in the grass, well hidden.

On and on the greybeard mowed, full tilt, but without force or effort. He pushed the swath before him like a river in flood. And when he got to that place, he swept his scythe around with such speed and power that it cut the anvil in half, right with the grass.

"Why, master, you've still got old stumps in your field!"

He didn't even stop to hone his blade.

Father and sons, now whiter than their shirts, were beginning to panic.

"Still," said one of the boys to his father, "you *could* stop him. Put your colic hex on him!"

"Yes, dad, quick, hex him!" said another.

Perhaps the hex worked, because the greybeard did go behind the bushes. When he came out, though, he seemed still bigger and more powerful. His scythe flew and the hay fell. Colic or not, he'd pause now and again in the bushes, then two seconds later be back out, as though he'd no more than wiped the sweat from his brow. On he'd go, like lightning, with the sun glittering on his sweeping blade.

People were running on the road to Marsac, some turning back to urge on those behind them. Others shouted, aghast. They were pouring in from everywhere to see the miracle.

And how they laughed at the master!

He and his sons hardly knew what look to give their faces—disappointment, shame, or rage. It was just as though they were the ones who'd had an attack of colic, right there on the mowed field in front of everyone. From that day on, they say, the four of them never again had their hearts so hardened with pride.

The greybeard mowed on and on, like a madman, but with a wonderful look of peace, goodness, and strength. He mowed the Taboulet field, big as it was, and three neighbors' fields as well. You could hardly watch him, he moved so fast. At that speed, it seemed he'd do the whole countryside.

Some thought he was Saint Martin, and others Saint Peter. No one ever knew for sure.

Then he disappeared into the bushes one last time, and people never saw him again.

Part
Five

THE MAD

AND THE WISE

54. The Carefree Sage

There was once a big-bellied miller who'd long ago been nicknamed the Carefree Sage. And he *did* always have a jolly face. What a pleasure it was to watch him at table, fork in hand, nimbly cleaning off his plate without ever stopping his jokes, laughter, and drinking! Oh, he was smarter than smart—smart enough to slip through the eye of a needle, smart enough to lead the devil off to mass and vespers.

Apart from that, he had at the mill with him a godson nearly thirty years old, and whom people still called Fantounet—Sonny Boy, in other words. You know the proverb:

> *Feet or backside, one or the other,*
> *You'll take after godfather or godmother.*

So there was the Sage with a fool for a godson—not a simpleton, really, but a boy so featherbrained he still seemed rather a loss. As the Sage liked to say, though, "It's not fools who've the thickest heads."

One year the king passed that way and happened to see the mill, all cheery and chuckling under a garland of vines, with its turning, splashing wheel, and its clumps of poplar and willow whispering and shimmering amid the twitter of chickadees. He asked who the miller was.

"Your Majesty, people call this miller the Carefree Sage."

"What?" said the king with a frown. "The Carefree Sage, you say?"

The king must have been in a very grumpy mood indeed.

"That miller's supposed to be wise, and he manages to have no cares? Well, he'd better look out, because I'm going to *give* him some cares!"

His Majesty the King sent word to the miller that he should be at the castle in eight days' time.

"I've three little questions for him: 'What does the moon weigh?' 'How much am I, the king, worth?' And finally, 'What am I thinking?' He's to bring me the answers, and if I don't like them, I'll have him hanged on the spot."

Now *that* was talking.

Having spoken, the king went on his way. Someone ran to the Carefree Sage, who listened to the questions. If his throat tightened up a bit, he didn't show it.

"They call me Sage," he remarked, "but it's wrong of anyone to think himself wiser than the God who made us all. I'd rather just be Carefree. These three excellent questions aren't going to trouble *me*."

And in fact, throughout those eight days, he didn't dine any less well than usual. No, he didn't swallow one mouthful or down one hearty swig less.

On the morning of the appointed day, he called Fantounet.

"Listen, you know those questions the king's asking? Go answer him instead of me. Just give him straight, simple answers. Anyway, your guardian angel will whisper what you need on the way."

Off went Fantounet, eyes bright and ears alert. On reaching the castle, he announced he was from the mill and had come to give the king his answers.

They took him in.

"Well?" said the king. "What does the moon weigh?"

"One pound, Your Majesty."

"One pound? And why's that?"

"Because the moon has four quarters and four quarters make one pound."

"Try the second, then," said the king. "This time it's about *me*. Tell me how much I'm worth."

"I'd say twenty-nine pieces of silver, Your Majesty."

"How's that, mister smart-aleck? Why twenty-nine?"

"How could anyone set a higher price on a man, Your Majesty, when Our Lord allowed himself to be sold for thirty pieces of silver?"

"Why, that's true!" exclaimed the king. "You're right! But tell me now what I'm thinking."

"Your Majesty, you're thinking I'm the Carefree Sage. I'm not, though. I'm his godson, Fantounet."

"Good heavens," cried the king, "it'd be a crime to leave a man like this to lead a miller's donkey! Why, he's made to drive the chariot of the State! Fantounet, my friend, I'll have you for my minister!"

2 6 6

55. Three Very Clever Lads

There was once a man, a carpenter by trade, who was so clever with his hands, he could have made a cat a new pair of eyes. Still, he had one regret: he'd never roamed France in his youth, staff in hand and sporting his colors. "They do say what I make seems well done. But *I* know that if I'd studied with real masters, my work would be something else again!"

He'd never been away from home. Evenings, he'd sit in his doorway smoking a pipe and gaze down the winding road that led far off toward all of France: toward terraced villages climbing the slopes of lava cones, with stout, square belfries rising gallantly above them; toward distant spurs and towns, crystal clear like scenes glimpsed through a glass of water; toward great sweeps of space, blue and inviting, out at the edge of the world. He thought about all the things the people on this earth know; and about the ones who've mastered secrets and skills, who've learned from a true master or else made their discoveries through their own patient toil and sudden, unsought inspiration. And he'd tell himself all over again that it's a shame, when you're young and all you need do is keep wishing and keep walking, not to go learn whatever the wide blue world can teach you.

This carpenter had three sons. When he saw they were old enough he said to them, "He who knows every trick of his trade, he who sings as he works along as well as the greatest of masters—that fellow is a man. Boys, you're to set out on the roads of France and come back in exactly seven years, on this same day. To the one of you who's the most skillful, I'll give the house! All right, you've heard me."

That house had a trellised front and every pleasant feature: a garden, vines with peach trees among them along the terrace, and that whole, splendid view! Just the sight of that house, there at the upper end of the village, told you what a delight it'd be to live and work there in heartfelt joy.

The three boys made up their bundles and buckled on their gaiters. Then they kissed their father and mother and set off down the road.

Month by month, seven years passed. Every evening as the father stood leaning against the doorjamb, his thoughts went out to his sons. He watched the world before him: the towns with their houses like specks of salt, the chain of hills stretching away into space, and far, far off, where sky and earth meet, the limitless blue. He distantly pictured the apprentices in workshops, by the roadside, or on strange streets; he pictured the amazing things master craftsmen can do with their skill. How beautiful it is, a mind which can devise ways of doing things and then can execute them! Would his boys come back with hands so clever they'd seem to have minds of their own? Or would the boys turn out to be all thumbs? Would they be the kind of clods who need more than three blows of the hammer to drive in a nail?

One July evening, seven years to the day after the three boys set out, they all came back together. One was a swordsman, one a smith, and the last a chef.

"All right, boys, it's time to show what you can do! And remember: the most skilled gets the house."

"I'm sure my brothers are more skillful by now than I am," said the chef modestly.

"We'll find out when we taste your cooking," the father replied. "How about a chanterelle omelet to celebrate your homecoming?"

"An omelet with chanterelle mushrooms," the chef repeated. "Fine! I'll go for some to the wood on the hill."

"We'll go with you," the two others chimed in.

The father wasn't going to let them go off by themselves, not *that* evening.

The four of them hadn't yet gotten all the way through the vines when they saw a storm coming—and from the bad direction, too. Great towers of cloud were swelling, grey over white, and you could hear the rumble of thunder. Then came another rumble to make anyone tremble: the rumble of hail.

Good-bye, baskets! The picking's over!

But as the first hailstone slapped to the ground, the swordsman seized a slender pole (the kind for propping up vines) that happened to be lying nearby, and with this wooden rapier challenged every hailstone that fell. The pole darted and whirled, thrust after thrust, while the young fellow leaped and danced to left and right. His pole was everywhere. With it he made what those in his line call the "covered rose"; he made his own sun. He sheltered his father and brothers like a roof, and even sheltered his father's vines—not that there were acres of them, but those hailstones weren't coming down one by one, either. They were solid! What a barrage! Yet with that furious pole of his, he stopped each one dead. The whole place was smoking.

Once the storm was by, he went to inspect the vines. Not a grape had been touched, not a single leaf.

"Talk about work!" exclaimed the father, amazed. "That's good work, all right! It seems to me the house will belong to *you*."

"You haven't seen what my brothers can do yet," answered the swordsman, tucking his shirt back into his trousers.

They were just coming out onto the road when they heard a rider galloping their way.

The smith listened carefully. "The shoe's gone from his horse's front hoof," he remarked.

Stepping into the blacksmith shop at the foot of the hill, he took a horseshoe and heated it red. As the horse galloped madly past, he tossed the shoe toward it from the doorway. The shoe stuck to the hoof and made a perfect fit. The horse didn't even have to slow down.

The father, just as amazed as he'd been by the swordplay, couldn't believe his eyes.

They went into the woods and picked their chanterelles beneath the clumps of oaks. Back home again, the chef took that day's fresh eggs from the straw nest in the henhouse.

"Leave it to me, mother," he said. "This omelet is my business. To make sure it comes out right," he went on, breaking a spray of broom over his knee, "you have to cook it over a fire of broom. Broom gives a flame that seals the omelet better and leaves it juicier inside, and the smoke gives the omelet just the taste you want. Excuse me, father, I don't mean to order you around, but would you just take the dish and stand over there by the door?"

The father took his place with the dish a step or two from the doorsill.

The pan was on the fire, resting on its trivet. The omelet was sizzling. When the chef saw it was done, he tapped the pan on the handle. The omelet leaped into the air and sailed past the chimney. Chatting casually, he strolled to the door, took the dish from his father's hands, and held it out without even looking. The nicely turned omelet slapped straight into it.

The young fellow had been right to come for that dish. His astonished father would have dropped it.

Tears of joy and wonder, as big as white currants, slid down into the father's mustache.

"My boys, my boys, the house belongs to all three of you! Who could possibly choose between you?"

He was right, too. Who indeed?

The house went to the three of them, and they all lived there together. They weren't going to run each other any competition with their trades. Each one sang his brothers' praises, and just shrugged his shoulders if the talk turned to himself. They lived their lives in complete harmony. Even their wives—what a miracle!—were happy with each other. And since they were all so friendly among themselves, and proud and contented too, despite all those who might have been jealous of them, they lived until they died.

56. Fearless Jean

There was once a rich man who had three sons, three strapping boys who did well and feared nothing. The three of them looked quite capable of facing anything that might come their way in this world.

This rich man also had an estate, and it was very well equipped. In fact, it lacked nothing, from the great stretch of woods on the sunset side of the mountain, to the clump of balm in the garden next to the beehive which faced the sunrise. And the orchard behind the house, especially, was a little heaven! Pears by the basketful, apples, plums, peaches, white and purple grapes. Oh, the place had everything—apples and pears in endless varieties, white apricots, even crabapples and medlars. And they were all round and fat and juicy, and tasty, too, I can tell you!

One year, a great year for fruit, the trees were so heavily laden that people were saying they'd never seen anything like it. Every branch had to be propped up. And now it was nearly time for the picking.

Just remember,
Fruit's ripe in September.

But the fellow was waiting for Saint Rémi's Day, October first. He waited a bit too long.

One evening, he went for a walk around his orchard. His whole pleasure was looking at those loads of fruit, and caressing them with his gaze. He came back home in awful silence, flushed and fuming. Then suddenly, in the middle of dinner, he brought his fist down with a crash on the table.

"Why, the thieves are loose out there! They stole masses of pears last night, and tonight the rascals are bound to be back for the rest. If there are any men present, it's time for them to show what they can do."

"All right," said the eldest son, "I'll sing those thieves a little song."

He took down the gun, loaded it with shot for hare, stuffed a good bottle under his coat, and took up his post under an old quince tree, in a spot darker than a wolf's lair.

Early fall nights are brisk. The heavy dew soaked through the coat and sent chills along the lad's spine. It wasn't fear, no, but he was shivering anyway. He'd sat down in the grass against the trunk of the quince tree. Now he uncorked the bottle and drank straight from it. For a while the wine kept him from freezing, but soon he was shivering again. He kept feeling as though some robber was about to grab him around the waist from behind.

In short, fear got the better of him. When he couldn't stand it any more, he turned around and scurried home to bury himself under the covers.

In the morning, there wasn't a pear of that kind left.

"My turn," said the second son. "I'll watch tonight. I'd like a good look at those rascals who're robbing the orchard."

He took the gun and another bottle. But fear got to him, too, and he, like his brother, rushed home to bed.

In the morning, all the winter pears were gone.

"A fine lot of boys I've got!" the father exploded. "Wide-awake, oh yes! The fruit's being stolen right out of our orchard, and meanwhile they're snoring!"

"All right," said Jean, the youngest, "it's my turn now. I'm not afraid of the cold, I don't need any bottle, and I don't believe I'm going to fall asleep."

He took just the gun, stuck a bit of white paper on the sight, and marched off to guard the orchard.

The night was as black as mortal sin. Now and again he stole from one tree to the next across the grass, as silently as a cat, his finger ever on the trigger. The only sound was an occasional apple brushing through the leaves and thudding to the ground.

At last, toward midnight, he thought he heard a noise, as though someone was cautiously pulling himself up through the branches; then came a whole avalanche of apples. Jean reached the tree in three bounds. By now his eyes were used to the dark. He put the gun to his shoulder, aimed, and fired. The thief tumbled out of the branches and went splat like a cowpat.

The shot brought everyone in the house to their feet. The father, the eldest son, the second son, the servants, everyone rushed up with lanterns. The thief lay very still, flat on his face in the grass. Jean had killed him instantly.

"You do a job, don't you, when you put your mind to it!" The father held the lantern close. They turned the thief over. Oh, *that* was a surprise! Whom did they see? The village squire.

Already they could hear men running toward them with a great clatter of wooden clogs.

"Hurry," cried the father, "hurry! They'll hang you, they'll hang you! Run, if you've got legs! Try to get to the other side of the mountain before dawn!"

"Dear father," replied Jean, "I'll be off then, since I must. Good-bye, father! Good-bye, brothers! Kiss our mother for me!"

He had no time to go to the house and pick up his bundle. Off he went without a penny in his pocket, and without even a staff. "But I'm not afraid," said he, "and I trust I'll never be afraid."

He walked and walked and walked, up hill and down dale, down dale and up hill. He walked the same way he worked—and when he'd taken on a job, that job just melted before him. The next evening he was still walking.

At last he reached a wild place, a spot of earth with a big tree. Overhead towered a rock with a chapel on it. He stopped under the tree, struck a light, lit a handful of ferns and dead branches, put his flint back in his pocket, and without fear of the wolf or of anything else, stretched out to sleep.

He was just dropping off when he heard a sound like breathing or sighing. Something was there in the dark—something neither man nor beast.

He sat up, rubbed his eyes, and looked at the tree. A shape was stirring there and climbing down from branch to branch. Then it was in front of him. The being, waxen white with gleaming eyes, didn't seem to be of this world at all.

The two stared at each other. The being stepped up to the fire as though to warm itself.

"Tell me, brother," said Jean, "who are you?"

"I'm from another land, one where it's not nice to be. Five years ago the judge had me hung from this tree because I stole the chapel's treasure. The treasure's hidden under a stone near the holy-water font."

"All right," said Jean, "I'll get it and I'll take it to the priest tomorrow morning."

"But you see," the other went on, "I was the priest's servant. I buried the chalice, the ciborium, and the monstrance in the garden, three paces to the right of the well. I'll suffer horrible torments as long as all the gold hasn't been returned. Young man, you who seem quite unafraid, if you could just dig them up and give them to the priest . . ."

"Then I'll go tomorrow morning," said Jean. "I promise."

"Oh, if you only knew what it's like there!" the other sighed. "Maybe you'd want to set me free this minute."

"Fine," said Jean, "I'll take what's under the stone and get to the rectory right away."

"Thank you for your kindness and your trouble," replied the ghost, and disappeared like a snuffed-out flame.

Up went Jean to the chapel, found the stone by the holy-water font, and rescued the treasure. Then he went straight on down to the village.

About midnight he reached the rectory door. He knocked. The priest stuck his head out the window.

"Who's knocking here so late?"

"Excuse me, Father, it's not that I mean to be rude, but do take a spade and come down into the garden."

"Must I do it right away?"

"The thing is, Father, that's it's a matter of freeing a poor soul from his suffering. It's your servant who sent me, you see—the one who was hung for stealing from the chapel."

The noise had roused the priest's housekeeper. When she heard what the lad was saying, a ghastly shiver ran through her.

"Don't go, Father, oh, don't go! Please wait for morning! Surely you're not going to go now!"

But the priest, after what he'd heard, would have felt bad about not answering the call. Still, he was shaking like a newborn lamb.

"Hurry, Father," Jean urged him. "There's a poor soul to save from Purgatory."

The priest took pick, spade, and lantern, despite the housekeeper, who was screeching like a badger. He opened up for Jean and went with him to the garden.

"Where's the well, Father? I'll just pace off three steps to the right
. . . This must be the spot. Here, give me the pick."

Jean took the pick and started breaking up the earth. His first blow
brought up the chalice, and the second the ciborium. The third yielded the
golden monstrance. It was just as though the ghost was right there with
them, in the blackness under the stirring hazels, and guiding their search.
Then Jean took from his pocket what he'd found up there, under the stone
by the font, and returned the treasure to the priest, who was shaking
helplessly from head to toe.

Just then both saw a shooting star cross the sky. "That," thought Jean,
"must be the soul of the thief heading for Paradise. Mark that up to my
credit, in compensation for the one I killed in my father's apple tree!"

"Come, young man," said the priest, "come, let's have a glass of ratafia
to help us over all that excitement. But how can I ever thank you for what
you've just done!"

They went into the house and had their refreshment.

"Listen," the priest went on, putting his hand over Jean's, "brave as you
are, you could do everyone here a very good turn. An hour from here, on
a mountain, there's a castle that's been taken over by the devil. He forced
out the castle's real owners, and ever since, every night that God sends us,
you hear the most frightful Sabbath up there. Yes, if you could chase the
devils out of that place, you'd give joy to the owners and to the whole
countryside."

"I could try," said Jean.

"There's just one little problem with going up there, though, and that's
that you never return. Of those who've been up—brave souls they were,
too—not one has ever come back down. So you see, you'd be putting
yourself in terrible danger . . ."

"Danger or not, Father, I'll go."

"You're not afraid?"

"Afraid? I don't even know what sort of creature fear is, or whether
it's got feathers or fur. No, Father. I'll just ask you to lend me your
consecrated stole and your crucifix."

"Gladly," replied the priest, "gladly. Come and sleep in Monsignor's
room. There won't be any ghosts to wake you up."

In fact, the lad slept like a log. When he woke up, the sun was watching
him from high in the sky, over the pear trees in the garden.

He arose, washed, had breakfast, picked up the stole and crucifix, and
set off for the devil's castle.

It seemed a long way through those woods—long and lonely. The path twisted and climbed among roots and rocks. Now and again he'd pass a spring or a clump of foxgloves. One hard climb just led to another, and one bend to the next. Out there, you could end up feeling very, very alone.

It was nearly noon when Jean reached the castle gate, which stood wide open. In he went. In the kitchen, a turkey was roasting over the fire, turning all by itself on its spit, and the soup pot was singing as it hung from its hook. Up stepped Jean, took a bowl, and began cutting himself a chunk of bread.

"Prepare four portions of bread-and-soup!" just then cried a voice from the chimney.

"I'll prepare them if I feel like it. Beg your pardon, but you might talk more politely."

"All right, *please* prepare four portions of bread-and-soup."

"Gladly, as long as you'll keep me company."

There burst from the chimney a fearful din and a horrible clanking of chains. You could even see the ends of the chains jerking and swinging about.

"Please, please," said Jean, "a little less noise. Drop that junk and come eat."

Three horned devils appeared that instant.

"Dinner's not quite ready yet," said the oldest, the head devil. "We've still got fifteen minutes for a game."

He slapped a pack of cards down on the corner of the table and took his seat right there, next to Jean. The two younger devils sat across from them.

Anyone else would have cracked. Those terrible faces! Those pitiless looks, piercing enough to give you the shivers! This was far beyond simply running into some ghost one night. But there sat Jean, as cool as a cucumber. He might as well have been sitting in the kitchen at the rectory. He had that consecrated stole in his pocket, though, and the crucifix was right there within easy reach. You can imagine how intently alert he actually was.

A younger devil tossed a card awkwardly, and it fell to the floor between the older devil and Fearless Jean.

"Pick up my card, you!"

"You could talk a bit more nicely. Beg your pardon, but pick it up yourself!"

The older devil bent down to pick up the card. Jean seized his chance just right. In a trice he slipped the stole around that devil's neck.

The devil found himself tied to a pillar by the sacred cord. Jean leaped up and seized the crucifix. The sight sent the two other devils scampering up the chimney, bumping the turkey and soup pot on the way.

"You know I've got you," said Jean. "Why did you want to have me pick up that card?"

"So we could push you into the well that's under the table."

"Bring out everyone you've thrown down there, then we'll see."

Grudgingly, the devil obeyed.

"All right," said Jean. "But I won't let you go till you sign a little promise never to come back to this castle again."

"I'll not sign any such paper!"

Jean adjusted his grip on the crucifix—the kind on a long staff, that's carried in church processions—and set about tanning that devil's hide. The devil's furious struggling sent loaf and knives, dishes and bowls flying from the table, but he couldn't dodge every blow.

"You'll never set foot here again and you'll let the owners enjoy their castle in peace. Write that in your own blood!"

"I will *not*, I will *not!*"

Oh, that's when Jean *really* set to. What a beating! The whole place was smoking with it. The devil shrieked like one possessed, and he couldn't have made more horrible faces if he'd been dangling from a gibbet.

"Stop, stop!"

"You're going to sign?"

"Yes, I'll sign."

With a claw he pricked the end of his finger, and with that same claw he signed the paper that the priest had given Jean. Jean made sure everything was in order. It was only after he'd stuffed the paper deep into his pocket that he untied the stole.

That devil took off like the wind, and it didn't look as though he ever meant to come back.

Well, when the priest saw that paper . . . ! And when the people saw their boys back again—the ones who'd dared go up to the castle . . . ! Jean got the biggest welcome you can possibly imagine. But the really big celebration was put on by the lord of the castle.

That lord could hardly think what to give Jean by way of thanks. He tried getting him to accept a purse full of gold, but Jean would only take a rose—from the hand of the lord's daughter, who pinned it over his heart.

This young lady was perhaps sixteen years old, going on seventeen, and

ever so pretty and gay. She gave him the rose, and that instant, without
even knowing it, Jean gave her his heart.

They'd made him promise to spend a fortnight at the castle. When the
fortnight was over they'd have gladly kept him longer. The lord kept looking
at the two of them—Jean and his daughter—and as far as he could see,
the pair of them were made for each other. But Jean came to say good-
bye. He wanted to keep traveling, to see whether he might find anything
on the road or in the woods that would give him a taste of fear.

Actually, he kept saying to himself, "What *are* you then, really? You
killed a man over some apples, and you weren't afraid of a ghost or of a
trio of devils. How could a wild man like you live with this young lady?"

He insisted on leaving. She gave him a handkerchief she'd embroidered
herself. There was a rose in the middle, with stars all around, and in each
corner of the handkerchief a little love-knot of flowers. He ought to have
seen all that the girl's eyes were telling him.

But he left and roamed the world. He went straight through whatever
came his way, without haggling or flinching. "I still don't know what sort
of creature fear is," he told himself. "I still don't know whether it's got
feathers or fur."

That worried him a bit—to the point where he wondered whether fear might perhaps be when you blush to hear people talking about a girl, and you run away when you see her coming.

One evening a nice girl he'd just saved from a wolf was talking about their getting married.

"Listen," said Jean, "I'd be glad to get married, but I've never felt fear in my life, and I've promised myself that I'll only marry the woman who can scare me."

The girl tried half-a-dozen ways, rattling chains on the stairs under a white sheet and playing ghost. Nothing happened. Fearless Jean was still Fearless Jean.

He had to say the same thing more than once, to other nice girls. That promise he claimed he'd made to himself ended up very serious indeed.

Meanwhile, he kept over his heart the handkerchief with the rose, and he came back at last to the land where he'd had his first adventures. He couldn't very well not visit the castle and find out whether the devil was keeping to his bargain. Well, yes, the devil was. And perhaps Jean, for his part, would have set off again. But the young lady wouldn't let him go. She sighed. He sighed too. One said one word, the other the next.

"But you see, I've made a promise: I'll only marry the woman who can scare me."

"All right, then, I'll scare you. Fearless Jean you may be now, but you won't be Fearless Jean forever!"

She didn't seem in the least stumped.

A day went by, then another. Nothing at all out of the ordinary happened.

On the morning of the third day, the young lady called him. "Jean, would you come and help me? We're going to make bread."

Up in those high villages it's the women who do the baking, because in the summer the men go into the mountains. In other places, it's the men who bake. Each county has its own customs.

"Jean, please, would you lift the cover off the dough trough?"

It was a big trough with a heavy lid. But helpful as Jean always was, he whisked it right off.

Heavens! Something like a clap of thunder swirled around him, stunning him, beating wings, rushing up into his face: it was a whole flock of pigeons flying up as one—fifty or sixty pigeons the crafty girl had stuffed into the trough.

Jean fell back three paces and ran his hand over his face.

"Whew! That scared me!"

The girl threw her arms around his neck and kissed him on both cheeks. "There's no more Fearless Jean! So we can get married!"

"Oh, how wonderful! That's it! All right, then, I know the truth: fear's a creature with feathers!"

They were married before the week was out, and they had a whole crowd of children who were never, ever afraid of bats.

57. The Land of Long Nights

There were once two tinkers: two lads who were perhaps a bit thick, a bit coarse—well, you might say they were good enough lads, more or less. And they were both exactly alike, except that one went for soup with lard while the other went more for the bottle. Both were close with their money, though, and once they'd been into their purses, they didn't like to go back for more.

That's why most of the time they slept at farms, up in the hayloft. That way they didn't have to spent ten centimes on an inn—that's what inns used to cost for a night. They saved it instead and were no worse off for all that.

But one night surprised them in a stretch of country like any number you can find, where it's all villages and no farms. They kept walking and walking and walking till they were groggy with sleep and exhaustion. They slept as they walked and walked as they slept. Their eyes kept closing as they trudged on like automatons. There wasn't a single house along those roads, not even a barn. Then at long last they reached a town. Oh, they hesitated a moment, but after all, that wind was blowing—the wind which bites and makes you shiver, the one they call Poor-Jeanne. They could hardly stretch out on the paving stones of the square, with no cover but a few dancing wisps of straw. They went into the inn.

"Heavens!" exclaimed the host. "You want a room for the night? But you see, I'm afraid we've a fair in town tomorrow, a big one, and I'm full up with merchants. As far as I can see, there's not a thing I can do for you."

"You know," replied one of the tinkers, nodding off even as he spoke; "you know, all we need is a place to lie down. We're not particular."

"Oh no," the other chimed in, weaving like a drunk; "oh no, give me a bit of straw in a corner and I'll sleep like a log."

"All right," said the host. "Come with me."

He took them upstairs to the end of the hall, then to the back of a room and into a garret which gave onto nothing at all. It was just a blind space under the eaves, with no other window than a wall cupboard. The kitchen boy had had to sleep there once upon a time.

Those tinkers weren't the kind to need a handkerchief: their sleeves were quite good enough. No, delicate feelings weren't their line. They were so sleepy they hardly gave the garret a glance.

"Fine!" they declared. "We'll sleep just as soundly here as anywhere else, and we'll be up in the morning just as early!"

Habit made them entrust the host with their matches and knives, the way they did on the farms.

Another habit of theirs was to seize by the hair any chance to get something cheaper.

"Just a minute, though. A night in this room's half-price, right?"

"Right," said the innkeeper as he took the matches. "And for half-price I'll let you sleep just as long in this room as you'd do in a room for the gentry. See you tomorrow!"

Off he went with the candle, leaving them to bed down in the dark the way they always did in barns. An evil idea had just popped into his head. He pulled the door shut, carefully dropped his candlestick, and under cover of the resulting clatter quickly turned the key in the lock without their hearing it. "Good night, good night!" thought he. "It's going to be a long one!"

Downstairs, he winked to the merchants who were sitting around drinking. "I believe we're going to have some fun!"

In a few words he explained what was up.

Meanwhile the two tinkers, who, their gear on their backs, had been killing themselves all day looking from house to house for jobs or working on village squares—the tinkers undressed, lay down, and sank into leaden sleep.

They slept so soundly that they didn't wake up till fairly late in the morning.

Wake up they did, though, in the end. They each opened one eye. Blackness, nothing but blackness. At first each tried not to move too much, for fear of awakening his companion. They hardly dared turn over on the straw. But one was hungry and the other thirsty. Hunger and thirst gnawed at them worse and worse, till they began to see visions. One dreamed of rich, steaming soup, the kind so thick the spoon stands up in it. The other dreamed of nice, cool red wine, big gulps and swallows of it, with the liter bottle right there on the table.

"I seem to have had my sleep," one muttered. "That's what it *feels* like, anyway, with this thirst I've got."

"I can't believe it," muttered the other. "I'm just too hungry tonight. It might as well be morning already."

They sighed, stretched, and sighed again.

"Are you asleep?"

"Are *you?*"

"I've slept enough. I'd be glad to have some soup."

"Me, I'd be glad of a proper drink."

"But you can see just as well as I can that it's dark yet."

"Yes, but still . . ."

They listened. The place was so far back in the inn, all they could hear was an occasional moo or a fragment of speech, and a confused roar of wheels and feet. All the sounds ran together like the sound of wind in the trees. They listened, waited, and let the time go by. But one was desperately hungry and the other desperately thirsty. They began yawning, yawning so long and loud that you could hear them from the fairground. "Hah, hah, HAH! Ah-hah, hah, hah, HAH!" They stretched their arms, worked their shoulders a bit, then started in yawning again fit to bust.

Finally the hungry one couldn't stand it any more. He got up in his shirt, groped his way into the blackness, felt around everywhere, found the latch on the wall cupboard, opened the door, and stuck his nose out this window which was six inches from the outer wall, taking the air and looking for daylight.

There was no more daylight out there than inside an oven.

So back he went to his straw and lay down again. "I've got to sleep. These things happen! Sometimes you think you've had your night's sleep and the night isn't over yet."

They tossed and turned, trying to go back to sleep, but sleep wouldn't come. What did come, louder and louder, were growls and rumbles of hunger—hunger for the soup man, thirst for the bottle man.

They couldn't help listening, though, and eventually heard a clock somewhere in the house ring twelve times. It was either midnight or noon.

Up they got, both of them this time, and went to the door. It was closed and locked.

They battered at the door with their fists, bawling and calling the host the way no one had ever called him before.

The host came up dressed for bed, with his nightcap on, candle in hand.

"What's gotten into you? Midnight's hardly rung and you're waking us all up! Lie down and be quiet! Otherwise my traveling men will be up to sing you their song. That's enough, now! Get in bed and wait for morning."

Pretending to be angry, he slammed the door on them. As it slammed, he nimbly locked them back in.

Thoroughly ashamed, they went back to their straw and tried with all their hearts to fall back to sleep. Through the head of one danced nothing but soup with lard, full ladles, overflowing tureens, chunks of cabbage, tender potatoes, and slices of brown bread amid the steam. The other was having visions of brimming glasses and ranks of liter bottles.

Dreaming away like that, well, they did at last dream themselves to sleep. By halfway through the evening they were snoring, noses on their pillows, loud enough to shake the whole inn.

The story of the two tinkers who'd gone upstairs in the inn to sleep had been the talk of the fair since the morning. People went to the Golden Lion the way they might have gone to a stage comedy. They'd go in and inquire about the two sleepers. Some even tiptoed up the stairs and to the door of the outer room, then to the door of the garret, waving signals to the people behind them and listening to the snoring that floated out of the darkness like the roar of water from a millrace.

The tinkers slept on and on and on . . .

Still, they obviously had to wake up again. This time they were so hungry and thirsty that they couldn't possibly stand it. This night was going on forever and this door never seemed to open . . .

They tried to be patient, at least till they should hear the clock strike an hour, so they could tell what time it was. But to make the joke even better, the host had stopped the clock.

At last, though, the wine man thought he was going mad. Leaping at the door, he scratched, shoved, and poked around.

"Come on, lie down! You don't want to wake everyone up again, do you?"

"Listen, I'll only wake them up very gently."

At first, yes, he went at it gently. Then both of them lost patience.

Hunger for soup with lard spoke just as loudly as thirst for red wine. Soon they were battering away at the door again and bawling.

The host came running, once more dressed for bed as he'd been at midday. He made sure he left all the doors open so that everyone downstairs could hear.

"But you're crazy, the two of you! Or are you sick? What do you mean, you're hungry and thirsty? What's the matter with you? The people here want to sleep! They'll make you regret this!"

The drinkers had come up behind him and were listening from the stairs. The steps were crowded with merchants, servant girls, and neighbors, both men and women. All were convulsed with laughter and their frantic efforts to keep from exploding were making them sicker even than the two tinkers. Tears were pouring down their cheeks, their shoulders were shaking, and the whole inn seemed to be vibrating like a mill.

"For heaven's sake," the innkeeper went on good and loud, "can't you wait for morning to raise all this rumpus? All right, come and see how much night there is left!"

He pushed them into the room, opened the window, and showed them the stars—because it was around eight o'clock.

"It must be two in the morning. I don't want to hear anything more out of you or there'll be trouble. As you're so eager to leave early, I'll come for you at cockcrow."

Then he shooed them back into their garret, locked it up, and rejoined his friends downstairs in the main room. Everyone had laughed themselves sick. Reviving them took more jugs of wine.

No one in the Golden Lion slept that night. A whole barrel had been emptied by dawn.

But what sort of night did the two tinkers have?

They slept some more, if they were able, or talked nonsense to each other.

"Oh, I tell you, the nights are *long* around here!"

"I was just going to say the same thing. Have you ever known a place where they lasted so long?"

"Where they make you so hungry?"

"Where they make you so thirsty?"

"What a dump!"

"Well, let's try to sleep some more."

"I'm sleeping so much I'm going to turn into a goat!"

On and on they went, their litany ending only to start over again, worse than a solemn rite of the Church. Merrymakers kept stealing up barefoot to press their ears to the door.

At last, before the break of day, the host came knocking and opened up.

"Wake up! Wake up! We're early risers here. No indeed, we don't lie around long in bed, not we!"

The two tinkers, on the other hand, felt these people lay in bed a very long time indeed.

They jumped up and shot from the room as though it was on fire. It didn't take them long to wash their faces.

"Could we have a bite to eat?"

"And a little drink?"

"We're so hungry and thirsty," they added in chorus, "that for once we don't even care what it costs."

"You want to eat and drink? Certainly, certainly. Downstairs is already full of people who care less for their beds than you do!"

The tinkers were brought whatever happened to be on hand—the left-overs from the fair. They'd have been served up the wolf, as the proverb goes, and they'd still have been glad to eat it, provided it was cooked! They cleaned off every dish and emptied every bottle. The word got around town in no time. People were still pouring in for a look.

The tinkers themselves had never seen such early or such cheerful risers. In fact, everyone was in such a good humor that they passed the hat and treated the visitors. Imagine having had such a feed for nothing! The tinkers had never felt so fat and happy—happier even than those jolly folk who

were having such a good time at the inn. The same mood prevailed out in the street, for the tinkers set off at last to such peals of laughter that every householder came to his door. In fact, they themselves were laughing the hardest of all.

"That's right," they kept saying to each other, "there's nowhere else where the nights are so long . . ."

"And where people then get up so early . . ."

"All cheerful and ready to laugh . . ."

"But when you're from somewhere else, it's hard to sleep soundly, as they do, all night long."

58. The Little Tailor

There was once a little tailor. You know what they say—there are silly people everywhere, after all, saying silly things. They say it takes three tailors to make one man. Anyhow, it was true with this one. He was just a tiny thing. Still, he was as plain and true as a good red apple, and as fiery as any burning coal. Always bubbling with good cheer, he was. And he didn't pass the time of day reasoning and calculating, no, not he. Ideas hit him on the cheeks, as hot flushes. He was so short, you see, that his heart was near his gut and got all heated up. Maybe that's why. Anyway, you'd never find yourself a friend clearer in the head, steadier through thick and thin, quicker to seize any chance, or braver in the face of whatever might come along.

The trouble was, in that miserable countryside where he lived, people didn't give a hoot about tailors. They mended their ratty old clothes themselves. But he just tightened his belt another notch.

One day he got fed up with making such a poor living. "There isn't room enough for me here," he declared to his wife. "I'm going to explore the world. I'll be back as soon as I've earned myself a purse full of gold. Then we'll take it easy."

"What are you talking about?" she sighed, clasping her hands together. "We'll live off plain water and barley bread if we have to—but don't *you* go roaming the roads, built the way you are!"

"I'll go as I am, yes I will!" he retorted, drawing himself up. "We'll just see what happens!"

"My poor little husband," she replied, "just look at you! Mallet blows don't bounce off hazelnuts. You think you're big enough to take what's coming? Why, one clout would squash you like a fly!"

"Whoever wants to squash me, let him try!" the tailor shot back, snapping his knife shut—they were talking over dinner. Now he was as red as a cock's comb. "I'll be off tomorrow morning," he went on. "Yes, tomorrow morning at cockcrow!"

Next morning at the first cockadoodledoo he jumped out of bed. His wife had gotten his satchel ready: two slices of bread and two goat cheeses.

"At least, little husband, don't go through Bigwood Forest! You know a giant lurks there, and he's the rottenest brute who ever walked this earth. He does so much damage, so much ravaging and pillaging, that His Majesty our king has promised his own daughter's hand to the gentleman who'll rid the land of him. But nobody's gone up against the giant yet. No, don't go through the forest. The brute would be only too pleased."

"Then *let* him be pleased! If the forest's on my way, then through it I'll go!"

He was getting redder and redder.

He took down his satchel and gripped his staff. His wife ran up with a fresh-laid egg she'd just found in the nest, under the straw. Afraid it might get broken, he slipped it into his breast pocket—the one that tailors call "hell."

Into one of his side pockets went his ball of string, and into the other his little finch, which would cheer him with a song when he sat cross-legged on the table cutting or sewing.

He took all those things; took three kisses from his wife (one on each cheek and one on top); took his leave; and took to the road.

Larks were singing in a cloudless sky. He strode ahead, still burning, swearing nothing would make him back off. As it happened, he came to the forest. Now, he'd said loud and clear that he'd go through Bigwood Forest if it stood in his way, and so he kept going. The forest started beyond a stream which turned three mills, and stretched on league after league to the shore of the sea. In he marched under the trees and kept straight on, head high.

Worked up that way, he charged along at a great rate. When you've far to go, you know . . . Well, he got tired and had to stop. He must have been hungry, too. Down he plopped, right where he was, on the moss. You know how people ask why tailors cross their legs to work? It's a riddle you ask little children. The answer is that if they crossed their *arms*, they wouldn't get anything done. Anyway, there he was in the forest shade, and even though all he crossed was his legs, he'd never have been able to do much else, because soon he was waving his arms around like a windmill. He had to, to keep off the flies that always buzz around in the woods. They were tickling and biting him, and driving him quite wild.

At last, with whacks of his handkerchief, he got rid of them all. Next, he quickly spread his two slices of bread with one of his two cheeses.

But he'd hurried too far and too fast. He'd hardly wiped his knife on the moss when sleep overcame him. Down dropped his head onto his shoulder, his shoulder slumped against the tree, and off he wandered to dreamland. His nap didn't last, though—the time to say a few rosaries, no more. Then the flies were back. They woke him up.

The tailor jerked awake. The two bread-and-cheese slices in front of him were practically black with those confounded flies. He was furious. Quick as lightning, he slapped both hands down on top of them. "All right," he cried, "I'll teach them to filch my lunch. That's twelve I've killed—five with one hand and seven with the other!"

He'd counted them at a glance, and crowed his triumph aloud into the wind. Then in three gulps he downed his meal.

He'd no sooner finished than sleep found him again, in that peaceful, shady spot. All he could do, before he dropped off, was to curl up with his white handkerchief over his face.

Even as he snoozed, though, he kept grumbling on about the heat of the day, the cool of the forest, the flies, and all the devil's endless vexations.

Now, it so happened that the giant passed by on business of his own. Perhaps he was off to gather hazelnuts, or maybe to steal and devour a whole herd of cattle.

Suddenly, a bass voice seemed to come from under the moss. "That's twelve I've killed—five with one hand and seven with the other!" growled the voice, which belonged to the dreaming tailor.

This "five with one hand and seven with the other," muffled by the handkerchief and floating up from the depths of sleep, shadow, and mystery, would have given the shivers to a hundred giants. This one started trembling like a leaf in the wind. As his eyes weren't too keen, he at first saw nothing at all.

He was about to turn and run when at last he made out a strange creature: a tangle of arms and legs, veiled in ghostly white.

"I'm done for!" the giant groaned to himself. "If this thing killed five with one hand and seven with the other, it must be some kind of weird, magic creature!"

Having squatted down to examine it, he now snorted with amazement. The snort broke four dead branches and tore a volley of leafy twigs from the surrounding trees.

The din woke the tailor up. He was surprised to find himself no longer in his nicely walled and curtained bedroom, but among moss and leaves. When he sat up, there loomed the giant's face before him, as big as a millstone. The giant was staring at him open-mouthed, his eyes as big as salad bowls.

It might not be quite right to claim that the tailor felt no tightness in his throat just then. However small he may have been, though, he wanted to be a proper man—one who doesn't yield to fright and who, even when startled awake, regains in an instant a simple sort of hearty, primordial courage.

He fixed his gaze on the giant's dull eyes and without even thinking hurled out this challenge:

> If you don't do what you see me do,
> Giant, I'll make a servant of you!

And the giant repeated obediently:

> If I don't do what I see you do,
> Midget, I'll be a servant for you!

Then the giant got a better look at the little fellow. The idea that this misbegotten speck should wish to take strides of twenty rods or uproot oaks now sent him into peals of thunderous laughter—which tore still more clumps of leaves from the trees and broke still more branches.

"Listen, giant," said the tailor. "You know what they say?"

"Of course I do," the giant replied. "What *do* they say?"

"The proverb says, 'Strong enough to squeeze water from a stone.'"

"Well then, little man?"

"Well then," said the tailor, who'd quickly put his hand down over his second cheese, there where it lay on the moss. "Well then, giant, pick up that other white stone, there on the path, and let's have a contest!"

The giant would have staked his life that the little tailor had just picked up an ordinary stone from the riverbed. He couldn't possibly have thought anything else, because no idea at all got into his head except very slowly. So he squeezed the stone in his hand till he was as red as a turkey's neck. He squeezed and squeezed till the veins stood out on his own neck like cables, near to bursting.

Not one drop ran from his fist.

Next, the little tailor stretched his arm out straight and made his own stone—a goat cheese—give a flood of whey.

The giant stared, mouth agape and lower lip hanging loose. His big bulbous eyes seemed to get bigger still.

"Look at that oak now, giant! Could you squeeze it in your arms till sap runs from its trunk?"

The giant took a deep breath, rushed at the tree, and threw his arms around it. He hugged and squeezed and wrenched at it, moaning and complaining the while just like a baker's apprentice. But when he let go and looked at his shirt, he could see well enough that all his strength hadn't pressed a single drop of sap from the tree.

"My turn now," said the tailor.

He too threw his arms around the oak.

It didn't take long. In a moment he stepped back. Opening his vest, he displayed a trail of sap dripping down his shirt. There'd been that egg in his pocket, you see, and he'd crushed it against the trunk.

The color of the giant's face passed from red to purple, then to something very near black.

"All right, little man," he grunted when he'd gotten back his breath. "But tell me: can you do what *I* do? Can you fell oaks the way *I* can? Blast and double blast, can you cover twenty rods in one stride?"

The little tailor didn't give him any clever reply. He just said:

> *If I don't do what I see you do,*
> *Giant, I'll be a servant for you!*

"Excellent!" cried the giant. "It's me against you and you against me. Come down to the plain, into open country."

Off they went together along a shortcut to the edge of the forest. The plain stretched before them into the distance, rippling with wind-tossed, ripening grain, like waves of smoke. Beyond lay further fields of wheat, estates, roads, meadows, and, at last, the sea.

"You see my cave yonder below that hill?" said the giant, pointing to his lair in the fold of a slope among the pines and junipers. "We're going to play quoits, little man, out on the flat. But first, I'll have a few cherries to get myself back in shape. Blast and double blast, I need some refreshment in this heat!"

There was a wheat field nearby, covered with rippling grain as thick as a wall, and along it grew a row of cherry trees.

You know what they say:

> *Years the cherries are red and full*
> *Bring a smile to one and all.*

That year must have been a good one, because the trees were loaded with perfect cherries.

The giant seized a cherry tree, pulled the branches to him, and started in stuffing and gorging himself on cherries.

The tailor set about doing justice to that same tree. He hadn't had so much as a drink of water after his bread-and-cheese lunch, and what with the heat, he was rather thirsty. Now the branches were bent so far toward him, he clambered up, sat himself down astride a limb, and helped himself to cherries with both hands.

The giant, though, swallowed everything, stems, leaves, and all, and didn't even bother to spit out the pits. He had his bellyful in five minutes. With a series of rumbles louder than thunder, his stomach let him know he'd had enough.

So he opened his fist and let go of the branches. The cherry tree snapped up straight. The tailor went sailing through the air like a stone from a slingshot. It's lucky for him he was as light as a starling, and the wheat was so thick. As the farmers say, you could have thrown a sickle into the field and it would never have touched the ground.

A hundred paces from the giant he landed on that bed of wheat as he might have tumbled into a heap of straw piled in a barn. After shaking himself to clear his head, he got up again more sure of himself than ever.

The giant, who'd never seen him go, was just shouting for him. Apparently giants aren't too smart, or too alert either.

"Where are you, little man? Where have you gotten to?"

"Look! Here I am!" cried the tailor, impetuously seizing his chance. "Yes, look! I'm right over here! The wheat seemed just right for measuring strides, so I thought I'd show you what kind of steps *I* take!"

The giant spotted the tailor yonder, then estimated the distance between where he'd been just a moment ago and where he was now. It made a good hundred rods. And between one place and the other there wasn't the slightest trace of footsteps. The rippling wheat remained perfect and unbroken.

The giant stared and stared. What a stride, blast and double blast! What a stride!

"All right, little man," he said at last, "come on home with me. We'll see how far you can throw the quoits I like to play with before my door."

So they started walking. The giant didn't dare say a thing. With his big eyes, bulging like a frog's, he occasionally stole a sidelong glance at the tailor.

A league of grassy meadow stretched along the hills, between the giant's lair and the river. There the brute played quoits with the millstones he'd stolen from the mills on the other side of the forest. Whenever he felt like it, he'd pick up those millstones between his thumb and his fingers, like pennies, and send them flying before him.

They'd fall into the river and splash water up to the tops of the hills. Sometimes, for a change, he'd send one off into a grove of trees, which the stone would then crush to firewood; or he'd fling another into a village square. The houses would all fall down while the steeple swayed like a drunken man and collapsed full-length on the ground. People would flee frantically in all directions to save themselves, and the cattle would rush off, mooing, amid clouds of dust.

Ever since the giant had started acting the devil that way, without the least restraint, there'd been nothing but death and destruction. The king would have been glad to give his daughter's hand in marriage, and all the gold in his kingdom too, to anyone who could rid them of the brute.

"Are *those* your quoits?" said the tailor when they arrived. "Why, they're just small change compared to the ones the children play with where *I* come from. These quoits of yours won't burden me much, no indeed."

The giant sucked back a string of drool hanging from his lower lip, as though he were an ox. "Little man," he said, "we've had too much fun already in the forest and among the wheat. The sun'll soon be down. It's a bit late now for us to go on with our contest."

"Whatever you say, giant."

"Till tomorrow morning, then, little man, in the cool of the day! We'll go to the forest and fell a few trees. Yes, we'll see who can knock down the most in one blow. After that we'll throw stones, blast and double blast!"

"Fine," said the tailor. "For now, let's eat and then go to bed. I'm very hungry and sleepy."

They dined off a quarter of a wild boar. The meat, half raw and half burned, wasn't much to the little fellow's taste, but he couldn't let himself starve. More adventures lay before him the next day, and more tests of strength!

He ate, then asked to go to bed.

The bed was a platform of pine logs. On it the little tailor made himself a nest.

Still, something told him to keep an eye open. Pretending to snore, he secretly kept watch. The giant still lingered before the hearth as though digesting his dinner. Squatting there on his heels, the brute poked around in the coals with his poker—the trunk of an oak all charred at one end.

The giant wasn't in a good humor that evening. Ideas were floating into his head, and as this normally never happened to him, he worried that he might be getting sick. "That tiny slip of a man," he kept telling himself, "is thunder and lightning in person! Imagine squeezing water from a stone and sap from a tree-trunk! And hundred-rod strides! I may be a giant and all, but if he moves in nearby, I'll be nothing, and that's a fact. All right, that's that. I've got to get rid of him!"

He pondered the matter deeply, over and over, still poking around in the fire. His eyes were bloodshot, like a bull's.

Finally, after all that pondering, he got up, tree-trunk in hand; and dull though he may have been, he still managed to creep to the bed without slapping his feet loudly against the floor of his lair. He stepped aside a little, to let the firelight show him where the little man had curled up. Then, wham! He brought his oak down on the spot with every ounce of his strength. After that, he went off into the other corner to sleep.

He was awakened the next morning by a frightful racket. The little man was drumming away with his stick on the cauldron.

"Up, giant, up! It's time for our contest! Let's get to the wood and start felling trees!"

The giant stared at him with eyes so big and round they seemed about to pop out on the ground.

"But, but . . . Little man, is that you?"

He could hardly speak.

"You mean you didn't feel anything last night?" he finally asked, getting creakily to his feet.

"Last night? No. Oh, some beetle may have come flying along and bumped my forehead. I fell right back to sleep."

The giant didn't even dare stretch and yawn, the way he did every morning when he got up. Those were powerful yawns, too. They went on and on and on, and you could hear them three leagues away.

Actually, the little tailor in his nest among the logs had only pretended to snore, and meanwhile had kept a sharp eye on the giant. He'd seen what was coming. He'd slipped lightly down between two logs, under the bed, and there he'd slept the sleep of the just in one of his host's slippers.

"Let's go," he said. "We'll eat after we work. Making up a bundle of wood will give us an appetite."

The giant followed behind him in silence.

They came to the forest. The giant hurled himself wildly at the trees, uprooting, smashing, and piling them high, then uprooting some more and breaking them over his knee. He soon had a mountain of wood. Next, he twisted three birches into a single band and tied the whole thing into one bundle. Finally, mute as ever, he jerked his chin at the little man to let him know it was his turn.

Unhurriedly, the tailor drew his ball of string from his pocket, gave one end to the giant, and told him to hold on to it. "Stay right there!" he said. Next, with a great air of determination, he started unrolling his ball along the edge of the forest.

The giant watched him go some way, then could stand it no longer.

"Little man, listen here!"

"Yes, giant? What is it?"

"Would you just tell me what you're up to?"

"Why, I'm running my string around your forest so as to bundle it all up at once."

"My forest? All of Bigwood Forest?"

"Of course."

"And then what? What am I going to heat my soup with? Will I have anything left to warm my toes with, when winter comes? Blast and double blast! Leave my forest alone and stick that string back in your pocket! I'd rather let you win this one and keep my forest!"

They still had to play quoits, though.

Back they went to the meadow. The giant picked up his millstones and hefted them in the palm of his hand. Then zip! off they went through the air. Some flew down into the valley, along the river, and others here or there onto a mountain spur; but all had behind them the giant's whole strength. Trees flew like chips from the ax, rocks split and bounced, the ground opened in zigzag chasms, and the hills shook as in an earthquake.

The tailor, meanwhile, whistled a tune, and barely shrugged his shoulders at this performance. As far as you could tell from his face, he might have been watching a boy toss quoits at a frog.

"All right now, sir small man, go ahead!" announced the giant, wiping his forehead with the back of his big, beefy hand. "It's your turn!" He shook the sweat off in big drops.

The tailor retreated three paces, leaned back, and put his hands to his mouth like a megaphone.

"Look out, world! Look out, world! Here comes my quoit! Shepherd girls beyond the sea, watch yourselves and watch your sheep!"

He seemed to listen for the answer, one hand cupped behind his ear.

Just then, as the rising sun grew warm, the finch in the tailor's pocket started singing.

"Why, that's right!" exclaimed the giant, who was listening too. "You can hear little cries! Do you understand what they're saying, sir small man?"

"They're on the lookout now over there where I'm from, beyond the sea. I believe I can throw my quoit."

Again he made his hands into a megaphone.

"Are you ready? Can I go ahead? And how's everything over there, anyway? How's dad? And mother? And my little wife? All right, here goes!"

Suddenly, the giant gripped the tailor's wrist in his fist.

"Just a minute, sir small man! First, I want you to tell me . . . I mean, you really ought to consider what you're doing. Just like that, you're going to throw my quoits over to where you're from, beyond the sea? Is anyone else there as strong as you?"

"I don't really know," replied the tailor. "I don't *think* so."

"What kind of fool do you take me for, then?" the giant went on. "The very idea, to just charge ahead like that with never a thought for what's bound to come next! *Think* a little, won't you?"

"Think of what, giant?"

"Tell me, once my quoits are yonder across the sea, who's going to throw them back? You think I want to lose them? Why, I brought those quoits all the way through the forest, from the three mills along the stream! Blast and double blast! Those are my quoits, my millstones! I'd just as soon call you the winner again and leave it at that! All right, all right, we still have to see which of us can throw a stone the higher!"

He seized a boulder, jerked it from the ground, adjusted his grip, and then, stiff-armed, hurled it into the sky. His broad back bulged with rolling lumps like a sack of turnips.

He threw another and another. They went so high, you had to wait quite a while to see them come down. And when at last they did fall, they shattered on hitting the ground and exploded in fragments. Again, the whole countryside shook.

"Your turn now to toss a rock, sir small man!"

The tailor stepped four paces forward, waving his closed fist. By doing so he got between the giant and the sun, which was rising over the mountains. Then he planted his feet and sent his stone into the air.

The giant watched it rise, and rise, and rise . . . till he couldn't see it any more because he had the sun straight in his eyes.

He kept peering, though, shading his eyes with his hand. He watched and waited. But the stone never came down.

He waited three-quarters of an hour. He waited till he got all silly and confused.

The stone had been the tailor's finch. When the tailor had taken the bird out of his dark pocket and thrown it into the sky, the bird had gone straight up like a lark. Then it must have set off for home from up there, high in the heavens.

In the meadow by the river, the giant was still waiting for the stone to fall back down. At last, dazzled and amazed, he bowed to the little man and conceded defeat.

"Just remember," said the tailor:

If you don't do what you see me do,
Giant, I'll make a servant of you!

"It's true, little man, I'm your servant. You're stronger than I am. You can outrace me, you can outdo me making bundles of wood, and everything else. I'm yours to command."

Hands dangling stupidly, the giant came to stand behind the tailor, ready to follow and obey. The tailor, singing a song, led him straight off to the king's castle.

They'd no sooner entered the town than a mad uproar greeted them. Everyone dashed out from the streets, the market, and the shops, gathered around them, and escorted them on—though at a little distance, the way boys escort a bear-tamer and his bear.

Drums beat for the little tailor at the castle gate. The guards saluted him and took him with his giant prisoner to the king. The king, the queen, and their daughter welcomed the little tailor in their most beautiful hall.

"Your Majesty, I place the giant at your feet."

"Cover yourself," said the king—for the mightiest grandees then were granted the privilege of keeping their hats on in the king's presence.

"Sire, I do so in deference to your wishes. This giant will serve you very well for all the little jobs that need doing around the house, like pulling up cabbages, rolling barrels, drawing sand from the river, or getting the magpie out of her nest in the tall poplar tree. Just give him a tub of soup three times a day, with a quarter of an ox, and on Sundays and holidays a small barrel of wine.

"Agreed," said the king. "He'll have it all. But you, my little baron— so red of cheek and wise in your simplicity—what would *you* like?"

"Sire, you may thank me as you see fit. I believe there's been some talk of your daughter's hand. I'd be honored, of course, but unfortunately, you see, I'm already married. On the other hand, you'd cause me no distress at all if you were to line my pocket. I promised my little wife I'd bring her home a purse full of gold."

"Give it to him this minute!" ordered the king. "Go fetch it from my treasury, and make sure it's the biggest and heaviest one there! He bested the giant, and he's the strongest man in the world. Anyway, the giant'll carry his luggage. He'll have to show the giant off to his wife, because a wife never believes her husband could do anything strong and brave. Then he'll bring the giant back—I need the brute to repair the laundry. But I'll make him my little baron, or, if he prefers, master tailor to my court!"

> Trip off lightly with a song,
> Children, run along,
> Now the story's done.

59. The Stocking with the Hole

There was once a woman named Jeanne des Caillades who had a stupid droop to her lower lip. She had wild, bulging eyes, too, like some old duke in a portrait. As they say, that day when the Spirit rained down on the Christians, she'd hidden under her umbrella. But her son Toine must have hidden even better because, talk about wits, he hadn't a single drop.

One Sunday he'd just jumped out of bed for early mass.

> *Come along now, you women, come!*
> *There's the first bell for mass, ding-dong!*

So. Hastily he slipped on his stockings, but in doing so noticed that one had a hole in it. That hole was as big as his finger.

"Say, mom!" he shouted to his mother, who was hurrying too. "Say, mom! There's a big hole in my stocking!"

"Well then," she answered, "turn it inside out!"

Not a bad idea!

He stuck in his hand, turned the sock inside out like a rabbit skin, and put it on. Then he stared, mouth agape, just like a clog without a foot in it.

"But mom! Come and look! The hole goes right through to the other side!"

60. The Seven Brothers in the Well

There were once seven lads from the Auvergne, seven brothers from up in the high country. Like the other young men from thereabouts, they set off as winter came on to earn their living in the wide world.

Yes, they were brothers, all seven of them. Every single one of them was a brother to all six others. It always amazed them to think about it, and it gave them a lot of confidence.

They weren't clever like those fellows who invented gunpowder, but clever tricks are the devil's business. And the oldest had promised his mother that he'd bring them all back in midsummer, on Saint John's Day.

So off they went along the roads, astonished by everything they clapped eyes on and very eager for a closer look: a chapel with its bell, a team of white horses, a high-arched bridge, a squirrel turning a treadmill round and round in its cage, and everything else.

Toward evening they passed a great big well, naturally quite unlike any up there where they'd come from. Water was gurgling from the rocks all around.

Up they stepped to admire it, and leaned over to stare down at the water gleaming at the bottom, till the eldest told them to get moving again.

But as soon as they'd started walking, it occurred to them that they should count one another to make sure that none of the seven had fallen into the well.

The eldest lined them up and counted them. He only got six.

So he joined the line and had the next eldest step out to try it.

The next eldest got just six too, and so did all the others, turn by turn: six and not one more.

"Thunderation! There *were* seven of us!"

Yes, each of those expert counters had forgotten to count himself! But that was because being upset had addled their brains a little.

The eldest went back to the well, leaned over the edge, and put up a hand to shade his eyes. There was someone at the bottom! All the others leaned over the same way and saw the fellow too.

No, there was no doubt about it. But they had no rope or ladder to pull their brother out with.

"All right, then, we'll make a chain. I'll hang on to the bar here. You, hang on to my ankles, and so on for all of us."

That makes quite a weight, though, six lads from the Auvergne. The seventh, clambering down from shoulder to shoulder, was only just grasping the lowest pair of ankles when the eldest way up there, strong as an ox though he was, felt his hands slipping off the bar.

"I'm losing my grip!" he shouted.

"Spit! Spit in your hands!" the next eldest shouted back.

Good advice, that—the eldest followed it right away. And suddenly there they were, all seven, at the bottom.

Did they drown? Oh, no. There was just enough water to break their fall, coming down like that on top of one another. But what a confused heap they made! They had no idea how to disentangle themselves and get back their own arms and legs from the pile. None of them could tell which were his any more.

Then the eldest got a bright idea—he was usually the one who came up with their ideas. Being on top, he unbuckled his belt and started whaling away with all his strength.

"Ow, ouch, my leg!"

"Ow, ouch, my hand!"

"Ow, ouch, my head!"

The belt was made of good leather half an inch thick, and cracked very nicely. It helped each of them recognize his own limbs and get himself sorted out. Water, mud, and seven Auvergnat lads make quite a mix.

They got themselves apart and stood up. Just then the moon rose. They saw the holes left in the masonry so you could put your hands and feet in them and climb out of the well.

From hole to hole, one after the other, they all scrambled back up onto the meadow.

They shook themselves like wet dogs, then shook their hats to get the water out of them.

When the eldest saw those hats drying on the grass, he thought of counting them. It turned out there were seven. That's how they found out they were all there.

Then they set off again in the moonlight, gladder than ever that all seven of them were brothers and more certain, too, that they'd get safely through every peril in the wide world.

61. The Land of Sillies

There was once a lad who was tempted down by a fair from our mountains onto the plain—from our country of poor rye down to the land of rich wheat. Down there, it's as flat as a tabletop without the plate of hard sausage or the pitcher of red wine! There's not a single brushy spur with a castle on it, not a single rock with its moss and its spring—no, not even a good big tree to rest your eyes on. And the people down there—well, they're as flat as their fields. There's nothing to say about them.

But anything new's a treat. To the lad—*you* go figure out why!— everything down there was a wonder.

It's true that as soon as he got to the fairground he spotted a wonderfully rosy blond girl with a very sweet face. Actually, her features were hardly more marked than those of a rosebud, but she looked so fresh, and had such an air of good-hearted simplicity, that he stepped right up to her and wished her a good day. She was eating a piece of cake, and she looked so innocently bewitching as she did so that he couldn't help saying, "If I could nibble cake as prettily as that, I'd keep nibbling it all my life!"

She burst into laughter and threw him a glance that wasn't at all un-friendly. He was a good-looking boy, pink-cheeked and brown-eyed, as clean as a pebble in a stream, and with a lively, decisive air that was a pleasure to see.

You know what it's like when you're young: those first, glorious moments when a boy and girl still believe a smile's all they need to know all about each other. The whole countryside's in flower, everything's bluer than the sky in May, and off you go, your heart sails away!

To make a long story short, those two got together. Everything fell into place. The two families had about equal property. From his house to hers, there wasn't a single step to go up or down.

One Sunday, he went to visit his girl for their engagement dinner.

About noon, with the table laid, the girl went down to the cellar to draw a pitcher of wine.

There she was before the barrel, bung in hand, hunkered down by the pitcher as it filled, when she got to thinking.

"So, I'm going to be married! And when I'm married, I'm bound to have children. And what'll I name those children when I have them?"

She thought and thought about it so long that the pitcher filled up and the wine began running through the cellar.

Meanwhile, the mother, who'd just prepared the bread and soup, came to see what her daughter could possibly be up to. She found her there, crouching by the barrel and lost in her dreams while the wine ran on and on.

"What's gotten into you, daughter? Good heavens, what's the matter with you? We'll lose the whole barrelful!"

"Oh, mother, if I'm thinking, it's because I've got lots to think about! If you only knew, you'd forget everything else too! I'm thinking that once I'm married I'll have children, and that once I've children I'll have to give them names. So what names will I give them, when I have them?"

"Why, you're right, that's something to consider, it really is! Daughter, I'm going to consider it with you. Let's both of us think hard."

To encourage deep thought the mother squatted down, duck-fashion, beside her daughter, there in front of the barrel. The bung was still in the girl's hand, and the wine was still running out.

The father, meanwhile, noticed that neither one was coming back up. He decided to go and see what they were doing.

"What's gotten into you, my wife and my daughter? By thunder, are you mad? My whole barrel's going to be empty. Put the bung back this instant! What on earth are you woolgathering about?"

"My dear husband, if we're lost in our thoughts, it's because we've good reason! You might do some thinking too. Once our daughter's married she's bound to have children, and when she has children she'll have to give them names. So what names will she give them, when she has them?"

"You're right, you're right, that's something to think about, that really is! All right, I'll think about it with you. Yes, let's all three of us think hard."

So there they were, thinking and dreaming, all three squatting in front of the barrel. The girl was between her father and mother. The bung was still in her hand and the stream of wine was still running out.

Upstairs, the lad missed his future bride. "What in the world are they doing down there in the cellar? It takes them as long to fill a jug as it takes a hen to hatch a dozen eggs."

So down he went himself.

"Heavens, what are you doing? You're going to lose all your wine! What in the world are you thinking about?"

"My boy, if we're lost in thought, it's because we've a serious matter to consider! Come here and think about it with us. How is your bride going to name your children? Because she'll have to give them names when she has them; and she's bound to have them when she's married!"

"Well, you keep on thinking till it's time for the wedding. I'll be back to marry her as soon as I've found just three people sillier than you!"

He took the bung from the girl's fingers, stopped up the barrel, then dashed back upstairs four steps at a time. He'd have jumped right over a wall, had one stood in his way!

Off he went home again, toward the mountains where the ash trees are bent by the wind.

But first he had to get through all that flat country.

The first thing he saw was some people straining to get the roof off a house.

"Good people, what are you doing?"

"Why, we're freezing in there, so we're taking the roof off to let in the sun."

"Well, at least don't hog it all for yourselves! Leave some for other people!"

And what did he see a little farther along, on a village square? Some people busily scooping water from a pond with a chicken cage.

"Good people, what are you doing?"

"Why, we want some water in our tub, so we've come to take some from the pond."

"Well, don't take it all. Leave some for other people!"

A little farther on, under some walnut trees, he found a man dancing around before a heap of nuts. Walnuts mold if they're stored wet. This fellow wanted to put them in the oven to dry, and he was trying to move them with a pitchfork.

Up stepped the lad, picked up a bit of a straw mat that was lying around, filled it with a few sweeps of his hands and emptied it into the oven.

"Goodness!" exclaimed the man. "You got the job done fast! I'm more patient, but it would have taken me quite a while longer!"

Some way farther on, beside the path, he saw a man and his wife. One was pulling their cow by the horns and the other was pushing it by the tail. They were struggling to get that cow up onto their roof.

"Good people, what are you doing?"

"Why, this confounded cow! We want to get her up on the roof to eat that tuft of grass, and she just won't go!"

The lad seized a ladder, grabbed a sickle that was hanging in the shed, scrambled up, cut the grass, and tossed it down to the cow. The cow ate it up in two swipes of the tongue.

The couple thanked him over and over. He, meanwhile, had already come down from the ladder, hung the sickle back up, and was two dozen paces off, heading out on his way.

He came to a town where he found everyone under the elm tree on the square. The men were arguing over something while the women and children waited patiently nearby. The debate was so heated, with long speeches and big gestures, that you could tell they were facing a grave situation. Clearly, they didn't know quite what to decide.

"You see," the local sages explained—the chief members of the council—"a cow dropped a cowpat smack in front of our church. We can't just do nothing. We'll have to tear down the church, move it elsewhere stone by stone, and put it back up again. But where shall we move it to? That's just what we can't agree on."

The lad seized a shovel, picked up the cowpat, tossed it onto a dungheap between two houses, and with another flick of the shovel scattered sand over it.

The people all lifted their hands in amazement, mouths agape.

"How could *anyone* be so clever? Why, we'd *never* have thought of that ourselves. You've saved us a tremendous amount of trouble—tearing down and rebuilding! The time it would have taken, and the work, and the cost! Thank you, thank you so much for the great favor you've done us!"

The lad could hardly contain himself. He'd have been glad to use that shovel on their behinds, to wake them up a bit. But instead he dropped the shovel and rushed, fuming, out of town.

Irked though he may have been, he was also hungry. After all, he'd left his future bride's house before dinner, without eating so much as a bite. He was obliged to give the matter some thought.

He noticed a house at a fork in the road. He didn't know the name of the place, nor even the name of the people.

"All right, I know what I'm going to say."

And in he went.

"Hello there, cousin!" he called cheerily to the lady of the house.

"Why, cousin, hello!"

"Are you in good health? How's everything going?"

"We're fine, cousin, thank you. And you? How's your family?"

They greeted each other some more and kissed. Then:

"Cousin, I've come to invite you to my wedding."

"That's very kind of you, cousin. Your cousin will be right back. He went to put our sow out to clover. Anyway, cousin, sit down. You must eat with us."

That, of course, was exactly what he had in mind.

When the husband came back, she told him their cousin had come to invite them to his wedding. Then she served up soup and a bit of hard sausage.

"But you see, cousin," said she, "we won't be able to go to your wedding after all. What would happen with our sow? We're fattening her up for Christmas. My husband's so busy. He has to take her to pasture and bring her back . . . And I have to feed her slops and give her the cooking water. Oh, I tell you, a sow's quite a burden to a household!"

"Cousin, if the two of you can't come, it'd still be a shame to have no one from the family at all. Why not send your sow?"

"Why, cousin, what a wonderful idea! When *is* your wedding, anyway?"

"Right away, cousin."

"Well, take her, then! You'll bring her back, won't you, cousin?"

"Why, of course, cousin, of course!"

"I'll tie a ribbon around her tail, cousin, to make sure she does us all credit!"

"Don't worry, I'll take good care of her."

As soon as the meal was over, off he went with the sow.

But once he was out, with the whole countryside to himself, he turned his hat around on his head, left the path that would have taken him home, and turned back toward his bride.

" 'As soon as I find just three people sillier than you . . .' That was what I told them. But I didn't find three, I found three hundred! As long as I'm in the genuine land of the sillies, I might as well marry my silly girl!"

Head high, he strode bravely off to marry her after all.

They killed the sow and cooked her for the wedding. I want you to know, I got my share. And we finished off what was left of that barrel.

I brought back wedding sweets galore
But ate them up—no, I've no more!

62. The Stupid Wife

There was once a man who wasn't quite as sharp as some people in the world. But the sharper you get, the more you risk getting your point broken. He, at any rate, just kept going his way. With warm feet and a cool head he did as well as any bishop.

The trouble was, he got married and took a stupid wife. Was she flighty and silly? Or a featherbrain without a thought in her head? No, no, she was a lot stupider than that. She was just too dumb. And too dumb is too much. She was so dumb that donkeys brayed with pleasure as she passed by. She was so dumb that she seemed a dead weight, a lump. She was as crude as they come, dirty and stinking too, and coarser than barley bread.

So what? He'd married her, so he had to keep her—keep her with all

her clatter of rough clogs, shlap-shlop; with the swish-swash of her coarse
skirts; with her gusts of ashes and dust; with her fibs and blunders; and
with all her dull stupidity. He knew that

> *A wife, like a goat,*
> *Needs a good long rope.*

He never once scolded her.

She gave him two or three children, which didn't help make the house
any cleaner. Evenings, the poor fellow watched them, snot running from
their noses, little faces gleaming with grease like baked apples, and grubbier
than if they'd just been scouring Hell. He watched them, that was all. He
was like an ox that ruminates and then, long afterwards, goes "mooah."

"Goodness, wife," said he nonetheless one evening, "aren't you *ever*
going to wash the children? I'd be glad to kiss them when I come back
from my day's work, but they're so crusted with mud and filth, I can't make
myself do it."

"Are children supposed to be *washed?*"

"Of course they are!"

"All right, have it your way. If you want me to wash them, I'll do it
tomorrow."

The next day she built a big fire—logs and all, since wood was cheap
and all you had to do was go fetch it from the forest. Then she put water
on in her biggest cauldron, grabbed the children, and stuffed them in . . .

It's hard to believe. I didn't see it myself, but that's the way the story
goes, anyway. My grandmother swore it was true. She said the woman was
from La Badin, up above the rocks of La Volpie . . . At any rate, she was
stupid enough to make you howl with despair!

She boiled her children like rags or napkins. Next, she carried them to
the river where she beat, rubbed, rinsed, and beat them again. At last she
spread them on the hedge between two apple trees to dry, the way women
spread their shirts and aprons on a rack.

The husband missed them that evening when he came home, for they
usually ran to greet him.

"They're not coming to meet me? What in the world are they up to?"

He got home, knocked the mud off his clogs on the stone doorstep,
went on in, and saw his wife.

"Well? What have you done with the children? Why didn't they come
out to greet me?"

"Why, I washed them the way you told me to."

"You washed them . . ."

"Go look out on the hedge. They're drying."

"Oh no!"

He ran to the end of the meadow, then was back like someone who's taken a blow on the head and can no longer make out what's in front of him.

"Is it possible?"

"What do you mean? *You* told me to wash them! So I did."

"Wash them, yes. But kill them?"

"But what's the use getting angry?" he thought as he sank onto the bench. "She's your wife. You're her husband.

> *Where the stake stays,*
> *There the goat must graze.*

Stupid she is, and stupid she'll always be. You're not going to change her."

He shrugged his shoulders, stared down at the earth between his clogs, and said not a word.

A husband like that deserves more praise than a purse full of gold crowns!

For eight days he remained stunned.

After the eight days were over he said to his wife, "I know what we'll do. Now we've no longer any children, we'll put money aside. It'll do for our old age—for the long lean years!"

She listened with her mouth agape like an empty clog.

"Yes indeed, for the long lean years! Try to look after our savings."

He knew she was listening with all her ears.

"It's not her fault if she's stupid. At least she means well. You have to give her that."

He went to bed, then the next day set off for work. Each evening he'd lift the lid of the grain chest. That's where he put the money he'd earned, there in the drawer for special treasures like the ones you buy from traveling notions salesmen.

"There! That's for the long lean years!"

The nest egg swelled, and the husband enjoyed watching it fatten. Some Sunday evenings he'd take the money from the drawer, spread it out, line up the coins on the lid of the chest, count and recount them; then scoop them all up, stuff them back in the drawer, and close the lid again.

"That's for the long lean years! For the long lean years!

The wife looked on, her lower lip drooping. And sometimes, when he was at work, she'd imitate his Sunday routine: she'd take out the nest egg, spread it out, and count it—or pretend to count it, rather, because she never could count except on her fingers, and even then only up to five.

One day she was alone at home like that, with the coins lined up on the lid. Suddenly there was a noise at the door. She turned around and saw a tall, skinny beggar with a long grey beard. He was holding out a hand grey with grime and asking for charity.

"Good man, I'll give you a bit of bread and a chunk of lard. Other than that, we've nothing at all in the house."

"All right," said he, "that nothing at all's good enough for me. Just give me what I see there on the lid of the chest."

"Oh, but you see," she replied, "that money's not for us. It's for the long lean years."

"The long lean years? Good woman, you're in luck. The long lean years, why, that's me."

"You? You're sure?"

"Am I sure? Just look: I'm as long and lean as a day without bread, and as dried up as Father Time on a clock. I always thought I was the long lean years, and now I'm quite certain of it."

"Well then, in that case, take the money. My husband's told me over and over it'd be for you!"

She didn't need to say it twice. The beggar scooped up every last fraction

of a penny. He stuffed the nest egg into his pocket, dropped his satchel on the spot, ran his hand over his beard like a Capuchin monk who's dined well, then with a hurried "Many thanks!" slipped off like a skinny cat toward the forest.

That evening the husband came back tired from his day's work. His stupid wife greeted him on the doorstep, both hands on her belly.

"Well, husband, there's news. The long lean years came. I gave him all the money you were keeping for him."

"What do you mean, the long lean years?"

"Oh, it was him sure enough, with his grey beard, as long and lean as a day without bread. Anyway, he told me he was the long, lean years!"

"Good heavens, where's the money?"

This time, when he grasped the disaster, he went out of his mind. But he was such a good fellow that all he did was collapse on the bench.

"What's the use of getting angry?" he thought as he sank down. "She's your wife. You're her husband.

> *Where the stake stays,*
> *There the goat must graze.*

Stupid she is, and stupid she'll always be. You're not going to change her."

It didn't even occur to him to club her on the spot.

A husband like that, you'd like to snip bits off his clothes for holy relics!

Nevertheless, after that blow he was no longer himself. Suddenly he picked up the satchel at his feet left by the so-called long lean years, stood up, and slung it over his shoulder.

"We're paupers now! All we can do is go begging from village to village for our bread. Wife, gather up your things and let's go!"

He set straight off without delay. From outside on the path, and without even turning around (he knew she'd obey him faithfully), he shouted back to her, "Come on, wife, get out the door!"

"I should get out the door?"

"Yes." At last he looked back. "But at least close the door behind you."

"I should get it out behind me?"

"I mean *close* it, the door!"

"I should get it out and hold it close? I should take it with me?"

"Oh, all right, take it to the devil!"

Being as strong as an ox, she lifted the door off its hinges, loaded it on her back, and followed her husband off toward the forest.

Up the path she slogged, shlap-shlop. Night was coming on. The jays, rooks, and green woodpeckers were calling to each other as they flew home to their nests. Animals were slipping through the brush—perhaps a foraging badger or a fox setting out to hunt.

And there were other noises too: footsteps and voices. The husband listened. He'd stopped in the middle of a clearing under a huge old oak. There were noises everywhere. He hardly knew which way to go. People said there were robbers in those woods.

Those people were right. And it just so happened that the robbers had agreed to meet under that same big tree. They came there to live it up and share out their booty. Two such scoundrels were coming from one direction. They'd run into Long Lean Years and, noticing how nervous he was, had seized him and brought him along, him and his nest egg. Two more were coming from still another direction and three more from a third.

"Quick," the man whispered to his wife, "quick, let's climb the tree!" He was already climbing himself. "Come, hurry, or let the devil take you and your door!"

"I should take the door?"

"Oh, forget the door!"

"I should get it?"

"Leave it! The devil take your door!"

"I should take it up?"

"All right, take it and to the devil with it!"

Tugging and hauling, she heaved herself and the door (all heartwood of oak, as thick as a meat pie and weighing goodness only knows how many hundredweight) up into the tree.

They climbed as high as they possibly could and settled themselves as well as they were able among the branches—she still holding on to that door. And just in time. The robbers were gathering under the tree from three directions at once.

They put down their cudgels and satchels, struck a light, picked up some deadwood, and hoisted the pot.

While putting the pot on to boil they talked shop and wondered what to do with that fellow who'd taken the nest egg. He, for his part, wanted to join them.

"Huh, that's the one," the wife grunted under her breath. "That's the one. I've found the long lean years again."

"So have I," her husband whispered. "I'm finding the time pretty long and lean myself. But what can we do? Just keep quiet and be patient."

If you want to stay polite, you can't talk about what happened next.

"Oh, husband," sighed the wife, squirming. "Oh, husband, I do believe . . . Oh, I'm just not going to be able to hold it in . . ."

"Control yourself, for pity's sake, or we're lost!"

But it was already too late. The robbers looked up.

"What? It's raining? You can see all the stars and still it's raining? Well, all the better. We'll have that much more soup!"

A moment later, the wife began sighing louder and squirming worse than ever.

"Oh dear, oh dear, husband, oh, I do believe . . . Oh, I'm just not going to be able to hold it in . . ."

"Oh no! Control yourself, for pity's sake, or this time we really *are* lost!"

But it was already too late. The robbers all craned their heads toward the pot and peered in.

> *Bubble, bubble, rich and brown,*
> *God's own fat is tumbling down!*

Delighted, they seized their spoons and dug in. Once the stew was disposed of they took a few swallows of wine and got down to business. That meant counting the loot and dividing it up. They gathered in a tight huddle with Long Lean Years, as ever, right in the middle.

"Oh dear, oh husband . . . Oh, it's my hands now and my arms. Oh, I just can't hold on to this door any longer!"

"Oh no!" whispered the husband. "If you let go of it, I'm dead and so are you!"

"I should let it go?"

"No, no, it mustn't drop!"

"Drop? I should drop it, then?"

"No, hold on to it, what the devil!"

"I should just let go?"

"All right, let it go and the devil take it!"

So she did. It crashed down like thunder through the branches. "Lost, we're lost!" the husband kept saying to himself. "But what's the use of getting angry? She's your wife," and so on.

The astonished robbers jumped up in a flash—but not for long. The door flattened them into a sort of strawberry jam. Not one escaped—just imagine!—not even Long Lean Years.

God Almighty! The husband scrambled down from his perch and his wife after him. They took back their nest egg, and they carried off as well all those purses full of gold coins that might have tempted others into evil ways.

Back home they went with their load. The wife had clapped the door to her back once more, because after all, a house needs a door, especially the house of a couple with money.

Her husband followed behind her.

"Your wife's a dummy," he was saying to himself, "yes, she is indeed and always will be.

> *What comes from the baptistry*
> *Lasts until the cemetery.*

But when God wishes, even stupidity can be a blessing for honest folk. She'll always be a dummy, but I might as well just forget about it!"

His money had multiplied. Now all he lacked was children. Before the year was out he had a son. The boy was no genius, but on the other hand—

> *Curly, curly, curly*
> *Like the tail on a hog;*
> *Shlapety-shlop*
> *Like a clog!*

63. The Ogre and His Tenant

There was once an ogre who had a castle on a mountaintop. There he lived with his ogress wife and their valet. The ogre's tenant lived down below, in a little house where he managed as best he could with his wife and their twelve children.

Unhappily, one year the wheat froze in May and they had almost no harvest at all. That year, believe me, life was no fun. There were only a few sacks left in the attic, and the tenant put off as long as he possibly could the moment for splitting them with his master.

He delayed so long, he found such good reasons and came up with such splendid excuses, and his dozen children ate so heartily, that one day all the sacks were empty. A rat couldn't have found himself a snack up there, not even by scratching around in the corners.

The tenant was a bit nervous. He knew he'd have a bad time when the ogre came down from the castle to claim his due.

"Listen, wife," said he one evening, "the ogre'll be here soon. Make sure you keep a kettle of water boiling on the fire. And you," he said to the children, "look sharp and keep a close eye on the castle. The instant one of you sees the ogre coming, run straight to me and let me know."

Three days later, the tenant was in his skimpy little garden, pulling up a few turnips. It was evening. Suddenly he heard his eldest sing out, "Here comes the ogre!"

The child dashed frantically up. "Daddy, I saw him come out the main gate! He's headed straight down here!"

The tenant dropped his turnips and raced into the house. He seized the kettle, where fortunately the water was boiling merrily away, and set it down three paces from the door between the pine tree and the spring. Next, he took down an old whip from its post in the stable and began to circle the kettle, whipping it vigorously.

Up came the ogre, purple with rage.

"My wheat! I want my wheat! It's wheat I'll have from you this time, tenant! No more excuses!"

But the tenant was too absorbed to see or hear a thing. The ogre had to grab him by the neck and shake him like a plum tree.

"Ah! I beg your pardon, sir! I'm so sorry! I was too busy whipping the pot to boil the water for our soup."

"What are you talking about? You cook your soup by setting it down in the grass?"

"Yes, sir. The pot came down to me from my dear departed great-aunt. It's magic, you see, and the whip is too."

"You boil water by whipping the pot?"

"Certainly, sir. Just look!"

The tenant lifted the lid. The water inside was still steaming and bubbling like a winded horse at the top of a hill.

"Why, you're right!" exclaimed the ogre. "You whip the pot and it boils? That's a sight I'm glad to have seen! Say, I'd like my wife to see it, too. Give me your pot."

"Oh dear, sir, and what would *we* do without it? Just imagine how much wood we'd need! Why, your valet chases the children if they go into the forest for deadwood."

"Take all the wood you want from my forest, and I'll let you off what you owe me in wheat as well."

"No, sir, no, I'm going to fetch you your sacks. Our cooking pot! My great-aunt's cooking pot!"

"Listen, I'll let you off the rent and I'll give you a pig in the bargain. My valet'll bring it to you immediately."

"Before nightfall, sir?"

"Immediately, I tell you."

The ogre was just dying to get his hands on that pot, so as to amaze his wife. He picked it up in such a hurry that he scalded his fingers. He grabbed the whip, too, and marched straight back to the castle with both of them.

The next morning, though, the tenant was trembling in his boots. He knew that if not the pot, at least the ogre's anger would be at a rolling boil.

There was no point in trusting the ogress to calm him down. The ogre had had a first wife who, for an ogress, had been only moderately nasty. His slaps and whacks had dispatched her to the next world. Then he'd taken a second wife. This one was as vicious as a wasp, and always ready to outdo her husband in savage rage.

"Well," said the tenant to himself, "we might as well eat that pig right away. We'll get that much out of the deal, anyhow. Then we'll just see what happens!"

They'd just finished making the blood sausage when the eldest, perched in the pine next to the house, came scrambling down shouting, "The ogre! The ogre! He's coming!"

"Quick, children, take this meat to the larder! Clean up now, get it all out of here. Move! You, wife, come here. Give me that blood sausage— the blood sausage and the knife. Hurry, hurry!"

He wound the blood sausage three times around her neck like a scarf, put the kerchief she wore at her throat back over it, and had only barely finished when he heard the ogre striding up, sure enough, even faster than a fellow strides home for dinner.

"There you are, you rascal!" The ogre burst into the house like a bomb. "I just about tore my arm out, whipping that pot of yours. But now, come here. It's not the pot any more, it's that carcass of yours, and *you*, who're going to dance!"

The frenzied tenant was so busy berating his wife that he seemed not even to have heard his master. "No bread!" he screamed, stamping his feet with rage. "Not a thing left in the house! We're lucky she leaves us the four walls! Why, the slut! I don't know what's keeping me from just thrashing her once and for all!"

He gnashed his teeth and foamed like a madman; he whipped up his rage like milk boiling over on the fire. Then he noticed a knife lying on the table. Instantly he picked it up and stabbed his wife deep in the throat. Blood spurted out like a fountain and the poor woman collapsed backwards in a heap.

It had all been so sudden that the ogre hadn't been able to stir hand or foot.

The tenant had only stuck his knife into the sausage, you understand, but all the blood had come out and was running in a scarlet stream toward the door. The tenant's wife, stretched out like a log, looked already cold.

"Why, you brute!" blurted the ogre at last. "Look what you've done! You stuck your wife!"

"You got it, sir. I stuck her. It's not the first time and it won't be the last."

Unfazed, the tenant went to the fireplace for a bellows, squeezed two or three gentle puffs into the corpse's nostrils, and turned back to the ogre.

"There, sir. She'll revive, you'll see. This kind of bellows doesn't grow on trees. It came down to me from my great-uncle. It brings people back to life."

The ogre's eyes were like saucers.

He did indeed see the tenant's wife sigh, blink, sit up, and then stand up. She wasted no time cursing her husband.

"Look what you did, you pig, you big slob! All the blood's ruined my dress! Every time you kill me, I end up spending a whole hour getting the stain out. And it's a fine mess you brought me back to! I was a lot better off in the other world. Give me that bucket of water and the rag! Oh, excuse me, sir, I hadn't noticed you were here. I'm supposed to give you greetings from your late wife, though. Yes, I met her there, and everything's upside down. She's a servant now for that old valet of yours, the one you sent there when you boxed his ears a bit too hard. The scum had just given her a black eye because she hadn't done a good job getting the mud off his clogs; and when he doesn't see his mug or his bowl coming fast enough, he's very quick to encourage the poor dear lady with a few swift kicks."

"What? My old valet? He kicks my first wife?"

The ogre was turning purple, and his neck was swelling up like a mating grouse's. The tenant gave him a few good puffs right in the face, just to make sure he didn't drop dead of a stroke.

"That's enough, thank you. You're luckier than you deserve. That cooking pot I paid you so much for . . ."

"Ah, sir, maybe you just didn't do it right! Or do you suppose you might have broken the spell?"

"How about if I broke your ribs? But give me that bellows. I'm hot-tempered, and around me you never know what'll happen next. This gadget of yours will be useful around the house."

"Sir, what are you saying? My uncle's bellows!"

"Calm down! I'll cancel whatever rent you may still owe me, and a quarter of my sheep are yours as well. You'll have them this very evening."

He grabbed the bellows and marched off, still red, swollen, and grumbling to himself. He was thinking about the way his old valet dared to treat an ogress in the other world. On his way into his courtyard he noticed his present valet, and the sight filled him with such rage that without a word of warning or explanation he seized a club, fell on the miserable lout, and gave him a thorough dusting off along all his seams.

"There, you rascal! Payment in advance! And now, get over to the sheepfold, pick out one sheep in four, and take a quarter of my herd straight to my tenant."

The hullaballoo brought the ogress running. She started right in screeching protests.

"A quarter of our sheep! Aren't you forgetting you need a whole sheep, a big one, every day for lunch? How am I going to feed you, then, you profligate, you wrecker of homes, you big clod who're good only for tossing your property out the window? Imagine giving our sheep to a tenant who hasn't even paid up his arrears and who's making fun of you all the livelong day with this magic whip and this magic pot of his! Ah, you poor fool, you blockhead! Such big, plump, round, beautiful sheep!"

On she went, giving him a piece of her mind—*all* of her mind, in fact, pepper and salt included. He gave her some back. The argument heated up, till soon they were trading gross insults.

To make a long story short, the furious ogre drew his knife and favored his ogress with so vicious a stab in the throat that she crashed to the paving stones of the courtyard. Out gushed a flood of blood that streamed off under the gate.

This was the perfect moment to try out the bellows. The ogre blew into one nostril, then the other, now gently and now at full strength. He blew every way he could think of. It took him a good hour to get the tragedy properly through his head. At last he got up, eyes blazing, beard abristle, and nostrils breathing fire. He headed straight for the house of his tenant.

The ogre's valet had just come by with the sheep, and of course had had a drink before he left. Good times were in the air. Certainly, nobody imagined that the bellows would have been put to the test so quickly. Everyone—father, mother, and children—was happily dining at the big table.

Suddenly one of the boys turned toward the window.

"The ogre, daddy! The ogre's here!"

Daddy had just barely time to jump to the door and bolt it. But the ogre was so swept away with rage that he no longer knew his own strength. With one kick of his boot, he sent the door sailing across the room. Then in he burst himself and seized his tenant who, whiter than his own shirt, was trying desperately to hide under the empty wheat sacks. The ogre stuffed the tenant into one of those sacks and slung the loaded sack over his shoulder.

"Get out of *that* now, magic or not!"

He set off for a pond he knew, in a lonely spot, intending to whirl that sack around a few times and heave it out into the middle of the water.

Ogres are strong, but the day's crop of rages had parched his throat, and the sack was heavy. By the time he'd gone a league he was dying of

thirst, so he stopped at the door of an inn. Dumping the sack on the ground, he entered to wet his whistle.

Cautiously at first, the tenant began to move. He wriggled, pushed with his elbows, and tried to get his hand out the mouth of the sack so as to untie the string. Unfortunately, the string was tied with a double knot. The ogre was going to come back, load the sack over his shoulder again, and send it to the bottom of the pond.

Suddenly, the tenant felt a foot poking at him and heard someone asking himself out loud what on earth could be wriggling around that way in that sack.

He recognized the valet's voice. But what help could he expect from that rascal, who was once again nastier and twice again stingier even than his master?

"Is that you, valet?" he hissed. "Would you like to earn fifty crowns?"

"Oh, tenant, is that you? Fifty crowns, you say?"

"Undo the string! Listen, I bet your master a hundred crowns that he couldn't carry me all the way to town without my getting away. Take my place, and half those hundred crowns are yours."

The valet didn't need to hear that twice. As it happened, it had occurred to him that to pay himself back for all the blows he'd received, and since in any case the number of sheep in the herd hadn't divided evenly by four, he might just set one sheep aside and bring it to the inn to sell.

Having stuffed the valet into the sack, the tenant tied the cord back up so tight that you'd have broken your nails trying to undo it. Next, he slipped on the valet's rough woolen cloak, took up his staff, and shooed the rest of the herd off ahead of him so fast that his boots might as well have been on fire. He didn't even stop to wish the ogre a good evening, though the fellow was right there, nice and cool, in the inn, draining bottle after bottle.

Life is certainly hard, sometimes! The tenant had gotten himself out of a very tight spot, but he still felt a dreadful threat hanging over him. What with one thing and another, he barely dared go home till well after dark, to leave again at the first crack of dawn. All day long he kept those sheep hidden in the bushes, along the edge of the wood, or in the brushy pastures.

This went on for a month or two. But all things must come to an end. One evening as he was leading his flock across the earth dam by the pond, he ran smack into the ogre. It was bound to happen. Ever since the incident of the sack, the ogre had been combing the countryside for his valet and his sheep.

"Why hello, sir!" began the tenant, stepping forward cheerily. "Are your sheep over at your place doing as well as mine?"

The ogre stared at him, and he could hardly have been more horrified if the tenant had sprouted horns.

"What? You're still around? Didn't I throw you to the bottom of the pond?"

"But sir, I was in the sack. The sack kept me from swallowing water, and if a fellow doesn't swallow any water, why in the world should he drown? Under the pond I found the other world—and look what beautiful sheep I brought back!"

"What? You brought those sheep back from under water? I'd have sworn they were *mine!* They all look just the same as the ones I used to have."

"Oh, sir, it's just full of them, under the bottom of the pond! And look! You can see the ones that are still down there."

The tenant had driven the sheep to the edge of the dam, and they were as clearly reflected in the water as in a mirror. The ogre gazed in silence at those sheep from the other world, his mouth agape.

"Sir, would you by any chance be good enough to put me back in the sack and send me straight into the pond again? I'll go and fetch the flock you see down there. It's at least twice as big as the one I have."

"Absolutely not," declared the ogre. "*I'm* going. Yes indeed, it's my turn. I'm so hungry, I'd gladly have swallowed all your sheep raw if I hadn't seen the ones down there. I've gotten so thin lately, you could fit two of me into my trousers. But those are *real* sheep! Give me your staff. I'm going after them!"

The only problem was that he didn't have any sack to jump into, and he *was* rather afraid of drowning.

The tenant had a helpful idea. He suggested covering the ogre with the cloak, having him crouch down inside it, tying his legs together securely, and pulling the hood all the way down over his face. Once this was done, he gave master ogre a hearty shove and sent him, wrapped like a package, head first into the middle of the pond.

The frightful splash made the sheep at the bottom scatter in all directions. That ogre must be still be looking for them, because no one has heard from him since.

64. The Priest and the Sawyers

E stivareilles once had a priest who was certainly the best and kindest man alive. But it wasn't often you caught him napping.

One day he decided his main room needed a new floor. As he had some logs good for sawing into planks, he struck a bargain with Sabatier, the chief sawyer. One franc per meter of plank: that was their agreement.

That evening when the work was finished, they did some measuring. There were just fifty meters of planks. Then they went into the kitchen for dinner.

When they'd had their soup, their cheese and their bread, and their seconds of cheese and bread, and the rest of the coffee to wash it all down with, and some firewater to smooth it all out, and some old stories followed by fresh gossip, the priest closed his knife.

"Well now, Sabatier, what do I owe you? I'll go and fetch it."

"Don't worry, Father, there's no hurry."

"No, no, I'd forget all about it, and so would you. You figure it out. It's easy, anyway."

"That's true enough, Father. It'll be a hundred francs."

"What do you mean, a hundred francs? One franc per meter, that's what we agreed; and there are fifty meters even."

"Right, Father. But each plank has two sides. Come and look."

He took the priest to where he'd been working and picked up a plank. "It's sawn along this side, right? Then look"—he flipped it over—"it's sawn along the other side, too. Fifty meters on one side and fifty meters on the other: a hundred meters at a franc per meter makes a hundred francs."

"Fine, fine, fine," said the priest. "I'll bring you what I owe you."

He went to the cupboard and came back with a fifty-franc bill.

"But Father, surely there's some mistake! You're giving me a fifty?"

"Why, certainly, my friend. We see eye to eye. Look: each bill has two sides. On this side it says 'fifty francs,' right? Well, turn it over and look at the other side. That says 'fifty francs' too. Fifty plus fifty makes a hundred. Sabatier, our account is clear."

65. The Surprising Sum

There was once a man whose father wasn't exactly penniless. The fellow made a rich marriage and inherited wealth from two uncles, so that he ended up having more property than anyone else in the parish. But he strutted and swaggered around as though his wealth was due entirely to his own cleverness.

One day on his way home he met a monk from the monastery, the one in charge of the sheep. Sure enough, the monk was bringing in his flock.

"Good day, Brother Jean. How many sheep do you have there?"

"Thirty-six, Master Pierre."

"You ought to sell them to *me*. You monks will never do much with them. You can't do sums. I'd make them into a *real* herd. Give me a price, and if I like it I'll take them."

"Well then," said the monk, "I suppose we might as well get rid of them. I'll take just one denier for the first, two for the second, and so on, doubling the amount each time."

"A denier for the first, two for the second, and so on? Really? One denier for the first sheep? Listen, Brother Jean, do you stand by what you just said?"

"Absolutely."

"Done, then! Shake on it! Brother Jean, we've got ourselves a deal!"

A denier was just one-twelfth of a sou, which was one-twentieth of a franc. Eager to seize such a bargain, Master Pierre called over a man who was clearing stones from his field, and another who was working on his vines. He took them as witnesses.

The monk was smiling a quiet smile and watching Master Pierre with twinkling eyes.

They started figuring. The tenth sheep cost five hundred and twelve deniers, or something over two francs. That was roughly a fair price. The twentieth cost more than one thousand pounds, the thirtieth was worth more than the parish, and the thirty-sixth more than the entire province.

66. The Apples Sold All Wrong

There were once two neighbors—good neighbors—who each had an apple orchard. This was over there in apple country, at Périer, under Maurifolet tower.

The year was no good for fruit. In April, the red-moon frosts blasted the buds. In May, the ice saints compounded the damage. In the end, one got no more than sixty apples from his orchard, and the other likewise sixty.

But the first one decided his apples were finer than the second's—and it was more or less true. So he priced them at two for a penny. The second priced his at three for a penny.

Off they went one morning to the fair at Issoire and took their place in the market side by side.

They'd hardly gotten settled when they saw a man rush up all red and out of breath.

"Quick, quick, friend," he panted to the one with the beautiful apples, "you've got to get on home! They're expecting you! Your wife's gone into labor!"

"Goodness! I hope it's a boy! But I was planning to sell my apples . . ."

"Never mind," put in his neighbor, "I'll sell them for you."

"Thank you! Thank you very much! Don't forget, now: two for a penny, and there are sixty of them."

He rushed off toward Périer.

"Two for a penny," said the neighbor to himself. "Will anyone really take them? Perhaps he'll think that all I really cared about was selling *mine*. No, no, with mine three for a penny and his two for a penny, I'll average out the price and sell them both together at five for two pennies. That way, whatever happens, he'll have no complaints."

Listen closely, now! This tale is hard to follow. It's like the game they call piquet: it's not for donkeys to learn.

By about noon everything was sold: sixty apples plus sixty apples. One hundred and twenty at five for two pennies—that is, ten for four pennies—made in all twelve times four pennies, or forty-eight. And that's what the fellow found when he counted them: forty-eight pennies.

"*My* apples, at three for a penny, come to twenty pennies. I'll take twenty pennies for myself. The rest, twenty-eight pennies, belongs to my neighbor."

Just then his neighbor came back, glowing. His wife had given him a boy. She was already talking about getting up. She didn't want to cause any trouble over a birth. It turned out he really had nothing to do, so he was back to look after his apples.

"What? Twenty-eight pennies? Sixty at two for one penny, that makes thirty pennies. It's simple. You owe me thirty pennies!"

The other fellow justified himself. To make sure he did it right, he'd put the two lots of apples together and sold them five for two pennies, which made forty-eight pennies. And there those pennies were, right there. He couldn't hand over what he hadn't taken in. Who could say he'd done wrong?

The argument heated up. They began shouting and a crowd gathered. They went over the calculations again. Both were correct. The fellow with the better apples should have gotten thirty pennies, but the other had only twenty-eight to give him. There were two pennies missing. Where could they be?

Those who grasped the problem talked it over loud and long but couldn't figure it out. There were two pennies missing. Where in the world were they? People came running from the sheep market and the goat market. Those two apple sellers held everyone's attention. The rest of the fair was nothing at all.

> The gentlemen from the police
> Stepped up to mind them,
> And those big-shot detectives
> Followed right behind them.

The judges tried to sort it out. But if one had every right to claim thirty pennies, the other also had every right to offer him only twenty-eight. Whose brains *wouldn't* get addled thinking about it?

Then the parish priest from Périer happened by. What a look the fellow had! Rubbing his nose with his finger, he thought the matter over about as long as it would take to say an Our Father.

"Come, just try imagining it. Imagine there was one pile of yellow apples at two for a penny and another pile of red apples. Selling them the way you did, three red ones and two yellow ones together, works perfectly well at the start. But the red ones are bound to go faster. There comes a time when all you have left is yellow apples, which you're selling five for two pennies instead of two for one penny! That's why the money came out short. You thought you were doing the right thing, but you made a mistake. You must treat your friend to a drink, in honor of the happy birth, and act as godfather for his son. Of the two missing pennies, each of you loses one."

> A little of yours,
> A little of mine,
> And everything'll be fine.

67. The Johnnies-in-the-Moon

There was once a stretch of countryside between mountain and plain. The reason I'm not telling you the name of the place is that I'd rather you didn't know it. One year there, in April, the frost brought by the "red moon" caused a disaster. It killed every bud on the vines.

The following Sunday, the wine growers met in their vat room to discuss the catastrophe. Everyone knows what *that* means, a get-together down in the cellar out there in wine-growing country—yes indeed, everyone knows what *that* means . . .

That evening, somewhat worked up, they gathered on the square with the feeling that something just had to be done.

Now, according to the neighbors (who no doubt were simply jealous), these fellows weren't outstandingly bright and couldn't even have told you which month Our Lady's August feast day comes in.

Actually, it was just that they didn't have much luck. Any one of them falling on his backside would have been bound to break his nose.

You could tell they had bad luck because of all the misfortunes they suffered in this run-in of theirs with the moon. It all amounted to three or four good stories—and a lot more reliable ones, too, than the kind you get in a big-time politician's speech.

Anyway, these Johnny-in-the-Moon people had been fortunate enough to find a genuine brain in their very own town. Even as a child, this fellow had had ideas popping into his head the way pooperelles—excuse me, but that's what we call them around here—drop from a goat's behind. I'm talking about those sort of black lozenges that goats scatter by the handful when they go scrounging from bush to bush on a nice sunny day.

Ideas? That fellow had had them by the dozen, till at last the people made him their mayor. There among the mountain spurs and vineyards, he led all those good old folks along like a herd of donkeys.

So that Sunday, the whole commune was looking to their mayor to fix things up for them and make sure the frost would cause no more tragedies.

They all were huddled under the big elm, red-cheeked and hats askew, arguing, calling to each other, and generally carrying on.

"Silence!" shouted the mayor. "We've got to think rationally. Listen closely. It's the moon which caused the damage. If we manage to get rid of the moon, we'll save our harvest for all time, and long live the bottle!"

Now *that* was talking—*and* thinking. Every eye was on the mayor, every mouth hung open like a baby magpie's beak as they waited for what would come next.

"All right," the blacksmith still objected, "but how are we to get rid of the moon?"

"And what difference will it make?" cried someone else.

"Be quiet," said the constable. "Our mayor's got a good head on his shoulders. If something can be done, he'll find it."

"I don't say it won't cost us some work," the mayor continued. "Look: she's suspicious already. You see her up there, peeking at us and laughing to herself?"

The moon was just then poking her head out from behind the steeple, like a boy who's scrambled up to peer over a wall. Yes, she'd come to watch them through the branches of the elm. She wasn't quite round, but seemed instead to be leaning toward them, so bright, so white, and so peaceful . . .

"You see her? She's laughing at us, I tell you! But there must be a way to knock her down from up there. All we need's a little ingenuity. Ah, I'm already getting an idea. Perhaps we're not quite up to it this evening. But let's meet again at this time tomorrow. I want each and every one of you to bring his wine-making tubs!"

None of them could yet imagine what the mayor wanted with these tubs, to keep the moon from doing any more harm. But they'd bring them anyway. Their mayor was clever! Meanwhile, they all went for a good big glassful.

The next evening, they were all back with their tubs. And there were a lot, really a lot! The tubs filled the square, where usually you saw only a dandelion or two, a couple of rocks, or a few wisps of straw turning in the wind.

The moon came into view, seeming as before to be watching them and laughing. She was rounder than last evening, and above all, more threatening. All evening the air had been mild, smelling of flowers, warm earth, and new grass; but now it was growing chill. The clouds melted away and the moon shone up there in a clear, empty sky, dazzling and well able to finish blasting the vine buds. That fiendish moon was going to freeze everything up!

The mayor gave his orders. The constable—an old rascal as red as a cock and nimbler than a squirrel—was directed to set a first tub right in the middle of the square, then to place another one on top of it, and another on top of that, and so on and so on . . .

Up and up rose the tower of tubs. Quite carried away, the constable kept topping it off with yet another tub. Higher than the houses it was! Higher than the steeple!

"Steady now! Steady! I'm getting close! Two or three more tubs and I've got 'er!"

He was so high up there, good people, he was so high! Just like a weathercock on a church tower! They could hardly hear his voice any more—it was just a whisper, a distant sigh . . .

"One more! This time'll be it!"

But the tubs were all gone. They scrounged around everywhere, but not one was left. Every last tub had been brought from the cellars and pressed into service.

Up there in the sky the constable was hollering, "One more! One! Just one little tub! She's that close! I've got 'er, I tell you!"

Everyone ran around like mad, searching in every corner, but there wasn't a tub to be found. It was enough to make you tear your hair out!

All at once the mayor had an idea. Ideas were his specialty, and he was hardly going to dry up in a crisis like that.

"We don't need the bottom one any more! Let's have that bottom one!"

They hopped to it.

What a clatter and crash! What shrieks! What cries! The din could have split the church walls. And right in the middle of it all, tub by tub, that old monkey of a constable came thundering down.

Still, once he hit the ground, he couldn't fall any lower. He got out of it with a few broken ribs and a sprained shoulder. Later on, though, those injuries never discouraged him from dropping in for a drink at one house after another. And he got off to a fine start that very evening, when they all whisked him right off for a good big glassful.

Another evening (this time he probably hadn't drunk quite *enough*) he was coming back from his rounds among the vineyards and their owners, stepping along bravely with his big red nose cleaving the wind. He was stumbling a bit over the rocks, and weaving somewhat from left to right, because it seemed to him that the path kept on suddenly straightening out in front of him. And what did he see when he got to the top of the hill?

Yonder, past the village, a moving, rising redness was glowing like coals when you open the oven door.

Heavens! He raced home, took down his drum, slung it around his neck, and grabbed the drumsticks. Off he charged through the streets, drumming the alarm.

"Fire! Fire! Fire!"

"Where? Where? Where?"

Everyone came out, shouting and slamming doors.

"By the pond! By the pond!" he answered, still battering away at his drum and heading that way on the double.

It was the moon—the moon rising as red as coals behind the black willows, and reflected in the water.

They got over all the excitement by all going for a good big glassful.

After that, they say, the constable had it in for the moon worse than ever—the way he might have hated some unpleasant neighbor, or some slut's daughter who kept slipping through his fingers.

Those two had a score to settle, he and the moon. He kept an eye on her. No, he wouldn't have her mocking him forever.

One evening he showed up at the mayor's place, panting for breath.

"Quick, Mister Mayor! She's touching the hill! Hang me if I don't get her this time!"

She did indeed look as though she was just resting on the hilltop.

They grabbed a wheat sack that was lying around and raced up there as fast as their legs would carry them.

But the hill was on the other side of the river and it was steep. When they finally got to the top, breathless and fainting, the moon had slipped away again.

They stalked the moon two or three times again like that, sack and all, but never caught her. To recover their spirits, they went for a good big glassful.

Now, the mayor was so clever that he at last realized one thing: "What with this game of ending up always Johnny-in-the-Moon, people around here no longer respect me as much as they used to."

He remembered the proverb, "You're better off calling the wolf a good friend."

"I'd be better off complimenting the moon," said the mayor to himself.

"We weren't very smart, were we, to try so hard to get rid of her! Who'd touch our seeds with moonlight?

> *Moon on the wane: sow your crop,*
> *Your seeds will all come up.*

"Without the old moon to show us when to plant, our lettuces would all go to seed, and our radishes too, and our chervil. Who'd touch our woods with moonlight?

> *Wood in thorn,*
> *Moon newborn.*
> *Wood in leaf,*
> *Moon near death.*

"Wood not touched with moonlight, as the proverb has it, tends to get worm-eaten. And the moon shows when you're supposed to cut your nails or your hair. The moon! If there wasn't one, we'd have to invent her. Yes indeed, my friends, let's keep her, since we're lucky enough to have her!"

When that mayor felt like it, he could speak golden words.

This happened in front of the inn, one Sunday in May. The mayor spoke under the arbor, in the shade of many bottles, and his speech deserved to linger in every mind. To make sure it got all the way into their heads, each one who heard him downed another good big glassful.

One nice quiet evening a fortnight later, as the smith was returning from his vineyard by the path along the pond, he suddenly saw . . . What do you think? None other than the moon that had fallen right there into the water.

Why, she had to be fished up and put back in the sky! They couldn't afford to lose her! The smith remembered the mayor's speech very clearly. Not having the moon any more would be a disaster!

So he had to think fast . . .

It didn't occur to him to look up and see whether the moon was still there. In that part of the country, ideas occurred only to the mayor. Anyway, he couldn't have thought of any such thing. There was no way the moon could be in the sky since he could see her distinctly, and very near, down in the pond among the willows.

So he ran to the village and brought everyone back—every Johnny-in-the-Moon thereabouts. What were they to do? How were they to fish her up?

"Somebody go for the village donkey," commanded the mayor. "Have the donkey drink the water. When he's drunk up the whole pond, we'll have our moon and we'll hang her back in the sky."

They ran for the donkey and rushed him over as fast as they could. Being a good old donkey, he happily started drinking.

Just then a cloud passed by. Before you could say boo the moon was gone.

"Woe is us! The donkey swallowed her!"

They went down into the pond to drag the donkey out. But they tumbled in so roughly, with such shouts and carrying-on, that the donkey got frightened. He reared, kicked the water, dodged, and blinded them with spray. Then he got away. Off he galloped through the countryside, up the brushy slopes and along the rows of vines.

They gave chase. All worked up, those Johnnies-in-the-Moon ran every which way after him, till at last their mad pursuit ran him to earth in the square with the big elm. There, right in front of the inn, they jumped on him.

They were so excited, you know, they didn't even hesitate. They stunned the donkey with a whack on the head and opened up his belly.

There was no moon in there.

"Well, by thunder, that galloping donkey scattered his droppings all over, and he dropped the moon somewhere too. Who's to know where? We'll probably never see her again!"

Everyone went back home, sadly downcast.

But as the smith came to the apse of the church, he let out a great cry.

"Here she is! We've found her! She's in here!"

And there she was, indeed, in an old cistern squeezed in between the round wall and a few hovels. The cloud had sailed by and she'd just come out again when he'd come on the cistern and spotted her.

"The donkey left her there! We've got to get her out right away!"

Everyone ran up again behind the mayor. The policeman brought the donkey's rope. It was pretty frayed, but long enough. They tied a hook to it and tossed the hook into the cistern.

A dozen of them began pulling.

The hook, meanwhile, had caught on a stone at the bottom. It was completely stuck and wouldn't move.

More men joined in, till there were twenty or so heaving away hard enough to skin their hands.

Suddenly the rope broke and they tumbled over together on their backs.

What did they see as they lay there?

There above them rode the moon, right back in her place among the clouds.

"Well, there she is, after all that work! We sent her right back where she belongs!"

That was the end of their tangle with the moon. Those Johnnies-in-the-Moon were so pleased and proud that evening, they got drunker than thrushes in grape-harvest time. After all, they could hardly *not* go and celebrate with a good big glassful.

68. The Woodcutter and the Salesman

There was once a woodcutter whose trade was felling trees in the forest and turning them into logs and firewood. That year he'd bought a field, right by his house, that had chanced to come on the market. The field made a big difference to him, but it had cost him a lot: three hundred francs, and not a franc less. He'd had to borrow them on a six-month term from a nearby farmer who had a bit more than he did. Now the six months were nearly over. He was going to have to return that money, and he was broke.

What to do? He couldn't even sleep. One evening he was on the way home from his day's work when, on the path between the woods and his house, worry got to him so badly that he began talking aloud. There he was, stumbling over the loose stones between the great rocks and the beech trees—you might say about as far as from Besace Wood to Jarrix—talking and scratching his head. Suddenly he saw before him a little fellow, a sort of salesman, all in black and with a handkerchief the color of fire. The salesman asked what was worrying him so, and making him talk to himself like that on the path.

"Ah, if I'm talking, it's just that I've plenty to talk about, and plenty to worry about, too! Anyone in my shoes would feel the same. I need money so badly, you see, and I've no idea where to find any."

He told the whole story.

"Oh," said the salesman, "if it's only money, my best friend has a bit in his pocket at the moment. Here—if you like, I'll count you out three hundred francs on this big stone here, no later than tomorrow. I'll set just one condition, though it's hardly worth mentioning: the first bundle you tie up tomorrow morning is for me."

"One bundle?" replied the woodcutter. "Take two or three if you want! However many you say! I tie up bundles all day long anyway."

"One's enough, my man: the first one you tie in the morning."

It was a deal. The salesman showed him the money, and even counted it out for him. Then the two parted, well pleased with one another. The salesman went on up toward the forest, and the woodcutter continued on down toward the village.

That woodcutter was so happy and so relieved that at supper he ate twice as much as he had the evening before. Soup with lard, cabbage, it all went down in a flash. His wife watched him as she stood, bowl in hand, by the table, and saw something was up. She kept after him till he told her the story.

"All right! If you really want to know what happened, I met a little salesman up there on the path, and he asked me why I was talking to myself. I told him the trouble I was in, and we made a deal. He'll give me three hundred francs for the first bundle I tie up tomorrow morning, as I start my day."

That woodcutter hadn't been born on a Sunday morning. That is, he wasn't one of those clever fellows who instantly sniff out what's really going on. Fortunately, his wife knew more than the devil himself.

She put her bowl down on the table and thought it over, arms akimbo. There are fine people in the world, filled with good will. But to run across someone who offers you three hundred francs for a bundle of wood—well, that makes you stop and think.

"Dear husband," she said finally, "don't you understand that the first bundle you tie up tomorrow morning will be you yourself? That's just what you'll do when you buckle your belt. And you'll belong to that man of yours, all in black with a handkerchief the color of fire. Do you know what you must do? Take a pile of branches out into the barn and lay the rope underneath them, so you just need to tie the knot when you jump out of bed, before you even put on your trousers."

The woodcutter obeyed. He put the branches in the barn just the way his wife told him to. Then he went to bed and fell asleep. As soon as he woke up the next morning, he raced to the barn, tied up the bundle, and left it all ready there, leaning against the wall.

He did his day's work as usual, and that evening, on his way home from the woods, he met the salesman at the same spot as before.

"Hello there, salesman. Your bundle's waiting for you. It's behind the barn door, up against the wall—a good big one. I tied it up this morning in my nightshirt, before I even put on my pants."

That so-called salesman looked quite disappointed. He kept quiet, but his eyes burned like two brands.

"Listen," he said at last to the woodcutter, "I've a wood up there. Come up to my wood tomorrow and we'll get to work, both of us. The one who makes the biggest bundle of firewood wins. If it's you, you get your three hundred francs. If it's me, I get *you*."

The woodcutter hardly knew what to say, and stood there scratching his ear. When he turned again to the salesman, he was gone. There was nothing to look at but the rocks, the tall beech trees, and the twilight over the mountain.

He reached home a bit stunned. His wife was waiting for him at the door.

"Well, is it all done?"

"Yes, that part's done, but now I've got another problem."

As he ate his supper, he told his wife what had happened. Oh, it's good to be clever, but it's even better to have a clever wife.

She thought it over, scratched with her nail at a grease spot on the table, then said to her husband, "Let him make his bundle. He'll make a big one, of course. But *you*, now, you're going to take the biggest ball of string we can find . . ."

Step by step, she laid out the whole plan.

On his way to the woods the next morning, the woodcutter met the salesman, who was coming to fetch him. Both climbed on up together toward the salesman's wood.

At last they got there. And friends, what a wood it was! Giant trees crowded together, their trunks as thick and round as towers, their branches as long as highroads, and crowned with masses of leaves that gave shade darker than the inside of a wolf's den. The salesman took off his coat and seized his ax. I tell you, he went at it like a crow knocking down walnuts. Soon he had a pile of branches big enough to make your jaw drop. Then he just spat in his hands, went at it again there among the ferns, and made the pile bigger still.

Hands in his pockets, the woodcutter looked on.

"Are you done? Fine. Now it's my turn. Beg your pardon, but would you just step over here, to the edge of the wood, and hold the end of my string?"

The salesman did so. The woodcutter then unwound the string as he walked around the wood.

"Hey!" cried the salesman after him. "What are you doing?"

"Just getting my wood together, as we agreed. I'll get around your wood, make a bundle of it, and take it away."

When the salesman heard *that*, he just about had a fit.

"Well, now, how this woodcutter goes at it! A great one, he is, for knocking down tenpins! He'd make one bundle of my whole beautiful wood, and shave me the ground as smooth as my hand, with nothing left but a few ferns and cranberry bushes! Oh no! Go hang!"

He dropped the string and charged after the woodcutter.

"No, listen, my good man, leave my wood alone! I'd just as soon give you the three hundred francs. No, here's what I suggest. I'll come to dinner with you this evening, and we'll settle everything. I'm getting old, so all I want is patias." (Patias, you see, is mashed potatoes with milk. Nothing goes down so nicely, or fills people's stomachs better.) "Whoever eats the most patias will have won. If it's you, you'll have the money. If it's me, I'll have *you*."

A patias-eating contest? The woodcutter could put it away with the best of them, but he could imagine what that salesman was capable of swallowing. Back home he went, no doubt much less easy in his mind than he'd have liked to be. When he got there, he had a drink to whet his appetite. Then he told his wife to make patias, and why: that other fellow was coming.

So his wife got everything ready and wiped off the table. She told her husband to have the salesman sit here, with his back to the wall; he himself should sit opposite. Then she arranged things so the lantern hanging from the beam would only light up her husband from the back. Besides, the lantern didn't give off much light anyway. What with the table and the closet-bed, the soot from the hearth, and the bars over the little window, you never can see much in all the smoked-pine clutter of a mountain cottage.

When it was all arranged, that clever woman took a sack—one for hempseed, or something like that—and hung it around her husband's neck, under his shirt.

The next minute, there was the salesman. They sat him down, and he put before him a pile of crowns, three hundred francs' worth. The woodcutter sat down opposite him, with his back to the lantern. The wife brought them their patias right in the pot, and both fell to, seated squarely on their benches, spoon in hand and chin nearly down on the table.

Woodcutters can really eat. Still, it's unlikely this one could have kept up with that salesman, who was going through the stuff like fire. The woodcutter knew what to do, though, because his wife had told him. Instead of gulping the spoonfuls of patias down his throat, he slipped them under his chin and down into the sack. You couldn't see much—you don't need to, to eat patias—and everything was set up just right, with the woodcutter against whatever light there was. Anyway, the salesman, intent on those spoonfuls of patias, never noticed a thing.

Eventually the sack was stuffed as tight as a pillow. The woodcutter turned to his wife.

"Wife," said he, "I'm full. I can't eat another bite. Give me the knife."

She passed him the big knife for (pardon me) sticking pigs, and he plunged it up to the hilt in the sack, as though running it into his own belly. Out sloshed the patias. Then he patted his stomach and really began to eat. Oh, it was a pleasure to see him dig into the pot and not work his jaws any more just for show.

The salesman could hardly believe his eyes. He'd eaten so much that his stomach was bursting, and he could hardly manage any more. As far as he could see, the only way for him not to lose was to do just the same as the woodcutter had.

He took the knife in turn, and gave himself such a stab in the belly that his innards flopped out in one mass. Instantly he collapsed on top of them. He never even knew what had happened.

As my grandfather used to say, there'd been a hundred of those devils before, so that left just ninety-nine.

Part
Six

BESTIARY

69. The Black Cat

There once lived in our village a little girl who (can you believe it?) loved her neighbor better than money.

Now and again, though, she'd have been glad of a crown. At home she had hardly a penny, and both her parents were dead. On the other hand, she knew the secret for getting along on nothing at all: take things boldly just as they come, and always be happy. Her thoughtfulness toward others helped a lot too. So did her high spirits, and her quickness to laugh.

> You're laughing, laughing, my shepherd girl,
> Dear shepherd girl, you're laughing!

Her good humor, abloom on her face, gave her the high coloring of a midsummer bouquet.

Now, one animal was a great friend to her in all her trouble, and that was her cat. This cat was a bit like Puss-in-Boots, you know, who did so much for his master.

Once when she was just a slip of a girl, she'd happened to do a favor for an old woman who lived deep in the woods. The old woman had some sort of fairy powers. Perhaps the girl had brought her a loaf of bread, or gone to fill her jug at the spring. Anyway, it was her own good heart that had moved her to do whatever it was. And the old woman, just like an old woman in a story, had given her a present in return: the cat. Cats were rare in those days, so long ago. Village people prized them, and got them to do things that no one asks of cats any more—like hunting and catching fish or game for their master.

"A cat's the devil's cousin," they say, but that applies only to black cats. This one was white, all white, as white as a white dove. His green eyes shone like the penitents' lanterns in the Holy Thursday procession. And he was sweeter and prettier than any cat had a right to be.

"Here, dear, this kitty's yours," the old woman had said. "He's my present to you. You'll see what he gives you. He'll go hunting for you. Trout on Friday and hare on Sunday he'll bring you—you'll see! And perhaps one day he'll bring you more than that."

"Thank you, kind old lady. Many thanks to both you and your cat. I was so lonely. The cat will be company for me."

"Look after him well. He's a good one."

So the girl decided she'd take good care of the cat. Right away the two were the very best of friends, petting and rubbing each other fondly.

That cat really was a hunter. When the girl went off for firewood or hazelnuts, he'd follow her into the wood, then suddenly pop out of the bushes with a thrush or a rabbit in his pink mouth. He'd do the same when she went to cut osier along the riverbank. And believe me, he was an expert at fishing eel or barbel. For herself, all she had was her billhook, and she had to live off the bundles of wood and the wicker baskets she sold. But now she also had this cat, which was such a help to her.

Then three months later something amazing happened. The white cat turned black!

People said it happened because the girl's cramped little cottage was as smoky as a fox's lair. But how could such a thing be true? Smoky or not, the place could hardly have been sooty enough to blacken the cat, the way people redden their clogs with cranberry juice for a wedding. Perhaps the cat got tired of keeping himself as clean and white as fine flour. His white coat certainly must have hindered him when he went hunting. You know a sheepdog has to be white, so it can be seen, but a guard dog should be black, so it can lurk invisibly in the shadows. Perhaps the cat turned black, by some sort of kitty magic, because he wanted to and needed to. At any rate, he ended up blacker than a crow's wing. Even crows throw off bluish or greenish glints, but not that cat. His black was deep and glossy, the blackest black you can imagine. The only white he kept was a little circle right there—you know where I mean—under his tail. It was no bigger than a miser's coin. It's true, believe me. My grandfather's grandfather saw it himself.

A black coat was just what that cat had wanted. Now he was craftier, deadlier, and better hidden than ever. By night, no wild creature could see him stealing down hedgerows dark or light, by the pond or in the deepest thickets, or along the edge of the woods. He crept as silently as dandelion down floats on the faintest breeze. One paw forward, then the next; a few lashes of the tail; then he'd gather himself, pounce, and sink his claws into the quivering body of his prey. Quail, wheatear, missel thrush, hare, rabbit— any creature of feather or fur: he'd clamp it delicately between his sharp teeth and bring it back to his mistress.

The girl began to thrive, and grew into a fine young woman. But growing's not all there is to life. You also have to set up house. You have to have children who themselves, one day, will light the fire on their own hearths and share their bread with their families.

There was a lad in the village in those days: honest, good-hearted, as straight as the poplar tree at Croix-haute, and as strong as the oak at Trois-Routes. He was the girl's neighbor, too, and the pair took a liking to each other.

But when the lad's mother noticed, she came looking for the girl with the black cat that very evening, to put a stop to their friendship.

"My dear," said she, "I might as well speak to you right away. You and my boy aren't meant for each other. You know I've always held my head up in the world—and do you know how fond I was of your poor mother? We're not big, rich people, but we've a bit of property, and my son's going to need a wife who knows how to run a house. You, on the other hand, are good only for gathering firewood. You can't spin, or do laundry, or iron, or bake, or milk, or clot cheese."

"I'll learn quickly if you show me how."

"But you've no sheep or cattle. All you have is that one black cat. And I must say, my dear, that even the cat is no credit to you. It's not like a Christian to have a black cat, as though she were a witch. Why, 'cat' means practically the same as 'friend of the devil.'"

"What are you talking about? My poor, dear little cat! All he's got of the devil in him is his way of catching rabbits and blackbirds."

"Oh, I'm not forgetting that more than once you've brought me game he'd caught. And I ate it, of course—but, you see, I wasn't really happy about it. Well, never mind. The trouble is that you've neither cattle nor capital, and that means there's nothing I can do for you. If my boy's to marry you, I'd have to see you with a hundred crowns."

"A hundred crowns! Mercy!"

"Yes, my dear. Bring us a hundred crowns, and you two are man and wife. I'll hold the wedding right away. But you won't find them under your black cat's tail!"

Now, the next day, the lord of the village was marrying off his daughter. Young and old in all the houses were up at the first light of dawn so as not to miss a single bit of the wedding.

It was all so exciting: the loaves, fat and thin, being carried to the oven by a procession of little boys; the bouquet of white roses a chambermaid brought in from the garden; the three minstrels in from town, with their flute, viol, and drum; the lords and ladies riding in from all the castles around; and everything else there was to see, from kitchen to chapel. Each scrap of news ran swiftly from door to door: how the wedding guests were to dine off a roast peacock done up in its own feathers; how the stableboy could hardly stand, he'd drunk so much; how the bride's veil was all Venetian lace; and finally, how the bride's candle had burned two minutes longer than the groom's.

That's how they found out, toward the end of the banquet, that the lord had sent for the village magician. He'd told the magician to perform some special wonder of his for the distinguished company. Not that the people around here were known in those days for their feats of magic—far from it. Anyway, the lord had boasted to his guests that the local magician had the power to show them night in broad day. Yes, he'd bring them night in a basket, right to their table!

"Night in a basket!" laughed all the assembled lords.

The magician managed to throw rainbows on the wall with a three-sided bit of crystal he held in a sunbeam. Then he put two chickens and a goat to sleep; picked up glowing coals in his fingers; spat fire from his mouth; and pulled a few other humble stunts.

"Night in a basket, night in a basket!" everyone began to shout, clattering their knives against the bottles.

The disappointed lord sent the magician packing.

"Go to the devil, you and your act! You didn't surprise or amuse us. You'd have had a hundred crowns from me if you'd shown us night in broad daylight."

"And from me too!" cried a baron.

"More than that from me!" called out a count.

Yes, they all promised a heap of crowns to whoever would show them night by sunlight.

Now, the day being hot, the room's windows stood wide open. The girl was sitting in her doorway, darning her stockings. She heard the lords shouting. So many crowns! And she only needed a measly hundred of them!

Just then, the cat came to rub up against her legs—the cat which had once been as white as a beautiful morning, and now was blacker than a moonless midnight.

The girl looked at him and got an idea.

Up she jumped, picked up the cat, kissed him, popped him in her best basket, threw her Sunday apron over it, and set lightly off for the castle.

"Tell the lord, tell all the barons here for the wedding! There's a girl outside who'd like to show them night in broad daylight."

"Mad girl, what are you talking about?"

"Go tell them! I have night here in a basket."

The servant went to pass on the message. There were shouts and hoots of laughter. Then back came the servant to open the door and usher her in.

There she stood now, before the whole uproarious company.

"Yes, my lords: night in a basket. Listen, and judge whether I'm telling the truth."

They listened closely, motioning to each other to be quiet. Sure enough, a cold winter wind seemed to moan through the cracks, and a wood owl to screech from its lair amid black branches. How could the lords have guessed that the basket held a frightened, yowling, spitting cat? They'd have sworn they heard night sounds over the fields in the gloom of Advent when the wind is high.

"And look!" she cried, smiling gaily.

She uncovered the cat, blacker than the black of midnight, with his eyes gleaming as bright as stars. Everyone jumped up in happy confusion, and all heads leaned over the basket.

"Why, what she says is absolutely true!" cried a count.

"That's right, that's right!"

"It's all there!" declared a duke.

"Yes, gracious wedding guests, it's all there! All of it, even the moon!"

With a quick gesture she lifted the kitty's tail and showed it to them—you know where.

The barons, counts, and dukes burst into gales of laughter, and really almost dissolved in mirth.

"Oh, it's night in a basket, it certainly is!"

"All right, then, we're not such fools after all!" cried the lord of the village. "I'm sure you'll agree this girl has earned my hundred crowns!"

"Mine too! I'll not go back on my word!" announced another.

Swept away by the happy occasion, by good food, copious drink, and sparkling wit, they were laughing so loudly that their glasses danced on the table.

"She can have all the crowns I've got!"

"Mine too!"

Each one reached for his purse, as though eager to be the first to empty it. How the crowns and ducats rained on the basket! Silver streamed the way our brook streams down the mountain when the snows begin to melt. The delighted girl looked on wide-eyed, and couldn't help clapping her hands.

"Well done, well done, well done! Why, now I'll be able to get married too!"

In high good humor, they started plying her with questions.

"Now we're so full of the wedding spirit, we've got to get them married!"

Someone ran for her friend and his mother. The drum, flute, and viol struck up their music—music to tempt the larks from the sky! With all that merrymaking, everything went like a dream. A notary wrote out the marriage contract. Two rings were produced from somewhere, and somebody went for the priest.

Now, cats don't much like noise. This one climbed in three jumps onto the canopy over the lord's seat. From there he looked down with some alarm on the proceedings, and presided too over the wedding, though he didn't approve of what he saw.

Being a magician, like all cats, he must have known his mistress would now go and live with the neighbors. And cats are supposed to be more faithful to the hearth than to the master. What they want is a corner by the fire to curl up in, with their nose beneath a paw. They don't much care for change or excitement.

So when everyone formed the procession, with shouts of glee and a ringing fanfare from the flute, viol, and drum, the cat had had enough. He leaped from the canopy onto the windowsill and from the windowsill to the elm tree. From the elm tree he quickly made his way home.

"Hurry up and marry me!" begged the flustered girl, half laughing and half crying. "See how all this fuss has frightened my black cat!"

Nonetheless, the very next day, the faithful cat slipped through the hedge and took up an honored place in her new home. And by some magic, white or black, he brought that home good luck. Yes, the cat's mistress always lived in harmony not only with her husband but even with her mother-in-law!

> Don't tell me it couldn't be:
> My grandad's grandad was there, you see!

70. The Devil and the Priest's Donkey

There was once an old priest so simple and saintly that he'd changed the whole life of his parish. No one would have stolen a single stray stick of firewood, or even picked an apple out of the ditch! The men swore no more than they needed to, to get their wagon out of a rut. They drank no more than three mugs each at the village festival, and when they got home afterwards they didn't even beat their wives. In fact things had gone so far—believe this if you can!—that even at the fair, where it's no sin to cheat your own parents, a fellow who had a cow to sell would actually tell you straight out, quite honestly, everything that was wrong with her!

The very sight of this parish made the devil seethe with rage. As there was nothing he could do with the place, he was always slinking around it. He was constantly trying at least to trap some old woman into the sin of slander, while the women filled their jugs at the spring; or to tempt some little girl into greed before the honey pot in the cupboard. He couldn't stop lurking, sniffing, and sneaking around in search of someone he could get at.

He didn't dare try to get at Father. That good, holy man would put him to flight with a sign of the cross. Finally, the devil was so put out by his failure ("If you can't get a thrush, go for a blackbird") that he actually started in on Father's donkey.

The parish was big and hard to get about in, being all cut up by ridges and ravines. The good priest had had to get himself a donkey. The devil tried everything on that donkey. He mixed twigs in his hay and thorns in his oats; buzzed around his ears like a flying beetle; flitted past his eyes like a bat; stung him under the tail or tripped him up against a stone; and in short, pestered him in more ways than any crowd of boys could possibly have thought up.

The donkey, however, bore it all stoically. He was a good donkey, just as patient as his master, and in fact a sort of saint himself, in his own donkeyish way.

The night before Christmas, animals always get a double ration of fodder, in honor of the animals around the manger. As soon as night fell, there was the donkey before *his* manger, all happy at the thought of the coming feast, and perhaps just a little bit greedy.

Suddenly he turned his head, and saw beside him the parish cantor.

"Dear donkey," said the cantor, "I've a favor to ask. You see, my cow's going to have a calf. I've no choice, I have to stay with her. So I've been wondering . . . Would you by any chance take my place at midnight mass?"

Everyone knows that the beasts in the stable speak in human voices at midnight on Christmas Eve—the ox and the ass, that is, who warmed the Child with their breath. So, at least, the donkey had heard, and he supposed there must be some truth to the rumor.

Take the cantor's place that night in church? Well, why not? He signaled with his long ears that he was willing.

"All you'll have to do," the cantor went on, "will be to go *Aaa-men*. It's perfectly simple. How about trying it?"

"Hee-haw, hee-haw," intoned the donkey.

"There you are, you see! You sing much more impressively than I do. Our priest will be very pleased tonight, and so will everyone else in the congregation. So it's agreed?"

The donkey signaled back Yes with his head and ears. How proud it made him to think that for once *he* would be singing the responses! Prouder he was than if he'd been called to carry His Holiness the pope through the city of Rome.

The cantor disappeared as suddenly as he'd appeared, though it never occurred to the flattered donkey to think this odd. He should have wondered about it, though, he really should have. A certain enemy had already played more than one trick on him. And that enemy has the power to take any form he likes, whether animal, beetle, or bat; or even the human form of a young girl or a greying cantor.

The donkey busied himself right away, shaking himself like a dog just out of the water to get rid of the straw stuck to his coat; licking himself like a cat that's gotten into the lard; and polishing his hooves like a woman brushing off her clogs on a snowy day before she enters her house.

As the first bell rang for mass, he blew his nose in proper form right down between his feet, shook himself again, polished himself some more, and stepped out lightly toward the church.

Unfortunately, all his primping had made him late. The whole parish was there when he came in, the men on one side and the women on the other. Father, all white and gold in his chasuble, was just going up to the altar. The candles were gleaming—a whole forest of candles. Obviously they were waiting for *him* in order to begin.

Ears erect, tail aloft, he galloped down the aisle straight for the choir, between the two halves of the congregation, as though he had a horsefly after him. And as he galloped he brayed at the top of his donkey voice, to let everyone know he'd come to sing the responses.

What an uproar! It was worse than the tower of Babel. The parishioners thought they were seeing the Horned One. Women screamed, children howled, old crones fainted dead away. Two men hurled themselves at the donkey's mane, and two boys at his muzzle. He tried to explain that he'd come to replace the cantor, and he brayed his plainsong just as loud as he could through all the rumpus.

They fell on him with blows of their sticks. They even beat him with lanterns. He shook his ears and danced about, doing his best to get away. Then he rose on his front legs and counterattacked with a frightful volley of kicks at the pews, the pulpit steps, and even the confessional.

A lot of good it did him to have so tough a skin and such sturdy bones! He almost got himself a broken back. The hail of blows drove him in retreat to the church door where, in a frenzy of rage, he bid them farewell with a mighty bray, turned tail, and fled.

Twelve boys lit out after him, with all the village dogs. They chased him to the edge of the village. Sparks flying from all four hooves, he sped over the bridge and up the hill, then at the top galloped on furiously into Epinettes Wood. His sides were heaving like a blacksmith's bellows, and as he was still dazzled by the church's countless candles, he bumped into all the trees. At last, he fell to his knees, broken and exhausted.

The clearing was lit by a sort of murky, reddish glow, like moonlight rising behind swamp willows. Next there came a peculiar laugh—a drawn-out snicker like a nasty-minded billy-goat's. The sulphur smell in the air was familar: the donkey remembered having smelled it in his very own stable when the so-called cantor had appeared and vanished.

Before him, he saw two red points of light, brighter than coals. Another look, and he recognized the devil. The devil, squatting on his haunches, was looking the donkey over, laughing, and apparently thumbing his nose at him.

The donkey lowered his head. He saw all too clearly now what had happened. "You poor vainglorious creature!" thought he. "The devil trapped you into the sin of vanity, and now he has you at his mercy. You see where it got you, wanting to play cantor. Now, to save your own skin, try playing donkey."

He pretended to be out of breath and out of voice; sighed three times as though about to expire; tried to get up on one knee and fell back; then tried the other knee and fell back again. At last he struggled to his feet, took four steps, tripped over various stones, and thudded head-first into a tree.

The devil burst once more into laughter.

"Who's there?" asked the donkey. "Whoever you are, in this wood, take pity on a poor blind creature! The thorns must have scratched out my eyes as I came through. I can't see. I'm all done in. Have pity, put me on the right path so I can go and give up the ghost on my own bed!"

"What'll you give me if I do?" Satan inquired.

"But who are you?"

"Why, I'm the devil."

"Then I'll give you my soul, master devil, since that's what the devil always seems to want."

"That donkey soul of yours isn't worth much. Well, all right. I'll mount you and guide you with my knees."

"Oh no, master devil, they broke me with their blows, and I'm afraid I'm too weak to carry you. Walk in front of me, if you'll be so kind, and I'll hold on to you by the end of your tail."

"Very well, if that's the way you want it."

So the devil went on ahead while the donkey followed behind, step by step, holding in his teeth the end of the devil's tail.

The devil felt very jolly as he skipped along, whistling:

> Come, master donkey, come along!
> You're not worth much any more.
> Come, master donkey, come along!
> Soon you'll not be worth a song!

"I'll lead him straight down to the river," thought the devil to himself, "and I'll send him in for a little dip. I'll never have played a better trick on that old priest."

"Not so fast, master devil, not so fast!" sighed the donkey. "I'm all worn out."

Still, he managed to move ahead, ears drooping, behind the Evil One. Humming and skipping, the devil had started down the slope, and the poor donkey meekly let himself be led on.

Now, the devil's afraid of water, even when it's not blessed. This was Christmastime, and the river was so cold that it might have turned to ice any minute. The devil didn't like the look of it one bit. On the other hand, he was a good jumper. "What a splash you'll make, master donkey!" thought he. He led the donkey out to a spot at a bend in the river, where the bank jutted out a little and fell off sheer into a deep, swirling pool.

"Now, hold on tight to my tail and let yourself come along. It's just a hop and a skip across. One jump, and we're over."

The donkey saw perfectly well what the devil had in mind. He clamped his teeth mightily onto the devil's tail and braced himself with all his strength against the rock.

With a great bound, the devil leaped forward. But if he was counting on the donkey following him, he made a big mistake. His tail, ripped out by the shock, hung from the donkey's teeth, while he himself, mutilated, arms and legs churning the air, plummeted into the river.

They say you could hear his shriek from the church. The wound on his backside must have burned terribly. No doubt all that ice-water made it feel much better.

The donkey trotted humbly back to the village, where the people were just coming out from church. Father was on his way home. The donkey went down on both knees and laid the bloody tail before him.

Father couldn't quite understand what had happened, but he had an idea that the Evil One had suffered some sort of revenge. The donkey, meanwhile, looked so simple, humble, and contrite that the good Father couldn't help forgiving him for the scene he'd made. And since it was Christmas Eve, he even comforted the donkey with a double ration of oats and a dose of hot wine.

As for the tail, they nailed it with a big wagon nail to the sacristy door, just like one of those demon gargoyles that poke out of church walls.

Every time the choirboys went by with a bottle of holy water, they'd have a wonderful time putting the bottle up against the tail. The tail would screw itself up like a piglet's, wriggle like a worm, and twist about like a snake. The donkey, grazing in the walled meadow, would come over and look on through the window bars. And with all his big yellow teeth, he would laugh.

There we are, the tale is done.
If you liked it, then you tell one.

71. The Nightingale's Three
Bits of Advice

There was once a villager who, seeing winter now over with all its cold and snow, and spring at last coming back to the fields, set out his traps to catch small birds. People normally do that in the dead of the year, in the snow. By now, the thorn hedges were in leaf, and daffodils were blooming in the meadows around the mill. But he was lucky. He managed to catch a nightingale.

He was going to stifle the nightingale under his thumb when it spoke to him.

"Man," said the nightingale, "what will you gain by killing me? Weigh me and see. I won't fill your belly. On the contrary, let me fly free, and you'll gain three pieces of advice which will serve you wonderfully well, if only you can get them into your head."

"Nightingale, I swear I'll let you go if your advice is as good as you say."

"Then listen," said the nightingale. "One, don't go after what's beyond your reach. Two, don't cry over what's hopelessly lost. Three, don't go madly believing things that defy belief."

The villager listened with mouth agape. He hesitated a moment, then opened his hand. The nightingale flew at top speed to perch on a pine tree a dozen paces off.

"Man, oh man, what a fool you are! You let me go, and here I have a treasure in my breast: a pearl bigger than a goose egg, in fact bigger than your fist!"

The villager was beside himself. All he could think of was the pearl he'd held in his hand and then let go again. Such a huge pearl! How could he get it back? If he picked up a stone, the nightingale would be out of range with a few flicks of its wings. It made him so sick to think he'd lost an enormous fortune that he suddenly went as yellow as a crabapple. Even the whites of his eyes were yellow.

Head high, but in a strangled voice, he tried to talk the nightingale round.

"Come, little nightingale of the woods, come, my wild nightingale, my friend, come and perch on my fingers! I'll take you home in great honor.

You'll find there everything nightingales love, and it'll all be yours. And I've a special present for you, too—one worth more to you than I can tell."

"Man, poor man," answered the nightingale from the top of the pine tree, "you're sillier than a stove-in basket. What have you done with my three pieces of advice? You've let them run straight out of your head like water! I'm beyond your reach, and you're still after me. I'm lost to you, and you're miserable about it. And finally, it defies belief that I should have in my breast a pearl three times bigger than my body, and you're still determined to believe it. A lot of good my advice has done you!"

With that, the nightingale fluttered up toward the clouds. The villager just stood there in his clogs, thoroughly ashamed of himself.

72. The Snake, the Fox, and the Man

There was once a man who was coming home through the woods. Walking under a pine tree, he heard someone call his name. It was a big snake. The snake had crept up the tree, from branch to branch, and now was wound around the very top. It couldn't get back down again.

"But snake, if I help you out of the tree, you'll bite me as soon as you're back down, won't you."

"Oh no, man, I won't bite you. I promise."

Gripping with his knees and pulling with his arms, the man clambered up to the top of the tree.

"Wrap yourself around my neck," he told the snake. "Don't worry, you won't fall."

The man clambered down again with his snake necktie on, and jumped to the ground.

"And now," declared the snake, "I just have to bite you!"

"Impossible! You *promised* you wouldn't bite me!"

"But don't you know you always get some pain for every pleasure you give?"

"No, no, I won't take that! We must get a judgment!"

Just then a fox popped out from among the rocks and junipers of the ravine.

"Tell us, fox. Is it true that you always get some pain for every pleasure you give?"

"Well," replied the fox, "that depends on one thing and another. Let's see. Tell me what happened."

They told him. He thought it all over and flicked his ears.

"Listen," he said, "this is rather a special case. If I'm to judge it properly, I'll have to have you two go back to where you were when you first met."

The snake went to the pine tree and slithered up to the top.

"Is that how you were a while ago, all the way up there?"

"Yes, fox."

"All right, snake, then stay there!"

The man thanked the fox. "That was a spot of trouble you got me out of!" he said. "I'll never forget what you've done for me. You know what? Just wait a minute. I'll run home and bring you the fattest goose we've got!"

The fox waited among the junipers, licking his chops. But that fox was smart. He could smell what was in the wind. He could just see that fellow who'd gone for a goose returning with a gun.

"I won't wait," said the fox to himself. "After all, a judge shouldn't take gifts."

He stole off that minute and disappeared.

"The snake had it right, though," he told himself as he ran. "That's about the way things go:

> *Do someone a good turn,*
> *Expect some evil in return.*

73. The Blackbird and the Fox

There was once a hen blackbird who'd let herself get caught in a snare—not the kind you hang in a tree, which is a willow wand folded in three with a bunch of rowan berries and a horsehair slipknot. No, this one was a snare to catch hare, set on the ground in a run among the broom.

The more the blackbird struggled, the worse she choked, and the poor thing couldn't help crying out.

Up came the fox.

"What are you going to do, fox?" cried she, shaking with terror. "I'm only a little bird, hardly a mouthful for your hunger! Listen, fox, I hear some village women on the path, taking their few wares to town—eggs, butter, and cheeses. If you'll free me, I'll make sure you get it all! You'll never have had a feast like that in your life."

Well, the fox was tempted. With teeth and claws he broke the noose and let the blackbird go.

She went straight to the path and flapped about in front of the women as though she had a broken wing.

"Oh, look at the blackbird! Its wing is broken. It can't fly any more. I'll catch it!"

The one who'd spoken put down her basket and started after the bird. She just missed clapping her hand down over it—but she *did* miss, not once, but two, then three times, bobbing up and down. The blackbird put on a very good act. She dragged her wing along the path and only skipped a step aside, barely escaping.

The other women joined in the chase, and they too put their baskets down by the path. Don't bother asking whether the fox managed to find all those chickens, blocks of butter, and cheeses.

The blackbird left the fox plenty of time to have a good feed. She'd promised. And anyway, she told herself it was safer to have him sated, even though she did have her freedom back now, and her wings.

But at last it was time to stop the game. Suddenly her wing was all better, just as though the bonesetter had come by. She shot off under the women's noses and went to perch in an ash, where she sang in triumph, loud and long.

The women were amazed and disappointed.

"I don't believe it! What on earth was all *that* about?"

It had been about their baskets, as they found out when they got back to them. No more chickens, no more cheeses, and not much butter, either.

There was no longer any point in going to town. The women raged and shouted, hands on their hips, in furious indignation. They even shed a few tears. And then they had to go home again, in grave danger of being very badly received by their husbands.

But how well the fox felt after that wonderful dinner! And the blackbird felt even better, like a queen in fact, for having escaped with her poor life.

74. The Blackbird, the Fox, and the Dog

There was once a blackbird who'd escaped the fox's jaws by giving him chickens, butter, and cheeses to eat instead—everything the village women were taking that day to market.

Ever since, the fox would greet her when they met, stop to chat, and ask for news of her blackbird children—whose godfather he was, by the way. In short, he was extremely gracious toward her.

One day she had to go on a little trip, and was rather worried about leaving her children behind.

"I won't be gone for more than three days. Three days go by fast, but disaster strikes even faster. Shouldn't I ask the fox to come and look after them? He's supposed to help them, after all, since he's their godfather."

So she spoke to the fox.

He wasn't all that keen on the idea.

"You see," he said, scratching his ear, "I'm awfully busy right now. I've got my own family to look after, too."

"I won't be gone for more than three days, fox, I swear it," replied the blackbird. "One of my aunts wants to see me. She means to make out her will, and she wants my advice before she dies. I'll come right back. Not more than three days, I promise!"

"That's what you say, blackbird. Maybe you'll say something else later on."

"Listen, fox. May the devil chew me up and swallow me down if I stay more than three days! And if I do, you'll have leave to eat my babies."

So she left, and the fox moved into her house. Foxes aren't known for their patience. "All right," he said to himself, "I've got three days to get through. Three days: Thursday, Friday, Saturday. On Sunday, I can eat the babies."

The very idea made his mouth water. Brother fox was getting hungrier and hungrier. At last he shut his eyes. "It's night!" said he. Then he opened them again. "It's day!" Three times in a row like that, he shut his eyes and opened them. "It's day! It's night! It's day! It's night!"

"All right! The three days are over!"

He gulped down the baby blackbirds.

The blackbird came home to find three feathers. That was all. She could have wept tears of blood.

Just then the squire's dog happened by, a great big powerful creature with mighty jaws.

"Why, blackbird, you look so sad!"

"The fox ate my babies, you see."

She told him the whole story.

"I'll punish the fox for you," said the dog. "Yes, I'll punish him. But what'll you do for me in return?"

"Well, I'll make sure you get to fill your stomach with good warm milk."

"Warm milk? That's very nice. But all that milk'll turn to cheese inside me. You must make me laugh a lot afterwards."

"Yes, all right, I'll make you laugh."

They agreed and got ready.

The next day, as the fox made his rounds, he heard the blackbird singing in the depths of the wood. Amazed, he stole carefully up to her.

"You're singing now, blackbird?"

"Why, yes, and I've good reason! I suppose you must have been out for a moment while I was gone, and the squire's dog came and ate my poor babies. But look! It killed him! Do you see him there, at the high end of the meadow, stretched out on his back?"

"The dog's dead?" exclaimed the fox. "Good heavens, it's true! How wonderful! You won't hear *me* mourning that brute! I'm going to go lift my leg on him. Yes, I'm going to treat myself to the pleasure of going right in his face!"

He rushed off, tail high in glee. There was the dog, legs stiff, jaws lolling wide open. The fox prepared to do as he'd said.

The dog jumped him and snapped his backbone with one crunch of his jaws.

"Oh, you won't take them with you to paradise, those baby blackbirds!"

The farmer's wife had just finished milking the cows. Up she ran.

There was the fox, with his back broken. A couple of paces away, a blackbird was dragging herself along the hedge. Apparently she'd gotten mixed up in whatever had happened. Her wing seemed to be broken. That blackbird was putting on her little act again.

"Well," thought the farmer's wife, "when you can't get a thrush, settle for a blackbird." She dove at the blackbird, hands out to grab her. The blackbird skipped up and fell back a couple of paces farther on. The same thing happened all over again several times in a row, with the blackbird darting into the hedge or slipping between two hawthorn branches. She gave the dog plenty of time to lap up the pail of warm milk, which was still at the entrance to the stable.

But all good friends must part. The blackbird flew off, leaving the farmer's wife behind. Next, she found the dog and took him over to the farm.

Four men were threshing grain in the barn.

The show began all over again.

Suddenly, there was the blackbird in front of them, dragging herself painfully through the dust.

The youngest laborer whacked at her with his flail, and when he missed, the oldest tried it. The rhythmic beat of the threshing came to a stop, and all four laborers took off after the blackbird. Stubborn as they were, the big lummoxes only managed to hit each other. A terrific uproar followed, filled with shouts and insults.

The dog looked on, splitting his sides with laughter. That milk in his belly never turned into cheese.

> *Me, I didn't stay;*
> *Down the hedge I slipped away;*
> *And we'll have one more another day!*

75. Off to the Doctor

There was once a black cat who'd caught a cold, and the cold had gone to his stomach. Having those black-cat ideas of his ("You won't live long," the other creatures would tell him, "you know too much"), he decided to seek the advice of a certain famous healer. This healer saw his patients at the Hermit's Hut. The black cat had had enough of coughing into the ashes, and needing to keep so near the fire that the heat singed his fur.

At the first bend in the road he heard someone calling his name. It was a little red hen, who asked him where he was off to. He explained.

"Well, what do you know!" she cried when he'd finished. "I've a terrible cold, too. I'm going to see that doctor."

At the second bend in the road, they were hailed by a brownish sheep, about the color of brown bread.

"Where are you two going, baa baa baa, my friends?"

"Well, baa baa, you see, we both have a cough, so we're off to the Hermit's Hut to get ourselves cured."

"I'll go with you, then, baa baa. I think I'd better. Just hear how I cough!"

"Join us, then. The more the merrier, and the madder the livelier."

On they went, the three of them, coughing their way along. At the third bend a yellow cow asked them where they were headed.

"Well then, moo moo, I'm in luck, moo moo! Ever since last winter, I've been hacking like old Mother Whooping-Cough herself. I'd better go and see the great doctor too."

All day long the four of them, coughing and wheezing their hearts out, climbed farther into the mountains.

Near nightfall they reached the high wilderness between La Chambonnie and La Chamba. The landscape was all skimpy grass, big round rocks, and whistling wind. Kites were wheeling in wide circles just beneath the clouds. The little red hen, too tired to take another step, had begged the brown sheep to let her perch on his back. She was afraid of the kites. But the others were afraid too—afraid of werewolves, or of goodness knows what else.

In the far distance, a lonely cottage stood on a stretch of grass, with a thread of smoke rising from its chimney. They hurried there as fast as they could.

Through the little window they spied an old woman sitting on a three-legged stool before a widow's fire: two logs in the shape of a cross. She was chatting with herself out loud, the way lonely people do when they're afraid of forgetting how to talk.

"You're much too alone, my poor Marion! One of these evenings you'll turn into an owl."

The black cat, the little red hen, the yellow cow, and the brown sheep had clustered at the window. They could see well enough what there was to see. The place was no palace, of course. There was a dark earthenware bowl on the table, and two big stones for andirons. By the hearth stood a pile of pine branches, and a calico spread covered the bed.

"It's senseless to live all alone," old Marion went on, "without even a friendly animal to talk to. If only I had a cow to give me a drop of milk! To think that some people whiten their soup with milk and still manage to complain! And a good curly sheep who'd give me his wool! I'd gladly knit myself a sweater. Why, these rags of mine are so full of holes, you could hang in them all the ladles for miles around! With a sweater I wouldn't fear the wind so. I could go to the forest for firewood. And if only I had a little hen to lay me an egg now and then! Or a black cat to keep me company! I'd pet him all day long."

The black cat, the little red hen, the yellow cow, and the brown sheep listened carefully.

"I don't know how you others feel," whispered the cat, "but I don't seem to have my cold any more. Maybe the change of air did me good. We are going to ask to spend the night, aren't we?"

"Yes, maybe the change of air did it, or maybe it was something else," said the sheep. "Anyway, my cold's gone, too. It's just as though the healer had laid his hands on me. So, we'll ask for lodging?"

"I'm all better, too," said the little red hen.

"Me too," said the yellow cow. "I'll knock politely on the door with my horns. But I'll stay outside, so as not to get the house dirty."

They saw Marion turn her head in surprise. She called to them to come in.

The black cat pulled the latchstring. The little red hen and the brown sheep followed him in.

Marion turned a little farther to get a good look at the cow, who'd stayed outside. Her eyes were as big as saucers.

"Good day and good health to you, mistress," began the cat. "We four were on our way to the Hermit's Hut to have ourselves cured of our coughs. But the good mountain air seems to have healed us all by itself. May we ask you to give us shelter tonight?"

"You'll have shelter and everything else, good creatures! I'll be so glad to have you with me awhile!"

"Awhile, or much longer, if you wish," the cat went on. "Someone living as alone as you needs company. We'll stay as long as you please, as long as it pleases God!"

"Ah, my friends!" cried Marion, pressing her hands together. "I got out of the right side of my bed this morning, I certainly did! So, you caught a cold and the cold led you to my door. Why, the luck's all mine! Darkness would fill my house if you went away again now!"

She began breaking branches on her knee to build up the fire, then set about finding them something to eat and a comfortable place to sleep.

"The devil take me," remarked the cat, who had a bit of a taste for swearing; "the devil take me if anyone was ever welcomed more warmly than this!"

What happened next? Well, they were old-fashioned animals, the kind there used to be long ago: they were never happier than when they could do something for someone else.

They stayed with the kind old woman, and did their best together to keep their hearth warm and their life long. "As God is our keeper," they cried, "so may we thrive!"

The little red hen had said it well enough that very first evening: "Here's a place where we'll have good tomorrows." And good tomorrows were what they found.

> Our own fire here is very low.
> We've eaten all the chestnuts, too.
> I'm not telling you to go away,
> But if I were you I wouldn't stay.

76. The Donkey and the Wolf at the Wedding

There was once a donkey, a brave little donkey who went trotting his way along, all loaded down with a big bundle of logs.

At a bend in the path he heard footsteps, and at the crossroads he met someone. It wasn't at all anyone he wanted to meet. In fact the encounter upset him a good deal. He'd run into mister wolf.

"Where are you off to, donkey, where are you off to so early?"

"I got up at cockcrow, and at larksong came to the wood. I had maul and wedges with me to fell trees, and a saw to cut the trees up with."

"So much the better for your work, then," said the wolf, "if you managed to finish it. So much the worse for your work," he went on, "if you didn't get it all done."

The donkey was no fool. He understood the wolf's meaning. He could read well enough the look in the wolf's eyes.

"You see," the donkey said quickly, "I'm invited today to a wedding.

> A donkey, when a wedding guest,
> Brings wood or water of the best!

But sir wolf, why don't you come along too? Our master's marrying off his daughter. There'll be fat pâté to start with, and pear tart for dessert! There'll be a roast suckling pig, with mustard under its tail. Just come along and you'll see! Follow me and you'll see!"

The wolf's eyes shone with greed, and his lips twitched in anticipation.

"All right, donkey, I'll try the wedding. I don't mind doing the people that honor. I'll come with the donkey and feast with the bride and groom."

It was no lie the donkey had told. They were serving food by the bowlful. The donkey ate. The wolf stuffed his face. The wedding guests welcomed the donkey and took no notice of the wolf at all.

They cleaned off all the dishes and danced between the courses.

"And you, sir wolf," asked the donkey, "wouldn't you like to dance?"

Weighted down though he was, the wolf got up to dance. Yes, stuffed or not, he insisted on dancing.

> Lively now and skip ahead!
> Looks as though your tail's a dead weight!
> Lively now and skip ahead!
> Looks as though your belly's lead!

But the first time he danced, everyone cried out.

The second time, they all charged him.

"Wolf, wolf!" screamed the girls.

"Club him, club him!" shouted the boys.

The master seized a shovel, and his servant the fireplace broom. Sir wolf began dancing a very lively bourrée indeed.

"You villain," he howled to the donkey, "you've played quite a trick on me! Just let me find you again in the woods and I'll play you another! Owowowowow! I'll make a drum of your skin and drumsticks of your bones—owowowowouch!—to beat out reveille in the morning and assembly in the evening . . ."

But it was on the wolf's own ribs they were beating reveille, and assembly on his skull. All broken and torn, he never again in his life got back to the wood.

There's cockcrow!
That's all, you know.

77. The Fox Teaches the Wolf to Sing

In the old, old days, there was a village priest who used to take whatever provision of bread, nuts, butter, or salt meat he had and lock it away in the sacristy. Yes, that's right, it was during the war. In all the village the church was the building least likely to suffer from fire, and people were allowed to store their provisions there if they needed to.

The fox, always sniffing around as he does with his pointed nose, caught the aroma of lard. He snuffled and sniffed so much around that sacristy that he finally found a little air hole to get in by. Getting out was something else, though, because the bars over the hole had been broken and forced back inward, which made the opening like the mouth of a fish trap. But the fox was slender, and he soon learned how to get in and out.

He helped himself to bread and salt meat for quite a while before the priest noticed his thievery.

Meanwhile the wolf, whom hunger kept wide awake, saw the fox come home one day with a loaf and some pork chops. The wolf wanted his share. In fact, he wanted to go food-gathering like the fox, to eat his fill on the spot, and to bring back all the bread and meat he wanted.

"Ah, brother wolf," exclaimed the fox, "how nice it'll be to have you with me! I was bored, all alone like that. It'll be much more fun with you. I'll feel much safer, too."

"So, fox, when shall we go?"

"Tomorrow at moonrise. Meet me right here."

The next night, at the time agreed, fox and wolf set off together.

"Get ready to stuff yourself," said the fox. "I'm taking you to a feast the like of which you can hardly imagine!"

When they got to the sacristy, the fox showed the way in by slipping through the hole. The wolf followed, though not without some trouble.

The fox was waiting. He took the wolf straight into the church.

"Listen, brother wolf, I know all about what happened to you a while ago with the goat, mostly because you couldn't sing the song she sings to her kids. And you got into trouble with the sheep, too, because you didn't know how to sing the litany with them either, there in the pasture."

"What are you talking about, fox? Quick, show me the food!"

"Don't be so greedy. Here you are in front of the lectern. Why not sit down in the cantor's stall and get yourself a feel for singing? Right here and now I'm going to give you a lesson."

"Do you really think I have to, fox?"

"Of course you have to! Let's begin, brother wolf. Repeat after me, good and loud, and in tune!"

The fox sang, in a squeaky little voice:

> *When Father comes to poke and pry,*
> *Miserere,*
> *I know a hole to get out by,*
> *Miserere!*

The wolf howled right back:

> *When Father comes to poke and pry,*
> *Miserere,*
> *I know a hole to get out by,*
> *Miserere!*

The fox went on:

> *That head of yours will be too big,*
> *Alleluia,*
> *It won't go through the hole, you pig,*
> *Alleluia!*

And the wolf promptly repeated:

> *That head of yours will be too big,*
> *Alleluia,*
> *It won't go through the hole, you pig,*
> *Alleluia!*

The fox continued the lesson:

> *Father's going to find you soon,*
> *Alleluia,*
> *And tan your hide, you big buffoon,*
> *Alleluia!*

Dutifully, the wolf sang:

> *Father's going to find you soon,*
> *Alleluia,*
> *And tan your hide, you big buffoon,*
> *Alleluia!*

Then the fox:

> *Your fur he'll make into a coat,*
> *Benedicamus Domino,*
> *And your arse into a flute,*
> *Benedicamus Domino!*

The wolf bawled meekly back:

> *Your fur he'll make into a coat,*
> *Benedicamus Domino,*
> *And your arse into a flute,*
> *Benedicamus Domino!*

Yes, that wolf was bawling fit to bring down the vault. At last Father himself, from his bed in the presbytery, heard the stirring proceedings. Up he jumped and rushed to the church. And what did he see when he opened the door? Two new cantors, the fox and the wolf, picked out by a moonbeam.

He quickly closed up again and went for the neighbors.

The fox decided he wouldn't wait. He slipped right out that hole.

The wolf would have been glad to follow, but couldn't get through. Now he was on the inside, he couldn't get his head past the bars.

"Fox, fox, show me another hole!"

"All right, brother wolf. But first, get me all the loaves and meat you'll find in the sacristy cupboard, and pass them to me through *this* hole."

The wolf had to do it.

"Many thanks, brother wolf," said the fox when he had everything. "I'm afraid I haven't any time to show you another hole. I can hear Father coming back with all the men of the village. You'll get from him as many holes as you want!"

And the fox made himself scarce.

> With holes all over, front to rear,
> Brother wolf went owowow
> So loud I heard him from here,
> And that's my story now!

78. The Cheeses

There was once a fox up around La Richarde, and he was very happy. He liked the mountain, especially when people came up to camp in the cabins with their chickens. The herds would be grazing there by May, and there'd already be cheeses.

By Pentecost,
Cheese has its crust.

And that fox loved eating cheese. The trouble was, the people up there were unkind enough never to think of giving him any. The lummoxes preferred to give their cheeses to the merchant.

The fox saw this merchant and his wagon. He plotted and planned.

Apparently all that thinking brought on a fever that went to the fox's head, because one evening as the merchant sat up on the bench of his wagon, he saw the fox laid out stiff in the road. His wife, beside him, saw the fox too.

"Why look," she said, "there's the fox! Get down and pick him up. He's got a nice pelt. We'll have it tanned."

"Yes, and I'll have to skin him first! Skinning a fox always makes me throw up."

Just to make sure the fox was really dead, and wasn't suddenly going to up and bite him, the merchant first sent him down a good crack of the whip. Finally he got off, picked up the fox by the scruff of the neck, and tossed him on top of the load of cheeses. Then, still grumbling, he got back up beside his wife and had the horse go on.

Even if the fox *had* been dead—which he'd taken good care not to be— the aroma of those cheeses would certainly have restored him to life and good spirits. He ate as many as he could, in perfect silence; rolled a few more off into the heather (because the road up there's no more than a track over the heath); then stuffed one under his tail and another in his mouth. Next, he jumped down from the wagon just as it came to the woods, quite forgetting to thank the merchant, and vanished into the brush.

Did he play that same trick on another merchant, too? There's no telling, but it's true at least that one day in the woods, the wolf met him carrying cheeses. The fox couldn't get rid of him till he'd told the wolf how he went about laying in his stock.

The wolf decided that he too could manage what the fox brought off so bravely.

His trick, of course, was also to stretch out, stiff and dead, on the road.

But the idiot sat up on a rock waiting for the wagon, like a weathercock on a steeple, and didn't make his dive till the wagon was almost there. He landed practically under the horse's feet.

The horse reared and whinnied, then came down with its two front hooves—big hooves, heavily shod—right on top of the wolf, trampling and crushing him.

The miserable wolf never had a chance. The merchant, who'd already been caught that way by the fox, jumped down from the wagon and went after the wolf with his whip handle.

Talk about a beating, that wolf got a good one.

Brother wolf never quite knew how he got away.

Lying in his lair in the evenings, or dragging himself through the woods during the following days, all he could do was groan and go hungry.

The only thought he had left in his head was to take revenge on that fox who'd caused all the trouble. He was too weak and creaky, though, to try an attack. Brother fox had wicked teeth.

The fox, meanwhile, had eaten so many cheeses that he could no longer stand the sight of them.

"What'll I do with the ones I have left? Why, I'll go and sell them at the fair in Saint-Anthême!"

The fox made himself a wagon, just like a merchant's. Next, he needed a team to pull it. Oh, a fox is crafty! This one got himself a team of two goats with very fine horns. He called them his oxen.

On the morning of the fair he set off with his load. As the wagon wasn't too sturdy, he himself trotted down the road beside it.

The wolf was lying in wait. He'd seen what was going on. And now, suddenly, there he was.

"Good morning, brother fox. Where are you off to this morning, you and your pretty wagon?"

"Where I'm off to? Why, to the fair. To Saint-Anthême. I made myself a wagon, got myself a pair of oxen, and I'm off to sell my cheeses."

"I'm going to the fair too, to buy salve for my wounds. Won't you let me ride in your wagon? After that incident you know about, my legs will hardly hold me up."

"Let you ride, my friend . . . But just look at my wagon!"

"Well, just look at my poor bleeding paws! Come on, let me at least put my front paws up on the wagon. I'll feel better."

"No, no, you rascal, walk along beside the wagon, like me!"

Still, the wolf insisted so much that in the end he was allowed to rest his front paws on the back of the wagon.

In the end? Right away, more likely.

"Oh, brother fox, do let me put my back paws up there too. Why, they're carrying my whole weight!"

The wolf started in again with such endless moaning and complaining that at last he got leave to put his back paws up beside his front ones.

"But not your tail! I don't want any of your tail up there! The load's much too heavy already."

That was all right for a while. Then the tail just had to come up next to the four paws. Why, it was getting all scraped up, dragging that way along the road.

The wolf wasn't fat, what with his two-week fast. But even if he'd been only skin and bone, he'd still have been too much for that wagon. The fox was clever enough at odd jobs, but he was no wagon maker.

Suddenly the axle broke.

"Blast! Go hang, you big stupid lump! Come on, wolf, get out of there and fix it! Look around, and cut a bit of oak the right size for an axle."

The wolf had to do as he was told. Weak as he was, he still went looking all over the countryside for an axle. But oak would have been much too hard to cut. All he brought back was a branch of willow.

"Willow for an axle!" raged the fox. "Idiot! Blockhead! Stay here with my oxen. They're pretty lively. Watch out they don't take off into the brush. I'll go get an axle of good hard wood."

Off went the fox.

The wolf stayed right there with the two goats.

They were tied up, too. He didn't even have to chase them. He ate the first goat.

Next, he ate the second goat.

Now he felt *much* better. All his strength was back.

There was nothing left of the two goats but their four horns. The wolf went and stuck them upright in the ditch.

Back came the fox, with a nice oaken axle.

"But where are my oxen? Tell me, wolf, what happened to my oxen?"

"Oh, fox, it was so strange! Maybe the air around here did it. Anyway, all of a sudden I felt so strong, and my coat got so shiny, and my eyes got so bright! The oxen were afraid of me. They dashed into the ditch so fast that they sank straight down into it. Look, you can see their horns."

The fox pulled on the horns. They came right out.

"The mud must have just swallowed those goats up," said the wolf. "Well, never mind. You're not far from Saint-Anthême. I'm sure you'll get your wagon to the fair somehow. *I* don't need to go any more. I certainly don't need any salve. Thanks for your team, though. They really did me good. Good-bye now, fox."

Away went the wolf, leaving the fox for once feeling pretty stupid.

> *It's all true, you realize.*
> *Why, I saw it with my own eyes.*

79. The Red Donkey

There was once a donkey as red as a squirrel—as red as a carrot, in fact. All shiny he was, and as handsome as a new penny. His temper was red too—very fiery.

This was back in the days when animals talked. The birds chattered and sang, birds of all kinds: the nightingale, the oriole, the quail—"Lovely quail, where's your nest?"—yes, the quail flitting along the wheat rows, the pretty partridge, the finch, the lark, sweet lark, the linnet, the wren, the shrike, the robin, and many others. They all gathered in a big wild meadow just to sing and sing the whole day long.

The red donkey went to say hello.

"Lend me your ears, birds, or whatever it is you hear with. *I've* got ears, and I've got a voice. And *I* can sing, too! I'll give some body to your music!"

He planted his feet and started in braying away. What a hee-haw, what a racket! You couldn't have heard thunder overhead.

"Be quiet, for goodness' sake, be quiet!" shouted the blackbird. And the thrush chimed in, "Won't you be quiet? Won't you?"

Be quiet? He was much too pleased with himself. So the birds had to give up their spot and leave him alone in their meadow. They all flew off together.

Meanwhile the donkey had brayed and brayed till his throat was all on fire. Down he went to the river, through the lilies, and drank till his belly was as round and tight as a barrel.

Next he rolled and frolicked about, still in high good humor, stamping up, down, and around with all four feet. In no time, the lovely clear water was all muddy.

The river was angry.

"Look what you've gone and done to me, you thundering blockhead! Just what do I look like now? I might as well be a pond, trampled over by a whole herd of thirsty cows. Wasn't it enough that you frightened the birds away? They sang in my field, and my murmuring made an accompaniment for their music. But you, you big red donkey, look what music *you* made for them!"

Vexed, the donkey waggled his ears and shook himself all over, sending water flying to either bank.

"Oh yes," the river went on, "I heard the blackbird and the thrush begging you to be quiet! And all you did was bray still louder!"

"So you heard me, did you? I sing louder than all of them put together. My plainsong is much nicer than their twittering!"

Out came the donkey from the water, dancing, prancing, and kicking, and he scrambled up to high ground.

It was dry and warm there under the pines. The ants were busy, carrying loads bigger than themselves—straws, pine needles, or wisps of heath.

"Where are you off to, little creatures?" asked the donkey, as nosy as ever. "You're working so hard! Why are you in such a hurry?"

"Let us by. We've better to do than to chat with a donkey. We've tons of work, and the fine weather won't last forever."

As curious as an old gossip, he followed the line of ants to their anthill. Then, the better to see what was inside, he kicked it with his two hind feet.

The ants were enraged. They went for him. Unfortunately, these were red ants. They stung him inside his ears and under his tail, and he couldn't get rid of them, though he shook himself like the devil. The blackbird and the jay up in the pine overhead laughed fit to bust.

Finally, our red donkey lit out helter-skelter for the river.

"So long!" shouted the ants after him. "So long, you miserable wrecker of homes, you who care for nothing but chaos! May that teach you never to come back!"

He dove into the cooling water and wallowed about. "Just look, my river, dear river, what those ants did to me!"

"You didn't half ask for it, did you, you little idiot of a red donkey! If only that would teach you to keep quiet a bit! Enjoy my water now, but learn not to make people angry!"

Maybe he did learn, but not for long. Three or four days, perhaps.

Next, he went beyond the pines, out onto the heathery moor. He saw bees visiting the flowers.

"What are you bugs doing, flying that way from flower to flower?"

"Why, fine red donkey, we're making our honey."

"What? Honey? What's that? Can I see?"

"Listen, it's a secret. We do all the work inside our hives. We can't tell just anyone about it. Get along, red donkey, get along."

"So, you honey bugs, you won't tell me your secret? Well, I'll find it out anyway!"

He followed them in their flight, ears pricked and tail erect, snorting like Saint George's own charger.

All the bees came out when he reached the hive, grumbling like a noontime storm moving up from the plain. But that donkey was pigheaded! He wanted to see, so he leaned down to peer through the hive's little doorway. And when he could make out nothing in there but darkness, he tipped the hive over with a toss of his head.

Oh, those bees were angry!

They were all on him in a minute, stinging him with a thousand stingers. A donkey's hide is tough, yes, but not everywhere. His nostrils and lips are tender, and so is the skin around his eyes.

It was no good his dodging and racing off full tilt. The bees, like a humming cloud, stayed right with him and kept at him.

By the time he got back to the river, with his swollen face and his drooping ears, he looked like some sort of dying lion.

"River, dear river, look what those awful bugs have done to me!"

"Well, you asked for it, didn't you, you little fool of a red donkey? All right, I feel sorry for you. Come into my water and I'll try to cool you off. In the meantime, bear your stings and learn patience. I mean, learn wisdom!"

Wisdom lasted perhaps six weeks. Then the donkey was back to his old self. One day, he went trotting off farther still.

Roaming, searching, nose to the wind, he came at last to a very poor stable, open to every breeze. It was made all of wood and straw, and built out from the rock. Inside were a grey donkey and an ox, and, in a cradle up against the wall, a little child. The child's mother sat by him. There was a man there, too, who was looking after the Mother and Child so that they wouldn't suffer too much from the wind and the cold.

The man made a sign to the red donkey.

"Gently, now, my fine red donkey, don't make any noise. You might wake the Child."

Well, yes, I'm afraid so. The donkey wanted to show off, and he started braying away. Hee-haw, hee-haw! He'd never brayed louder.

God the Father opened a window in paradise, somewhere up there around the moon.

"That's enough, this time, red donkey," said he. "We won't have any more red donkeys on earth."

And there really never were any more.

8 o. The Wise Sow

There once lived a weaver at Saint-Etienne-sur-Usson, and he had a hen, a duck, and a sow.

The duck came right into the house whenever she felt like it, and sat down under the table.

One day, the day before carnival, while the weaver and his wife were dining, the duck heard him say to her, "Heavens! We have to invite the neighbors over tomorrow and give them a good meal. We'll put the hen in to boil and the duck on to roast. We'll slaughter the sow, too. That way we'll have blood pudding and sausages. With a few bottles of wine, we'll be doing very well!"

> *Quack, quack, quack,*
> *I heard all that,*
> *And I'll pass it on!*

said the duck.

> *Pass it on, duck,*
> *And you're done!*

answered the weaver.

But the quacking duck got away and flew to the stable. She told the sow and the hen.

"Quickly, quickly," said the sow, "we must take our children and leave. We'll take cover in the ravine over by Chambelièvre. Our master and mistress are old. They won't come looking for us there, among all the weeds and bushes."

So they did as the sow had told them.

But by the time they were below Thoiras, the hen and her chicks could go no farther. The brush was too thick for them. Anyway, hens go to bed early, and night was coming on.

"Sow, my friend, please make me a henhouse with a few wisps of heather! Yes, yes, heather'll do. I'm all worn out, and so are my chicks. We'll stop right here."

The good kind sow made the henhouse with a few wisps of heather; and the hen and her chicks made their nest on heather too.

Below La Rainerie, the duck and her ducklings likewise found they could go no farther.

"Sow, kind sow, please, make me a shelter too. Make it with fern and broom. Yes, yes, fern and broom will do. My ducklings and I will spend the night here."

The sow herself didn't get much higher. Over by Sautemouche, she and her piglets felt terribly sleepy.

> *Men must keep*
> *Seven hours for sleep,*
> *Women eight and piglets nine.*

The sow wanted her own shelter built of stone, weathertight, and solidly anchored in the ground.

How wise she was, mother sow!

Around midnight, the wolf came cruising the ravine. He knocked at the hen's door.

"Who's there?" asked the hen.

> *"It's me, the wolf, all shivering.*
> *Quick, mother hen, let me in!"*

> *"It's past midnight. I'll not open—*
> *Why, my little chicks, you'd eat them!"*

> "I'll find my way through your wall
> And eat you, hen, chicks and all!"

Scrabbling away with paws and jaws, the wolf in no time had torn the heather henhouse to pieces. It took him no longer to crunch up the hen and her family.

Next, he went to the duck's house and knocked on her door.

"Who's there?" asked the duck.

> "It's me, the wolf, all shivering.
> Quick, mother duck, let me in!"

> "It's past midnight. I'll not open—
> Why, my ducklings, you'd eat them!"

> "I'll find my way through your wall
> And eat you, duck, ducklings and all!"

It took him no longer to tear down the duck's house than it had taken him to break down the henhouse. And in nothing flat he crunched up the whole duck family.

Then he went to the sow's and knocked at the door.

"Who's there?" asked the sow.

> *"It's me, the wolf, all shivering.*
> *Quick, mother sow, let me in!"*

> *"It's past midnight. I'll not open—*
> *Why, my little pigs, you'd eat them!"*

> *"I'll find my way through your wall*
> *And eat you, sow, piglets and all!"*

Oh, he tried, he really tried! But with his paws he only managed to dig up a little dirt, like a dog scratching after a field mouse; and he didn't dare use his teeth on those stones.

Off he slunk again, ears drooping, without having gotten at mother sow and her piglets.

He'd smelled fresh meat, though, the old devil. Three days later he was back, talking very nicely.

"Listen, mother sow, I know what you and your children need: a pile of potatoes that's in the cellar at Sautemouche. We'll meet there tomorrow evening. Agreed?"

"Understood and agreed," answered the sow. "Thank you, brother wolf!"

Two days later the wolf was back again.

"Well, mother sow? So you played me false? Why didn't you come to meet me at Sautemouche?"

"What do you mean, why didn't I come? We were all there! Just look in front of the door. You'll see all the peelings."

The wolf had a look and scratched his ear.

"Then we must have misunderstood each other somehow. But now I know something even better. There's a whole store of walnuts in the cellar of the oil mill at Chambelième. You and I'll go help ourselves before the miller presses the oil. Let's meet there tomorrow evening. Agreed?"

"Understood and agreed," answered the sow. "Thank you, brother wolf!"

She didn't wait for the next evening that time either. She took a long way round to the mill, with all her piglets. They brought back quite a load!

When the wolf came back to bluster at their door, she showed him a whole pile of shells.

"Why, we must have eaten three bushels of them! You're the one who didn't come. What was the matter, brother wolf? Why weren't you there?"

"Listen, mother sow, we'll get it straight next time! There's a fair the day after tomorrow at Sauxillanges. Shall we meet there, just the two of us?"

"At Sauxillanges? I was just going there myself. Yes, I *must* go to the fair."

"Well, let me see you there, then! What path will you take?"

"Oh, I'll take the path of the needles."

"I'll take the path of the pins. We'll see each other there and come back together."

Mother sow set off very early in the morning two days later, despite some rather hard showers.

> *Rain in the morning*
> *Never stopped a pilgrim.*

She went quickly through the fair and bought a washtub—one of those enormous earthenware tubs, all ribbed and decorated, that the Sauxillanges potters make. Then she loaded it across her shoulders and started home.

Path of the needles, path of the pins—the wolf and the sow had each wanted to trick the other, and the sow now ended up going home on the same path the wolf had chosen to come by.

She spotted him from some way off. Heavens! What was she going to do? Fortunately, another shower was passing by, and the wolf had his nose down. Mother sow put down the tub, slipped beneath it, and lay very still indeed.

The wolf stopped when he got to the tub, and sniffed at it. Then he saw the drain hole, and goodness knows what got into his head, because up he stepped and lifted his leg.

Of course mother sow waited till he was gone. She came out again as soon as she could, shook herself, and prayed for another shower to come along and wash her off. Then she started home again.

The next day the wolf was back at her door, just as she'd expected. He was furious.

"All right, mother sow! I suppose you're just laughing at me! We *had* agreed, you know! I looked for you at the fair, and I never saw you!"

"You didn't see me? You certainly watered me well enough, you filthy beast! Yes, I was under the tub. I was hiding there from the rain."

"What? You were . . . But listen, this just can't go on. We agree to meet, then I never find you."

"But you see, brother wolf, you're the one who never gets it right."

"Yes, well, I'm out of patience. Open your door, mother sow. We're going to get things straight right now."

Mother sow knew perfectly well what getting things straight meant. But she'd been the day before to see the big dog at La Rainerie, and she'd sent him to talk to the hounds at La Grangefort and Parentignat. She glanced out the window and made sure everything in the house was the way she wanted it: the kettle on the fire and water in the kettle. Then she had her piglets go and hide by the firewood, in the corner.

"Open the door!" bellowed the wolf. "Open the door, I tell you, mother sow!"

She went and opened it.

In the wolf swaggered as though he owned the place. She invited him politely to sit down, then went back to her housework. She was making the bed.

The wolf, meanwhile, couldn't take his eyes off the piglets, who were peeking out at him with their tails wiggling.

> *How I'd love to have a sweet*
> *Wiggly little pig to eat!*

"Oh, mommy," squeaked the piglets, "did you hear what brother wolf said?"

"No, children. What did he say?"

"Mommy, he said:

> *How I'd love to have a sweet*
> *Wiggly little pig to eat!*

"Heavens! Is that true, brother wolf?"

"No indeed, mother sow. When I saw you making the bed, I said:

> *How warm they'll keep their little feet*
> *Under mother's quilt and sheet.*

But the wolf could smell fresh meat, and with those fat, pink little piglets before him he just couldn't contain himself.

> *How I'd love to have a sweet*
> *Wiggly little pig to eat!*

"Mommy," cried the piglets, "just *listen! Now* listen to what brother wolf said!"

"And what did he say, children?"

"Mommy, he said:

> *How I'd love to have a sweet*
> *Wiggly little pig to eat!*

"Why, brother wolf, is that true?"

"Of course not, mother sow! I saw the water boiling in the kettle, so I said:

> *That water's boiling at such heat*
> *It'll boil over on our feet!*

And the kettle *was* boiling. Mother sow noted that. Then she glanced out the door. Suddenly, she turned back to the wolf, her arms lifted high in amazement. "Wolf, brother wolf, what have you gotten us into now! Gentlemen are pouring in from everywhere with their hounds! Yes, they're here with the hounds—all the hunters from La Rainerie, La Grangefort, and Parentignat!"

Oh, that wolf forgot all about wiggly little pigs. He jumped up, terrified.

"Quick, hide in the washtub!" cried mother sow.

He dove right in.

"But cover me up with something, mother sow!" he whispered.

She covered him with the sieve.

And you know what she did next? She poured the whole kettle of boiling water right through the sieve onto the wolf.

How the wolf howled, how he danced! In one bound he was flying out the door, with his scalded fur peeling off in clumps, and sailing away on the wind.

But now it was more than a pound or two of fur he had at stake. He knew that all too well, and was doing his best to make himself scarce.

Mother sow and her piglets, doubled up with laughter, stood in their doorway and watched him run. And as she laughed, mother sow shouted at the top of her voice:

> *Bravely, hunters, the wolf's foiled!*
> *See him flee now, halfway boiled!*
> *At him, hunters! Bravely ride!*
> *Tan the wolf's hide! Tan his hide!*

81. The Gander, the Fox, and the Lark

There was once a gander, and for a gander, he was pretty lively. One day when all the people of the farm were off at the fair, he seized his chance, flew off, and came back down smack on a heap of sheaves. Now he was all right. He'd have plenty of feed.

The fox happened by.

"Aha!" said he. "What do I see? Where's the ladder? You didn't get up there without a ladder, did you, my friend?"

"Oh yes I did, fox. I flew up here on my own two wings."

"Is that a fact? Oh yes, my friend, I know a bit of the world. It's when hens have teeth that I'll be seeing you fly."

"I flew up here, fox, believe me. I really did."

"I'll believe it when I see it, my fine friend. I dare you to try it before my eyes."

"All right, fox, you'll see!"

Already the gander was beating his wings to come down from the top of the heap to the ground.

"You poor innocent creature, what are you doing?"

The good, kind little lark spoke up. She dove down from the sky to warn the unfortunate gander, who was still such a young bird, and who couldn't see where the fox was leading him.

"Look out! Look out! You'll hardly touch ground before he's on you! He's got teeth, the rascal, and he'll let you feel them!"

"Gander, don't believe this busybody. She wants to keep me from telling everyone, in wood and field, that I saw you with my own eyes fly just as well as she!"

The gander was lively, no doubt, but he wasn't very bright. He kept hesitating, wondering which one to believe.

"Listen," the fox went on. "Just look at the almanac! Today's a fast day. You think I'm going to eat meat? Don't be silly! Pay no attention to this crazy bird and her foolish chatter!"

"Gander, poor gander, if you listen to *him*, you're lost. Don't do it!"

The gander did it. He flapped to the ground three paces from the fox, to show him how he could soar right back up to the top of the heap. Yes, he was going to show that fox he could fly!

The fox saved him the trouble. The gander never flew again. The fox covered the three paces between them in three bounds.

> *The lark cried out dear, dear me!—*
> *And the tale is over.*

82. The Partridge and the Fox

There was once a lady partridge, and very pretty she looked, too, on her red feet. She was singing that day on a rock, among a few clumps of heather.

The fox heard her, and up he stepped.

"Now that, my dear, is *singing!* I never heard a nightingale or a warbler spin a lovelier melody. Yes, I seem to hear your dear departed mother's own voice. Yet I do think *your* voice still lacks . . ."

"Lacks what, fox?"

"Some especially moving quality I always heard in hers. Ah, yes, now I see what's the matter."

"What *is* the matter, fox? Tell me!"

"You see, the dear lady always closed her eyes, the better to lose herself in her song."

The partridge, for once a silly fool, promptly closed hers.

Wiggling his behind, the fox gathered himself to pounce. In one leap, and with one swipe of his jaws, he seized the lady with the red feet and trotted off with her in his mouth.

But the partridge is a clever creature. Although aghast and trembling, she didn't lose her head. When the fox passed the bridge, she heard the washerwomen shouting, "Look, look, he's making off with the partridge!"

"If I were you, fox," said she, "I'd shout right back, 'So I am, washerwomen, so I am! And I'll be eating her soon, whether you like it or not!'"

A fox loves being cheeky. This one jumped at the chance, the way he'd jumped on the partridge.

"So I am . . ." he shouted.

He'd hardly relaxed his jaws when the partridge freed herself, took wing, and perched on a high branch.

The fox knew perfectly well he'd never sweet-talk her back.

"Good-bye, partridge," he called, "and many thanks. You've just taught me a lesson. After this I'll only talk when I need to."

"Good-bye, fox," the partridge called back, "and many thanks to you, too. You've just taught me a lesson as well. After this, I'll only close my eyes to sleep."

83. The Squirrel and the Fox

There was once a rather young squirrel who was actually quite clever but lacked experience.

One day at the edge of the forest, he'd just come frolicking in among the leafy branches of a beech tree, when he saw an animal down below him in the brush. It had red fur, and its tail was even bushier than his own. The animal was turning and darting about, making plenty of noise, and completely absorbed in whatever it was doing. The squirrel, as curious as an old gossip, wanted a closer look.

He jumped to the ground and hopped over to see. Suddenly, so fast he never knew what hit him, the poor silly thing was a prisoner in the fox's paws.

Yes, the fox had chosen that spot to finish off a hen—an old hen who'd run free all her life behind the woodpile at her farm. She was ancient, and as tough as leather. The fox had no cook to pop her into the pot for him. And if it was no young chicken he'd come across, it certainly wasn't his fault.

The squirrel, born that April, was just three months old and very tender. How delicious he'd be, after that miserable, leathery old hen! The fox's eyes sparkled, his nose quivered, and he couldn't help twitching his tail.

Just before he made one gulp of his little cousin, the shaking squirrel managed to say, "Goodness me, Excellency, what a jump that was! Absolutely amazing! You should be king over all the squirrels. Their tails aren't nearly so large, and they certainly can't jump so far!"

"True enough!" remarked the fox.

"My mother told me you can jump straight up higher than the wheat, to catch birds. Can you really? Higher than the wheat? Not a long jump like just now, but a jump straight up?"

"Can I?" replied the fox. "Look, cousin!"

He jumped straight up higher than the broom, which was as tall as a man.

But to jump he'd needed his paws, and so had let his cousin go.

That instant the squirrel skipped aside, as lightly as a wisp of down on the wind, and frisked on up from branch to branch till he found just the right spot. And there he sat, tail fluffed, very bright and merry, to applaud and bow and shower the fox with respectful compliments.

"Come back, little cousin!" called the fox. "Come back!"

"Oh, Excellency, you do me too much honor! I'm your humble servant, not your companion."

"You're my cousin, I say. Come back to my paws, and I'll teach you to jump!"

"Oh, I know you'd make me jump, sir fox. But first, I want to get all my brother squirrels to acknowledge you as king over us all. Then, perhaps, I'll come back."

"No, no, come back now, dear little cousin, don't wait! What do I care for a crown? Come back! Come back!"

"Uncle fox, you're a wonderful acrobat. When you really want my company, I'm sure you'll manage to join me up in this tree."

Having made fun of the fox, the squirrel danced about and darted up through the branches to the very top. From there he sailed like a bird from beech to beech. Master fox, down among the broom, could only follow with his eyes—but also with his nose, neck, and shoulders, the way a bowls player does as he watches his ball roll among the others. The squirrel was laughing a high, whinnying little laugh, like a tiny, flame-colored horse charging through the air. All the squirrels in the wood quickly gathered around and joined in, laughing loud and long at the expense of uncle fox.

The fox would have liked to laugh too, to save face, but he was just too put out to manage it. As his mother fox used to say,

> *Boastfulness*
> *Is foolishness.*

84. The Wolves' Castle

There was once a poor donkey who carried sacks to the mill. The miller, I'm afraid, was no good, which is rather rare among millers. Anyway, he didn't know how to run his business, and all he ever fed his donkey was storehouse sweepings, with a whack of the broom for dessert.

The poor donkey had had enough. One night as he pondered his lot he decided he was simply too miserable to stand it. He broke his rope and left the stable. And since he didn't suppose he could possibly be worse off anywhere else, he simply started off straight ahead, wherever his steps might lead him.

On his way through the village he heard a cock crow, and struck up a conversation.

"Won't you let me come with you?" asked the cock. "Won't you? You see how I crow before dawn, to announce the coming rain. Yet my master gives me so hard and mean a life that for me all weather is foul weather."

"Follow me, then," said the donkey. "We'll find whatever we find."

A little farther on, after they'd crossed the river Dore, they met an old dog—one of those good-natured terriers with hair even over their eyes. They and the dog got talking, and told each other their sad stories. Since the poor dog had a touch of mange, one of these mornings his master was going to tie a stone around his neck and dump him in the river.

"Won't you let me come with you?"

"Certainly, dog, certainly we will. Come along. We'll find whatever we find."

A little farther on, at the edge of a wood, they met a nice little cat. They and the cat got talking, and told each other their sad stories. The little cat had been beaten by his mistress for having put his paw or his nose into the cheese. His mistress thought him too greedy, and never fed him anything but a few miserable scraps.

"Won't you let me come with you?"

"Of course we will, dear kitty! Follow us! We'll find whatever we find."

Some way on, in the hills, they met a poor old ram. A dealer had lost him on the way home from the fair. The dealer had gotten terribly drunk and had whipped him cruelly, over and over again.

Once again, they told each other their stories.

"Won't you let me come with you?"

So they had the nice sheep come with them. "We'll find whatever we find!"

A little way on, behind a farm, they met a pig. The pig had been lucky: since the farmer had forgotten to close the gate of his sty, he'd decided to do some traveling.

"Oh, I know what I've got to look forward to next Christmas!" cried the pig when they told him their stories. "My master will slaughter me. They'll turn me into ham and lard, blood pudding, sausage, and salami. How would you like that to happen to *you?* Won't you let me come with you?"

"Of course, dear pig, of course! Come along! We'll find whatever we find!"

A little farther on they met, this time, a goose—a goose whose master was going to begin force-fattening her, and who knew what that meant.

The goose too asked, "Won't you let me come with you?"

So they had her come along. "We'll find whatever we find!"

Then there was a billy-goat, whose master was going to kill him as soon as he could, to make his skin into a water bottle. The master thought his goat was getting too old and smelled too bad.

The goat wanted to come along, too.

Finally, there was a little duck with a limp. She too had a complaint against her master.

"Won't you let me come with you?"

So the little duck came along, too.

By this time, the whole lot of them had reached the big, scary forest, and it was too dark for them to go on.

"Oh cat, kitty-cat," said the donkey, "couldn't you climb up there to the highest branch and tell us whether you see a light, or some sign of a place where we might find shelter?"

"Follow the path straight ahead," the cat called down from the top of the oak tree. "It leads to a light. It leads to a house."

"But what will we *find* in that house?" asked the sheep, shyly.

"We'll find whatever we find," answered the donkey. "It'll be no worse than at my master's. We've had a bad time of it, but let's be brave now, and go ahead!"

And in fact, the time for high courage had come. What they found at the end of the path was indeed a house.

The sheep began shivering the instant he laid eyes on it.

"Oh woe and misery! It must be the wolves' castle! I'm sure the bones of my poor father, my poor mother, and my poor brothers are in there!"

"What'll we do?" asked the donkey. "We're all completely worn out! What are we going to do?"

"We'll go and see what the wolves are doing," said the duck. "I was the last to join our band, so it's up to me to go first. I'll go on in!"

"Well then, little duck, you're the bravest of us all! But how will you get in?"

"You, donkey, if you please, stand up against the wall. Then, sheep, stand in front of him, and the dog in front of the sheep. You'll make a stairway for me to climb up to the roof. For the time being, my friends, keep very quiet. But when I start making noise, make all the noise you possibly can!"

With one or another's help, she clambered onto the thatched roof, which came down to the donkey's head. Then she waddled on up silently, with muffled steps, to perch on the smoking chimney.

The wolves had just put out the light and gone to bed.

All of a sudden the brave little duck dove straight down the chimney into the house, with loud flaps of her wings and thunderous quacks. Layers of soot came tumbling down with her.

Outside, the rest of the band struck up a deafening music, braying, yapping, baaing, bleating, yowling, grunting, and trumpeting. The duck managed to bring down so much soot, and to raise such a ruckus and a wind with her quacking and her wings, that she woke the wolves from their early sleep into a horrendous panic.

The wolves hurled themselves as though possessed toward the door, which they could neither find nor open. When at last they got it unbarred, they trampled each other to get out and vanished into the night.

The company of friends then joined the duck inside, where they stoked up the fire and made a light. The castle was strewn with bones from mutton roasts and mutton chops, but a single glance showed that it was also filled with everything they themselves could want. So they rested and dined.

"What a wonderful house this would be for us!"

"Yes," said the donkey, "I can see us living here far from our masters, in the freedom of the forest!"

"So then, my friends," crowed the cock, "we'd all live here in good fellowship! Why not? Why not?"

"Why not?" retorted the sheep. "Because the wolves will be back."

"If they come back we'll be ready for them," declared the dog. "But it's nearly midnight now, and the first thing to do is to get a good night's sleep."

"I'm a bit chilly," said the cat. "If it's all right, I'll sleep where I always do, on the warm stones of the hearth."

"I'll sleep near you by the firewood," said the dog.

The pig, the sheep, the goat, and even the donkey found themselves places nearby. The cock perched on the mantelpiece. The goose preferred a spot in the courtyard, on the branch of some spindly tree.

"Goodness gracious," said the duck, rather proud of herself for having put all the wolves to flight, "I think I'll get back up on my chimney. It's a good spot, and I can sleep in the open air."

She also thought, though she didn't say so, that she'd see the wolves from there if they came back, and would be able to sound the alarm and fight beside her friends.

By the time the wolves reached the edge of the forest, they were thoroughly ashamed of their fright. They were also sorry to have fled their home, the castle. So they gathered in a circle, muzzles high, and held a council.

"As far as *I* can see," said a young wolf a bit more resolute than the others, "we left the castle awfully fast. Even if it was the devil himself who came to throw us out, I'd rather like to know what he looks like."

"We panicked," said another. "We could have done better."

"All right, we can act now. Comrade wolves, let's go back! We must retake the castle, even if it means fighting all the devils in hell!"

Back they trooped to a spot before the castle, where they stopped and prepared for battle.

"I'll tell you what," said an old wolf to the young one who'd spoken so boldly. "*You* go on in, since you want to know what those devils look like. Stoke up the fire, make a light, and take a look around. When you're done, report to us. We'll wait for you here."

The young wolf couldn't think of an answer. He went to the door and slipped inside.

And he listened.

The blackness in there was full of sounds and breathing. He'd have been glad to go right out again. But how could he do so without having at least lit a light and seen enough to make a report?

He stole to the fireplace, blew on the coals, and sent a few sparks flying.

Luckily, a spark woke up the little duck, who'd fallen asleep.

She opened her eyes and saw on the path the whole pack of waiting wolves. Peering down the chimney, she saw below her another wolf scraping away at the coals with a bit of wood.

That instant she dove down the chimney again, as she'd done the first time, with a great beating of wings and a terrifying volley of quacks! Down tumbled soot and mortar, straight into the eyes of the wolf, who'd lifted his muzzle to see what sort of creature was coming down on him in the dark.

The wolf backed away and stepped on the cat. Spitting and yowling, all claws spread, the cat leaped at the wolf's muzzle and scratched it horribly.

That same instant, the cock dove at the wolf from the mantelpiece, let him have a fresh dropping smack in the face, and pecked out one of the wolf's eyes.

The pig caught one of the wolf's legs in his snout and gripped it as in a vice. The dog at the same time bit the wolf's tail, and nearly ripped it off. Then the ram butted the wolf in the belly and sent him flying right to the goat, who drove his sharp horns into the wolf's behind. Next the donkey, with deafening brays, stove in the wolf's ribs with a double kick.

Rebuffed and reeling, from whack to whack and grief to grief, the young wolf ended up outside again—where the goose was waiting, hissing fiercely. She struck him savagely with her wings and bowled him over.

"Comrades, comrades, take me away, I'm done for!" groaned the wolf when at last he stumbled, barely conscious, back in among his fellow wolves. "Quickly! Take me away! There's a pack of devils in there, and they're all on a rampage! First there was a mason devil that dumped mortar all over my head. Then a wool-carder devil scratched my muzzle up with his carding brush. At the same time a doctor devil slapped some sort of stinking poultice on my face and put my eye out with his scalpel. Oh, they worked me over! One blacksmith devil got his pincers on my thigh, while another, a carpenter, got his clamp on my tail and practically pulled it out. Meanwhile an oxherd devil was running his pitchfork into my backside, and a barrel-maker devil was bashing in my belly with his mallet. Another devil deafened me and pounded me in the ribs, till finally some devil washerwoman, who

was waiting for me outside, smacked me with her wet laundry and knocked me flat. Oh, I'm finished, I'm done for."

Just then the moon peeped from behind a cloud. Seeing their comrade covered with blood and in a very bad way, the wolves knew right off what sort of devils awaited them at the castle. Devils of all sizes and kinds, in hopeless hordes!

Panic seized them again and put them to frantic flight. Over hill and dale they sped, right and left, faster and faster. At this very moment,

Unless they've died,
They're still fleeing far and wide!

P a r t
S e v e n

LOVE

AND MARRIAGE

85. The White Cat

There was once a king who had three castles, and this king had three sons, too, all born on the same day.

Triplets! You don't see that often, but it happens. It certainly happened then, right in the king's own house.

Now the king's mare gave birth to three foals just at the same time.

"Fine," said the king to himself. "I'll give a foal and a castle to each of my sons. But which shall have the strongest castle and the largest stretch of land? Which shall have the kingdom and the crown? All right, I swear they'll go to the wisest of the three."

The years passed and the boys grew up. People called them Big-John, Not-John, and Good-John. All three were brave and quite respectably clever. But Big-John and Not-John did strut a bit. Big-John put on military airs and longed for glory. Not-John fancied dancing, flirting, and pretty girls. Good-John, on the other hand, never puffed himself up. Born not of Adam's false rib but of his true one, he was as straight as a skittle and as good-natured as a starling—in short, the true son of a king. He didn't talk much, though, and he took things with a smile, simply entrusting himself to God. That's why the people of the court called him a dreamer and a woolgatherer.

The time came to announce which son would inherit the kingdom.

The king's officers and counselors really had no idea which one to choose. The king himself leaned now toward Big-John, who seemed more kingly, and now toward Not-John, who seemed better company. But he remembered his oath. One evening he summoned his three sons to the castle's great hall.

"Well now," said he, "which of you will be king after me? A king has to be wise. He has to keep a good head on his shoulders so that everything in all the households of the kingdom should be safe and well ordered. I'm going to test you. Each of you shall have one of the three horses my mare bore all those years ago, and one of my castles, too. But you must all three roam my kingdom and come back with a way to thread twelve ells of cloth through a needle's eye."

"If in all this kingdom there exists a length of cloth fine enough to pass through a needle's eye, then I myself will bring it to you!" declared Big-John proudly.

"Father," said Not-John, "Your Majesty, if by craft or any other means it is possible to satisfy you, then I will do so."

Good-John, for his part, looked thoughtful and bowed without a word.

"Leave tomorrow," the king commanded, "and be back in three weeks."

They rode off the next morning. Away went Big-John and Not-John, trotting smartly, oh yes, galloping! Their eyes darted everywhere, for they were eager to see everything and make it all their own. The third brother, being in less of a hurry, looked as though he were daydreaming.

"Look at that woolgatherer, will you!" said Big-John, turning around to stare, his fist on his horse's croup. "When we're long gone he'll still be here, right in front of the castle gate, listening for the ring of the cook-pot handle."

"I don't suppose we need worry about him much," replied Not-John, twirling his mustache. "No, let's stick together on this. The kingdom'll be either yours or mine."

But Big-John took the road toward the border, thinking he might find merchants there who'd sell him just what he needed.

So Not-John took the road to town. He told himself that the ladies there would direct him to the cleverest seamstress.

Good-John, for his part, took a path which led toward open space—an upward slope between hawthorn hedges thick with beautiful white, blue, and purple flowers. He rode as though the flowers, or the fringe of sky beyond them, were all he cared to see. On and on he went from hill to hill, trail to trail, and breeze to breeze.

He followed the wind, you might say, led now by a linnet and now by a warbler, till at last, toward evening, he came to a wild stretch of woods and heath. The leaves stood out more cleanly, the birds sang more sweetly, and the wind blew freer there than anywhere else in the world.

He hardly felt lost or lonely at all. But where and how was he to spend the night?

He faltered, took a few steps, stopped, walked on a little, stopped again, then stepped forward once more. Night was settling very gently, like a cloud of ashes.

All at once, through the clumps of cherries, dogwoods, and rowans, Good-John saw a whole garland of lights come on. They seemed a signal to him, so he bravely urged his horse toward them.

Trotting on across a lawn, he came to a castle with lights blazing in every window. And there were so many, many windows! Strangely enough, though, there was no one to be seen passing the windows, against the light. It was as though, despite all those candles, the castle was actually deserted.

Good-John might have turned back right then, but he wasn't afraid.

He rode straight into the courtyard, dismounted, and went to knock at the door. Who opened up for him? A big grey cat.

"So the doormen in this castle are *cats?*" Asking politely for a night's lodging, he spoke to the cat just as though it were a person. And the cat answered him just like a person:

"Please enter, Your Excellency. The lady of this castle bids you welcome. She hopes you will be kind enough to take supper with her."

Good-John followed the grey cat down one hallway and up another, passing behind him from room to room. Everywhere was oak paneling and gilded ceilings! The parquet floors shone brighter than mirrors, while the draperies and paintings stood out more brilliantly than scarlet jewels. "My father's castle," said Good-Jean to himself, "is nothing beside this one."

There wasn't a soul about, though. There wasn't a sound. You could barely hear a slight brushing as of velvet slippers vanishing down a hallway, or a light whisper as of a tail slipping through a half-closed door.

The grey cat showed Good-John into a room done up all in gold and mirrors. A gilt place setting for one was waiting on the table before an armchair with three cushions.

The twin panels of the door opposite opened wide, and in came a pretty lady cat—the prettiest cat you could possibly imagine! A whole company of big grey cats followed in single file behind her. The lady cat jumped very gracefully up onto the cushions, sat down, wrapped her tail around her dainty feet, had a place laid for the king's son too, and ordered that supper be brought in.

The grey cats whisked in the soup tureen, the dishes, and the bottles. Good-John thought he must be dreaming. He knew he wasn't, though, because there aren't any smells in dreams. Those sauces, pâtés, and potted meats smelled good enough to wake the dead. Good-John had never tasted anything like them in his father's own castle.

The lady cat, meanwhile, was behaving just like a cat. She was served a white mouse between two silver plates, and though she seemed not to touch it at all, she quickly crunched it up. She was so delicate about it that Good-John never even saw the mouse disappear.

Once they'd wished each other good health and the supper was over, the white cat invited her guest into the formal sitting room. The place was dazzling.

"Practically no one ever visits me here in this castle," said the lady cat after jumping onto her chair. "So I'd be delighted if you'd be kind enough to tell me about yourself and your travels. May I ask you why you set out and what you're searching for?"

Would Good-John, in his own father's castle, have felt like confiding in any lady, young or old? Not much, I'm sure. But this white cat seemed so poised, so wise, and so kind! Well-groomed and elegant too, she was, and so graciously reserved! And she fairly radiated peace, as when a willow leaf drops onto a pond and the rippling circle widens all the way to the water's edge. Anyway, she was the white cat, that was all there was to it.

So Good-John told her everything: how they'd always called him a dreamer and a woolgatherer; how his brothers laughed at him; how his father was perplexed about having to choose the wisest of his sons, who would then inherit the kingdom; and finally how, the evening before, he'd set his three sons a test.

"So," murmured the white cat, "you're supposed to show the king how to pass twelve ells of cloth through the eye of a needle? I'll think about it. Would you do me the honor of staying here in the castle and keeping me company?"

"The honor would be all mine," Good-John replied. "I know now that nothing would give me greater pleasure."

He said this not just to be obliging, but because he really meant it. Who could solve the cloth and needle problem better than this cat? Anyway, Good-John liked her way of never seeming flustered, and her distinguished air which lifted you up above the world's troubles. It was as though here, in the cats' castle, all of life's folly and noise just fell away. Why yes, Good-John certainly *did* want to stay with the white cat!

Three weeks passed—the most pleasant he'd ever spent in this world of ours.

"It's time," he said to the white cat one morning—"time for me to set off. I mustn't delay any longer. I have to go home to my father's castle."

The white cat bid the biggest grey cat bring her an ivory box.

"Pull on this golden thread," she said, "and your father the king will be satisfied that you've brought him what he asked for."

Good-John reached the castle that same evening. His two brothers were there already. Each had a large roll of cloth so white and fine that it was a wonder. They saw in his right hand an ivory box no bigger than a spectacle case, and burst into laughter.

"The woolgatherer got it all wrong!" everyone murmured. "Instead of twelve ells of cloth, he's brought back a pocket handkerchief!"

"Father, Your Majesty," said Big-John proudly, "here's the finest cloth the weavers sell. But as for getting it through the eye of a needle, you can't ask people to do the impossible."

"Here's cloth which may be finer still," said Not-John pleasantly. "And if it won't quite go through a needle's eye, at least there's no hole in *it* for a needle to go through, either."

The king signaled that these pretty speeches didn't impress him. No doubt the cloth they'd brought was the best there was, and the finest imaginable; but they certainly weren't going to get rolls as thick as a strongman's thigh through the eye of a needle!

Good-John stepped modestly forward and pulled on the golden thread. Then he drew from its case a needle as big as one of the king's guards' own daggers and ran the thread through its eye. A flood of billowing cloth followed, whiter than snow at Christmastime and so very fine that no spider could have woven any half so light. Satisfying the king was no problem— if you had a big enough needle and fine enough cloth.

The white cat, as if with her own delicate paw, had sorted out the whole thing.

Lords, ministers, and pageboys, mouths agape with wonder, watched the cloth go through the needle's eye.

The king too was amazed, but he still visibly hesitated to let the woolgatherer inherit his crown.

"Myself," said Big-John, "I went to the very cleverest merchants, and my brother Not-John went to the cleverest seamstresses. There's nothing left but magic."

"We should try another test," Not-John murmured. "A single success could be due to pure chance, or luck, or a passing bright idea, or who knows what else?"

"That's right," rejoined the king. "To the wisest the crown! You have to be bright indeed to keep a whole kingdom going. So the crown will go to the one of you who can show me a horse with its head where horses generally have their tails. Yes, that's it! Leave tomorrow morning and be back in three weeks."

"If such a horse exists in your domain, I shall pride myself on bringing it back to you," declared Big-John proudly.

"It *must* exist, if only to please you," chimed in Not-John. "I hope to add it to your stable."

Good-John, meanwhile, just looked thoughtful and bowed without a word.

The next morning at cockcrow, all three jumped into the saddle.

Good-John followed the linnet from meadow to meadow, all the way to the cats' castle.

The big grey cats welcomed him and led him to the lady, their mistress. "You cats," thought Good-John to himself, "you're such subtle thinkers! Who knows? Your lady may well be able to meet my father's wish!"

"Lady cat," said he as he bowed before her, "cloth finer than any, and a needle bigger than any, were nothing for your wisdom to spy out! But do you know what my father is asking for now? He wants one of his sons to show him, in three weeks' time, a horse with its head where horses generally have their tails!"

"Very well," replied the white cat, "I shall consider the matter. Would you like to spend these three weeks with me in the castle?"

Would he like to! Oh, dear little white cat! Good-John wished for nothing else so much in all the world, not even his father's kingdom. Let horses devise their own way, if it pleased them, to get themselves born with their heads where their tails should be! Just now, he cared little for horses, for riding, for thrones, or for being a king, as long as he could stay on and chat with his beautiful white cat!

He enjoyed that pleasure for three whole weeks, and perhaps it cleared his mind better than anything he had ever done before. He felt he'd learned, simply by being with the white cat, to grasp the golden thread and pull on it with a sort of sweet serenity. The woven cloth then unrolled of itself, he had what he wanted, and all things were plainer than day.

"It's time," he said to the cat one morning—"time for me to go. I mustn't be late, I mustn't dawdle. I have to get back to my father's castle."

The white cat had the biggest grey cat bring in a silver box.

"Pull on this golden thread," said she, "and your father the king will find that his demand has been met."

He so trusted her that he didn't tug on the golden thread till his father's castle was in sight.

From the box tumbled a piece of paper. He unfolded it, read it, and sent thoughts of thanks, love, and admiration to his white cat. He then returned his horse to the stable, put the stable key in the silver box, and went on up to the hall where the king awaited his sons.

"Father, Your Majesty," said Big-John, "having combed the whole kingdom, I am now sure that there lives no horse which has its head where horses generally have their tails. In fact, I have consulted the greatest experts, and am quite certain that no such horse can exist in nature. Therefore, I am unable to bring you one. No one should be asked to do the impossible."

"As for me," said Not-John, "I promise Your Majesty that you shall have this horse: a very clever magician will find it for me. However, he will only be able to do so in a year when Easter falls on the new moon."

"And you, my son?" said the king to Good-John with a touch of fatherly friendship in his voice.

"He?" exclaimed Big-John, shrugging his shoulders. "What else will *he* tell us? What a woolgatherer! We left him dreaming his way from bush to bush."

"And we just saw him through the window," added Not-John, "ambling back again at whatever lazy pace his horse preferred. We saw no trace of any fabulous horse."

"Father, Your Majesty," said Good-John evenly, "would it please you to come down to the stable which houses your best horses?"

Big-John (somewhat irritated) and Not-John (somewhat anxious) were both so surprised, their mouths fell agape.

But the king arose and went down with all his court to the stable. Good-John gave him the silver box. The king took out the key, opened the stable door, and went in.

Big-John followed right behind him, then Not-John, then all the others. Again, every mouth fell open. Those who weren't in the front row stood on tiptoe, craning their necks right and left. Because it was true! It was absolutely true! They saw before them a horse which had its head where horses generally have their tails.

A murmur ran through the crowd. People climbed over each other, even lords and royal officers, for a better look.

Suddenly, a page giggled. Of course, he should have waited till the king let them know it was all right to laugh, so he tried to swallow the giggle and its noise. He just ended up sounding like milk boiling over onto a fire. Soon others too were choking with suppressed mirth, till at last they were all laughing aloud, red in the face, with tears pouring down their cheeks.

Good-John had simply tied up his horse backwards, with its tail by the feed rack and its head toward the door. Ears back, the poor horse was watching the lords and pages crowded against its stall, very puzzled as to what in the world they thought was so funny. The hoots of laughter, meanwhile, rose and multiplied. Every belly shook with uproarious hilarity.

The king was the first to wipe his eyes and signal for silence.

"A joke," declared Big-John loudly, "is not an answer. *I* took the king's order *seriously!*"

"Two trials demand a third," suggested Not-John. "We need a third test."

"All right," said the king. "Our woolgatherer certainly solved the mystery this time. But I'll assign a third test, which will be decisive. Look to your wits! It isn't just cleverness you'll be needing now, but discernment and good judgment too, and persuasiveness, and perhaps even some courage. The kingdom will belong to the one who brings back the finest princess to be his queen. There you are! Leave tomorrow morning and be back in three weeks."

The next morning at cockcrow, all three jumped into the saddle. This time, Big-John and Not-John suspected there might be some secret to ferret out, so they promised each other not to lose sight of Good-John.

They watched him roam aimlessly from shrub to shrub, wander from a clump of birches to an old service tree, pick a cranberry here, then nibble a raspberry there. After a while they couldn't stand it any more.

"Looking over the girls of the kingdom is serious business. If we hang around with this dawdler, we'll spend our whole three weeks doing nothing else. Myself," said Big-John, "I'm going to call at the castles of the greatest dukes and nobles."

"And *I'm* going to look for the very prettiest girls," rejoined Not-John. "I'll leave my brother to seek his beauty in weasel-land!"

He didn't know how truly he spoke. As soon as both had disappeared around the bend, Good-John applied the spurs. From meadow to meadow he galloped to the castle of the cats. He went to seek out his dear white cat—her beauty, her wisdom, and her matchless friendship.

He'd no sooner dismounted than he told her what his father the king was asking for this time.

"Kitty, my white kitty, my lovely, he now wants me to take a wife. But that's the farthest thing from my thoughts. It's beside *you* I'd like to spend my days. Yes, I want to spend all my life with you!"

"But this is your kingdom you're talking about! Do you realize that?"

"Oh, I'd gladly give up my kingdom to stay with my white cat!"

"Very well, then. Keep me company these three weeks. Will you promise me that when the time comes, you'll do whatever I ask?"

"I promise! I swear! How could I not do *anything* for you, who twice have done so much for me? Dear white kitty, you have my word."

"And I'll not give it back to you, either! It's mine and I mean to keep it!"

The three weeks went by like a single day.

This time, the cat reminded Good-John that it was time for him to leave—time for him to appear at his father's castle with the girl he'd chosen for his wife.

"But I'm not choosing *any* girl! I'm giving up the kingdom for my dear white cat. All I want is to stay with my white cat!"

"If you really mean that, then remember your promise. You swore, did you not, that you'd do whatever I might ask?"

"Yes, I swore. But if you ask me to leave the castle to go and get married and live far from you, I think I'll die."

"I have your word," the white cat repeated. "You must do as I tell you, without a murmur, like a man of courage."

She summoned her grey cats. They and Good-John followed her to the woodpile behind the kitchen. There stood a massive chopping block (an oak stump, no doubt) and on it lay a great ax. The white cat sat on the block as though it were one of her cushions, but instead of curling her tail around her paws, she stretched it out straight.

Good-John, looking on, had no idea what might happen next. He sensed the grey cats around him waiting anxiously, with bated breath.

"What you must do," the white cat began calmly—"what you must do is cut off my tail with a blow of that ax."

Good-John lifted his hands as though in prayer.

"Hurt you? Oh no, I *couldn't!* Never mind all this business about my kingdom! Just be my white cat. That's all I ask!"

"I'd like to be exactly that," she replied, "and more so than you realize. But I have your word, and you're the son of a king. Pick up that ax."

The grey cats pressed him too.

"Pick up the ax! Cut it off, cut it off! Hurry, cut it off! Come, pick up the ax! Do as she says! Cut it off!"

Their voices set his head spinning, and their actions swept him along until, as though in a dream, he picked up the ax. With or without her tail, and whether or not she was a cat like any other, she'd always be, in her own perfect way, his little queen of peace and his own dear white cat.

Filled with love, fear, and care, he severed the tail with one blow.

Oh, the stupefying wonder that followed then! No more tail, no more cat. No more grey cats, either. He saw before him a young lady as white as swan's down but more delicate still—as delicate as a fairy.

The truth is that some fairy had become jealous and put an enchantment on her. The fairy had condemned her to remain a white cat till the day when the son of a king should choose her over all other princesses, and set her free by making her bleed. No doubt the enchanted are, in that respect, just like werewolves: they say that to give a werewolf back its human body, you have to cut it with a knife, a sword, or an ax so that it bleeds.

And the grey cats too, cut or not, turned back into the princess' entourage. They laughed with pleasure to see their own two feet again, and were quite delighted with their mistress and with this king's son!

She herself had eyes only for her prince, as he had eyes only for his princess: a princess so lovely that the evil fairy's worst could only turn her into a white cat. And now, how perfect a queen she'd be! Great people are the ones who manage always to fall back on their feet like cats, to remain at peace, and to rise by wit and tranquillity of spirit above all the folly of life.

The princess had a third box brought in. It was made of gold.

"Pull on the golden thread," said she. "Then perhaps your father will feel his demand has been met."

A pull on the golden thread brought forth Good-John's royal ring. Good-John, who cared little for his own kingdom, was to have two. Once again, at his father's castle, the prize was to be his, thanks to the white cat.

The girls Big-John and Not-John brought back were real princesses, but Good-John's was a queen: a queen with an air of sweetness, silence, and reserve—though a reserve quite unlike distance.

All the king said when he saw her was, "There she is!" And all he wished to know was what size ring she wore. She'd brought him the ring from her own kingdom, and he compared it to the other ring that Good-

John had just drawn from the golden box. He'd have had her brought his whole kingdom if he could.

Then he ordered that everything should be made ready for the wedding, the very next day.

And what a wedding it was, too! Yes, I tell you, it was quite something!

Such a feast I had there, mind,
I left my own knife behind,
But got such heaps of wedding sweets,
I ate the last batch just last week!

86. The Grain Merchant

There once lived in France a rich grain merchant, and he had a son named Jean. He sent Jean to town, to the merchants' school, to give the boy still greater skill than his own in the buying and selling of grain.

When Jean finished school he went back home to his father, who was pleased with the way Jean went about his work. Still, the father felt like testing him. He put him in charge of a ship filled with grain and told him to go sell the cargo to the English, far across the sea.

Jean set off on the ship and ran it so ably in every way that in a short while he'd crossed the sea. There he disembarked, sold his grain at a good price, had himself paid in gold coins, and found himself all ready to go home.

On his way back to the port where his ship lay waiting, he went through the vast, dark, and dangerous Forest of England, and there he came upon three robbers: men like wolves. They were dragging off a girl whom they'd just seized. The girl's old nurse was following behind, shrieking and tearing her hair. Both women were paler than death.

Jean raced up and drew his sword. The robbers prepared to defend themselves. One was ready to cut the girl's throat with his knife rather than let her go.

Jean emptied his purse onto the path and proudly set his foot on the heap of gold.

"Let the young lady and the old woman go," said he to the robbers. "If you do, this gold is yours. If you don't, steel will settle the matter."

The robbers exchanged glances. They didn't hesitate long. There was the gold, and there was the resolute lad. They let their prisoners go.

With a kick, Jean scattered the gold across the path. Leaving the robbers to scratch about under the leaves, he led the two women swiftly away.

Swiftly too, he brought them aboard his ship, hoisted the sails, raised the anchor, and returned home to his father in France.

"Good day, good day, my son! Did you sell our grain well?"

"Yes, father, very well, very well indeed."

"So you must have brought back lots of money in your purse!"

"No, father, hardly any. In fact, none at all."

He told his father what had happened to him in the depths of the Forest of England: how he'd tossed all the money onto the path so as to save two prisoners from robbers.

"Very well, my son. You've shown a splendid grasp of what a good Christian should do for his neighbor. But now you must go back to school. You're to spend another six months there and become a good merchant."

So for six months Jean went back to school.

His father, meanwhile, looked after the young lady and her old nurse. He gave them both refuge in his house and made sure they lacked nothing they might need, whether food or clothing.

Six months later, Jean was back.

"My son, I shall entrust you with another cargo of grain. Go and sell it in England."

Before boarding his ship, Jean went to say good-bye to the young lady he'd saved from the robbers. She was as lovely as a white rose.

"Take this kerchief," she said, giving him the red silk kerchief she wore around her neck. "When you're through the Forest of England, ask to speak to the king. Present yourself to him with this kerchief in your hand and offer him your grain. He'll buy it from you at a better price than you could ever imagine."

"For love of you, I'll do it," said Jean.

In England, he did just as the young lady had told him. Once through the forest he asked the way, then went to present himself to the king, kerchief in hand.

The king was at the window and watched him approach.

"Handsome merchant, you who travel the land, draw near, draw near! And you, guards, seize him! Now, merchant, try to answer me, or I'll summon the executioner. He'll send your head flying from your shoulders. Tell me: where did you get that kerchief?"

"It's my love's kerchief."

"It's my daughter's. It's six months since I last had news of her—six months since she vanished from this world in the great Forest of England."

Jean told him how he'd found her deep in the forest and saved her from the robbers; how she and her old nurse had taken refuge at his father's house; and how she lacked nothing there, neither bread nor cake nor dresses nor ribbons.

In a transport of joy, the king took a weighty purse full of gold and bought the whole cargo at the asking price. Then he urged Jean to go and fetch the young lady who'd given him the red kerchief.

"Go, then return to me. The quicker you bring her back, handsome grain merchant from distant France, the quicker you'll marry her!"

Jean didn't just go, he flew. Ever since his first glimpse of her in the forest, he'd loved her with all his heart!

He got through the forest this time without meeting any robbers. But then, on his way through a town, he saw a crowd of excited people running. They were dragging a dead man along on a mat, through muck and mire— dragging him to the garbage heap.

"Why aren't you burying him in hallowed ground, the way Christians are supposed to do?"

"Because he died a debtor. He's caused many people to lose a lot. People who die here without paying off their creditors, why, we don't bury them at all!"

"And if someone paid his debts for him?"

"Oh, he had so many! Pay them off? Who on earth would do such a thing?"

"I would. Here's my purse."

Now that was done in a truly Christian spirit. Jean had been moved to pity when he saw those people treating a dead man that way. On the other hand, once he'd paid off the creditors, he hadn't a penny left. All the king's gold went to settle the poor man's debts.

Jean boarded his ship once more and sped across the waves. Home again, he came before his father.

"Good day, good day, my son! Did you sell our grain well?"

"Even better than last time, father."

"So you must have brought back lots of money in your purse!"

"No, father, hardly any. In fact, none at all."

He told his father all his adventures: how he'd had a poor man, who'd died in debt, taken to church and buried in hallowed ground, instead of being dragged off to the garbage heap.

"Very good, my son. You've shown a splendid grasp of what a good Christian should do for his neighbor. But now you must go back to school. You're to spend another six months there and become a good merchant."

"As you wish, father. And when the six months are over, I'll ask you for leave to accompany the king of England's daughter back to her father. She's the one the robbers had seized. Since I freed her, the king will give her to me for my wife."

"In that case, you needn't go back to school. You may not know enough to be a good merchant, but, my son, you know enough to be a good prince."

The merchant gave Jean a suit of velvet, a purse with one hundred pieces of gold, and a valet dressed in taffeta. Jean took the king's daughter and her old nurse, and set sail that very evening for England. His delighted father saw them off from the harbor. Jean and the young lady moved as though in a dream. They thought they saw the heavens opening before them.

But they hadn't been sailing the ocean a day when a storm swept down on them: wind, floods of rain, bolts of lightning, and all the fury of the raging seas! A dozen times they saw themselves engulfed by the deep, or buried under mountains of water that came crashing down from on high.

Jean faced each danger with such cool courage that he managed to save his ship. But he was so exhausted, when at last calm weather returned, that he collapsed at the foot of the mast. There he sank, half naked, into a leaden sleep on a coil of rope.

Now the valet who, like a coward, had hidden during the storm, re-emerged on deck, saw Jean, and was seized with a horrid thought. Yes, envy had been gnawing at the brute's heart from the moment they'd cast off. He so wanted the sweet lady with the red kerchief for his own—and still more the treasures of all England! "Anyway," he told himself, "it's all a matter of luck. What the grain merchant did in the forest—giving up his money for the young lady—why, I could just as well have done it myself. All I need do is get rid of him and put myself in his place. I've as much right as he to the young lady and all the king's money!"

Picking up an oar, he struck the sleeper's head a terrible blow. Then he took him, stunned, in his arms and tossed him overboard.

Having disposed of his master, he went before the king's daughter and her nurse. Both were lying in a corner of the boat, worn out by the storm.

He told them a wave had swept the grain merchant away. Yes, he'd slipped into the sea, he was gone.

The young lady fainted when she grasped what he was saying. She was as stunned by the news as her love had been by the oar.

She regained her senses only to see the valet himself donning his master's velvet clothes. Then he commanded her and her nurse, threatening that otherwise he'd feed them to the fishes—yes, he commanded them to swear they'd never, ever give him the lie, no matter what he might say; and that should anyone question them, they'd describe him as their savior.

The nurse swore, her poor old body all atremble. The young lady, well, she was so crushed with fatigue and sorrow that she hardly cared any more. Her love was dead. What else mattered? She swore too. Both raised their rights hands and swore.

At last the young lady understood what she'd promised, and that being a king's daughter, she could never take back her oath. She realized she was in the power of the brutish valet—she who, just that morning, had been looking forward to a lifetime with her love. Yes, just that morning the gates of heaven had stood open; and now, that same evening, she was looking through the gates of hell. That's the way life goes.

Actually, though, Jean wasn't dead. A wave had carried him off and left him in a hollow of the rocks. There he awoke the next morning, half dead with hunger and cold. He was alone, lost and all alone, on a wave-washed rock in the midst of a boundless ocean which stretched away, billow on billow, to the very edge of the sky: alone, nearly naked, without help or hope, like a scrap of driftwood washed up in a storm.

Suddenly, a great shadow passed overhead. A crow, broader of wing than any crow ever was or could be, landed by him as though taking him already for a corpse.

"Crow, crow, why are you here on your black wings?"

"On my black wings rides your salvation. We need only strike a bargain."

"What bargain could I strike with you, crow?"

"A bargain to do with your first child. The day it's two, you must give me half. That's my price for taking you on my wings. I'll carry you to the king's castle, straight to the young lady with the red kerchief."

"I'll not give you my child, black crow, if my wife is one day to have one. I'd rather die on this rock."

"But do you realize your love is in the power of your valet—the one who stunned you and tossed you into the sea? Will you leave her to that fate?"

"Crow, don't ask for our child!"

"As for the child, I'll leave you one chance. If it's a girl, she's all yours. If it's a boy, then we're agreed: you give me half."

Three times Jean gnawed at his fists in rage and despair. Then, without a glance at the crow, he made a sign. He was thinking of the king's daughter, his love with the radiant face, and how she'd fallen into the hands of that Judas of a valet.

The crow plucked out one of its own feathers and tore off a strip of its skin, like a shred of parchment. It pricked Jean in the arm for blood. Then they both made their pact and signed.

Next, the crow took the pact in its beak, loaded Jean on its back, and spread its wings. That instant it clove the clouds over sea and shore, fields and forests, and carried Jean to the castle of England.

There stood the young lady atop the highest tower, gazing toward the sea. As sorrowful as death she was, ever since that storm. In three days they'd be marrying her to the valet, and she hadn't opened her mouth. All she cared for in life any more was climbing this tower, to gaze afar toward where her love had been swept away by the wave and was now a mere corpse, the sport of the ocean waters.

Suddenly, there he was, coming back to her from the clouds. All she could do was throw herself into his arms.

The brutish valet, coming up to see her, found her laughing and crying in a man's arms. When he saw his master he backed away, his mind reeling, before this miracle which had struck him like a lightning bolt. From the head of the stairs he stepped out into the void.

Nine days later they held the wedding.

Nine months later a child was born, and it was a boy.

At first, all Jean's thoughts were of happiness and joy. But there came a time when he trembled to kiss his son, half of whom he'd promised to the crow. Often he drew away from his wife with lowered gaze. He began roaming the woods to weep in secret. He sought out the depths of the forest to groan in despair.

His wife saw well enough that some sorrow gnawed at him, but when she asked him about it, he was silent and evaded her questions.

At long last, on the day before the child was to turn two, Jean took his wife by her white hand and led her into their secret room. There he gazed at her with tear-filled eyes.

"We must talk now," he said.

He told her of the bargain he'd struck with the crow, on that rock in the sea. He explained how he had to keep his pact. They spent the whole night together lamenting their misfortune.

At dawn's first grey light they lifted their heads, hearing a tapping at the window. They didn't send the crow away or try to kill it. They let it into their room where no one had ever come, and where the child was asleep in his little bed. The crow held out to them the parchment of the pact, signed in blood. Tears of blood poured from the mother's and father's eyes, but they didn't repudiate their debt. They made a sign that they meant to make it good.

They were expecting to see the crow tear the dear, sweet body of their child to pieces, when it changed form before their eyes.

"I'm the dead man who, for his debts, was to be thrown on the garbage heap: the one you managed to have buried in hallowed ground. On the day your life was in danger, there on the rock in the sea, it was given to me to save you; but only on the condition that you be tested again. I found that you, the grain merchant, were a loyal merchant indeed: faithful and sure, and as trustworthy as gold. You were going to honor your pact, though it would cost you more than your life. You did well, and now you shall be happy. Good-bye, forever."

The dead man stood by his word. They kept their dear child and all the others, boys and girls, who came after, into the twilight of their lives there in the castle of England; and they were happy.

87. The Unhappy Couple

There was once a poor man who'd married none too well. His wife was the type to give her husband a hard time—a sort of lioness, you know. Anyway, whether it was his marriage or some other ailment that got him, one fine evening he kicked off.

At the gates of Paradise he took off his hat and stood there, twisting it round and round in his hands. "I was so often impatient with her," he reflected humbly, "and I had that craving for the bottle which used to come over me on Sundays, to help me forget my wife. Who knows what I'll get for all that? Maybe I've earned myself two or three hundred years in purgatory." Such were his thoughts while Saint Peter studied his great register.

"Fine, you're clear," said Saint Peter suddenly, closing the book. "Go right on in. You've earned entry into Heaven."

"But I did wrong sometimes," protested the fellow, who couldn't believe his ears. "Surely I'm supposed to do some time in Purgatory."

"You were married to Zélie, right? Go on in. You did your purgatory on earth, at home."

Another fellow who'd just arrived stepped forward. He touched a finger to his cap.

"Then I expect I can go on in too," he said.

"Oh? No purgatory?"

"Why no, I did it before I died, just like him."

"Is that so?"

"Why, I even did it three times over. I don't know about that Zélie you just mentioned, but anyway, I married Julie—what a drill sergeant *she* was!—then Génie, then Mélie. It got worse every time."

"I see. After your first wife, you got married twice more?"

"Yes. Julie, Génie, and Mélie. Don't you see what I went through?"

"What I *do* see, my man, is that we've no room for you here!"

Saint Peter's gesture told the fellow clearly enough to get lost.

"Heaven is for the unfortunate. It's not for blithering idiots!"

88. The Husband Who Was Never Pleased

There was once a grumpy fellow who was never pleased with anything. He couldn't believe a field was properly sowed unless he'd sowed it himself; he couldn't believe a door was properly closed unless he'd closed it with his own hands. He was always frowning, lecturing, scolding, and grumbling.

If you want to tame the wolf,
Marry him off!

His mother, wanting to tame her wolf, got him married. That little wife of his was brave and smart, but it'd have taken more than that to please him.

One evening, three months after the wedding, the two quarreled at last. He'd been biting his tongue for twelve or thirteen weeks, trying to keep from telling her that no matter what she did, from spinning hemp to watching their cow, she did it wrong. Now he got started on that.

His wife cut him short. "All right," she said, "that's enough. I'll take our Marquise out to pasture today, but tomorrow I'll take over *your* chores. You can take mine. We'll see how you do with them."

The next day, the wife set off for the fields while the husband stayed home.

Butter! He began by making butter. But churning milk into butter is thirsty work. To do it right, you have to refresh yourself with a swallow of wine. He grabbed the bottle and went down to the cellar to fill it.

He was hardly down when he heard a thump overhead, then a sloshing sound. "Good God! It must be the pig! He's just gotten into the house, he must have knocked over the churn, and now he's eating up all the butter and cream!"

Our man scrambled back up the ladder. That was the trouble, sure enough. Furious, he seized the three-legged stool and gave the pig such a whack behind the ears, it was curtains for that pig right there.

Quick, quick, then, the pig had to be bled! He hauled the carcass up onto the bench and bled it smack in the middle of the house. That didn't help clean the place up any, I can tell you. Then he dragged the pig out the door, threw it on a harrow, covered it with a bale of straw, decided it was too hot not to have a drink, and finally realized—with a thunderous volley of curses—that the spigot in the cellar was still running.

Yes, blast and double blast, the cellar down there was now a pool of wine! Upstairs, a pool of blood lay next to a pool of cream, because in his haste he'd knocked over the bucket for the blood sausage. The devil take the whole lot!

The cow, meanwhile, ought to have been out to pasture. She was moo-mooing away.

Now, the house was backed up against the ramp to the barn. To take care of the cow faster, he got the idea of putting her out through the roof, and by hard labor or just sheer rage he actually did it. Let the chips fall where they may!

Now he raced full tilt back into the house to look after that confounded wine, and the blood, and the cream.

Down in the cellar, he realized at once the cow might fall off the roof.

In one bound he was up on the roof, grabbing the well rope on the way. (Oh, you've got to look sharp! No woman tangled up in her own petticoats could ever get herself out of a jam like this!) He whipped that cord around the cow's neck, dropped the other end down the chimney, slid down the roof, jumped to the ground, dashed to the fireplace for the rope-end, tied it around his leg so as to leave his hands free, and went about sopping up the cream.

He'd hardly begun when a tug on the cord knocked him over. The cow had lost her footing and tumbled off the roof. Off he went, flat on his back, sucked into the chimney (blazes, what's happening!?) and bumping, thumping up, up into sooty blackness, to hang, half stunned, by one leg between sky and earth.

What could he do but yell "Help! Help!"

Suddenly, he heard the church bell ring the alarm and, behind the bell, a deep roar, the crackling of a nearby fire, shouts, and running steps.

Oh, he howled from the dark then, all right, for them to come and get him out of there!

But the people dashing up had something quite different in mind.

While flaming straw roasted the pig, a bit of a wind had risen. It had sent burning wisps of straw dancing through the twigs and dead leaves in the courtyard. At last the woodpile went up. From the village, people saw a column of flame and billowing, curling smoke. They rang the bell and ran to help. The fellow's wife saw it too, from the corner of the field where she was wielding her pick, and quickly joined them.

She got her husband down, wiped the soot off him, and perhaps wiped away as well those ideas of his about women. She gave him the swallow of wine that puts everything right again. And she was the one who, that very evening, took the cow out to pasture with no interference from him. Head bowed, he went to cut firewood in the forest. The village constable, happening by on the road, shouted out to him the lesson to be drawn from it all:

> Let each fight his own fight
> And the cows will be all right.

89. The Wife Who Was Never Pleased

There was once one of those eternal old biddies—you know, the kind with the pinched nose, the thin, tight lips, and the beady blue eyes behind their spectacles, who're always ready to complain about the least thing; one of those who, as they say, find mistakes even in the Magnificat. That poor husband of hers must have heard plenty over the fifty years of their marriage.

By and by God called her from this life. One fine evening, she up and died.

Her husband was such a decent fellow that he mourned her with all his heart.

A week later, he went to see the village priest.

"You won't believe it, Father, but my good Claudine appeared to me last night."

"What are you saying? Claudine? She appeared to you?"

"Yes indeed. It was she, all right. You'll see. 'So,' I said to her, 'it's you?' 'What, you don't recognize me?' 'Oh yes, wife, I recognize you, certainly I do! Tell me, where are you?' 'Where do you *think* I am? In Heaven, of course!' 'In Heaven! Take me up there with you, then, right now!' That's when she—you know that look she had, Father—that's when she said, 'Well, husband, if I were you I wouldn't be in such a hurry. I'm afraid even Heaven could stand some improvement.' "

9 0. The Beauty and the Thirty Mariners

In France there once lived a king's daughter who was very, very beautiful: as straight as a reed in a meadow, as high in color as a rose, and as radiant as an Easter day.

Was she proud, too? Well, she *was* a king's daughter, but still she didn't need to insist quite *that* much on her rank. Dukes and princes bowed lower to her than to anyone else. There wasn't a lord in the whole kingdom who didn't kiss her feet in her service.

She wanted to get married. Her father found her a fine, handsome suitor, more impressively noble than the king of Spain.

Now, two days before her wedding, this beauty wished to roam the fields freely, like the partridge who, as the song has it, flits hither and thither and sings in the wood!

Out she went at the break of dawn, under the red sky. Then she came to the fields wearing her silver bracelet and her golden belt, and with her hair floating around her. She felt as free as the wind. When she wasn't running she was flying, and when not flying, running. From meadow to meadow she flitted, from wild rose to wild rose, and from hawthorn to blackthorn tree. Then the sun rose and shone over the world.

She ran so far and long, that daughter of a king, that at noon she reached the ocean's edge. There she sat on the shore and filled her gaze with the ever-rolling waves.

Along came a ship carrying thirty mariners. The captain stood at the stern and sang a song—a song unlike any the king's daughter had ever heard though she wasn't able to catch the words.

She arose with a flush on her cheeks, and more slender in the wind than a willow wand. Her blood was spinning like a wheel and her foot tapped the beat for a dance.

"That song of yours, handsome mariner—I'd like to learn it too!"

"Come aboard, my beauty, we'll teach it to you!"

She boarded the ship, she flew like a bird, that king's daughter to whom all in the kingdom bowed their heads.

"Sing, mariner, sing! Teach me to sing!"

The captain sang and gained the open sea. On they sailed, those thirty mariners, straining at the oars. The song went on so long, so long, there on the rolling, roving billows, there on the waves of the deep blue, rolling sea.

"Handsome mariner, I no longer know whether your song makes me sad or glad. Sing it again, again!"

Sail on, mariners, sail on! From billow to billow they tugged at their oars, ever farther across the ocean deep. The sea slid by and twilight fell.

Suddenly, there aboard ship, the king's daughter hung her head.

"Why are you crying, my beauty, why are you crying so?"

"Oh, I hear him! I hear my father calling me home for supper!"

"Don't cry, my beauty, you'll have your supper with the thirty of us!"

"I hear her! I hear my mother calling me home to sleep!"

"Don't cry, my beauty, it's with the thirty of us you'll be sleeping now."

On they went another hundred leagues without laughter or song.

"Oh, what will my father say when he looks in vain for me to come home to the castle? What will my fiancé say when he finds me no longer in my high bedchamber?"

"It's not of your father you should be speaking now, my beauty, nor of your fiancé. You're the wife of thirty mariners who sail the sea."

On they went another hundred leagues without laughter or song.

The beauty saw a great castle on the shore: turrets and towers, floating banners and creaking weathercocks.

"Oh, aren't those my father's castle, and the towers of Notre-Dame, and the steeple of Saint-Denis?"

"That's the mariners' castle, my beauty, where you'll be sleeping tonight."

That evening after supper she was led up into the great tower.

"There's no king here to save you now, and no prince either, nor any

servant to wait upon you. Undress, my beauty, take off that silver gown of yours, and your golden belt."

"But the lacing of my corset is all knotted. I can't get it undone. Lend me your sword, mariner, so I can cut it."

That mariner had no idea what a king's daughter can be like. He handed her his sword. When she got it, she plunged it into her heart.

Rosier than any rose she'd been just the other morning, she who now was whiter than any lily. All her red, red blood ran across the tiled floor.

Never again would she see her home, the green fields, the gilded castle, or her father's resplendent drums.

The thirty mariners buried her on the shore and wrote on her gravestone:

> Here lies the beauty who chose to die
> Rather than marry any man.
> You who pass by her tomb,
> Weep for her fate, weep for our own.

91. The Pretty Spinning Girl

There was once the son of a king. He had a fondness for racing about in the great outdoors, and especially for hunting in the fresh air of the forest. In fact, the ladies felt he spent too much time pursuing the hind and too little pursuing *them*.

On his way home one evening from the forest of red-coated game, he strayed away from his huntsmen; and as he passed through a village he saw a filthy old woman emerge from a garden, dragging behind her a lovely but terribly distressed young girl. The girl's great gentle eyes were pouring tears like diamonds. With her distaff at her side, she held a heap of white roses in the hollow of her skirt. The old woman tore them from her, screeching like a magpie, and dashed them into the mud.

"Roselie, you little wretch! I'll teach you to have a good time, my girl! Get on home this instant!"

She wrenched the distaff from the girl's hands, and with it dealt her a few smart blows on the head.

"Gently, good woman, gently!" said the king's son, stopping short. "What makes you mistreat this pretty spinning girl so?"

The hag straightened up like a viper that's had something step on its tail. Then she looked at the rider and recognized him.

"What she's done to make me scold her, Your Highness? Too much, I tell you. She's a great one for spinning, she is. Why, she never even stops any more! Yes, whirl, my distaff, whirl and spin and spin!"

She burst into laughter, while the pretty spinning girl wept twice as hard.

The king's son leaned forward on his saddle and without actually knowing much about it, admired the thread wound on the spindle. The girl looked at the ground, blushing as red as a wild strawberry.

"Good woman," said he, sitting up again, "if you hate girls who like to spin, then give this one of yours to my mother the queen. She keeps in the rooms of the castle a store of bast which is just waiting for a peerless spinning girl."

"Ah, Your Highness, if you think that baggage would do well serving our good queen, then by all means take her with you! She's such a burden to me, all I want is to be rid of her!"

Just then a dozen huntsmen came up to join the king's son. He had the oldest of them take the spinning girl up behind him on his horse.

She, meanwhile, seemed to want to speak. But she was choked with tears, and diamonds still poured from her eyes.

"Don't cry, pretty one, my mother loves good spinning girls. She'll make your fortune!"

The king's son would have liked to go on speaking gently to her and to dry her tears. He saw quickly enough how she felt: she didn't understand half of what he was saying. She was too alarmed at finding herself among so many men! What a thing it was, too, for a girl, to go and start a new life in the king's castle. Till that minute she'd lived in peace, filling her fragrant spindle along the hedgerows, in the green of the fields, or perhaps sitting beneath an oak, her distaff by her side.

So daydreamed the king's son as he let his gaze rest again on the pretty spinning girl.

The queen welcomed the girl. She examined the spindle closely, and found the thread so even and fine that it might have been spun by fairies. After that she praised the girl, even complimenting her on her looks, her hair the color of harvest wheat, and her fresh youth and fine deportment.

The queen sent for Roselie the very next morning. She led her through a series of rooms filled with hemp from Brittany and flax from Flanders and Picardy.

"You decide, little girl, where you want to begin. Choose among all these kinds of bast. But I don't suppose it makes much difference to you. You're so clever with your fingers and, so my son says, such a hard worker!"

The girl was embarrassed and flushed like a child.

"Anyway," the queen continued, "you're to spin them all. I'd like to keep you always, since you're such a wonder at spinning. No, no, you mustn't get flustered like that. Oh, *I* see what the trouble is: it's this country outfit of yours—that green skirt and white bodice—that's attracting too much attention. I'll dress you up in the right style for the castle. Then you won't feel out of place any more."

So the chambermaids dressed the girl and did up her hair. She looked more beautiful than ever. The king's son hadn't been able to sleep that night, and when he saw her again, a shiver ran through him.

The next morning, when Roselie wanted to get dressed and do her own hair, she got so confused that she couldn't manage it. Everything went wrong. The chambermaids smiled and the fine young ladies laughed to see her got up that way.

Her cheeks on fire with shame and pique, she loaded her distaff and started to spin. But when, toward noon, the queen asked to see her work, she'd hardly filled a quarter of a spindle.

All downcast, she stood before the queen and explained that she'd had some trouble. Anyway, this being her first day, she'd only just gotten to work.

"Then you'll do more tomorrow, my girl."

The same thing happened all over again the next day.

"Madam, my arm's begun hurting and the pain won't let me work. No, no, madam, I don't need a doctor or medicine. The pain's always gone by the third day."

The good queen was kind enough to feel sorry for her and told her not to strain her arm.

Still, as Roselie left the queen's presence, she overheard the young ladies saying that this sore arm was nothing but an excuse, and that this pretty girl was simply a fake. Perhaps they'd spotted one of the looks the king's son had been casting secretly at the pretty spinning girl.

In her room, Roselie cried her heart out.

"What am I going to do? What's to become of me? Go back to my mother? She'd beat me all the livelong day, just as she's done ever since my father left on his travels. My mother can't stand me. Oh, she knew perfectly well what she was doing when she sent me to the queen. Even so, though, she didn't know *everything*. She didn't know my heart would no longer be free. I'd so love to stay here, so I could sometimes catch a glimpse of my dear prince. But if I stay in the king's castle, all my pleasures will blossom as cares. And what will happen to me when all is discovered?"

The third day came, and what was Roselie to say to the queen? Such was her worry over what to do that she could bear it no longer. She fled, with her hair and clothes looking odder than ever. Into the dark forest she slipped, among the great trees and the rocks.

"Go back to my village? Oh, no! But if I stay at the castle, I won't be able to keep up for long this story about a sore arm. The queen will send me away in shame before my dear prince's very eyes."

Her legs failed her. Down she sat beside a brook which emptied beneath a mighty rock into a black lake teeming with trout and perch.

"There's only one thing for me to do, and that's to die. I'll climb that rock—it's higher than a church steeple—and throw myself into the lake. I'll be dead by the time I hit the water, and then the fish can eat me."

But just as she was getting up from the grass, she saw a man in front of her. He was dressed all in black, his looks were dark, and his eyes glowed like live coals. Still, he stepped toward her, looking concerned and helpful.

"Where are you going, my pretty child? You seem a little sad. Your sorrow must be special indeed if it's beyond my power to heal."

"Oh, it *is* special, sir, it *is*," said Roselie, "and, I'm afraid, quite hopeless."

"You mustn't so quickly believe *that*, my pretty child. Tell me what's wrong. I'll not only share your sorrow, I'll make it go away."

Roselie held back a little. But after all, she *was* about to jump off the rock. Why shouldn't she tell all? So she did. She told the man everything: what had happened the other day in the village; how horrid her mother had been, knowing perfectly well she could only spin very slowly and hated doing it; how she hadn't dared to explain the truth to the queen and make the prince out a liar; how those heaps of bast in all those rooms had made her feel faint; how she'd gotten off for three days by pretending she had a sore arm; and how those three days were now over.

"If I didn't so hate spinning, how I'd have loved to stay on in the castle, working for the queen! I got complimented on my looks. I was dreaming

I might one day marry one of the king's officers, or—who knows?—some lord's son. I'd even wondered whether perhaps . . . But I'm mad, that's all there is to it, and the only way out of my folly is so very bleak!"

"My pretty child, instead of that bleak way, why not take a happy one? Would you respect your obligation to someone if he helped you?"

"Oh yes, sir, of course!"

"If that's how you feel, then I am at your service. Shall we strike our bargain?"

He put a wand in her hands.

"As soon as you touch a heap of bast, no matter what kind it is, this wand will spin it into thread for you—thread of the finest quality. I'll be back for the wand forty days from today. If you then say to me is, 'Here, Ricdin-Ricdon, here's your wand back,' you won't owe me a thing. If all you say to me is 'Here's your wand back,' then I'll be your master and you'll have to follow me."

"Why shouldn't I remember his name?" said Roselie to herself. "Ricdin-Ricdon—why, that's easy!"

Right off she asked the man in black whether the wand couldn't help her dress herself and do her hair better.

"If it could do *that*, we'd have our bargain struck."

"Is that all, my pretty child? My friends and I never let young ladies go without knowing how to fix themselves up properly. All they need do is reach a bit of an understanding with us. Just look!"

He touched her with the wand and led her to the water's edge. She saw herself so exquisitely gotten up, in fact so ravishingly lovely, that her own beauty was all she could think of any more.

"I'm your servant, then, my pretty child, till we meet again. That'll be in forty days, on the very day!"

He gave her the wand and instantly disappeared.

Back Roselie went to the castle, bursting with hope and joy.

On the grounds she met the king's own son, who was looking for her. The young ladies had mocked her and her clothes with hoots of laughter, so he wanted to see her again and comfort her. But when she did appear, he found her beauty astonishing. Trembling a bit, he complimented her, and she trembled a little, too.

Happiness kept her from sleeping that night, just as care had the night before.

As soon as day dawned she dressed herself with the help of her wand, then went to touch a bundle of flax, which turned on the spot into finer thread than ever came out of Flanders.

Toward evening—joy had so swept her away that the whole day had seemed scarcely more than a minute—she presented her skeins of thread to the queen. The queen cried out with amazement, caressed her, and told her she was a miracle of diligence and skill. For a long time the queen fingered the thread and chatted on about spindles, wheels, and spinning; then she picked the thread up again, admired it some more, and at last decided she must show it to the king and to her son.

The castle that evening rang with praises for the pretty spinning girl.

The only words that touched Roselie herself, though, were the ones she'd heard from the king's son, and the only sight that lingered in her mind was the look in his eyes.

Every day that followed was just the same, thanks to the wand. Roselie lived in a dream. Not yet seventeen, she was by nature at once a bit impetuous and a bit shy. She was quite carried away by the queen's affection for her, and still more so by that of the king's son. Her cheeks were aflame, and her head seemed full of a fiery vapor like the clouds at dawn.

It occurred to her one morning, as she picked up the wand, that one day she'd have to give it back. And she realized that in all the excitement, she'd forgotten the name of the man in black. So she tried to remember it: Redin-Redon, Redelin-Redelon, Radin, Ragdin, Ricotin-Ricoton . . .

"I've got it on the tip of my tongue. I'm sure it'll come back. Forty days—that makes six weeks, and every day has twenty-four hours. I'd have to have really bad luck not to remember the name in the end."

Young as she was, forty days to her meant an almost endless stretch of time.

Mornings and evenings went by; the days passed and the weeks. Time flew amid repeated marks of the astonished queen's kindness—and sometimes, under the gaze of the king's son.

But the young ladies of the castle had eyes too. They caught some of those glances the king's son was giving the pretty spinning girl. Did he ever look at *them* that way? If he wasn't with the queen or with Roselie, he was hunting deep in the green, green forest.

"When the queen realizes that her own son might want to marry that shepherd girl, she'll quickly put things to rights. But the queen herself is still dazzled by her. It'll soon to be time to open her eyes."

One of the young ladies, Astramonde, resented Roselie more bitterly than the others. More than once in the past she'd made advances to the prince, and since she had no modest idea of her own charms, she'd taken it into her head that she'd end up making him her own.

She didn't know, nor did anyone else, that the king's son had met Roselie one day beneath the rock by the lake. Together they'd strolled to the brook alive with perch, which, as it moistened the grass, watered a thousand tiny wildflowers. Their talk had at first been all looks and sighs.

Suddenly, the king's son told Roselie he'd give up his kingdom rather than give up *her*.

"Don't you know that in olden times, crowned kings sometimes married shepherd girls? We must see that time again, or I know I'll die."

There in the depths of the woods, each swore the other a great oath always to be true. But they hid their promise of faith from everyone. The prince didn't even dare to keep company often with Roselie.

But Astramonde spied out their love. And to find out more, she who already had a taste for magic made herself a sorceress, in league with the devil.

The king's son often went hunting alone. There on the forest paths, lined with hazels and honeysuckle, he was free to dwell on his fondest thoughts, which were all of Roselie.

One evening, near nightfall, he was on his way back to the castle. Beneath the rock at the edge of the lake he suddenly was accosted by a wonderfully lovely young lady. She was all decked out in diamonds and pearls, and her eyes flashed still more brilliantly than her jewels. She threw herself at his feet.

"I'll not get up again until you've made me a promise!"

He tried to make her rise, but he had to promise to do for her whatever lay within his power.

She told him she was the daughter of the closest neighboring king, who'd been massacred with all his family by another king, savage and evil; that she alone had escaped, having been saved by a wizard named Amonfadar; that she'd seen the prince in the forest and known he was a valiant man; and that she therefore had dared to believe he would deign to take up arms for her.

"See my arm, Your Highness: see this birthmark like a crown-shaped rose, the emblem of my royal family! But here's my dear protector, Amonfadar. He shall tell you more."

A tall, lean man with a thick beard came forward. He drew the king's son a little apart.

"Your Highness," said he, "restore the princess to her birthright. I shall help you to do so with my magic. As soon as you draw your sword, you shall witness her whole kingdom rise up on her behalf. And you yourself, at the same time, shall receive her kingdom and her hand. The princess has given you her heart, as you yourself know. Her life is in your hands."

"I shall do what honor demands," replied the king's son. "I hope I shall be able to restore her kingdom to her. But I myself am no longer my own master. I have sworn a great oath to another young lady."

"What are you saying, Your Highness?" rejoined the wizard. "I may have heard something of a shepherd girl, a spinner of thread. But what weight can be given to such a promise when a great princess is offering you her kingdom?"

"I have sworn," the king's son answered. "I must now be more faithful even than gold or silver, which never rust."

At these words the princess, who had stolen close, burst into tears and tried once again to throw herself at his feet. Were he to reject her hand, she would have no use for a crown! But she refused to believe in such cruelty. Wringing her hands, she lifted her lovely, tear-filled eyes to his. In short, she threw him into such confusion that he began to think himself a brute.

Just then the wind brought him the sound of the angelus ringing in a village nearby. Without a thought, he made the sign of the cross.

Instantly, the princess and the wizard seemed to have been struck by lightning. They vanished completely, leaving behind only the smell of something scorched.

Too astonished to know what to think, the king's son went home to his father's castle. Lest he seem to boast of the adventure, he breathed not a word of it to his love.

Three days later, at the same twilight hour, Roselie was at the very same spot. There, a tall, lean man with a thick beard came to her and greeted her with an air of grave benevolence.

"My daughter," said he, "I see more of your future than you do yourself. You are about to encounter terrible difficulties. Are you prepared for them? Tomorrow, are you not to return a certain wand? What will happen then to the pretty spinning girl? What will she say to the queen? What will she say to the son of the king?"

Roselie trembled and could think of no reply. A storm was rising over the forest. Its approach, and above all the thought of the next day, oppressed Roselie so cruelly that she could scarcely breathe. Those last few days, she'd been tossing about in her head a thousand unholy names—Ricalon, Ricadin, Rigadon—without ever being able to remember that of the man with the dark looks. She would have to follow that man, leave the castle, and say good-bye forever to the king's son.

"Listen, my daughter. Amonfadar (for that is my name) might know a way for you to keep the wand, to stay on in the castle, and to remain in the queen's good graces."

"Oh, Your Excellency, I'll do for you whatever I can."

"My daughter, here is a handsome baron who is madly in love with you. Accept his ring, and tomorrow everything will be yours."

He introduced Roselie to a young lord with sparkling eyes, as handsome as a prince. Flustered as she'd been, Roselie hadn't even noticed him until that moment.

"Swear you'll be true to him."

Roselie began shivering all over.

"My faith is no longer mine to give. I've given it to another, forever."

"Take care! Take care! Don't indulge yourself with dreams! Don't imagine that you, a shepherd girl, a spinner of thread, are to marry the son of a crowned king! If you withhold your faith from this baron, then tomorrow you shall see what pit is waiting to swallow you!"

"I acted like a foolish girl, I deceived the queen and all her people, I was cowardly and told lies. But I've given my faith and I won't take it back. I shall be as true as silver and gold."

She'd hardly spoken before a frightful thunderclap cut her short. Fainting, she made the sign of the cross. Two cries of rage rent the air. The tall, lean man and the young lord were gone. Like smoke they dissolved into the twilight.

She turned and started toward the castle grounds. By the gate, she suddenly saw three men burst from behind the trees.

They fell on her, armed with knives and swords.

How she screamed!

She slipped and fell, while the men collided with each other and got in each other's way. Lightning flashes dazzled them. Mad with fear, she kept screaming and screaming. Another man then appeared. The three scrambled up to attack *him*. He lit into them with such skill and fury that his first blow felled one. Another soon fell too. The third, wounded in the side, took to his heels.

In her savior she recognized the king's son. They fell into each other's arms and he held her to his heart. She was sobbing aloud.

"Oh, my darling, my beloved, are you wounded? I see blood on your arm!"

"And you? Didn't they pierce you with their knives? No, that's not blood on my arm. It's a rose, a birthmark. That's why I'm named Roselie."

Now his beloved's torn sleeve was hanging loose, he'd seen on her arm, by the flash of another lightning bolt, a rose-shaped mark like a crown.

The people in the castle had heard the shouts and cries. Armed valets dashed up with torches. The king's son took Roselie home while the valets removed the bodies.

The king's son could hardly swallow even a glass of wine. Too many things were spinning around in his head. "The one who fled—I'd wounded him badly. He was bleeding freely. Perhaps I could follow him, since the storm is passing and the moon is so bright. Who posted those three out there? These assassins, this rose, and the anguish I see well enough she's in—what does it all mean?"

He took up his sword again. Something made him do it. He had to set out once more.

By the light of the moon he found the traces of blood and set off after them.

They led him far away to a part of the forest, all rocks and ravines, where no one ever ventured. There in the brush stood a ruined castle, doorless and open to the winds. The king's son was astonished to see it all lit up with a strange glow still bluer than the lightning. From it rose a din: gusts of laughter, hoots and yells, and the sounds of dancing.

He peered in from among the leaves and through a broken window. A mass of horrid shapes were writhing about in the hall. In their midst, a man in black, tall and terrifying, was leading the dance with frenetic zest.

No goat ever leaped as he did. His frisking and jollity made the blood run cold.

Just then, as though God himself had intended it, a young woman drew apart from the throng and threw herself down on her knees before the man in black. The king's son knew her. It was Astramonde.

To the man in black she addressed prayer after beseeching prayer.

"Well, you see, my dear," he replied with a laugh, "their faithfulness to each other is keeping them safe. Oh, I don't much like what I do under the name of Amonfadar. My other name suits me much better! And I think that little fool of a girl has forgotten it. Yes, I believe she's just let it fade away into the air."

He started in again with his prancing and amazing leaps, while in a voice that would give you the shivers he began to sing:

> Pretty child, my name
> Is Ricdin-Ricdon: the same.
> Whoever's lost it, let her look
> In yonder fishy brook!
> If she can't say her line,
> Why, she'll be mine, all mine!

The song was so impressive—at once so silly and so terrifying—that it was quite unforgettable. All the way home, the king's son heard it ringing in his ears. He saw again the rose on his beloved's arm, and thought over again what he'd heard from the false princess—a mere demon, like this Amonfadar: that the sign of the rose on her arm made her heir to the neighboring kingdom. And the three assassins . . . And Astramonde, an enchantress and a magician . . . These things churned like straws in a whirlwind, and out of them could come nothing good for himself.

He wanted so much to talk to Roselie, but he couldn't go to her room. No one was supposed to enter there. She'd requested this because of her wand, saying she'd be unable to spin if anyone came to disturb her.

At daybreak he climbed the highest tower, sadly confused. And there— what a happy stroke of luck!—he found Roselie. She'd gone up there too, to take the air after a night as sleepless as his own.

There she sat on the floor, arms around her knees and head against the parapet, gazing, all unseeing, out over the fields toward the blowing clouds and the flying birds.

Then she recognized her beloved. Up she rose and turned to him, as white as milk and as pink as her namesake flower.

"Roselie, my dearest love, what's weighing on you so? Now you've come safe and sound through so great a danger, what's causing all the pain I see you in?"

"Yes, Your Highness, yesterday evening you saved me from the knives! But you won't always be beside me! Is it true, at least, that you yourself were untouched?"

"Who could harm those whom love protects? Last night I risked far worse dangers, and they were as nothing to me."

He told her how he'd roamed the forest and about the ruined castle, though he didn't name Astramonde. He spoke of the man in black. Then, suddenly, he sang the song that had been in his head ever since:

> Pretty child, my name
> Is Ricdin-Ricdon: the same.
> Whoever's lost it, let her look . . .

He'd hardly spoken when Roselie cried out. She clapped her hands, laughing and crying.

"I'd been racking my brains for that name, and now you've brought it to me! How good you are, Your Highness, to have gone so far for your friend! And how kind God is to have led you there, then brought you back safe and sound!"

At last, she made her whole confession to him. She hadn't yet realized that the man in black might be a devil.

"I was completely mad! But I wanted so much to stay near you! And the pretty spinning girl was so hopeless at spinning! Anyway, I never imagined . . . Just think where this pact would have led me, the one I made with the man in black!"

She couldn't forget her terror or revere enough the goodness of God, who'd planned it so that thanks to a miraculous encounter, the king's son should bring her, in the hour of her perdition, exactly the name she'd been trying in vain to remember.

"My darling, my beloved, our good angels managed everything to keep us true to each other. It's clear enough we're to be married for good and all."

He took her in his arms and kissed her before the whole kingdom.

But Roselie heard people calling her name, as though the whole castle was looking for her. She had to run to her room.

It was the queen who'd sent for her. And as soon as the queen saw her coming, she exclaimed:

"I've heard strange news, my girl! There was a monster among my people!"

One of the men the valets had carried off for dead the evening before was actually still alive. Detesting Astramonde and what she'd put them up to, he'd revealed it was she who'd armed them. He'd wanted to confess everything before giving up the ghost.

"So those men were there to kill me!" said Roselie to herself as she listened to the queen. "Astramonde wanted me dead! But I deserved it. Oh, I was mad, quite mad! All I thought about was dressing up and making myself pretty—making myself pretty for one I ought not to have even dared look at. Mad, yes, mad! Oh dear, we're *both* mad, my love and I! That Astramonde will denounce us as soon as they find her. She'll announce our love to all the world! What will the king and queen do then?"

Roselie trembled to think of what lay before her. All in one day, she'd not only lose her wand and so no longer be the pretty spinning girl, but she'd also be driven far from her love, if not cast into some frightful dungeon. "Oh, if only he'd been just some farmer so I could serve and help him, and live off black bread with him in a cottage! I who so hate spinning, I'd have spun for *him!* But now, will I even escape the devil? That name! That name which is always flitting out of my head in the midst of all this turmoil! If my love isn't there to tell it to me again, if he's not constantly by my side, what's to become of me?"

She was deep in these thoughts when she saw him enter the room. He took her white hand in his, and the look in his eyes told her everything: before his mother and all the young ladies, he would proclaim her his wife.

He led her to the queen. But just then the king came in with a humble old man whom the pretty spinning girl recognized as her father.

"No, no," cried the old man as she ran to him, "I'm *not* your father!"

He announced before everyone that Roselie was the daughter of the king from the neighboring kingdom, as proven by the rose on her arm— just as a lily flower, the fleur de lys, appears on the breast of a child of the royal house of France. Having been a soldier at the time, he'd been able to save her and carry her off when the king had perished with all his court. Without even telling his wife, he'd substituted the baby girl for his own, who'd been under the care of a wet-nurse and who had just died. "And if the woman you took for your mother was harsh with you sometimes, remember she's not the mother who bore you."

At the right moment, he'd gone back to that other kingdom and spoken to certain nobles. They'd worked among the people, and now the people were ready to rise in revolt that very day.

A murmur arose, and those present ran to the windows. Astramonde had been seized in the depths of the forest and was being brought back, bound, on horseback.

They untied her to let her climb the steps. Suddenly, she drew from her breast a vial of poison and swallowed it.

The strong poison went instantly to her heart. She declared she'd prepared it for Roselie and the king's son. Having found out by her magic art who Roselie really was, she'd tried to deliver her into the devil's power, or to the assassins' swords. She'd wished for death or hell to part the two true lovers; but she'd only succeeded in bringing about her own death and her own hell.

The words had hardly passed her lips before she was dead. It was not at all clear that she had died repentant.

Meanwhile, dramatic events were taking place. Messengers were arriving at breakneck speed, followed by the nobles who'd come to acknowledge Roselie as their queen. In just a few hours, they'd won her her kingdom back.

Roselie, with so much going on, cared for one thing only: that she was there, hand in hand, beside her beloved.

She'd just retired to her room after dinner when she heard three little knocks at the door. Without thinking, she went to open it.

There in the doorway stood a tall, lean man with a dark look. His eyes shone from the depths of the shadows like burning coals.

She knew him immediately.

Dumbfounded, then seized with panic, she ran for the wand and picked it up with a trembling hand.

Did she know the name or didn't she? But then it came to her lips just as her beloved had told it to her, high on the tower in the morning breeze.

"Here, Ricdin-Ricdon, here's your wand back."

The devil wasn't expecting that. He gnashed his teeth and then, with a smell of singed horn, abruptly vanished.

She never saw him again, or the wand either.

But to please the good queen who loved it so, and to show her husband, the king's son, that if she'd resorted to magic before, she was now all love and diligence, she went back to spinning flax.

She might as well have been spinning those heaps of flax into golden and silken days for them all: her husband, herself, and their children. And till the day she died, people never left off calling her the Pretty Spinning Girl.

9 2. King Nosibus

There was once a king who was passionately in love with a princess. He couldn't marry her, though, because she was bewitched.

He sought the advice of all those who knew the most about bewitchings and enchantments, and he found out at last that to break *that* spell, (can you believe it?) he had only to tread on the cat's tail—because the princess had a cat.

He stepped on that tail good and hard—too hard, I guess, because suddenly the cat changed into a giant. The giant looked furious. He was rubbing his backside.

"King," roared the giant, "you'll marry your princess. But the two of you will have a son with much too big a nose. Nothing will go right for him till he finally admits it."

The wedding was held with heaps of candies and pâtés in delicious crusts, and with lots of fanfare and bells.

When the year was out the queen had a child: a fine, bouncing boy. He was such a pretty baby! But just a minute! There was that nose . . . What a nose! It was a good foot long, or ten inches, at least! They say a church steeple can never be too tall for its parish, and that no big nose ever ruined a handsome face. Well, perhaps that's true of just a *big* nose. But what happens when the nose is a bass horn like that one, a whopping proboscis?

The king and queen, dumbfounded, hardly knew how to take their misfortune. They must have forgotten what the giant had said, or maybe they got it backwards. Anyway, instead of letting the nose go for the embarrassment it was, and trying to laugh it off, they insisted on turning it into an emblem of royalty. They were the king and the queen, after all, and everything was theirs to command. No favors were handed out any more except to those with big noses. All talent, merit, and wisdom simply came down to the size of the nose. From the nurse to the halberd bearer, they surrounded the prince entirely with people who had too long a nose. Noses like that became the height of fashion and respectability. The prince, the court, and the whole town came to believe it: the longer your nose was, the more smoothly your life went. A nose just couldn't be too long!

When the king's son turned a vigorous twenty, he lost his father and found himself king instead. The good people of the countryside nicknamed him Nosibus. They laughed at him some, but not too loudly. He *was* the king! Who'd have dared tell him the truth when he came by hunting down a hare or inspecting his wheat? Who'd have let him know quite simply how things really stood? That rotten nose skewed everything. In short, the king was determined that his face should be the model for every face. The best way to get along with people is to take them for what they themselves want to be taken for—see them as high and mighty, just as they like to imagine themselves.

On the other hand, people did dare to remark that the king ought to get married, that he was the right age for it and that the kingdom needed a queen. He was shown portraits of all the neighboring princesses. And wouldn't you know, despite all his fancy ideas about noses, and despite that bass horn of his own, the one he wanted right off was Princess Sweetheart. She had only a straight little nose, just the right size. She was pretty, though—pretty enough to make you sing out! Anyone seeing her wanted another look. King Nosibus couldn't take his eyes off her picture.

He sent to ask for her hand. He galloped off to meet her ten leagues down the road, with four hundred trumpets blaring before him.

Here came Princess Sweetheart. One glance told King Nosibus she was a thousand times lovelier still than her portrait.

But that one glance was all he got.

Suddenly, there sprang forth on the spot that giant who'd appeared long ago when the king's father had stepped on the cat's tail. Thanks to some magic or other, the giant swept the princess up and carried her off through the air.

Nosibus was terribly put out. Or, rather, his face grew even longer than his nose. Nose to the sky, and burning with love, he spurred on his charger. In nothing flat he'd left his four hundred trumpeters eating his dust on their chubby white horses—because, after all, his was a steed fit for a king. Tracking the princess as she flew along in the giant's hands (it's hard for a giant to hide, even high in the sky), he urged his mount on and on, eyes to the heavens and nose to the wind, leaping hedges and brooks all the way.

Two days and two nights he galloped on without pause, all the way to a distant mountain. The giant seemed to have put the princess down on top of it.

At last he halted at the foot of the mountain and saw in a nearby cavern a little old woman: an old woman so snub-nosed she had no nose at all!

The two stared at each other.

"*That's* a funny nose!" both exclaimed together, bursting into laughter.

The king asked the old woman if she could give him supper.

"With a nose like that," she declared, "you must have smelled my cooking a long way off!"

They ate their soup sitting across the table from one another, each on a log. With rustic frankness, the woman kept joking about that mighty length of nose the king had there in the middle of his face. Yes, she twitted and tweaked him no end.

The king had always assumed his nose was an advantage and an ornament. It had never occurred to him that anyone could laugh at it. At first he tried to be amused by this noseless woman's way of looking at things. Then he got so bothered that he began to wonder whether she might not after all be more right than he.

And after that, well, all those jabs and jibes irritated him no end. King or not, it was just too much to have someone laughing like that at his nose. As soon as they'd eaten their pears, and without even waiting for the cheese, the king thanked her and leaped into the saddle.

"All right," said the old woman, "look ahead on the way up the mountain. Perhaps you'll find there the lady you're after, and perhaps something'll happen to you that you don't at all expect."

"What?" asked the king, turning around in the saddle.

"You'll see, you'll see! Perhaps I'll have opened your eyes a little. You couldn't see much farther than the end of your nose. That's not nothing, of course, but it's not enough!"

The king spurred his horse, then started up the mountain among the yellow flowers and the rocks. He thought about what he'd just heard and about the princess, great as she was in beauty and small as she was in the nose, and whom one certainly couldn't wish other than she was. He thought about himself, too, with that big devil of a handle there on his face; about how his mother and father had decided that when it comes to noses, big is beautiful; and about the way the old woman had sung him roughly that same song, but backwards. It was beginning to dawn on him that when all was said and done, most people must see his nose the same way she did. It even seemed to him that he himself, in his heart, had always felt embarrassed by that nose of his, though of course he'd never breathed a word to anyone about it.

He was absorbed in these reveries when he spotted, on a mountain ledge above crags where ancient hawthorns clung, a strange castle made of crystal and air. At the risk of breaking his neck, he urged his horse on up an almost vertical trail. Like a madman, then, he burst out before the enchanted castle. Now and again veils of pink and blue vapor hid it from view. And whom did he see at the window, from a hundred paces off? His own princess, Princess Sweetheart.

When he went to kiss her hand, his nose got in the way.

"Oh no, it's true!" he cried. "This blasted nose of mine is too big!"

That instant—he barely had time to take the princess in his arms—the castle dissolved into thin air. King Nosibus saw the giant and the old woman with the tiny nose watching him and laughing. They too were vanishing into space. But all he really wanted to see was his beautiful princess.

"Why no, Your Majesty!" said she, considering him with touching sweetness and grace. "No, no, your nose isn't too big at all!"

Just then he saw himself reflected in Princess Sweetheart's silver medallion. At first, he couldn't believe his eyes. Then he ran his hand over his face and found that it was true. His nose was now like everyone else's.

With all his heart he thanked the fairy of the cavern for having shrunken his nose and broadened his view. After that, he had only to take the princess up behind him on his horse. Off they went to get married, with more candies and goodies, more fanfare and bells than there ever had been long ago for the king his father.

93. Isabelle and Her Three Brothers

There was once a lady, a widow, who had sons—not as many, though, as Marguerite in the song:

> *"Marguerite with your blond hair,*
> *So many children you have there!"*
> *"Five are soldiers brave,*
> *Five are in their grave,*
> *And five watch the house for me.*
> *There are fifteen of them, you see!"*

This lady had only three, but they were good ones: three handsome triplets. She brought them up in her little castle on top of a mountain and she looked after them very well.

Perhaps someone put an enchantment on the lady, but anyway, she wasted away. And whether she was unable to break the spell, or there was some other reason for it, she finally died. But she didn't go without suffering sadly as she thought of her three sons. They say dying people see the future. Maybe so. At any rate, she, on her deathbed, foresaw misfortune.

Happily, before bearing triplets, she'd had a daughter named Isabelle.

"Isabelle, my Isabelle, I leave your brothers in your care. It's up to you to feed and guide them till they're of age. Do all you can for them. Later, let them do all they can for you, and may God watch over all four of you."

With that, she turned her face to the wall and gave up the ghost.

The four children now had to manage as best they could.

Isabelle taught her brothers to know which plants are good for soup or salad—pigweed, dandelion, lamb's lettuce, and daisies. They went gathering them along the hedgerows, together with hazelnuts, chestnuts, and beech-nuts. Sacks on their backs, they went to stock up on provisions in the Red Forest.

The boys were growing. They'd have been glad to go hunting or to the wars, but they had no money to buy shoes, or knives, or gut strings for bows. Isabelle could hardly bear it. Though bold, brave, and cheerful, her brothers were skinnier than cats and their pockets were emptier than a grasshopper's.

One day an old woman came to talk to her.

"My daughter, you have only to wish it and you can have plenty of money. My castle is on the other side of the mountain. Follow me there and take everything in hand."

"But what's to become of my brothers?"

"They'll become what they are already. As the years go by, children grow into adults. I'll fill your apron with gold crowns. You can use the money to feed your brothers and buy them bread, salt, iron, meat, oil, and wine."

Isabelle sighed three times, not knowing what to do. As she rolled the edge of her apron between her fingers, she rolled thoughts about in her head. Gazing down, she hesitated. Gazing back up, she made her decision. She followed the old woman.

At first the three boys couldn't manage their beds or their clothes, or the pot or the bowls either. Their room was more like a wild boar's lair than anything else; their coats and trousers were falling to pieces; the turnips in the pan were either raw or burned, while the soup in the tureen was a clear broth without salt or sage.

They just laughed it off, or tried to. But gruff as they were, like sea urchins or badgers, underneath they were drying up like old herring bones.

"All right, we'll just be that much lighter on our feet. Of course things aren't the same any more, with our sister gone!"

What bothered them most was no longer being able to gather sorrel or hunt partridges all three together the way they used to. Each of them in turn stayed home to cook and mind the house. But one often forgot the broom, and another let the dishrag lie wherever it might be. The only thing they really enjoyed was being together, the three of them—since they weren't four any more: being free in the fields, whether hunting, trapping, or gathering, but at least all together. That's the way it is, when you're twins or triplets!

One evening at sundown, coming home from a day like that, all three stopped short in the doorway. The room looked different. There were no crusts or bowls strewn about, no dustballs or straws or feathers to roll back and forth between the fireplace and the door.

"Look, brothers, someone's put wood on the fire!"

"Brothers, look, someone's even hung the pot!"

They couldn't imagine what had happened.

It was the same the next evening.

Now, on leaving the castle they'd locked it up tight, and they found it just as securely locked on their return. Go figure *that* out!

"There must be some fairy mixed up in this!"

"Brothers, I'll have no peace till I find out what's going on!"

They talked it over while stoking the fire, and as they ate their soup they laid their plans. Every day one of the three would stay home at the castle till they found out who was coming to tidy up.

The first evening, the brother on guard fell asleep.

The second evening, the one on guard heard his brothers hunting in the pasture and climbed into the turret to watch them. When he came down again, he found all the cooking and cleaning done.

The third evening, the third brother hid under the bed. Suddenly, he heard a sound like leaves rustling near the little window. But the opening was no wider than a loophole. Even a cat could just barely have squeezed through. Still, he took a peek. He saw their sister, Isabelle, slip into the room.

Out he came from hiding.

"Sister! It's you! I *knew* the soup was just the way you used to make it. Even with the same meat pie, the same cabbages, and the same lard, two different people will never make the same soup! Everyone knows *that*! I knew the way yours tasted, you see. So it's you, it's *you* who've been coming here each evening. We were silly not to realize it. You took such good care of us! We were all you ever thought of. Oh, my dear, dear sister!"

He kissed her, talked to her, and kissed her some more.

She laughed, all out of breath.

"But let me look at you, Isabelle! Why, you're so thin and skinny! I can practically see daylight through you! I'm no longer surprised you should have gotten through the little window. Tell me then, sister, how are you?"

"Oh, brother, if only you knew! The old woman in the castle on the other side of the mountain—why, she's a sorceress! Every morning I have to suck her little finger. It makes me waste away."

As she spoke, the two other brothers came back.

One threw his arms around her neck and kissed her, crying, "Isabelle, Isabelle!" The other wanted her to tell them all about her life with the old woman.

Then all three told her with one voice:

"You're not going to leave this evening. You'll stay at home with us!"

"Brothers, the old woman's a sorceress. She'll know how to find me! My footsteps will talk to her and she'll follow them. She'll take me back."

"And *we'll* defend you. God stands up for Christians."

"Alive or dead, she'll put some curse on you! Oh, brothers, that old woman is terrible! She has a son who's a sorcerer too. He lives in the mountains, and his wife's a lady from some castle. He's even worse than she is!"

"The mother's a laugh and the son's a joke. Now, we've got knives and we've got swords. We'll pierce one through the heart and cut the other's head off!"

"Oh, brothers, brothers, I'm sure the old woman's already on her way here. She's running, she's flying, she's going to lay her hands on me again!"

Down they went into the courtyard and quickly, quickly dug a trench the way people do to trap wolves. They covered it lightly with willow branches. One scattered leaves on top, while another spread handfuls of sand. The sun had set a deep red. The wind was blowing and night was coming on.

Through the night and the wind the sorceress raced toward them, her nails stretched before her, as though borne through the air. Her feet were touching the earth, though, because she tumbled into the trench.

Over and over she rolled, with sand, leaves, branches, and earth raining down upon her. She smothered to death.

"Sister, dear sister, sleep easy now! You're back with us for always!"

The next morning under the rising sun, with everything dew-spangled in the morning chill, they went to the trench to clear away every last trace of the sorceress.

One of the brothers noticed that parsley had sprung up.

The second brother cut the parsley with his knife.

The third took the parsley and made it into a pretty green sauce.

"Brothers, we'll eat the sauce, and there'll be no more sorceress left!"

The three brothers ate it, but their sister didn't want any.

The lads then began to sing. They set off hunting, as happy as ever to be together.

They hadn't reached the courtyard gate before they began to moo. They weren't yet outside on the path before they were changed into oxen.

Isabelle went to mind them in the pasture. She found the best places for them, where the grass is high but as fine as mousehair. She led them to the clear spring, where pretty flowers grew red, white, and all the colors God ever made.

Still, she couldn't help crying—crying for her brothers and for herself too. That was a sad, sad time.

"They might as well be dead. What sort of life is *that* for them? And what's to become of me? So poor I am, and so alone! Oh, so very, very alone . . . On the ash tree yonder, on the highest branch, a little bird is singing. I know what he's saying: 'Girls, girls, get yourselves married!' But there's no husband for me."

One day she was sitting under a bush, dreaming and weeping, when she saw a rider coming her way.

The man greeted her from the other side of the pasture. When he got to the bush he said:

"Girl with your three oxen, what are you doing in this meadow?"

"Minding my three brothers who've been changed into these oxen."

"Pretty Isabelle, you'd be better off in my castle. Come there and be my wife. I'll turn your brothers back into lads."

She was so happy to hear the man say that, she never wondered how he knew her. For her, it was quite enough that her brothers should be her brothers once more. She little cared what might happen to *her*. Perhaps she wasn't even that sorry to find someone to marry. She looked at the man and knew he was a lord because he had a long beard—a beard so black that, like a crow's feathers, it shone blue. A beard always makes a man look like a king.

"I'll be your wife," she said right away, "if you give my brothers back their human form."

"Swear it on their life."

"On their life, I swear it."

She'd hardly spoken when he dismounted. She'd hardly risen before he'd picked three herbs: the herb of thought, the herb of sorrow, and the herb of craft. He gave them to the three oxen to eat.

The three oxen turned back into boys.

The rider took Isabelle, and her three brothers too, up behind him on his horse. The black horse seemed to grow longer to make room for them. Then he set off with them to his castle, for the wedding.

On Saturday the magnificent wedding was held. On Sunday, the three brothers sadly prepared to go home again.

"Sister," said the first, "our house is far away on the other side of the mountain. I don't know when we'll ever see you again."

"And I," said the second, "I really don't know how your life will go, sister. I wish I did."

"I'm already anxious for news of you," said the third. "Sister, I'm terribly worried about you."

"I keep remembering that you've done everything for us," the first chimed in again. "What will we do for *you*?"

"There's only one thing we can do," put in the second. "We'll give you our dog."

"Yes, our little dog's our favorite," added the third. "If ever misfortune strikes and you need us, you'll have only to put a word to us on his head and he'll come straight here. And now, sister, good-bye!"

Isabelle climbed the highest tower to watch them go. Her husband, handsome man with the blue beard, still worried her a good deal.

Day by day, he worried her more and more.

They were eating one morning when he told her he was leaving on a journey. Swallowing a glass of wine, he unhooked from his belt the ring of keys to the castle.

"Go anywhere and open any door. Everything is yours, lovely Isabelle: everything you'll find in halls or rooms, in chests or cupboards—all, except for what's in the study at the top of the little tower. That's my own treasure, not yours. No, there's nothing there for Isabelle, she'd only make trouble. So don't open that door. Here's the key: it's this little one. But I tell you on your life, don't go in!"

He took another swallow of wine, then handed her the keys. Mounting his black horse, he told her, "I'll be back in the evening, the day after tomorrow."

She spent the first day going through the great halls. She found more things in the cupboards than four notaries could note down in a week, from preserved plums to silver flasks.

The second day she spent going through the rooms. The chests there held still more riches and curios, from lengths of green velvet to moonstone necklaces. There were so many sets of ladies' jewelry, both for blondes and for brunettes! It was very strange.

On the morning of the third day, Isabelle stayed at her window. At eleven o'clock she picked up the little key. At the stroke of noon she climbed the little tower.

She'd no sooner opened the study than—God save us!—she let the key drop and would herself have dropped on the spot if she hadn't clutched the door.

Eight severed heads, hanging by their brown or blond hair, stared at her with dead eyes: the heads of eight poor women.

Now, all at once, she understood. Her husband, the handsome man with the blue beard, was the sorceress' son, and himself a sorcerer as sharp as the devil's horns—the devil his own mother had married many long years ago. He hadn't taken just one young lady into his castle, but eight! Yes, he'd taken them in for good and all, and still had their heads with their bloody necks hanging there in his black study. They say any sorcerer, even if he can do no better, must at least kill nine plants. *That* one planned to kill nine women.

She shut the door, locked it again, and left the tower, though she never knew how, for her legs would hardly hold her up any more. Dazzling flashes blurred her vision. Even so, though, she couldn't help seeing that the key was now stained with blood. She tried her best to wipe it clean. She scoured it with ashes and sand, scraped at it with a knife, then a file; but nothing worked. The blood always reappeared.

That key was bewitched. There was a spell on it. Oh, dear Lord! God help us!

"Madam, what has upset you?" asked the maid.

"I see my death coming," she replied, whiter than her shift.

She'd hardly spoken when her husband entered the room. She'd not yet risen to greet him when he saw the key and understood everything at a glance.

"Ah, madwoman, you've betrayed me! Didn't I tell you, on your life . . . ? Very well, your head shall be the ninth. Have you any favor to ask me before I cut you down?"

"Two, husband: two favors. Let me eat lentils and let me say my prayers."

She went up into the highest tower. Quickly, with a trembling hand, she wrote a note and put it on the little dog's head. The dog raced off toward the castle of her three brothers. Then she set her maid to watch at the highest window, under the eaves.

Next, she started eating her lentils. It takes some time to eat lentils when you eat them one by one off the point of your knife.

Her husband was waiting down in the courtyard. He was crying:

> *"Sharp, sharp, my little knife,*
> *Cut Isabelle and take her life!"*

Then he roared up to ask whether she'd be finished soon.
"No, no, husband, I'm eating my lentils."

> *"Hurry, or taste bitter strife!*
> *Sharp, sharp, my little knife,*
> *Cut Isabelle and take her life!"*

After a while he started again, roaring louder than ever:

> *"Have you finished? Answer, wife!"*

"No, husband, but I've only a pinch of lentils left."
And to the servant girl up under the eaves she whispered:

> *"Servant girl, look! Who's coming?*
> *Do you see no one this way running?"*

> *"I see pastures green and broad,*
> *But no dust out on the road!"*

Down in the stone-paved courtyard her husband roared again:

> *"Sharp, sharp, my little knife,*
> *Cut Isabelle and take her life!*
> *Have you finished? Answer, wife!"*

"Oh, husband, I've finished my lentils. Now I'll start my prayers."
And to the servant girl under the eaves she whispered once more:

> *"Servant girl, look! Who's coming?*
> *Do you see no one this way running?"*

> *"I see pastures green and broad,*
> *But no dust out on the road!"*

The man with the blue beard was thundering now:

> *"Are you done praying, wife?*
> *Come down, Isabelle, on your life,*
> *Or I'll be up with my knife!"*

"Just a moment, husband! I'm just finishing my prayers!"

> *"Servant girl, look! Who's coming?*
> *Do you see no one this way running?"*

> *"Yes, yes, at last*
> *They're coming fast!*
> *I see dust out on the road,*
> *I see a sword gleam in the cloud!"*

Down in the courtyard, Bluebeard was howling with rage:

> *"Come down or not, for your life,*
> *Isabelle, I'll be up with my knife!"*

And up he came, foaming, dagger in hand.

"Hurry, now, hurry! Take off your clothes!"

"Oh, husband, for my honor's sake, don't take off my shift!"

"Then take it off yourself!"

He'd hardly spoken before the door shook under a rain of kicks and blows!

And before he could lay hands on Isabelle, the door burst from its hinges.

"Dress again, quickly, dress yourself!"

Swords drawn, the three brothers charged into the room.

"What were you about to do, filthy traitor, murderer?"

> *"We see by your deathly pallor*
> *You were going to kill our sister!"*

"I only wanted to give her a new shift."

"Well, we'll give you a new skin! Let me have those keys that are hanging from your belt."

They searched the castle from cellar to attic. They opened the black study in the little tower.

"Our sister's head was to be the ninth. But the ninth will be your head, instead!"

They cut off his head, set fire to the castle, and reduced it all to coals and ashes. Of course, they never meant to keep for themselves any of the sorcerer's accursed riches.

Then they set out again through the pastures. Off they went to the other side of the mountain, and they took their sister and the servant girl with them.

After that, it was the servant girl who cooked and kept house for them. Their sister, the lovely Isabelle, could always go with them, gathering or hunting, through fields of flowers red and white, flowers of every color. God grant them health and joy! They lived together all the days of their life.

94. Mongette

There was once a girl they called Mongette.

A "monge" is a monk. Even beans are called "monges" because they're brown, grey, russet, or tan, just like monks' habits. So "mongette" means something like "little girl monk." She wasn't a nun and she hadn't taken any religious vows. But having lost her father and mother as a child, she'd been more or less brought up by the local priest. This was a village near a fairly large town where there was even a garrison of soldiers. She'd ended up spending a good deal of time in the church. She swept the nave and chapels and kept them clean and tidy; washed and mended the vestments; gathered flowers in the garden; and decorated the main altar and the altar of Our Lady with red lilies, moss roses, or violets according to the season. She looked after the altar lamp, too, and gave out alms of bread and lard to the poor. In short, she did what a nun would have done, had there been one in the village. That's why she was called Mongette.

But Father had only given her all this to do because he'd seen how deeply devoted she was to the Holy Virgin. No longer having an earthly mother, Mongette had turned to Our Lady and become her child. She loved Our Lady as a mother who was never away.

Perhaps Mongette wasn't quite like other girls. As shy as a young hare, she spoke little and was slow to smile, though her eyes were large and kind. She seemed to live her whole life behind those eyes, lost in some sort of reverie or dream. Mongette's big eyes didn't even seem to see what they were looking at.

Unfortunately for poor Mongette, one day her eyes saw only too well a soldier passing by.

Glittering sword in hand, and all in white armor clad, he rode along like Saint George. She was dazzled. She saw him for only as long as it takes to say an Our Father, but the sight never left her.

Mongette was eighteen. She had no idea what had happened to her. It was as though a cord had tied itself to her and was pulling her forward from the center of her chest. There was nothing she could do about it. Her fate was sealed. She had to go to be with that soldier. She had to do it the way someone starving must have bread. He *must* have that golden-brown loaf with the warm fragrance that reaches out to him as he passes the oven-vent of the bakery.

It was June. Mongette went one last time to her church and knelt there in the chapel of the Good Lady.

"Holy Virgin Mary, I am no longer what I should be in order to approach your image, change the water in the vases, and fill your lamp with oil. Our Lady, you are my mother, I know, I know. You will never abandon me, but I feel forlorn. I surrender, like one who asks only for mercy. As I leave, I shall return to you the keys of the church. Have pity on your poor child."

She laid the keys on the altar and left, closing the door behind her. She went to join her soldier, the rider armed in white.

But in her life of sin, she still said a Hail Mary each morning, and each evening had the same self-accusing, imploring thought of refuge in her mother Mary. Anyway, she didn't live that life very long.

No, she hadn't long to travel beside her friend—her friend already in waking life and forever in her dreams. That fellow made a Saint George more dazzling than the sun, and a rascal at once merrier and more terrible than any. He'd call her Nonnette, "little nun," with a hoot of laughter, empty three mugs of wine, then savor his wine under the table or smash table and benches together. Now horrified, now overjoyed, now beseeching, she no longer knew whether or not she lived on this earth at all.

But it didn't last long. Mongette had only six or seven weeks with him. One evening someone came to tell her he'd been in a fight. She found him on the street, his side cut open and his hands dark with blood.

Mongette thought she would die. She wept till she was half crazy. Then poverty followed mourning, and sickness came after. She did not die, though. All she could do was turn to her mother Mary. Despite sin, shame, and tragedy, she begged Mary over and over, palms folded in prayer, to let her go on being her child.

Mongette had left the village at midsummer, on Saint John's Day. It was on the feast day of the Virgin's Nativity, the eighth of September, that the poor creature realized she wanted to go back. The idea came to her that morning. "I must go home to the village," she said to herself. It was a scary thought but it filled her head. That was all she could see to do. "I've got to go back to the village. That's the only place, there in the shadows at the back of the chapel, where I can still be near my mother Mary."

She kept repeating this to herself all day, and all night, too, even in her sleep. The wish to go home wouldn't leave her. The next morning it came on again, stronger and stronger.

Once more a cord was drawing her on from the center of her heart.

But would she ever dare show her face there again? How could she? She'd just dropped all her responsibilities and left. What could the priest and village people have thought of such dereliction? She who so feared any dark look or unkind word, she almost fainted at the thought of appearing again before them, her forehead branded with her sin.

But she had to set off for the village. A voice told her to go. And Mongette had never really gone far. She'd been hiding out in a humble quarter of the town where her soldier had belonged to the garrison—hiding out in her tiny room at the back of a little courtyard she never left. Though her legs nearly gave way under her, she set out.

After the noon meal she left by one of the town's three gates. Up she went toward the spot, there on the mountain spur, where criminals were punished. Hanged men swung there from gibbets. She told herself that she, even more than those deserter soldiers, deserved death.

The distance was hardly an hour's walk, but she kept a pace like a pilgrim's: four steps forward and three steps back. Still, by midafternoon she reached the village.

She was still in an agony of foreboding. A slender breeze flitted along a hawthorn hedge loaded with berries. It brought her the savor of September fields: a savor of earth and stubble, of veiled sun—the peace of fall.

There was no peace for her, though, no savor of dusty straw or pink sunset sky; no, nothing to give her the least hint of peace. The chill of shame had frozen her to the bone—shame which pins your arms and legs, which stops the blood.

There was the beadle, digging in the garden below the tower. She paused. His hood hid her from him. Anyway, she'd changed so much, nobody would have known her; and that white-haired old man didn't see any too well. Disguising her voice, she asked him whether there hadn't once been a girl named Mongette living in the priest's house.

"There certainly was a Mongette, and there still is," answered the beadle, resting his hands on the handle of his spade. "If you've got business with her, you'll find her in Our Lady's chapel. That's where she is, praying to God."

Mongette thought he was soft in the head.

"He's just like all those old people who live in the past. Old age has him all muddled up."

She didn't dare ask him anything further. Bowing her head, she passed on.

The church was open.

Mongette stood in the doorway. She didn't take a single step further. No, she just looked. There really was someone in Our Lady's chapel, someone down on both knees, praying. Every detail of her dress seemed the same as Mongette's.

She stood on tiptoe, trying to peer through the gloom. On the altar she saw the keys, exactly where she'd left them when in her madness she'd gone away. Her heart nearly failed then; it almost burst. Helpless, Mongette sobbed aloud.

A moment later, though, she dried her eyes and advanced, trembling, through the church and into the chapel. She had to. The praying figure rose and turned toward her.

"I was expecting you, Mongette."

Mongette stared at her, wide-eyed. She felt as though she'd stepped from the dungeon of shame out into the full light of the sun.

"Mongette, I'm the one to whom you entrusted your keys: the one in whom you've never, even in the depths of sin, forgotten to seek refuge."

Mongette was shaking. She fell on her knees and broke again into sobbing, though dissolved this time in unspeakable happiness as she touched her forehead to the flagstones before the Lady.

"You asked me to be your mother, Mongette. Oh, you begged so hard! My child, my child, could I have failed to take pity on you? See then what

I did. I took your place on the day of your madness. I stayed here in your own dress, in your own face. All your service was done. No one ever knew you were gone or had sinned. Now, take up your duties again. Pray, my poor, dear child, pray and do your penance."

Our Lady threw her arms around Mongette's head and pressed it to her side.

Mongette's life after that was all expiation and prayer. But her heart had been filled forever with such sunlight that she shook some evenings, remembering.

Before she died she asked the priest, "Tell them all my story . . ."

She asked out of real humility, and so that each of the faithful should come to know better the mother we have in Our Lady Mary.

95. Saint Joseph in Heaven

There was once an old country priest who'd always been young at heart. Theology wasn't exactly his line, but he believed that you can't go wrong if you practice charity, and that when all's said and done, charity is still the best way we have to assure our own salvation.

He was particularly devoted to Saint Joseph, who'd had to look after the Child: Saint Joseph the loving father, the patriarch, the shadow of the Father; Saint Joseph who was all wholesome goodness, like good bread, and always kind as well, like a country carpenter who knows you must do the impossible to help people out—who knows that goodness is best and sweeps all before it.

Maybe the old priest dreamed it, or maybe he thought it up himself in the goodness of his own soul, but anyway, he liked sometimes to tell a story.

Once upon a time, he'd say, it seemed to God that things in Heaven were no longer going quite right. There were some funny characters around. Elect souls they may have been, but they sure didn't have much going for them. They didn't seem to feel quite right in Heaven, either, because they were slinking around in the corners.

"Has Peter gotten too indulgent? No, I know I can trust Peter. Someone else must be slipping people in on the sly. I'll have to do something about it."

It didn't take God long to find out. That same evening he spotted Saint Joseph sneaking along the wall with his big cloak over his face—the one he'd worn on the Flight into Egypt.

"Hmm, he might as well be out to rob magpies' nests. What's he up to?"

Saint Joseph stopped in a curve of the wall and drew a ladder from the shadows. He must have remembered he'd been a carpenter and made it himself. Then he flung it across the wall, leaned over, and gave a low call.

In no time at all three, then four characters had scuttled over.

"People!" thought God to himself. "Give them an inch and they'll already take an ell. If we're more indulgent still, we'll end up in a fine pickle!"

That evening, though, he let Saint Joseph proceed. He even let him put the ladder back in that dark corner.

Later, he said his piece.

"Anyway," he concluded, "it's perfectly simple. If this goes on I'll have to take action. The guilty party will find himself expelled from Heaven."

Saint Joseph looked at God for a while in silence, grinning. He knew that when it comes to goodness, no mere creature could possibly teach anything to God.

"Leave here? Leave Heaven?" he said at last. "But Lord, have you fully considered the consequences?"

Grinning more broadly than ever, he looked down at his feet as though talking just to himself. "You see, when the father's sent away, the whole family's bound to follow. I'll take the wife with me, you know, and the little tyke too!"

96. A Tricky Wedding

There was once an engaged couple who came to the priest to be married.

About to begin the ceremony, the priest noticed the groom was tipsy. He stopped right there.

"There's a little problem. Come back tomorrow. I'm not marrying anyone today."

The next day, our groom was back again, three sheets to the wind. He could hardly stand.

"I just can't marry this man," said the priest. "Come back tomorrow if you like."

There they were again on the third day. The groom's head was lolling, his legs were wobbling, and in fact he was only being held up—with the greatest difficulty—by his bride. Drunk, he was, dead-drunk, as drunk as a thrush in grape-harvest time!

"For heaven's sake," exclaimed the exasperated priest, "can't you get him here in any other state?"

"But Father," replied the bride, "how *could* I? If he's not pretty well soused, he just won't come!"

97. The Three Widowers and the Three Widows

There were once three widowers, and as they watched people play skittles in the church square, they chatted together.

Said one, "I had unbelievable luck. My dear departed wife was an angel. It'd be madness to count on the same a second time. Marry again? Believe me, I'll take good care not to."

"*I* got lucky," said another, "when my wife dropped dead. She was a devil, I tell you, and home was hell. No indeed, you won't catch *me* trying marriage again."

"And I," said the last, "I got an angel for my first wife and a devil for my second. I don't want to find out what the third might be like. Anyone who wants to try it out, go ahead. I'm not going back for more."

At the other end of the square, three widows were sitting on a bench before the notions store.

Said one, "I did rather well, I think. Men aren't as bad as they're made out to be. I was happily married once and I could be so again. If I found a fellow who'd have me, well, I'd take him."

"Life with that brute of *mine* was pure misery," said another. "I'd really have to be out of luck to find another like that. There are all sorts of men. If one stepped up to me this evening, I'd not let him get away."

"And I," said the last, "I was happy with my first and unhappy with my second. Men are just like melons: there are good ones and there are bad ones. If I got a chance to remarry, I wouldn't mind risking it."

98. The Peg

There was once a king at Saint-Martin-des-Olmes. This king had a daughter who was going on seventeen and ready to get married. She had plenty of suitors, too, since her father had twelve cows in his stable. But the father had sent one packing, and the daughter another. There were only three left: one from Les Balays in the high country, one from Saint-Martin itself, and one from down at Etagnon.

On Sundays, all three would be off to see the girl. Oh, she was worth looking at! They would help her watch the cows.

One Sunday the king appeared in the pasture.

"All right, listen. Tomorrow, each of you bring me a peg. The one with the best-made peg will have my daughter."

So he wanted a peg! Fine! The next day the three lads were back.

"Good day, good day, my boys. Well, let's see your work!"

The one from Les Balays held out his peg. The king took it, looked it over, and gave it back.

"No, that's not it. Your peg's too big."

The fellow from Etagnon held out his. Was it too small? Well, no, not really.

"But," said the king as he handed it back, "it's not right either. Don't you realize you made it out of green wood? Pegs are supposed to be made of dry wood."

That left the boy from Saint-Martin-des-Olmes. The king turned to him.

"Well, my boy? Where's your peg?"

"I didn't make one, Your Majesty."

"And why not?"

"Because to make a peg, you first have to see the hole."

"Very good, my boy. You're smart. My daughter's yours."

99. Lovely Rose

There was once a poor man, a small farmer, who was so poor that he owed money, as they say, both to the dog and to the wolf. He didn't even have a suit for going to town, which is why he never went to town at all.

At last, his persistence and courage in scraping away at the earth allowed him to put a few francs aside. He paid off his debts and got himself on his feet again. Then, late one fall, he had to go and sell a calf. Never mind the sorry sight he made. On the day of the big fair, he set off to town.

Before he left, he asked everyone in the family what they'd like him to bring back. Now, he had three daughters: Marguerite, Julienne, and Rose. They were his three flowers, as he himself was fond of saying. He loved all three dearly, though he couldn't help favoring the youngest just a little. She had real courage, as he did, she never never put on airs, she was brave, and she was easy to please. Anything good was good enough for her. She was a pleasure to look at, too, and also a pleasure to be with. You felt like singing to her the words of the song:

> *Lovely rose of the white rose tree,*
> *Sweet, sweet rose of spring!*

So, there he was before his door, holding the calf by a rope. "It's the first time I'm going to the fair," he said. "What shall I bring home for you?"

Marguerite answered, "A pretty dress the color of the moon!"

And Julienne answered, "A pretty dress the color of the sun!"

Lovely Rose said nothing.

"You then, sweet, what would you like from town? A pretty dress of gold, silver, and silk, like your sisters?"

Rose didn't think much about herself or her clothes. She kept remembering that she had milk to churn into butter and then to clot for cheese.

"Come, sweet, hurry. Tell me!"

"Father, I don't want anything."

"I won't leave till you tell me!"

"All right, father, my name is Rose, so bring me back a rose."

She'd forgotten it was already late in the year. The roses were all gone. Her father worried about that all the way along. "Still," thought he, "in town, in some rich man's garden, I might well find her her rose after all."

Having sold the calf, he managed to buy the two dresses the colors of moon and sun. He'd have given a lot of his money for a rose, but he never found one.

He had to head home again without the rose.

The sky, meanwhile, had turned grey, the wind had risen, stormclouds had gathered, and snow now began falling in big flakes.

The snow stuck right away and the footing turned bad. The poor man had delayed too long, looking for that rose. Night was coming on. He decided to cut across the heath. The next thing he knew, he was lost.

On and on he walked till he was soaked through and worn out. Around him stretched a landscape he'd never seen before, all of heather, ponds, and sparsely wooded moor. But all he could think about was his misery at having to go home without a rose for his youngest daughter, while the two others each had exactly what they'd wished for.

All at once he realized, "They're going to believe, my wife and the girls, that robbers stopped me on the way and took my life to get at my purse. Anyway, doesn't it look as though at this rate I *am* going to be finished? I've no idea where I am any more, and I'm so tired, I don't quite know how long I can go on. I'll collapse any minute now here in the snow and give up the ghost."

He was just giving up all hope, soaked and exhausted as he was, when he suddenly saw light through the dancing flakes of snow. It brought back his courage. He gathered his strength and pushed on.

He soon came to a brightly lit castle.

The gate was wide open. Not being brash, the man hesitated. Still, necessity left him no choice. He had to go on in or drop on the spot.

Into the courtyard he went and climbed the steps. All the doors were open, too, but there was no sign of anyone inside. How strange it was! He called out, softly at first and then louder. There was no answer. He took three more steps. He was nearly fainting with cold and hunger. When he saw in the hall a lighted fire and a table all laid, he walked that way. Soup was steaming in the tureen. He dared to sit down and help himself to a bowlful. "I'll be braver with something in my stomach." When he'd finished the soup he poured a glass of wine into what was left in the bottom of the bowl, the way farmers do, and drank it down. That made him feel better. Next, he attacked a roast chicken, the smell of which was making his mouth water, and ate whatever else was before him—ham in jelly and a pear tart. He even emptied the bottle.

Now he was a new man, he thought of looking into the adjoining room. There he took off his clothes, already half dry, laid them out before the fire, and got into the bed—a feather bed with a warm comforter. Forgetting to worry any more about seeing no one in the castle, he fell asleep.

He slept soundly. Once he'd gotten dressed in the morning, he looked high and low for someone to apologize to and to thank. He found not a single living soul.

What was he to think of this castle and all that went on in it?

Out he stepped, and there, right next to the door, he noticed a rosebush. Despite the snow last night, it had just burst into bloom. Yes, that rosebush was covered with barely opened buds, as big and red as Easter eggs.

He did hesitate once more, but he so badly wanted a rose like that! Was he to go home with nothing for his youngest daughter, nothing for

her alone, when he had before him exactly what she'd asked him to bring? The strangeness of the place was quite enough to put him on guard, but he could just see himself giving his dear Rose the rose and telling her his adventure. In the end, he couldn't stand it. He chose the most beautiful of the buds and cut it off with his knife.

Oh, how he should have chosen instead discretion and wisdom! What had the miserable man gone and done?

A beast emerged before the rosebush, as though straight from the earth. It was so hideous, so perfectly made to inspire disgust and terror, that he dropped the knife. The beast's jaws were like a great mastiff's, its legs like a lizard's, and its body and tail like . . . what do you call those yellow-spotted creatures people are so afraid of—the ones that live under moss and in holes in the earth? Oh yes, salamanders.

"You came into my house," said the beast, "you ate and drank well and got dry. You slept snug and warm. And your only thanks, on your way out this morning, was to cut the most beautiful of my flowers! Miserable man, your last hour has come!"

The beast advanced on him with slavering jaws. Trembling, he retreated. He stammered that he'd been very wrong, offered to pay for the rose, and promised the beast his purse or whatever else of his the beast might want.

"Save your breath," the beast replied. "But tell me, don't you have daughters?"

"Yes, three. I cut this rose for the one we call Lovely Rose."

"Very well, then, listen. If you don't want to pay for this rose with your own life, then have one of your three daughters come here in just one week, on Saturday like today, and give herself to me. Do you hear?"

"Yes, I hear you."

"You cut the rose, so take it with you. When your daughter gets here, let her cut another. Then I'll appear to her. After that, it'll be up to her to do what's expected of her, if she knows how."

There was no argument to make. Anyway, the beast had just vanished. All the poor man could do was set out again for home.

He walked along sunk in thought. "What can that beast want with my daughter? What does it mean to do with my dear little girl?"

It never occurred to him to wonder which daughter would go to the beast's castle. He already knew. He foresaw well enough which one of his three flowers would put forth blossoms of brave devotion, the way a rosebush puts forth roses. A shiver ran through him as he walked on. Snow melting off the branches dripped down his neck, and he never knew it was snow. He tripped over rocks and never knew they were rocks, started linnets from the bushes and never knew they were linnets. He was still living that moment when the horrible beast had appeared and spoken those terrible words. "What can it want with my daughter? What will it do with my child?"

At last he made his way home, shaking and yellow in the whites of his eyes. He looked ten years older. His wife and daughters thought he was exhausted. They imagined he'd suffered all night long in the snow. When they tried to get him to eat a bit of meat, all he would do was drink, and no more than plain water at that. He sat down before the fire.

Still, Marguerite and Julienne asked him whether he'd brought them their pretty sun and moon dresses. He took the dresses from his bag and gave them to the girls.

"For you, dear Rose, I've brought back the rose you asked for. But it'll cost us dearer than your sisters' pretty dresses!"

Then he began the story of what had happened to him.

"And finally, the beast told me it would come for me. It'll devour me if, a week from now, I don't give it one of my daughters."

No one said a word. Only the fire murmured low in the darkness of the fireplace.

"I could *never* go into that castle father just described," said Marguerite, "where things happen without your ever seeing a soul."

"And I'd drop dead on the way there," chimed in Julienne, "at the very thought of seeing that beast. Why did Rose have to go and want that miserable rose?"

"That's right," Marguerite went on, "it's her wanting that rose that's brought a terrible misfortune on our father!"

"*I'll* go to the castle," said Rose, who couldn't keep from weeping. "It's not very kind of you to say so, but yes, you're right, it's because of me that father's suffering all this pain and anguish. When it's time for him to pay his debt, I'll go to the beast."

How that week went by—both horribly slow and lightning fast. There was nothing left to life but tears and agony.

Then came the morning when Rose and her father, terror-stricken, set out for the castle. On his way back there the father stumbled over the very same rocks and got caught on the same bushes, because of those same thoughts rising in his mind. "What does that beast mean to do with my daughter? It'll have our Rose to do with as it likes—Lovely Rose, my dear, sweet girl, who used to bring me my bowl of soup at noon, there at the edge of the field. And this summer, when I was reaping, she was right behind me, binding the sheaves. I'll never see her there behind me again, with that smile in her eyes. Oh, evenings when I hear boys singing on the path,

> *Lovely rose of the white rose tree,*
> *Sweet, sweet rose of spring!*

I'll feel my heart leap from my body."

In silence they reached the beast's castle and went on into the courtyard. The doors were all open, the table all laid. You could see the tureen steaming. But Rose went straight to the tall beautiful rosebush and cut off a rose.

Instantly the beast appeared.

Oh, that beast, with its big, bulging, bloodshot eyes, its slavering snout, and its skin as pimply as a goose's but slimier than a toad's! So disgusting and terrifying was it to look at that poor Rose trembled all over.

"Is that you, Lovely Rose?"

"Yes, I'm Rose."

"Don't be afraid if some things in this castle surprise you. I'd be so glad if I had a still bigger castle to surprise you with one day. Rose, everything in this house will be yours. You'll spend your time here just as your father spent that night. You may even find lifelong happiness if you know how to take things as they're meant. And when you want to talk to me, you'll only need to cut a rose."

The beast sighed and disappeared.

Rose and her father spent three days together in the castle. Though they saw no one, the table was always laid and the beds always made. When the bells rang for the angelus, three times a day, they found whatever they wanted to eat served up on the table. But they didn't think much about eating. Here they were living like lords, very differently from the way they did in their own poor house, but they only wanted to be home without the thought that they'd have to part weighing on their hearts.

The father had to leave again, though. Rose even asked him to, out of consideration for her mother. Back he went home, to push the plow behind his cows, and still he knew nothing of how it would go between his Rose and the beast.

"The beast talked kindly, but its mouth may be black with lies. And what did it mean by that baffling speech? Yes, what does it want with my daughter—my poor child, baptized and a Christian, whom I had to leave in the hands of the beast? Oh, I know you can see in Rose's eyes the angel who's always with her. But even if the beast's not all beast, will it be able to see Rose's angel and understand she's all goodness and sunshine?"

That's how he spoke to himself all the way home through the fields. Now and again he even felt his heart lighten a little.

Rose had gone with him to the gate. Then she returned to the rosebush by the door, as though it were the castle's secret and its soul. Reverently, she cut a rose.

The beast appeared instantly.

Rose wanted to know what it expected of her. Remembering its eyes, its voice, and its words, she felt some compassion. Not that she could have brought herself to touch it, but she'd have been glad to help it in its trouble.

The beast saw in her all her deep, simple kindness, and saw too how this kindness put her beauty beyond compare.

"Thank you for having lodged my father before I let him leave," said Rose. "I'll do everything for you I can."

"Are you really speaking from your heart, Rose? How good you are, Lovely Rose, not to resent my ugliness."

The beast had lain down at her feet before the rosebush and was gazing tenderly at her, its eyes on hers. And there it stayed, saying such sad, sweet things that Rose felt drawn to it more and more.

"I know what I am, and it's what I deserve to be: a beast of fear and horror that surely makes you tremble more than any spider or toad. And yet, Rose, my Rose, you have pity on me! If only you could know me truly . . . But one more word and I shall lose all hope . . ."

Sighing, groaning, the beast gazed at her with tears pouring from its eyes. Nasty-minded people—and there certainly *are* some—would have just laughed. But Rose was a saint of goodness. Though trembling, she returned that affectionate gaze and found words to soothe the beast's pain. She promised never to reject its presence and always to be its friend.

"I won't leave you, whatever happens."

"Listen, Rose, I trust you. Soon I'll give you three days. Go and see your father, your mother, and your home. But on the third day you must come back. Promise me that."

"Dear God," said Rose to herself, "what have I gotten myself into now? I'm not only a prisoner on trust in this castle, but I actually feel friendly toward the beast. I couldn't help myself when it spoke so sadly. When it looks at me, I see distress brimming in its eyes. Surely it has some secret it must keep from me. But I can't guess that secret, either."

She felt such pity that she wanted to go away for a while. So she reminded the beast of its promise to give her three days for a visit home.

"I shall miss you, Rose, oh my Rose," said the beast, "during those three days. I shall dry up like mown hay drying in the fields, when I no longer have you with me and can no longer look into your eyes. But go, since you must! I trust you to come back promptly. In that I risk misery for myself, but I am in your hands. If you only knew the gift within you, and the faith which is still mine . . ."

When Rose reached the door of her house, how her father and mother kissed her, and her sisters, too! They'd thought they would never see her again. Rose only asked them to forgive her for all the sorrow she'd caused them.

They questioned her shyly about the castle—that is, about the beast. She told them she'd never felt the beast meant her any harm. She said the look in its eyes was often just like a human's, and that actually it deserved heartfelt affection.

The three days sped quickly by, while they made as much of her as they could. Rose's parents breathed easier after she told them the beast wasn't evil. But now their fear was gone, they weren't eager to let her go off again.

They found so many ways of insisting she stay a little longer that she spent one more night at home. She was supposed to be back at the castle early in the morning, but still they managed to delay her. In the end, she wasn't able to set out until after the noon meal.

She reached the beast's castle toward sundown. All the way she hurried as best she could, filled with foreboding and even with deep remorse. As she fairly flew through the ponds and pastures, she thought of the misfortune which might follow her being the least bit late.

Sure enough, there next to the castle door, the great rosebush, the soul of the place, was wilting already. It drooped as though touched by frost.

For a second her heart seemed to stop. The rosebush stood for friendship, as its dying surely proved, and their friendship had not turned out as it should. The roses had lost their petals—all but one which Rose quickly cut.

The beast didn't appear.

She began to shiver. Straining her ears, she heard a slight sound, as of someone groaning and struggling to move. She took a few steps toward the garden. There were more groans. Moving toward them, she saw the beast next to the well.

Worse off even than the rosebush, the beast lay languishing beneath the ferns, near death for all she knew, and apparently about to fall back into the well it had just emerged from. It seemed all but lifeless, robbed of strength.

"I've come to apologize," said Rose, transfixed.

"Rose! Oh, Rose!" the beast replied. "Don't you know you're the death of me?"

"Don't mistrust me. You've no reason to. And don't wish me ill."

"I don't wish you ill, Rose, but look what your being late has done to me! Do you know you've stolen my heart, and I can't live far from your gaze?"

"Beast, my beast," said Rose, "I'm here!"

Her heart was burning so with pity just then that neither fear nor disgust could hold her back. Seeing the beast soiled with mire, she bent down and took it in her arms, to wash it in the water of the well.

But then, oh wonder! She'd no sooner touched it with her good, kind hands, no sooner made her gesture of loving charity, than she had before her no longer a beast but a lad like the son of a king, a prince as radiant as bright day. He was so beautiful that Rose was amazed. In fact, she felt in herself something beyond amazement.

"Rose," said the prince, going down on one knee, "I fully deserved the curse that was on me. I dreamed of nothing but feasting and battles, and hardly recognized the compassion in kindly glances. Beggars disgusted me, with their rags and scabs. One day I laughed at a poor man who came begging bread at my door, and found myself changed into a beast. My castle was to remain open to all comers, offering food and lodging, while I lived on in a hole in the earth. Meanwhile, love-roses flourished before the door. The first rose was to be taken to a lovely girl who was a poor man's daughter; then she was to agree to come; and finally, one day, she was to make a gesture of heartfelt charity toward the beast by touching it with her hands. She had to do this of her own free will, without being asked and without being disgusted! Then the curse would be lifted. Otherwise, I would die in bestial form; and the girl, whose heart compassion would not have been able to move, would die as well."

But he didn't need to say so much. Lovely Rose did not wish to die. Like him, she was shining.

Hand in hand they strolled to the rosebush of love. It was green again

and covered with flowers, showing that a great love had bloomed. The rosebush said and sang it: Lovely Rose and the beast, the prince of the castle and the poor man's daughter, were going to be man and wife.

Rose's father and mother came with her sisters to the wedding, and Rose kept them with her always. The castle remained a welcoming refuge for the poor.

As long as Rose and her prince lived on, the great rosebush by their door blossomed like a tree of love, rose upon rose.

100. Disturbing News

There were once a husband and wife who had a cow. The day after Christmas, the cow died. The wife got after her husband to buy another, and she kept at it so long that at last he gave in. He decided to do it at Candlemas, and to make sure he got a good fat one, he went to town. He promised to bring the cow back by evening.

The afternoon passed. Four o'clock rang, then five. The good woman had settled down at the window, knitting and watching. Like the servant girl in "Isabelle and Her Three Brothers," though, she saw pastures green and broad, but no dust out on the road. She kept waiting for her husband to show up, leading the cow by a rope, but he never did.

At last she spotted a man. He was riding, but he didn't have a cow with him and he wasn't her husband. It was someone from the village lower down.

She went to the door.

Raising his hand, he signaled to her from a distance. A fit of anxiety seized her.

Up he came to her, panting a bit, and took time to catch his breath.

"Well, Marion, it's no good news I've brought you."

"Ah, heavens!"

"Yes. Your husband was bringing back a cow he'd bought at the fair . . ."

"And?"

"And he let her get away."

"How awful!"

"Just a minute. He ran after her and caught her."

"Thank goodness!"

"No, no, wait. The cow struggled. They were on the little bridge and the planks were wet—slippery, you know. The cow fell into the river."

"Why, that's terrible!"

"No, listen. Your husband kept hold of the rope . . ."

"Oh no!"

"He went right in after her. The river was high. It swept them both away."

"The cow too?"

"The cow tumbled along about the distance from here to the well. That poor husband of yours went maybe twice that far."

"Did they get the cow out?"

"Yes, they got them both out. But you see, Marion . . ."

"Oh, mercy, tell me quickly! Was the cow dead?"

"No, but by the time they pulled your husband from the water, why, it was already too late. He'd drowned, that's all there is to say. Drowned. They're coming now with a stretcher. They're bringing him back."

"But what about my cow?"

"Oh, they're bringing her too. She'd found footing on the bank."

"Thank God! So, my husband's dead?"

"I'm afraid so."

"But there's nothing wrong with the cow?"

"No, nothing."

"Well, neighbor, all I can say is that the way you brought me the news, you certainly managed to give me a good scare!"

101. The Candle

There was once a man who'd always been tight with his money. He'd scrimped on every last thing, from candles and firewood to cheese and bread. When he got old, he began scrimping even on drinking water.

His poor wife fell ill. Not that she'd eaten herself to the brink of the grave, poor thing—no, not she. She never got enough to eat, not even in January when pigs are slaughtered and people do some feasting. Anyway, one evening she was ready to breathe her last.

Meanwhile, one of the cows was about to give birth. The husband just had to go and see how the calf was coming, and help it into the world. As he closed the stable door a thought struck him.

"Listen, Toinette," he said, "I'll leave you the candle. But if you think you're going to die, blow it out, won't you, before you go."

102. The Perilous Post

There was once a woman, no doubt as good a woman as any and in fact better than some, but somewhat difficult. Now, one day—perhaps she hadn't gotten the right medicine—she up and died.

Her husband certainly mourned her decently enough. But, as they say, "A late wife rates a new hat."

They were carrying the dear departed to her grave when, on the way out of the courtyard—the passage being narrow and slippery—the bearers got into trouble. The coffin bumped into the gatepost. Suddenly the departed, who wasn't departed at all but just unconscious, was woken up by the shock. She cried out.

With shouts of dismay, people rushed to the coffin and opened it up.

She let out a sigh.

Instead of continuing on to the cemetery, they naturally carried her straight to bed.

She revived.

A few years later, the wife who hadn't really been dead died again. This time it seemed to be for good. The doctor came and certified she was deceased.

On the day of the funeral, as the bearers were heading out of the courtyard, the bereaved husband stepped smartly forward and stood against the gate.

"Take care now, you people! For the love of God, watch out for that post!"

103. The Big Quarrel

There was once a household where the husband and wife never quarreled—no, never a hard word, never the least reproof. Each approved of what the other wanted and agreed with what the other said.

They lived two leagues off the road in the depths of the woods. There they quietly spent their lives, never bothering their heads with the ways of this wicked world.

They did have a daughter, though. She'd found a job, gotten married, and settled down far from her parents, in the city.

One fall she sent a note to ask them to come and visit.

They thought about it a lot and talked about it a little. At last, they found they were both agreed ("So, we're going to see that daughter of ours?") and decided to make the journey.

One morning, as soon as the sun had dried the dew from the grass, they locked up the house, hid the key under a stone, and set off, in their Sunday best, for the village.

When they got to the road with its cross, they saw two black crows on a service tree.

"Say!" the husband exclaimed. "Look, wife—two crows."

No answer.

A half-hour later they reached the village and took the road to town.

As they passed the well, the wife said to her husband, "You know those two black birds you showed me back there on the tree? Well, *I* think they were a pair of jackdaws."

No answer.

On they went, to the clop-clop of their clogs, gazing around at the countryside and keeping an eye on the clouds yonder, over the mountains.

An hour and a half later they reached the town and went straight to the inn on the square, from where the mail coach left for the city. They waited to board the old rattletrap.

"You're right," said the husband to his wife. "Must have been a pair of jackdaws."

They waited and waited. The rattletrap showed up. In they got and sat down. A half-hour passed.

"Now that I think it over again," remarked the wife, "I believe you were right. They *were* two crows."

The coach finally left. They rolled on and time passed. Sitting across from each other, they rested their chins on their hands and their hands on the handles of their big blue umbrellas. They'd never been so far from home. Now and again they looked out at the view.

"Well," said the husband when the coach stopped two leagues farther on, "maybe it was one crow and one jackdaw."

"You're right," said his wife. "One jackdaw and one crow."

"Oh for goodness' sake!" said the husband. "If coming all this way just means we have to bicker and squabble, we might as well turn around right now."

"You're right," said his wife. "We'll go and see our daughter another time."

They got out of the coach and went home.

104. Jeanne d'Aymet

There was once a girl named Jeanne d'Aymet. Aymet's a village in the Rouergue country, near the Roc d'Anglars. You're high up there, looking out over the plains of Montauban and Toulouse.

At the Roc d'Anglars there's a clear spring. Jeanne d'Aymet went for water there.

Once she woke up in her poor little house.

"It's day! Dear Lord, it's already bright day!" Light was flooding in from outside, a white light that filled the countryside. Quickly, she caught up her water dipper and her jug of unbaked clay. She ran to the Roc d'Anglars for water to prepare her father's meal.

She'd not reached the first turn in the path when she heard the cry of an owl. She'd not reached the second turn when she saw the moon over the woods.

It hadn't been bright day, it had just been the moon.

But as she came to the Roc d'Anglars, a rider appeared on the path. As she dipped water from the spring, the rider reined in his horse. Perhaps he was coming home from the wars, tired of riding and sick of battle. Perhaps he was wounded. Wasn't he shivering with fever? How fair he was! How his eyes shone! Jeanne d'Aymet didn't know he was the king's son.

Down he jumped from his horse and wished the girl good day.

"What are you doing there, pretty girl, so early that it's still night?"

"Fair rider, the moon deceived me."

"The moon deceived me, fair rider," she repeated, too astonished to think of anything else.

Under the rider's gaze she felt—why, she was half mad!—a silvery radiance flooding her as it flooded all the world round about. Her heart beat strong and fast, up into her very throat.

"I'm thirsty, girl. Give me some of your water."

"Fair rider, I've neither cup nor glass."

"Then give me some in your dipper, girl."

"Fair rider, I left in haste. I never wiped my dipper."

"Wipe it now, if you like. What does it matter?"

"But, fair rider, I've nothing to wipe it on . . ."

She was putting up a fight, Jeanne d'Aymet, she was trying to slip away. The words they were saying seemed—she couldn't tell why—to hide others they weren't saying at all.

He asked her her name.

"Jeanne d'Aymet, you find a way out of everything!"

She smiled and said she was sorry. It was her country way, of course. Farmers have that knack of finding an answer to anything. They're ingenious and attentive, for everything they have they must grow from the earth of their little plot: food, clothing, and whatever else people need in this life.

"Jeanne d'Aymet," said the king's son again, "you find a way out of everything I ask."

"Fair rider, that's what I've always been taught to do."

"Jeanne d'Aymet, tell me, what is your father's work?"

"My father tills the soil, fair rider."

The tale reveals no more of what they said to each other that morning. It only says that Jeanne d'Aymet followed the king's son to Paris.

After that, it just tells of her lament. "Fair rider, the moon deceived me": the complaint of the poor abandoned girl, far away in the city. What she'd taken for the sun of love was only the moon of night.

Their story has it that one fine day she brought the king's son an apple.

Perhaps a woman had brought it to her from back home. Perhaps in Paris, under the streets' black rain, that apple meant everything to her: the smell of hay at midsummer, the infinite peace of those evenings when the air in the depths of the bottomless sky is all suffused with pink, the countryside at harvesttime, all the sun and hope that still lay ahead . . .

That was all she had to give her love, the king's son: a certain freshness, and the savor of those loves lived out beside a spring.

But what was that apple to the son of a king? It didn't even speak to him of their love back at the Roc d'Anglars. That love had been so brief.

Or if the apple did speak to him, their love there in Paris meant less to him than smoke melting into the distant air away at the edge of the plain.

The king's son gave Jeanne d'Aymet back her apple.

Head lowered against the wind, Jeanne d'Aymet took again to the road. Towns, villages, passing riders—she never saw them at all. Her only thought was to be home again, at the Roc d'Anglars, beside the clear spring.

Jeanne d'Aymet threw herself into the spring, and in that spring Jeanne d'Aymet drowned.

105. The White Goat

There was once a lord's wife who was expecting the birth of a pretty child.

One day she was strolling from meadow to green meadow when something white suddenly loomed before her in a gap in the hedge. She saw a white beast, horned and bearded, with the wild gaze of its golden eyes full upon her.

The shock was so great, she fainted in the grass.

The lord her husband had great difficulty bringing her back to herself.

It had been a he-goat that frightened her so: a goat whiter of hair than the hawthorn flower and wilder of eye than the high mountain forests. No shepherd had seen it in those meadows before, nor would any ever again.

The lady, as though obsessed, kept seeing that same vision. The beast loomed before her, taller than any human, so white and so wild.

When her time came, the poor woman bore not a pretty Christian child but a creature like a white goat.

The lord and lady, trembling with horror, ordered it removed from their sight. They had it taken away to an ancient castle of theirs in the heart of the forest.

There, servants fed the creature. The place lacked nothing: you had only to help yourself. If you weren't afraid to go in, you got everything you could want. Those who passed by during the day saw the white goat there. Those who passed at night saw only a shadow.

When he was seven, the White Goat stopped bleating like a kid. He spoke words.

When he was twenty, he asked his father to come and see him.

"Father, I want to get married—to the king's daughter, I mean."

"What are you saying, my son?"

"Father, I saw her pass by on the road. Go to the king and ask him for his daughter. Whatever price he may set on her, she shall be my wife."

The lord looked down, then nodded three times. He set off for the king's castle.

"Sire, my son, the White Goat, has spoken. He wishes me to ask for the hand of your daughter. What answer shall I give him?"

"Tell him he shall have my daughter, but only after he has had built, in one night, a highroad between this castle and the one yonder where he lives, in the depths of the forest."

The lord took this answer back to his son.

The White Goat went out his door and cried aloud, as though calling a host of hidden beings. The sun was just going down, its last rays fading as they rose through the leaves like a golden haze. In the gathering shades of night, teeming shadows raced in from all directions. They set to work like an insect army, felling and clearing trees along the way, then rolling boulders aside, ridding the route of pebbles and gravel by the shovelful, filling in and raising embankments, building and, finally, laying the road. By sunup the highroad stretched from castle to castle.

"Father," said the White Goat, "what the king asked for has now been done. Go and tell him I wish to have his daughter."

The lord saw that the task was done. Without a word, he followed the new road to speak to the king in his castle.

The king climbed his highest tower and saw the highroad stretching away, straight through the woods toward the castle of the White Goat.

"There's a lot more for him to do before he gets my daughter! Tell him that instead of his old castle, he's to put up in a single night one exactly like my own—so precisely like it that not one of its doors shall have a single nail more or less!"

The lord carried back the message. At the same moment of sundown, the White Goat cried aloud at his door as though to summon an unseen host from the depths of the woods. Among slanting shadows and the sun's last red rays, they rose up, bored, swarmed, and set to, shaping stones, mixing mortar, squaring beams, cutting rafters, building walls, raising the roof frame, laying the tiles, and putting up the weathercocks.

By dawn the castle was done. Its windows blazed in the sun's first light.

The lord returned to the king and announced that his orders had been followed to the letter.

The king stared at him.

"I'll believe it when I see it myself!"

He asked for his great horse, rode to the spot, and saw. He saw a castle just like his own, from the lock on the door to the golden pinnacle on the tip of the tower.

"Yes," said the king, tugging at his beard, "but in front of *my* castle there's a large garden divided by box hedges and all planted with blue rosemary, roses, and violets. My daughter likes to stroll there. She has a pretty taste for gardening. Tell your son that in one night he's to make a garden exactly like mine—so alike that not a single rosebush has one leaf more or less."

The countless spirit host of the dark and the woods worked through the night, mingling with air, grasses, and trees, planting, rooting, clipping and pruning, drawing in water, drawing up sap, bringing on to flower and fruit.

The next morning, the garden stood ready under the rising sun, so exactly like the king's own, down to the last myrobolan plum and amaranth blossom, that even a bee would have mistaken one for the other.

When the king came, at the lord's invitation, he at first hardly knew what to say.

"Very well," he declared at last, pulling hairs from his beard, "but in *our* garden, all the birds in the world come to build their nests: the quail, the dove, and the pretty partridge. My daughter couldn't bear not to hear them sing. Your son must have them all too. Let him fill his garden with them in one night. If he does, I'll give him my daughter."

"I'm asking for all the birds of the sky," said the king to himself. "I don't suppose he has the servants to go and bring them down from the clouds."

When the White Goat heard the king's answer from his father, he didn't even wait for nightfall. He stood in the middle of the garden and gave a shout through his cupped hands. A cloud of birds gathered from the four corners of the sky. They built their nests, they fluttered and sang among the leaves of the trees.

The king learned of the miracle.

"Sire," said the lord, "my son has done everything you commanded. He now asks for your daughter. What answer shall I give him?"

"Tell him I'll come and hunt in the forest tomorrow. I invite him to join me."

"Give my daughter, my lovely daughter, to that White Goat?" said the king to himself, as he spurred his horse on. "Oh no, it's out of the question. I know what I'll do tomorrow, and never mind if I endanger my own soul!"

The next day the king came to hunt—to hunt big game. He took the White Goat with him into the thick of the forest. He'd selected for his quiver three very sharp arrows.

When the moment arrived he shot them one after another at the White Goat.

The first vanished into the leaves.

The second touched the White Goat but fell at his feet without harming him.

The third turned back on the king and wounded him in the face.

Next, the king seized his spear and charged the magic creature. The spear broke like a straw.

The king turned bridle and fled for his castle, clinging low to his mount, digging in the spurs.

"My daughter! What have I done? I thought to mock the White Goat and set him impossible tasks, but by magic he performed them! Now I'm a prisoner of my own word. A moment ago I tried to kill him and failed. He's stronger than I am, my daughter! He wants to be your husband and *will* be!"

"Oh father, my father—to marry the White Goat!"

"My daughter, you must sink or swim."

"I'd rather die. But I'll marry him since I must. Before I give my consent, though, I want just one thing from him. I too have a word to say."

She went to the castle in the woods and there, at the door, she spoke to the lord, the father of the White Goat.

"If I'm to marry your son, I want him to bring me in a golden cage the Bird-Who-Tells-All."

The White Goat strode off into the heart of the forest.

In the darkest nook of the oldest grove lay a pool as black as pitch. The White Goat whistled a tune: a tune so sweet, so light, so magical that the green serpent rose from the depths of the mire. Eighteen feet long, that serpent was, and it writhed upon the black waters. All the birds in the world flew to it like larks to a mirror, twittering, fluttering their wings, and falling to the ground.

At last one came, still more brilliant than the rest: the Bird-Who-Tells-All. It too twittered, fluttered its wings, and fell. The White Goat had only to pick it up and put it in his cage.

He took the bird, caged, to the king's daughter.

She then said she would keep her word, and that secretly, that same night, she would marry the White Goat.

"I'll only ask you one thing," he said to her. "Don't yet look in my ear."

Then sleep overcame him. That White Goat, that sorcerer goat about to become her husband, sank down onto a bench in the great hall and fell asleep. She, the king's daughter, soon would have no sorrow or joy that this goat didn't share.

Then she saw something glitter in his ear. How could she help looking?

It was a golden key.

She took it. As though drawn by a thread, she went to a sunken door in an angle of the wall. Opening the door, she saw loom after loom and weaver after weaver.

"Good health to you, young lady, good health! We've been working for you these last seven years!"

All around were scattered scraps of brocade, lengths of bombazine, lampas, and velvet.

She went to the very back of the workshop, to another little door. This too she opened with the golden key. On she went into another workshop, where she saw frame after frame and woman after woman embroidering.

"Good health to you, young lady, good health! We've been working for you these last seven years!"

All around were lawns, batistes, and muslins.

She went to the back, to another little door.

She opened the door with the golden key and went on into another workshop. There she saw endless lacemaking pillows and woman after woman making lace.

"Good health to you, young lady, good health! We've been working for you these last seven years!"

All around were rolls and rolls of lace finer than frost on the windowpane, or than spiderweb wheels between sprays of dew-spangled broom.

Seven years they'd been waiting for her! For her they'd been working their magic seven years!

Shaking, she made her way back to the great hall. Gently, very gently, without waking him up, she slipped the key back in the White Goat's ear.

Then they held the wedding. During the ceremony the king saw not the White Goat, but only a shadow.

In the castle everything was more magnificent still than in the king's own. The guests were served all they could wish for: meat and sauces in golden bowls, wines in goblets of gold.

But the king hardly saw these splendors. All he saw was that shadow who was the White Goat.

Home he went in silence on his great horse, sorrowing.

The queen awaited him at the head of the steps.

"What were you doing with our daughter at that castle in the woods? Why haven't you brought her back? My daughter! Where's my daughter?"

"Your daughter—our daughter—stayed behind. She's found her husband there. God grant that she be happy!"

The king had to tell her everything.

Shrieking like a madwoman, the queen set off. Early in the morning she came to the White Goat's castle.

"My daughter, my daughter, can this thing be? Run! Flee! Come with me! Let us be gone!"

"I'll not leave, mother. I shan't abandon my dear White Goat."

"But my daughter, you're mad! Come to your senses, my daughter!"

"My father married me to the White Goat and I must love him. I am forbidden to say more."

Before slipping the ring on her finger, the White Goat had whispered to her alone:

"I won't always be a White Goat or a shadow."

And in fact, after the wedding, he'd become a handsome young man. But then he'd looked at her:

"I know now that you disobeyed me. You touched the golden key. The enchantment is only half gone, when marrying you should have dispelled it completely. So I can't yet take human form during the day. But if you keep the secret, I won't always be a White Goat. No, I'll soon turn back into a man forever."

The king's daughter knew she really must *not* reveal that secret, and that she might already have said too much.

But there was her mother, pressing her ever more cruelly, begging, crying, imploring—without success thus far.

The new bride only protested once more that she meant to stay in this castle with her dear White Goat.

"Very well, my daughter," said the mother, suddenly changing tone, "if you're not to be parted from him, then he's not a white goat both day and

night. Tell me the truth, my daughter. Is he a white goat during the night, too?"

Still her daughter refused to talk. She kept her eyes to the ground and wouldn't open her lips.

"Tell me the truth or I'll cut your throat! I'd rather see you dead than know you're the wife of a monster."

The queen drew a knife from her bosom. The poor girl threw herself at her feet.

"Mother, mother, what are you asking me? Don't kill me, mother! Think what you're doing! Yes, it's true, he's a white goat by day and a man by night."

Oh curses and malediction!

Suddenly they were plunged into uproar, darkness, and terror. Every wall, every floor, and the very castle itself crashed down in ruins. The mother cried out, stumbled, picked herself up, and fled. The White Goat appeared.

"What have you done, miserable wife, what have you done? You took the golden key! You gave away my secret! And if you hadn't spoken, I'd have been free of this enchantment tomorrow and I'd have been a man forever."

She groveled at his feet, wringing her hands.

"My husband, oh my husband, is there no way the harm can be undone?"

"Undone? I hardly know. Penance, perhaps—but long and hard. And who knows whether it will work?"

"Penance? Oh, tell me how! I'll do anything to free you."

"Then put on these shoes of lead. Each weighs four hundred pounds. Walk straight ahead by highways and byways. Walk and walk till the shoes wear away."

"I'll do it! I'll walk, I'll wear my legs down to the knees!"

"Try to make your way to the castle where my fate will take me. Climb up to the finest room; come to me in the time when I have human form and show me your wedding ring. Then the enchantment will be gone and I'll be a goat no more."

She put on the leaden shoes that each weighed four hundred pounds and set out along the roads.

She dragged those shoes through rocks and ruts, limping, stumbling, but always walking on. She walked so long and far that evening by evening and season by season she wore out those four-hundred-pound shoes.

When they were worn out, she found herself in a country like no other: a country without grass or flowers, and where the sky had no stars.

She saw a castle on a hill. It was the castle of the winds.

First she spoke to the white wind, the wind of the south. She asked him for news of her husband, the White Goat.

"How should I know your husband? Why, I don't know him at all."

"It's not hard to recognize him. He's a White Goat by day and a man by night. He lives in a castle with the Bird-Who-Tells-All. Tell me where that castle is, for I've finished my penance and worn out the four-hundred-pound shoes."

"I can't tell you where the castle is. I haven't seen it on my way. But since your penance is done and your dress is as worn out as your shoes, I'll give you a dress of moon-cloth."

The white wind gave her a dress the color of the full moon when she shines aloft like a silver platter, so brilliant that she puts out the stars.

She spoke next to Le Matinal, the east wind, and asked him the same thing: whether he knew where the White Goat was.

"I can't tell you. I didn't see him on my way. But since your penance is done and your dress is as worn out as your shoes, I'll give you a dress of star-cloth."

The dress was the color of clusters of stars when the wind of the great frosts polishes them there aloft.

Next, she spoke to the west wind, La Traverse.

But La Traverse didn't know where the White Goat was. All he could do for the poor girl was to give her a dress of sun. It was just like the dazzle you get when, blinking your eyes, you try to look at the sun up there as it gazes down on the countryside.

Next she talked to the north wind, the cool Bise.

"Your White Goat? Yes, I saw him on my way. He's in the castle with the Bird-Who-Tells-All. It's only eight days' walk from here. But hurry, hurry! He's forgotten he's married and he's about to take another wife."

The poor creature set straight off again through the wilderness. She'd worn out her shoes, she'd even worn out her feet.

At last she reached the castle. She looked like a slop girl, covered as she was with the dust of the road. She got herself hired as a scullery maid. Only three full days remained before the wedding.

On the evening of the next day she put on the dress of moonlight.

The White Goat's fiancée was already there, taking charge of everything. When brightness filled the castle, she rushed to see where it was coming from. She found this girl in the depths of the kitchen and couldn't believe her eyes.

"I must have that dress, whatever your price! What will you take?"

"For this dress I'd like one night in the castle's finest room."

The fiancée ran and showed the dress to her mother.

"One night in the castle's finest room," said the mother. "That's hardly a lot for a dress like that! But that's the room where the White Goat lives. He mustn't know that this scullery maid is going there."

At supper she made the White Goat drink a goblet of wine infused with elder leaves.

The king's daughter found herself in the room. She knew her husband must be in it too, deep in some secret alcove.

"Where are you, my dear White Goat whom I injured so? I've done my penance, I've worn out the four-hundred-pound shoes. Come, see the ring you yourself put on my finger! Dear White Goat, where are you?"

But the drugged wine had put him so soundly asleep that he never answered. Morning came, and the poor creature had never had a sign of life from him.

The next evening, she put on her dress of starlight.

Radiance filled the castle. The alert fiancée ran to investigate.

She insisted she must have the dress at any price. They made the same bargain.

Everything went as before: the drugged wine, the finest room, the White Goat's sleep from which no call or cry could wake him.

The following evening, the king's daughter put on her dress of sunlight.

The fiancée wanted that one even more than the two others! Again, she bought it for a night in the castle's finest room.

Now, the wedding was to be the next day. The king's daughter was in agony at the thought of not recovering her husband before then.

The White Goat, meanwhile, wanted to make sure everything in the castle was ready for the wedding.

He roamed from hall to hall and from room to room. In his rounds he saw the cage with the Bird-Who-Tells-All.

The Bird-Who-Tells-All was twittering and singing, and in its pretty song it sang:

> *Remember the daughter of a king and queen*
> *You took to your castle in the forest green?*
> *These three years she's sought you everywhere,*
> *These three days she's been calling you here:*
> *"Dear White Goat whom I injured so,*
> *Dear White Goat, where are you now?*
> *See me, love, see my golden ring!"*
> *But you were sleeping off drugged wine,*
> *And, White Goat, you're sleeping again!*

The White Goat started. He went no further in his rounds. There was fire in his head, though a fire which shed no light.

He went to sit at the back of the second room, but that evening he was unable either to eat or to drink.

When night came, there in the secret alcove of the castle's finest room, he resumed his human form but couldn't sleep. This time he heard the voice—the king's daughter's voice:

"Where are you, dear White Goat whom I injured so? My penance is over. Dear husband, where are you? Come, see the ring you gave me on our wedding night! Come, see your true love! Oh, my dear White Goat, where are you?"

Suddenly, it all came back to him: his true love, their wedding, and his hard fate. Like a madman he hurled himself into the room and threw himself at the king's daughter's feet. Everything was his again, their love and their sworn faith. Recovering their perfect love of husband and wife, he recovered forever his human form.

No doubt the fiancée, and her mother too, raged and tore their hair. But what could they do? The White Goat was already married, and that was that. The Bird-Who-Tells-All told and sang the whole story. To make themselves feel better they ate up the feast being prepared for the wedding: pies and pâtés, roasts and tarts.

The White Goat and the king's daughter paid them no heed. She was his at last, she who despite her travels and penance was again lovelier than bright day. And he was finally hers, he who was the handsomest lad you could ever hope to see.

The evil enchantment was gone. Both were simply what they were, and each belonged to the other. They were together and truly happy.

Their story's over, you know,
Just now when the cock starts to crow.

A Note on Sources

French Folktales is a selection from the vast *Trésor des contes* which Henri Pourrat compiled over nearly fifty years, starting in 1910. Pourrat, who lived in the Auvergne region of central France, drew his tales from both written and oral sources. The written tales are mainly from popular literature circulated among the Auvergnat peasants by traveling salesmen. Most of the oral tales were collected in the field by Pourrat himself, although a few were written down for him by correspondents, or reached him in the form of essays assigned, at his own prompting, to local schoolchildren.

Pourrat carefully noted all his sources (for example, name of the teller, occupation, date and place of the telling), and his complete records are now preserved at the Centre Henri Pourrat in the Bibliothèque municipale et interuniversitaire de Clermont-Ferrand. However, he did not include such information in his published collection.

Therefore, it was not possible to list the sources of the tales in this volume. Moreover, the problem is complicated by the fact that Pourrat rewrote every tale he collected, written or oral, and often conflated several field versions into one. As a result, his work has not been rated highly by French folklorists. Actually, Pourrat's treatment of his material was anything but cavalier, and his tales are inauthentic only in an academic sense. Pourrat knew his region, its people, and its folklore thoroughly. Every detail of life and manners in his tales is accurate, and the tales themselves are entirely faithful to the spirit if not to the letter of their sources. Furthermore, Pourrat was an exceptionally fine writer. For the nonspecialist, his *Trésor des contes* is undoubtedly one of the pinnacles of folktale literature.

Fundamental research on Pourrat's collection and its background has been done recently by Bernadette Bricout, who is the first person to have examined and analyzed Pourrat's voluminous papers. Bricout's doctoral thesis on the subject is cited below in the Bibliography. The third volume (which, because of problems of time and distance, was not available for the preparation of *French Folktales*) contains a complete inventory of Pourrat's sources, both written and oral. Those interested should consult Bricout's work, in conjunction with a complete edition of *Le trésor des contes*.

R.T.

Tales Classified by Volume

Each part division in this book corresponds to a volume title from the seven-volume French collection of Henri Pourrat's tales, entitled *Le trésor des contes* (Paris, Editions Gallimard, 1977–1986). This table lists each tale as it appears in *French Folktales*, followed by its original French title and the page on which it can be found in the corresponding volume of the French edition.

Bibliography

1. Works consulted for the introduction to *French Folktales*

Bricout, Bernadette. "Henri Pourrat et Arnold Van Gennep: histoire d'une querelle." *Cahiers Henri Pourrat*, no. 1, pp. 85–99. Bibliothèque municipale et interuniversitaire de Clermont-Ferrand, 1987.

————. "Le peuple et la culture populaire dans le *Trésor des contes* d'Henri Pourrat." Doctoral thesis (thèse de doctorat d'état) presented to the University of Paris (Université de Paris–Sorbonne [Paris IV]), 1987 (3 vols.), vol. 1. (The published version of vol. 2 is cited below; vol. 3 contains a complete analysis of all Pourrat's sources and a complete bibliography.)

Delarue, Paul. *Le conte français. Catalogue raisonné des versions de France et des pays de langue française d'outre-mer: Canada, Louisiane, îlots français des Etats-Unis, Antilles Françaises, Haïti, Ile Maurice, La Réunion.* Vol. 1. Paris, Editions Erasme, 1957.

————. Review of *Le trésor des contes*, vol. 1. *Mois d'ethnographie française*, 1949, pp. 65–66.

————. Review of *Le trésor des contes*, vols. 2 and 3. *Arts et traditions populaires*, no. 3 (July–September), 1953, pp. 18–19.

Gardes, Roger. "Le monde de Gaspard des montagnes et l'oeuvre d'Henri Pourrat." *Cahiers Henri Pourrat*, no. 1, pp. 100–21. Bibliothèque municipale et interuniversitaire de Clermont-Ferrand, 1987.

Hadjadj, Dany. "Du 'relevé de folklore' au conte populaire: avec Henri Pourrat, promenade aux fontaines du dire." In Roger Chartier, ed., *Frontières du conte*, pp. 55–67. Paris, Editions du Centre National de la Recherche Scientifique, 1982.

Pourrat, Henri. *Ceux d'Auvergne*. Paris, Albin Michel, (1928, 1939) 1987.

————. *Le trésor des contes*. Edited and with notes by Claire Pourrat. 7 vols. Paris, Gallimard, 1977–86. (Volumes arranged thematically and entitled: *Les fées, Le diable et ses diableries, Les brigands, Au village, Les fous et les sages, Le bestiaire, Les amours.*)

Simonsen, Michèle. *Le conte populaire français. Que sais-je?* Paris, Presses universitaires de France, 1981. series, no. 1906.

2. Other relevant works

Actes du Colloque du Centenaire: "Henri Pourrat et le *Trésor des contes.*" *Cahiers Henri Pourrat,* no. 6. Bibliothèque municipale et interuniversitaire de Clermont-Ferrand, 1988.

Bricout, Bernadette, ed. *Contes et récits du livradois: Textes recueillis par Henri Pourrat.* Paris, Maisonneuve et Larose, 1989. (Vol. 2 of the thesis cited above.)

Mian, Mary, trans. *A Treasury of French Tales.* Boston, Houghton Mifflin, 1964. (A previous volume of translations from Pourrat's *Trésor des contes.*)

Mittler, Sylvia. "Le jeune Henri Pourrat: de Barrès et Bergson à l'âme rustique." *Travaux de linguistique et de littérature,* vol. 15 (1977), pp. 193–215.

Pourrat, Henri. *Contes.* Folio series, no. 1892. Paris, Gallimard, 1987. (A low-priced, one-volume selection from *Le trésor des contes.*)

————. *Gaspard des montagnes.* Livre de poche. Paris, Albin Michel, (1922, 1923, 1930, 1931) 1984. series, nos. 2015 and 2016. 2 vols.

————. *Le trésor des contes.* 13 vols. Paris, Gallimard, 1948–62. (The order of the tales in this edition was worked out by Pourrat himself, and differs from the order in the more recent edition cited above.)

Zipes, Jack. "Henri Pourrat and the Tradition of Perrault and the Brothers Grimm." In Jack Zipes, *The Brothers Grimm: From Enchanted Forests to the Modern World.* pp. 96–109. New York and London, Routledge, 1988.

L i s t o f I l l u s t r a t i o n s

The illustrations in this book were selected from those appearing in the seven-volume Gallimard edition of *Le Trésor des contes* and are taken from the following sources:

Henri Pourrat (1887–1959) collected the multivolume *Le trésor des contes* ("The Treasury of Tales"), from which *French Folktales* is a selection. His many other writings include stories; reminiscences; historical, religious, and ethnographic essays; and novels, of which the best-known is *Gaspard des montagnes* ("Gaspard from the Mountains").

Carl Gustaf Bjurström, a literary critic and translator, selected the tales in this collection. He was born in 1919 and raised in France. He has translated the work of Claude Simon, Samuel Beckett, Céline, Jean Anouilh, Albert Camus, Michel Foucault, and others into Swedish and that of August Strindberg, Stig Dagerman, Lars Gyllensten, Gunnar Ekelöf, and Ingmar Bergman into French. He currently lives in Paris.

Royall Tyler, the translator, was partly educated in France and teaches Japanese at the University of Oslo in Norway. He edited and translated *Japanese Tales*, also part of Pantheon's folklore series.